SHADERS
FOR GAME PROGRAMMERS
AND ARTISTS

$$w = \cot\left(\frac{F}{}\right.$$

$$h = \cot\left(\frac{F}{}\right.$$

$$n = \begin{bmatrix} w & 0 & 0 & 0 \\ 0 & h & 0 & 0 \\ 0 & 0 & Q & 1 \\ 0 & 0 & -QZ & 0 \end{bmatrix}$$

$$Q = \frac{Z_f}{Z_f - }$$

$$Z = \text{Far } Z$$

THOMSON
COURSE TECHNOLOGY
Professional ■ Trade ■ Reference

Normalized
View Frustrum

rum

SHADERS
FOR GAME PROGRAMMERS
AND ARTISTS

$$w = \cot\left(\frac{F}{}\right.$$

$$\mathbf{n} = \begin{bmatrix} w & 0 & 0 & 0 \\ 0 & h & 0 & 0 \\ 0 & 0 & Q & 1 \\ 0 & 0 & -QZ & 0 \end{bmatrix}$$

$$h = \cot\left(\frac{F}{}\right.$$

$$Q = \frac{Z_f}{Z}$$

$$Z = \text{Far}$$

SEBASTIEN ST-LAURENT

Premier
Press

INCLUDES CD-ROM

THOMSON

COURSE TECHNOLOGY™

Professional ■ Trade ■ Reference

SVP, Thomson Course Technology PTR:
Andy Shafran

Publisher:
Stacy L. Hiquet

Senior Marketing Manager:
Sarah O'Donnell

Marketing Manager:
Heather Hurley

Manager of Editorial Services:
Heather Talbot

Acquisitions Editor:
Mitzi Foster

Senior Editor:
Mark Garvey

Associate Marketing Managers:
Kristin Eisenzopf and
Sarah Dubois

Project Editor:
Sandy Doell

Technical Reviewer:
Mathieu Mazerolle

Thomson Course Technology PTR Market Coordinator:
Amanda Weaver

Interior Layout Tech:
Marian Hartsough

Cover Designer:
Mike Tanamachi

CD-ROM Producer:
Brandon Penticuff

Indexer:
Kelly Talbot

Proofreader:
Sean Medlock

To my wife, Nicole,
for all her love and support
while I wrote this book.

ACKNOWLEDGMENTS

First and foremost, I want to thank my wife Nicole for all of her support throughout this project. Writing a book can be a major undertaking, and without her help and love, I would never have completed this one or might have lost my sanity doing so. I love you!

I also want to extend a big thanks to the Thomson Course Technology PTR team, first for giving me the opportunity to write this book, but also for all your help and support in making it come true.

Mathieu Mazerolle also deserves special mention for his efforts as a longtime friend and technical editor. His help proved invaluable in making sure I was in line and ensuring this book was the best possible book it could be. I also want to send my thanks to the kind people at NVIDIA and ATI Technologies for their technical information, which helped immensely with this production.

Finally, I want to thank everyone who has taught me in some way, including the awesome teachers at Sherbrooke University and, more importantly, Larry Landry and Glen Eagan for offering me an internship as part of the video game industry; thus launching my career.

ABOUT THE AUTHOR

SEBASTIEN ST-LAURENT has been programming games professionally for several years, working on titles for the Xbox, PlayStation 2, GameCube, and PC. He started in the video game industry while studying computer engineering at Sherbrooke University in Sherbrooke, Quebec. By interning in a small company called Future Endeavors during his college years, he got into the industry and stood out in the line of graphics engineering.

After graduating from college, he moved to California to work full time with Z-Axis as lead Xbox engineer, where he worked on several titles including the *Dave Mirra Freestyle BMX* series. He is a graphics engineer in the ACES group at Microsoft, Inc, where he is currently working on the next incarnation of Microsoft's *Flight Simulator* product.

About the Series Editor

ANDRÉ LAMOTHE, CEO, Xtreme Games LLC, has been involved in the computing industry for more than 25 years. He wrote his first game for the TRS-80 and has been hooked ever since! His experience includes 2D/3D graphics, AI research at NASA, compiler design, robotics, virtual reality, and telecommunications. His books are top sellers in the game programming genre, and his experience is echoed in the Thomson Course Technology PTR *Game Development* series.

Letter from the Series Editor

You may have noticed that the Thomson Course Technology PTR *Game Development* series has not published a book on shaders until this one. This is no mistake. We were waiting for a number of things to occur: first and foremost, for the technology to mature. If you recall the initial release of DirectX, you know that the software was revised almost on a quarterly basis, and worse yet, everything you learned was nearly useless until DirectX 5.0 stabilized a number of the systems. Shader programming is a similar animal; it's been changing very quickly; however, both NVIDIA and ATI seem to have the hardware down, and Microsoft has stepped up to take a leadership role in the development of HLSL (High Level Shader Language) to make programming shaders as effortless as possible.

The second, and probably most important, reason we have held off on a book in this area is that, as the series editor, I wanted to have a book that was the quintessential guide to beginning to intermediate shader programming. Finding the right author to do that has taken a long time, but the wait was well worth it. Sebastien St-Laurent is expert at shader programming, but even more important is his ability to make the topic interesting and engaging.

Moreover, the information you read in this book will not be out of date in six months; this is core material, and 90 percent of it will be applicable three to five years from now, so you are going to get an incredible return on your time investment. There are a lot of shader books on the market. I have read all of them. When Sebastien and I developed the outline and table of contents for this book, we both wanted to make sure to cover the important material that others had covered while filling the holes and gaps that other books have repeatedly left out.

In the final analysis, this is one of my favorite Thomson Course Technology PTR *Game Development* books. Not only does the book move at a fast (although not a blinding) pace, the writing style is fun, and the author continually gives examples and suggestions of how to use the technology. In addition, because the book relies heavily on ATI's RenderMonkey shader tool, non-programmers and artists can learn a lot as well.

On a technical note, the progress of graphics technology over the last 25 years is rather cyclic. If you recall, the first 3D games were software-based with software rasterizers: *DOOM*, *QUAKE*, and related games. Then, as 3D fixed pipeline hardware matured, games started taking advantage and became hardware-based, and the pipeline moved to the hardware with the result that a huge loss of control ensued.

Now, however, we can run software on a per pixel basis, and that's a mind-blowing concept. So shaders bring us full circle; we have the speed of hardware with the flexibility of software. I suppose the next step will be for the hardware to be completely reconfigurable via reprogrammable logic cores embedded in the GPUs . . . we will see.

In conclusion, if you had to pick a single book on pixel and vertex shader programming, this is the complete solution. You will learn everything from the tools, the technology, and actual implementation details. And of course this is all *fresh* material, not regurgitated, updated material from articles or other books. Hence, without hesitation, I recommend this book if you are interested at all in shader technology.

Sincerely,

André LaMothe
Thomson Course Technology PTR *Game Development* Series Editor
2004

CONTENTS AT A GLANCE

Contents

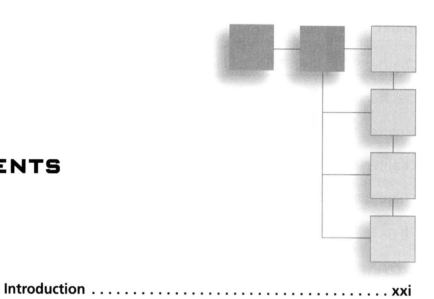

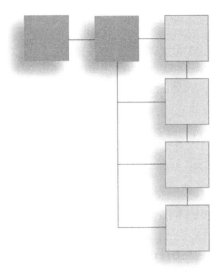

INTRODUCTION

During the summer of 2003, I was approached by André LaMothe to write a book on the topic of shaders. My experience on the PC and Xbox and writing game engines and shader architectures made me a great candidate for such an endeavor. Having always wanted to write a technical book, I simply could not resist and jumped into this great adventure.

My first task was to determine the approach I would take in writing this book. At that time, there were already several books available on the topic of shaders, and I felt the need to innovate and explore this topic in a form not done before. One of my gripes with many of the books already in print was that they all spent so much time explaining how to use rendering APIs, such as DirectX, and little time making shaders. This is where the idea of using ATI's RenderMonkey came into being. This new tool offered a rich set of features, allowing the quick, easy, and intuitive development of shaders.

I set off to do a *brain dump* of all my shader knowledge, taking advantage of RenderMonkey to make the learning process even easier. Throughout this book, you can expect to spend most of your time learning about shaders and how to create them. I do not just focus on the basics; several useful techniques, from basic to advanced, are presented in a straightforward manner aimed at allowing you to quickly absorb and apply the knowledge you gain from this book.

Who Should Read This Book

The topic of *Shaders for Game Programmers and Artists* is shader development; therefore, the book is written for anybody who has some interest in the topic. Because the topics and techniques covered throughout this book are so varied, it is bound to be of interest to everybody from hobbyist programmers to professional shader developers.

The approach I take in this book, using RenderMonkey, allows the content to be distanced from rendering APIs, such as DirectX or OpenGL. This allows you, the reader, to focus essentially on shader development and not on the development of framework applications. My approach to this book has the added advantage of making shader development available not only to engineers but also to technically minded artists.

Finally, with the approach taken throughout this book and the extensive exercises at the end of each chapter, *Shaders for Game Programmers and Artists* can also be a valuable asset in the classroom where real-time graphics have taken an even more important place in the computer science curriculum.

What Will Be Covered (And What Won't)

The topic of *Shaders for Game Programmers and Artists* is shaders, and it is all I will focus on. I will explain a variety of techniques that cover a wide range of topics, from image filtering to advanced lighting techniques. The following list summarizes some of the topics covered in this book:

- Introduction to several basic shader-related topics, including shaders, their history, and extensive documentation on how to use RenderMonkey and develop shaders using the HLSL shader language.
- An extensive set of screen-based techniques that can be used to enhance existing scenes. This book covers simple techniques, including everything from basic color filters to more advanced topics such as depth of field, heat shimmer, and high-dynamic range rendering.
- Lighting techniques ranging from simple per-vertex and per-pixel lighting approaches to more advanced topics such as bumpmapping, spherical harmonics, and polynomial texture maps.
- The rendering of varying materials is also covered through several techniques ranging from bi-directional refractance functions to procedural materials.

With this in mind, all shaders are developed making use of the RenderMonkey platform. This tool, developed by ATI Technologies, provides an easy-to-use framework for shader development. This approach allows you to focus solely on shaders and not on any specific APIs or the writing of framework code.

The preceding paragraph implies what we will not cover in this book. Because I want to focus solely on shader development, I will not go into any detail regarding general C/C++ programming; nor will I go into detail about how any of the rendering APIs work.

In simple words, this book covers shaders, using both RenderMonkey and the HLSL shader language.

Exercises

To facilitate the learning process throughout your reading of this book, I have included several exercises at the end of each chapter in a section called "It's Your Turn." These exercises invite you to expand upon the shaders developed throughout the chapters and increase your understanding of shaders. Extensive solutions to each exercise are to be found in Appendix D, "Exercise Solutions."

Support

Finally, a Web site is maintained at http://www.courseptr.com that provides support for this book. This site will be updated regularly to post errata and updates to the example programs as needed. Be sure to check it if you have any problems.

And if you have any questions or comments about this book, feel free to contact me, Sebastien St-Laurent, at sebastien_st_laurent@hotmail.com.

PART I

FROM THE GROUND UP

Welcome to *Shaders for Game Programmers and Artists*. The title of the book is very much self-explanatory; we will explore shader development together throughout this book. You will learn how vertex and pixel shaders work and how information flows from the initial piece of geometry to the final pixels displayed on the screen. Throughout the book, I will show you how to harness the latest hardware innovations and take advantage of the newest shader technologies to create photorealistic and stunning 3D graphics.

The goal of this book is not only to teach you some impressive effects and techniques, but also to give you the skills you need to explore your own creativity and create new shaders and techniques from scratch.

The first part of the book focuses mostly on introducing the technologies and tools we will use throughout the rest of the book. You can think of this as your warm-up before you get your hands dirty!

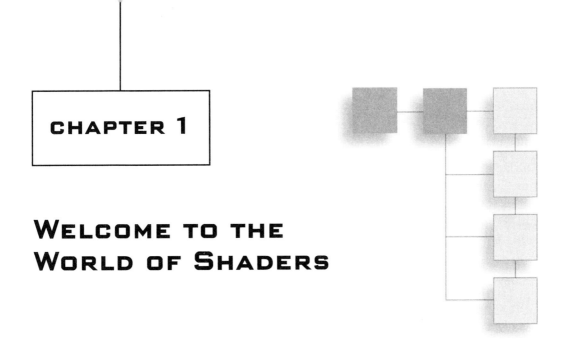

CHAPTER 1

WELCOME TO THE WORLD OF SHADERS

Computer graphics and its associated hardware have made significant technological leaps since the introduction of the first consumer-level 3D hardware accelerated graphics card, the 3Dfx Voodoo, in 1995. This card had limited rendering capabilities, but it allowed developers to break new ground and move away from software-only solutions. This finally made real-time 3D graphics and games a true reality.

Since then, the following generations of hardware improved significantly in their performance and features. However, all of them were still bound by a limited fixed-pipeline architecture that restricted developers to a constrained set of states that are combined to produce the final output.

The limited functionality of the fixed-pipeline architecture restricted developers in what they could create. This generally resulted in synthetic-looking graphics. At the other end of the spectrum, high-end software rendering architectures used for movie CG had something that allowed them to go much further. RenderMan is a shading language developed by Pixar Animation Studios. It enables artists and graphic programmers to fully control the rendering result by using a simple, yet powerful programming language. RenderMan allowed the creation of high-quality, photo realistic graphics used in many of today's movies, including *Toy Story* and *A Bug's Life*. One thing to note about RenderMan is that it is very complex and was never intended for real-time rendering, but as a means to give full control to movie CG artists.

With the evolution of processor chip making and the accompanying increase in processing power came the natural extension of the RenderMan idea to consumer-level graphics hardware. Along with the release of DirectX 8.0 came the introduction of vertex and pixel shader version 1.0 and 1.1. Although the standard came with limited flexibility and omitted some features such as flow control, it was the first step in giving developers and artists the flexibility they needed to produce the stunning and realistic graphics they had always dreamed of. We were finally at the point where consumer video cards could produce graphics that could compete with the renderings produced by Hollywood's movie studios.

During the next few years, graphics hardware and 3D APIs made giant leaps forward in functionality and performance, even shattering Moore's law with respect to technological advancement rate. With the introduction of the DirectX 9.0 SDK and the latest generations of graphics hardware, such as the GeForce FX series from NVIDIA and Radeon 9800 series from ATI Technologies, came vertex and pixel shader version 2.0 and 2.x.

note

The term Moore's Law came from an observation made in 1965 by Gordon Moore, co-founder of Intel, that the number of transistors per square inch had doubled every year since the introduction of the integrated circuit. He also predicted that this trend would continue for at least a few decades, which has so far turned out to be true. Also, since the transistor density relates to the performance of integrated circuits, Moore's Law is often cited as a prediction of future hardware performance increase.

This new shader model brings new flexibility never before available to real-time graphic application developers. Some of the new features include support for flow control operations such as branching and looping, many more constant and temporary registers to play with, up to 16 dependent texture lookups, and much more. With all those new features, developers and artists now have the same freedom to create stunning effects and materials, finally bringing movie-grade CG to consumer-level hardware in a real-time fashion.

Although this technological innovation meant developers could now push more geometry through the rendering pipeline, we have hit the point where the increase in geometry does not add significant graphic detail to a scene. On the other hand, proper use of multipass texturing with the use of shaders allows a never-before-seen realism. Keeping this in mind, shader development is sure to be the next best thing when it comes to computer graphics.

This book takes advantage of the latest technologies and tools available to introduce you, the reader, to shader development and design. Although this book is written for intermediate to advanced users, anyone with a basic understanding of 3D can benefit from exploring the shaders and effects presented here.

To simplify the learning task, I'll take an innovative approach throughout the book. Instead of focusing on a specific 3D API, as most books do, I will use a tool called RenderMonkey, developed by ATI Technologies. RenderMonkey allows shader development through a simple graphical user interface. It abstracts shader creation from any specific API and allows for easy development and prototyping. And no additional coding beyond the shader program itself is needed. This has the added advantage of making this book a great learning tool for both students and technically minded artists! You can now learn shaders without having to acquire the more general programming and 3D API skills that most currently available books require.

In the following sections, I discuss the basic requirements needed to develop shaders through RenderMonkey. I also do a quick outline of the vertex and pixel shader architectures, and a flythrough of tools that you will find useful as you use this book.

Prerequisites

As I just mentioned, you are expected to have a minimal understanding of 3D graphics and especially the mathematics behind them. Although I cover some of the basic topics in the next chapter as reference, I don't go in-depth on those subjects. You are expected to know the basics, which include basic matrix and vector operations, such as dot products and cross products in the R^3 and R^4 space. If you feel your linear algebra skills are a little behind, it might be a good idea at this point to grab a more general 3D book or a linear algebra textbook to brush up on your skills.

Because this book does not dwell on the fine details of specific rendering API and does not target any specific programming language (with the exception of the High-Level Shader Language), few programming skills are needed. This philosophy allows the book to present shaders in a neutral environment that enables both programmers and technically minded artists to take advantage of the new shader craze!

Beyond the intellectual requirements, here is a basic list of software and hardware you'll need to use the contents of this book:

- DirectX 9.0 SDK (included on the CD).
- RenderMonkey by ATI Technologies (included on the CD).
- Windows 2000 (with service pack 2) or Windows XP (Home or Professional) operating system.
- Pentium 3 class or better processor.
- At least 256MB of RAM.
- 500MB of hard disk space.
- A high-end 3D graphics card. I recommend either a Radon 9800 or GeForce FX class card. Since I use vertex and pixel shaders extensively throughout the book, hardware with support for these shader models is strongly recommended. You may still use lesser hardware, but you will need to use software emulation, which will significantly lessen performance.
- And of course, the latest drivers for your video card.

With those prerequisites in mind, you will be able to start exploring and developing the shaders from this book by using RenderMonkey. You will also be able to start exploring your own creativity and creating your own shaders from scratch with the skills you will gain throughout the book. Appendix C contains all the instructions you need to install the software included with this book and get you on the right track to shader mastery.

In the following section, I review the improvements and architectures of vertex and pixel shader version 2.0 over 1.0/1.1. In Chapter 2, I elaborate on a more complete survey of 3D rendering and hardware architectures.

Vertex and Pixel Shader Pipelines and Capabilities

Vertex and pixel shader model 2.0 brings many significant new improvements to the language since the introduction of version 1.0 and 1.1 with DirectX 8.0. Because of the recent release of DirectX 9.0, and the release of vertex and pixel shader 2.0-compliant video cards, this book focuses mostly on developing shaders based on this technology.

note

Although the use of a vertex and pixel shader 2.0-compatible video card is strongly recommended, you can still take advantage of the shaders developed throughout this book with the reference rasterizer. The reference rasterizer will emulate the needed vertex and pixel shader functionality by using a software renderer. However, remember that any emulation is always significantly slower than the real thing!

I assume you already have a basic knowledge of 3D, so let's start by going over the significant changes introduced by the second generation of shader languages over their legacy counterparts.

Vertex shader 2.0 and 2.1 include the following improvements:

- Support for integer and Boolean data types and proper setup instructions.
- Increased number of temporary and constant registers.
- The maximum instruction count allowable for a program has increased. Developers have more flexibility (the minimum required by the standard has gone from 128 to 256, but each hardware implementation can support more).
- Many new macro instructions, allowing complex operations such as Sine/Cosine, Absolute, and Power.
- Support for flow control instruction such as loops and conditionals.

The following list outlines pixel shader 2.0 and 2.x improvements:

- Support for extended 32-bit precision floating-point calculations.
- Support for arbitrary swizzling and masking of register components.

- Increase in the number of available constant and temporary registers.
- Significant increase in the minimum instruction card allowed by the standard, from 8 to 64 arithmetic and 32 texture instructions. Pixel shader 2.x allows even more instructions by default and allows the hardware to go beyond the standard's minimum requirements.
- Support for integer and Boolean constants, loop counters, and predicate registers.
- Support for dynamic flow control, including looping and branching.
- Gradient instructions allowing a shader to discover the derivate of any input register.

With this rich set of improvements, developers are free to set their creativity loose and create stunning effects. At this point, it is probably good to do an overview of their architecture to give you a better understanding of how the information flows throughout the graphics hardware.

note

Because we will focus mostly on the use of Microsoft's HLSL, we will not elaborate on the instructions and syntax about writing shaders directly in assembly. When using assembly, you write your shaders in simple instructions, which the graphics processor executes directly. However, this makes programming more difficult because you have to manage variables and registers, and some simple concepts can translate into several instructions. On the other hand, HLSL is a high-level language that enables you to write shaders in a more logical way without dealing with all the micro-management hassles of hand-writing assembly shaders.

For more information on this, you should consult the documentation provided with the DirectX 9.0 SDK, included on the CD with this book.

It is functionally too expensive to represent a 3D environment in terms of true volumetric representation. Such a representation would be too expensive in memory use and processing requirements, as I will discuss later. Most objects are solid and opaque, causing you to only see their external shapes. If you see an egg, you see its outside, but by simply looking at it, you cannot tell if there is anything inside. Because of this, 3D graphics are simplified by using this idea and representing an object out of its outer shell rather than trying to represent it as a whole. Think of it as building a papier-mâché structure where you must first erect a wire mesh to define the shape you want to build.

In 3D graphics, this wire mesh is represented by a set of polygons, which connect to form an outer shell. Each extremity of each polygon is called a vertex. Vertices are the core of 3D graphics because they transport all the structural information needed to represent the geometry, such as the position, color, and texturing information.

note

I have to add a quick mention about my use of the term *polygon*. Although the definition of polygon implies a shape that can be constructed of any number of sides, it is common practice in 3D rendering to use a polygon in its simplest form, which is a triangle. So throughout this book, I will use both terms with the same meaning.

When rendering 3D graphics, this information passes to the graphics hardware through the use of a rendering API such as Direct3D or OpenGL. Once this information is received by the hardware, it invokes the vertex shader for every vertex in your mesh. Figure 1.1 includes the functional diagram for a vertex shader 2.0 implementation, as dictated by the specifications.

As you can see from Figure 1.1, vertices come in from a stream that is supplied by the developer through a 3D rendering API, such as Direct3D or OpenGL. The stream contains

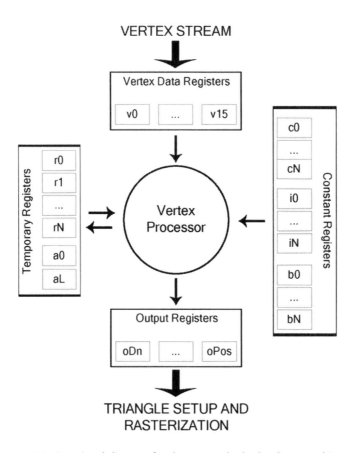

Figure 1.1 Functional diagram for the vertex shader hardware architecture.

all the information needed to properly process the geometry for rendering, such as positions, colors, and texture coordinates. As the information comes in, it is put into the proper input registers, v0 to v15, for use by the vertex shader program. This means that each vertex is processed individually and can be defined by up to 16 pieces of information through the input registers. The vertex shader program then has access to many other registers to complete its task, which consists of taking the input information and processing and transforming it into a form to be used by the pixel shader to perform the final shading and rendering.

Constant registers are read-only registers that must be set ahead of time and are used to carry static information to the shader. Under the vertex shader 2.0 standard, constant registers are vectors and can be floating-point numbers, integer values, or Boolean values. Take note that registers within the vertex shader are stored as a four-component vector, where you can process each component in parallel or individually by using swizzling and masking.

On the left side of Figure 1.1 are the temporary registers, which are used to store intermediate results generated by the vertex shader. Obviously, because of their temporary nature, you can both write and read from these registers. Take note of the registers named a0 and aL. These are counter registers for indexed addressing and for keeping track of loops. They are special cases, and all other registers can be used for any purpose you wish within your shader. Also keep in mind that because HLSL is a high-level shading language, you do not need to take care of register allocation. It will happen transparently as the shader is compiled to its final form.

With access to the vertex data registers (also known as input registers), temporary registers, and constant registers, the vertex shader program is now free to process the incoming vertices and manipulate them in whichever way the developer sees fit. Once the processing is complete, it must pass the results to the final output registers. The most important one is oPos, which must contain the final screen space projected position for the vertex. The other registers carry information such as colors and the final texture coordinates.

Once the vertex shader has done its job, the information is then passed along to the rasterizer. This part of the hardware takes care of deciding the screen pixel coverage of each polygon. It also takes care of other rendering tasks, such as vertex information interpolation and occlusion.

Interpolation is the process by which the information defined at the vertices for a polygon is transitioned so that each pixel has a proper value. Imagine a line with one vertex at each end. If one is black and the other is white, at some point in the middle of the line you need a color that is somewhere between, like gray. Interpolation performs the same process on the whole scale of the triangle. The occlusion process, on the other hand, takes care of which portions of the polygon are onscreen. Determining this enables us to not waste valuable processing time shading portions of a polygon that you can't see in the first place. This helps reduce the overall work that must be done by the hardware. After the rasterizer determines the pixel coverage, the pixel shader is invoked for each screen pixel drawn. Figure 1.2 includes the functional diagram for the pixel shader architecture.

As you can see from the diagram in Figure 1.2, the hardware sends the pixels it calculates through the input color and texture registers. Those values are based on the perspective interpolation of the values defined through the vertex shader. Registers v0 and v1 are meant to be the interpolated diffuse and specular lighting components. The registers t0 to tN carry interpolated texture lookup coordinates. You may notice in Figure 1.2 that the arrows for the texture registers go both ways. This is due to a design decision, which also allows you to write to the texture registers and use them as a temporary register by writing to them. Finally, s0 to sN point to the textures that the pixel shader will sample during the actual processing of the pixel. Although those registers have clear semantics, they can be used to carry any information from the vertex shader onto the pixel shader.

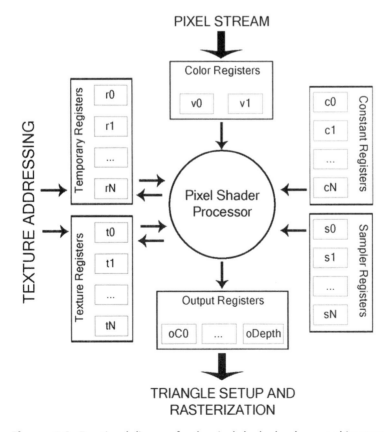

Figure 1.2 Functional diagram for the pixel shader hardware architecture.

The constant registers, c0 to cN, can only be read and are set up ahead of time by the developer with values useful to the shader. Finally, the temporary registers, r0 to rN, are read/write and keep track of intermediate results during the processing of the pixel. When using HLSL, all register usage and allocation is done automatically and is transparent to the user.

Finally, the output registers, such as oC0 and oDepth, are used by the hardware to render the final pixel. They define its final color, fogging, and depth, and in the end, it is your job to have your pixel shader determine these values. Once the pixel has gone through the pixel shader, the output information is then used to blend the final result onto your frame buffer, which is then presented on your computer screen.

note

Temporary registers within vertex shaders are meant to keep temporary values for the processing of a single vertex. By design, values within the temporary registers are not guaranteed to remain from one vertex to another, and you should not assume they are.

Most registers in pixel shaders, with the exception of some addressing registers, are vectors comprised of four floating-point values. The advantage of the vectorial architecture is that it allows processing of multiple values at the same time. By default, all floating-point values are processed as 32-bit precision floating-point numbers. The pixel shader specification allows processing of 16-bit precision values, which can be enabled by special instructions. On certain hardware implementations, the use of 16-bit floating-point arithmetic can be significantly faster.

The last thing to note is that as with the vertex shader vector values, pixel shader vector components can also be swizzled and masked to enable us to manipulate and extract individual components. The swizzling operation allows you to take any combination, in any order, of the components of a vector. For more information on swizzling and masking, refer to the HLSL reference found in Appendix A.

Keep in mind that this is a simplified survey of the rendering architecture, and much more does happen behind the scenes. Also remember that this architecture may vary slightly from one hardware implementation to another. However, the standard does guarantee that for two different implementations with the same capabilities, the final output must be the same.

note

Although DirectX 9 also introduces vertex and pixel shaders version 3.0, we will not focus on taking advantage of their features. They were introduced as support for possible future hardware and cannot by used for any real-time applications at the time of this writing.

Tool Overview

You will soon realize that learning shaders isn't simply done on paper; tools are required to get the job done. In this section I present the tools you will most likely need to use throughout the book, either to complete the exercises or simply to explore your creativity.

RenderMonkey

This great tool was developed by ATI Technologies as a great user-interface-driven way to create shaders by taking advantage of DirectX 9.0's features. This tool gives the user a great way to assemble shaders by assembling basic building blocks without having an extensive knowledge of programming or 3D APIs. Figure 1.3 shows a sample of RenderMonkey in action with a sample shader.

Because of its power and flexibility, I use RenderMonkey as our primary shader development tool throughout the book. For this reason, I have dedicated Chapter 3, "RenderMonkey Version 1.5," to introduce this wonderful tool to you.

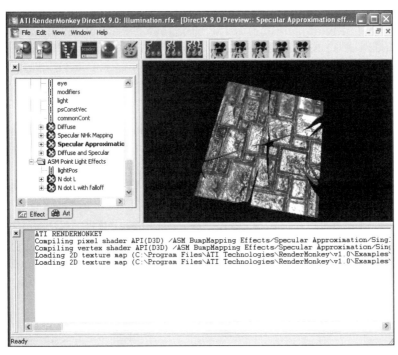

Figure 1.3 Screenshot of RenderMonkey in action.

Microsoft Texture Tool

Microsoft has developed a simple, yet powerful, tool as part of their DirectX SDK. This tool, as shown in Figure 1.4, can do many basic texture manipulation tasks. Some of its functionality includes:

- Support for extended 32-bit precision floating-point calculations.
- Changing the format of textures.
- Creating cubemap and volume textures.
- Exporting textures to the Microsoft .DDS file format.

note

To have access to the Microsoft Texture Tool, you will need to install the DirectX 9.0 SDK, included on the CD with this book.

Because .DDS files are the primary format used by RenderMonkey, this tool comes in handy from time to time, especially to convert textures if you use an image editor that does not support .DDS files. Also, since most image editing tools do not support special textures such as cubemaps and volume textures, this tool is most useful when you need to compose such textures.

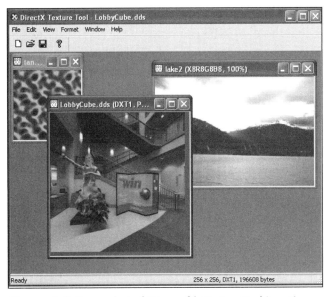

Figure 1.4 Screenshot of Microsoft's Texture Tool in action.

note

Microsoft developed the file format for .DDS files. DDS stands for Direct Draw Surface. The intent behind this format was to have a file format that more closely matched the texture requirements of 3D hardware and exposed some of the more advanced features, such as cubemaps and texture compression.

NVIDIA Photoshop Plug-In

Photoshop is a commercial image, editing program developed by Adobe Software, for which NVIDIA has developed a plug-in allowing you to manipulate .DDS image files directly. Although Photoshop itself may seem a little pricey, if you are serious about image editing, it is a must! NVIDIA's plug-in allows you to do many things with .DDS files, including:

- Import/Export of .DDS files.
- Automatic mipmap generation.
- You can export your .DDS files in any standard DirectX format, including compressed textures such as DXTC.
- Export and import of cubemap textures with a particular image layout.
- Support for image reformatting on export. This includes resizing, filtering, and image color format changes.
- Normal map generation based on a height map, which is useful for bump mapping.

Figure 1.5 shows you the dialog box that shows up when you invoke the NVIDIA plug-in. Take note of all the options and features the tool offers. The NVIDIA Photoshop plug-in is included on the companion CD. You can also download a trial version of Adobe's Photoshop by going to Adobe's Web site at www.adobe.com.

3D Studio Max

Besides editing textures, you need to be able to edit geometry. As of this writing, RenderMonkey supports .3DS and .X files, which are export formats supported by 3D Studio Max by Discreet. 3D Studio Max is a commercial (and fairly expensive) 3D editing package that is used by many video game developers because of its ease and flexibility. Figure 1.6 shows 3DSMax in action with a sample scene loaded.

Because of an increasing demand by the gaming community to have 3D editors available to them so they can modify games, Discreet has developed Gmax, a free feature-reduced version of 3DS Max. Although GMax has a more limited set of functionalities than its big brother, it is a good starting point and will enable you to do most of the tasks needed to build your own geometry. You can download GMax from Discreet's Web site at www.discreet.com.

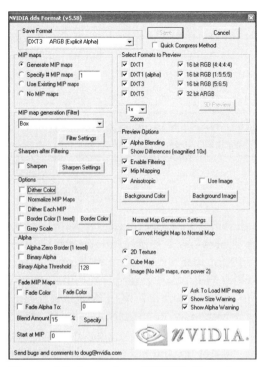

Figure 1.5 Screenshot of NVIDIA's Photoshop plug-in in action.

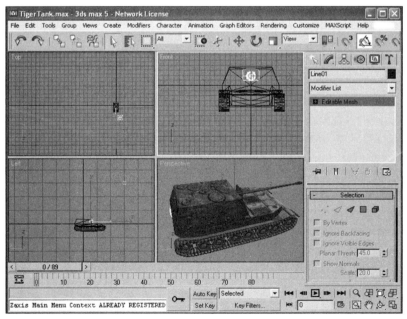

Figure 1.6 Screenshot of 3D Studio Max in action.

For the purpose of this book, you will not need to create geometry on your own; you will use some pre-supplied sample geometry. On the other hand, if you are serious about creating your own shaders and geometry, you should consider getting 3DSMax and learning how to use it.

note

.X files are a 3D model format developed by Microsoft. A 3DSMax-compatible export plug-in is included with the DirectX SDK on the CD accompanying this book.

Microsoft Effect Editor

As part of the DirectX 9.0 SDK, Microsoft has developed a tool called Effect Edit, which is similar to RenderMonkey in the sense that it provides a simple framework to edit shaders. This tool is based around Microsoft's .FX format, which is an extension of the High-Level Shader Language allowing the developer to specify multiple techniques and render states to use when rendering. As you can see in Figure 1.7, the Effect Edit tool is simple when compared with RenderMonkey, which may be better suited for more advanced DirectX developers. Because of RenderMonkey's simplicity, it has been chosen as the primary tool for this book. Although we will not use the Microsoft effect editor, I like to mention such tools so you are aware of what is out there.

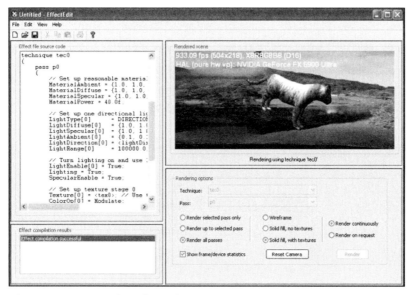

Figure 1.7 Microsoft's Effect Editor utility running a sample shader.

NVIDIA's Cg Toolkit

Because Microsoft's HLSL is aimed at the DirectX SDK, it is limited to the Windows platform; it does not provide a cross-platform solution to high-level shader development. NVIDIA has responded to this lack of cross-platform support by developing, with the support of Microsoft, the Cg shader language. In essence, Cg is compatible with HLSL, and shader programs can easily be ported from one form to another. The real advantage of Cg is its rendering API independence, which allows it to operate either under DirectX or OpenGL.

With the introduction of the Cg shader language came the release of the Cg Toolkit. This toolkit includes the Cg compiler and runtime components, documentation, and many shader samples for developers to experiment with. Also included in the toolkit is the Cg browser, which serves as a simplified shader development framework. However, we will not use this toolkit in this book because it is aimed more towards software developers than simple shader development.

If you wish to try out the Cg Toolkit, you can download it from NVIDIA's developer Web site at www.NVIDIA.com.

It's Your Turn!

Throughout this book, you will find "It's your turn!" sections at the end of most chapters. These sections will invite you to do extra exercises based on the topics covered in a chapter. This will encourage you to apply what you have learned and explore your own creativity. You can find the proposed solutions to the exercises in Appendix D.

For this chapter, we simply suggest that you install the content from the CD and play around with the samples and tools included with the book. This way you can get used to the layout and have all the data and tools handy while you read the following chapters.

What's Next?

At this point, I hope you are excited and ready to start writing shaders. I have gone over the basic requirements, tools, and technologies involved in shader development. This knowledge will come in handy later when you start writing actual shaders and in the future when you take on shaders on your own. Now that you know some of the tools you need, it is time to get the ball rolling and teach you some of the skills you need to write shaders.

In the following chapter, we explore the basics of 3D graphics, how it works, and the architectures used. As I said before, this book is aimed at intermediate to advanced 3D developers, so you're probably already familiar with the next chapter's content, but it is still worthwhile to take a bird's-eye view of the basic concepts needed to render 3D graphics.

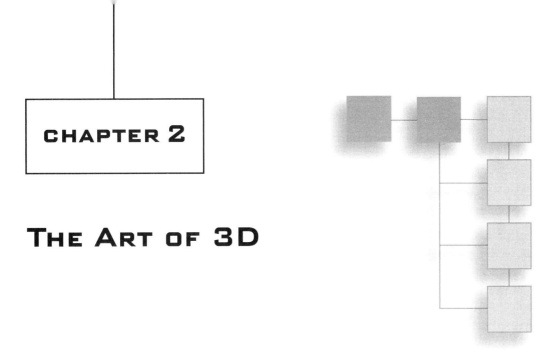

CHAPTER 2

THE ART OF 3D

Although I assume that you have a basic understanding of 3D rendering and its implications, it is still good to go over the basics once again as a reference, and that's what I'll be doing in this chapter. People take such things for granted and forget all the reasoning that led to today's modern 3D graphics hardware architecture and software APIs.

Here you will find a discussion of the fundamental principles behind today's 3D graphics and the math behind those principles. You will also learn about the current standard APIs used in the industry, and the common hardware architectures used to implement such graphics. Finally, I'll provide a history of shaders and how they integrate into today's rendering pipeline.

This chapter may seem boring to some and too technical to others. However, today's rich and photorealistic real-time graphics come from years of research and development. To be proficient and take advantage of the latest technologies, you should first understand where they came from.

From the Ground Up

You want to draw something realistic onscreen, and your challenge is to represent a 3D world on a flat 2D screen. In the next few sections, you will learn about the basic approach that most rendering architectures take in order to render their geometry onscreen. I will start with the basic elements and expand into a more real-life view of what happens under the hood with today's rendering architectures.

Looking at Our Universe

The first thing to consider before rendering is what our universe is made of. The universe we want to draw is composed of objects that are made of molecules. If we were to draw objects by taking into consideration all the little particles that comprise them, our rendering would look awesome, but we would run into some serious problems. A simple little object contains millions of atoms, which would need tremendous amounts of memory and processing power to display.

Such rendering is approximated in fields such as medical imaging and is called volumetric rendering. However, even if you were to estimate a 3D object by a 256 × 256 × 256 grid of particles, you would get a coarse approximation and still need about 64MB worth of memory just to represent this simple object (and this doesn't even include the processing power required to render your object). Obviously, this approach may work for some specialized fields, but it is still out of reach for general-purpose rendering.

Because volumetric rendering is still too prohibitive, we need a better approximation. If we take into consideration that most of the objects we render are solids and are opaque, we can take a much better-suited approach. What if we represented objects by their solid outer shells?

Essentially, this approach is similar to making a papier-mâché figure. First, using a metal mesh, you define the shape you wish to create. After you have the shape you want, you cover the mesh with papier mâché and let it dry. To complete your shape, you apply some colorful paint and . . . voilà!

Although this analogy sounds childish, this is essentially the approach taken in most current 3D rendering architectures. As shown in Figure 2.1, the metal mesh is equivalent to the vertices and edges that define the shape of your object and set the groundwork on which your object will be built.

Although this mesh defines a shape, we still need to make it solid. This is where the papier-mâché comes in. As shown with the teapot in Figure 2.2, intersection points on the mesh are connected with triangular polygons. These polygons will be filled by the rendering hardware, thus giving your object a solid outer shell.

It may interest you to know why polygons are generally defined as triangles in common rendering architectures. First of all, triangles are the simplest shape that can be defined with an actual surface area, and thus it serves as a fundamental building block for the creation of meshes. Although you could use more complex polygons, and some unusual architectures do, you are bound to encounter two problems. The first significant issue comes from the fact that by using a more complex shape as your fundamental primitive, such as a square, you may not be able to define more complex shapes as accurately. In addition, the mathematics for rasterizing more complex polygons, which means determining the pixel coverage of a polygon, becomes much more complex because you would have to deal with non-convex polygons.

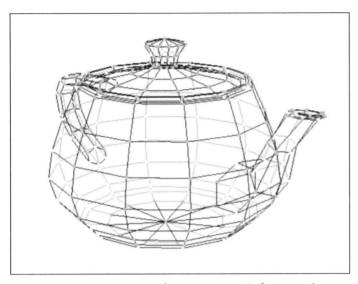

Figure 2.1 Representation of a teapot as a wireframe mesh.

Figure 2.2 Representation of a teapot with polygons
interconnecting the mesh segments.

Although you don't need to let your polygons dry, they still need some color, and this is
where textures come in. Simply apply a texture (or many), lighting, and other coloring,
and you have a realistic-looking solid object like the one shown in Figure 2.3.

Figure 2.3 A snapshot of the teapot with texturing.

Of course, how realistic your object looks mostly depends on how fine-grained your mesh is and how much texturing you apply. This is a compromise that needs to be made to balance your renderings based on the application, the realism wanted, and the target performance.

Here we have examined the case of a single object. But the universe is composed of many objects. What if you want more than one teapot, or what if you want a teapot and a rubber duck? All of the objects in your universe are positioned, and the next thing we need to discuss is how this happens.

The positioning of an object in the world is representable by three components: position, rotation, and scale. Although there are different ways in which positioning components can be represented, the most commonly used form is a matrix representation.

The object's vertices define the relative position from the object's center, which is also referred to object space. By assigning a transformation matrix to each object in the world, you can represent a specific object in the world by transforming its vertices from the object space onto the world space, which is the coordinate system representing the universe.

In the following sections, you will learn how each of the three components can be represented by the use of matrices.

Translation Matrix

Positioning an object in space requires that the object be given a 3D spatial coordinate. The coordinate itself is about the origin of the world, which is defined arbitrarily. Figure 2.4 demonstrates translation and its matrix representation.

note

When talking about a 3D world, the term "origin" is used to define the center of the world. In simple terms, it represents the point in space that has a zero coordinate and from which all positions are defined.

Scale Matrix

Sometimes objects need to be scaled because they need to be represented in the world in a different size than that in which they were originally created. Scales can be applied arbitrarily in any of the three axes. Figure 2.5 shows how scaling is represented in matrix form.

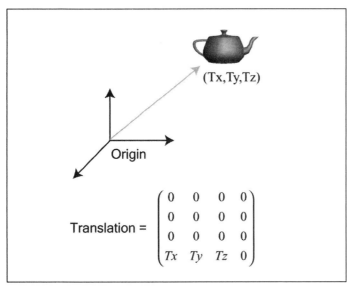

Figure 2.4 Translation and its matrix representation.

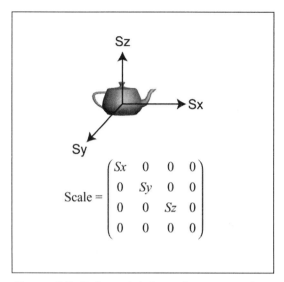

Figure 2.5 Scales and their matrix representation.

n o t e

Before I get ahead of myself, you may wonder what I mean by *axes*. When dealing with coordinates in a 3D world, you need to be able to represent any position from a position that is at the center, or origin, of the world. There is a reason why our world is considered three-dimensional; it implies that we need three distinct coordinates defined along three axes, which are generally perpendicular. The best way to understand this concept is to imagine that you are in a room and want to define the position of an object relative to you. You can use three axes to define where a specific object is, such as saying that a lamp in the room is 3 feet to your left, 5 feet above your head, and 10 feet in front of you.

Rotation Matrix

In addition to positioning and scaling objects in your world, you will need to rotate them. In matrix form, the rotation is represented by a sequence of rotations along the object's X,Y, and Z axes. Figure 2.6 illustrates rotations and their matrix representation.

Now that you understand how the basic transformations can be represented in matrix form, you still need to understand how to combine these operations to achieve the final transformation matrix used to convert an object's representation from object space into world space. Combining several transformation operations in matrix form is straightforward and is performed by multiplying the matrices together. This is as far as I will go in regards to matrix operations and linear algebra, because this is the bare minimum you need to know to place an object onscreen. If this all seems like gibberish to you, I strongly

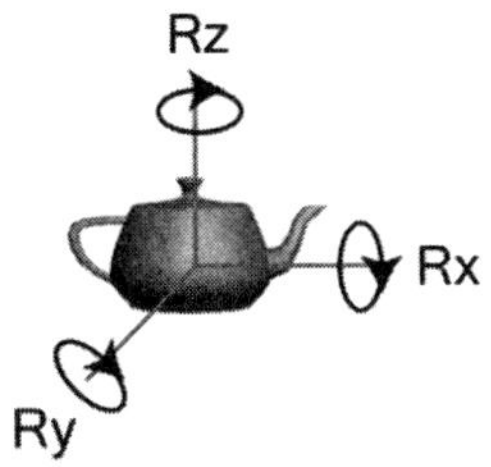

$$Rx = \begin{pmatrix} 1 & 0 & 0 & 0 \\ 0 & \cos\theta & -\sin\theta & 0 \\ 0 & \sin\theta & \cos\theta & 0 \\ 0 & 0 & 0 & 1 \end{pmatrix}$$

$$Ry = \begin{pmatrix} \cos\theta & 0 & \sin\theta & 0 \\ 0 & 1 & 0 & 0 \\ -\sin\theta & 0 & \cos\theta & 0 \\ 0 & 0 & 0 & 1 \end{pmatrix} \quad Rz = \begin{pmatrix} \cos\theta & -\sin\theta & 0 & 0 \\ \sin\theta & \cos\theta & 0 & 0 \\ 0 & 0 & 1 & 0 \\ 0 & 0 & 0 & 1 \end{pmatrix}$$

Figure 2.6 Rotations and their matrix representation.

suggest you pick up a more complete 3D rendering book or a linear algebra textbook to brush up on your 3D math. Try *Course's Mathematics for Game Developers* by Christopher Tremblay (ISBN: 159200038X).

Viewing It from a Camera

At this point, you should understand how an object is represented in a 3D world for rendering purposes. I also gave a brief overview of how such objects can be positioned in your virtual world through the use of matrix transformation operations. However, this is not enough to enable you to render this world onscreen; there is still something missing. Because we are viewing the world through a screen, this is very much equivalent to having a camcorder positioned in the real world. To reproduce this behavior, we need to place a virtual camera in our virtual world. The camera itself is positioned in the world in the same way as any other object—by using a transform matrix. This is illustrated in Figure 2.7.

With a camera placed in our world, to render our scene, we need to represent our objects relative to the camera, or in camera space. To do this, we need to apply the inverse camera matrix to each object's transform. How to determine the inverse matrix is beyond the scope of this chapter, but it essentially involves applying the reverse transformations applied to the camera in the first place.

Once we have this inverse camera matrix, we can combine it with each object's transform matrix and get the camera space transformation for each object. This combined

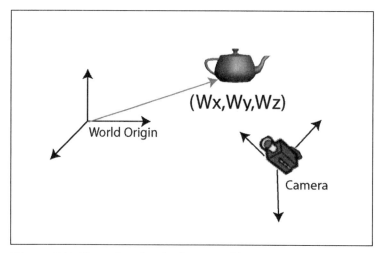

Figure 2.7 Illustration of a simple scene with a camera.

transformation, shown in Figure 2.8, essentially represents the objects in a form about the camera's origin instead of being relative to the world's origin.

Are we rendering yet? Not exactly. Our camera is positioned in the world, but we still need to render to the screen. Unfortunately, computer displays are still a flat 2D medium, and we have to somehow represent our 3D geometry on that flat 2D surface. This is called projecting, therefore, the projection matrix. I will not go into details as to how the projection matrix is derived, but Figure 2.9 demonstrates a standard perspective matrix and what each component represents.

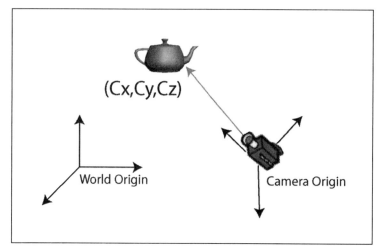

Figure 2.8 Transforming an object from world space to camera space.

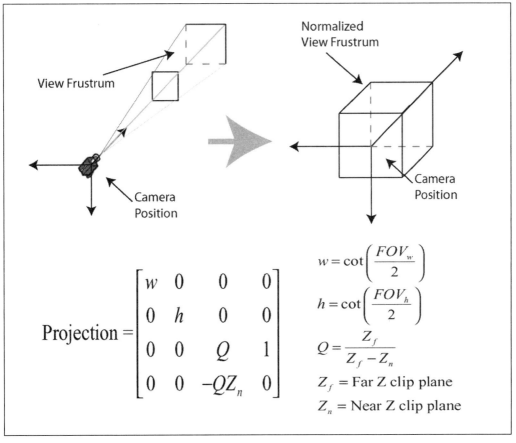

$$w = \cot\left(\frac{FOV_w}{2}\right)$$

$$h = \cot\left(\frac{FOV_h}{2}\right)$$

$$\text{Projection} = \begin{bmatrix} w & 0 & 0 & 0 \\ 0 & h & 0 & 0 \\ 0 & 0 & Q & 1 \\ 0 & 0 & -QZ_n & 0 \end{bmatrix}$$

$$Q = \frac{Z_f}{Z_f - Z_n}$$

Z_f = Far Z clip plane

Z_n = Near Z clip plane

Figure 2.9 A projection matrix and its components.

From Figure 2.9, you can see that the equations can be daunting. The essential is that the w and h components of the matrix define the width and height of the screen in terms of the field of view of the camera (FOV), which is the size of the viewing cone defined by the camera. The Q and QZ components of the matrix define the near and far clipping plane of the camera, in essence the depth region for which your camera will render.

note

There are several different types of projection matrixes that can be used, depending upon the coordinate system used and 3D API specifications. In our example, we show a matrix based on the Direct3D's left-hand coordinate system.

This projection matrix can be applied to objects in the same way other transforms are applied. Multiplying this matrix by our object's camera space transformation gives us a screen space matrix. As Figure 2.10 shows, the object-camera-screen matrix essentially takes an object from our world and transforms and projects it onto our screen.

Under the Hood

With the projection matrix applied to our vertices, we now have a representation of our geometry that fits on the computer screen. Because we assume our objects are opaque, we generally cannot see the inside of them. You cannot see the polygons from inside the mesh, so you don't need to render them. Most 3D architectures take advantage of this to optimize rendering by removing the faces that are facing away from the camera; this is called *back face culling*. Whether a polygon is facing the camera or not is determined by whether the vertices in a polygon are being rendered clockwise or counterclockwise; this is known as the polygon's *winding order*.

Once this optimization is done, most renderers also perform clipping. Clipping serves two main purposes. The first is to optimize the rendering by completely removing polygons that are totally outside the screen. The second reason for clipping is to ensure that polygons that are partially in the screen are trimmed to the size of the screen to reduce the computational load.

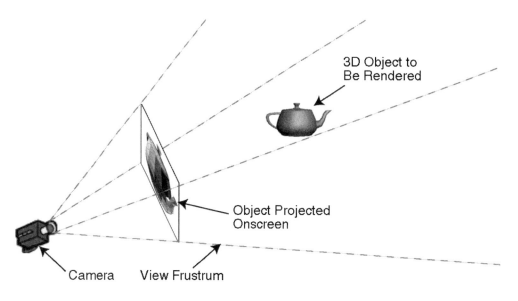

3D Object to Be Rendered

Object Projected Onscreen

Camera   View Frustrum

Figure 2.10 The process of projecting an object onto the screen using the projection matrix.

Now we know where the polygons are on our screen, and whether they are visible, but we now need to draw something on those polygons. Rendering architectures perform what is called *rasterizing*. We know where our polygon is going to be onscreen, so we can now determine which pixels the object will be occupying onscreen. The rasterizing process usually divides the polygon into horizontal strips of pixels that can be rendered. For each of those strips, the renderer can also interpolate the vertex information (position, color, and texture coordinates) correctly, considering such things as the polygon's 3D perspective onscreen.

For each pixel, we now have all the information we need to draw. At this point, however, most renderers make another optimization to avoid drawing useless pixels. For each pixel drawn onscreen, depth information is also stored in the Z-buffer. This Z-buffer keeps track of the front-most pixels as the scene is rendered. For each new pixel (or fragment), we can compare against the Z-buffer to determine if the pixel is visible or hidden behind another pixel.

If the pixel is not occluded by other pixels, we can use the texture coordinates that have been interpolated and combine them with the vertex color and other vertex information to render the pixel on the screen. After the output color is determined, other rendering operations, such as alpha blending and stencil testing, may occur before the pixel is put onscreen.

Lather, rinse, repeat! Do this for every pixel of every polygon, and you have a rendered scene. Keeping in mind that this is a fairly simplified overview of how rendering happens, it should give you a good understanding of what happens under the hood. And as you can see, a lot happens! Later in this chapter, you'll learn how vertex and pixel shaders tie into all this.

3D APIs

Now that we have seen how rendering usually happens within the hardware, there is still a big piece of the puzzle missing. We need to be able to tell the hardware which geometry to render and how to render it. Because of this, we need an API that is able to communicate with the hardware.

The first consumer 3D card on the market, the 3Dfx, had its own proprietary API named Glide. This API enabled you to communicate directly with the hardware and render your geometry. However, such a proprietary API had a big shortfall. As other companies came out with their own 3D hardware, it was almost impossible for developers to write 3D applications that could work equally on all 3D graphics cards. There was a need for a more standardized, non–hardware-specific API for 3D rendering. This need was answered by OpenGL hardware drivers and Microsoft's Direct3D.

OpenGL

OpenGL was initially developed by Silicon Graphics, Inc. (SGI) in the late 1980s. It was developed as a multipurpose, platform-independent, 3D graphics API. The first functional public release of the OpenGL API was in 1990 with the release of Version 1.0. Since 1992, the development of OpenGL has been overseen by the ARB (OpenGL Architecture Review Board). This review board is made up of major graphics card and industry leaders, such as NVIDIA, ATI Technologies, IBM, Intel, SGI, and many more. The role of the ARB is to keep the standard up to date and maintain the OpenGL specifications so that they consider current and future industry needs.

The current mainstream version of OpenGL is Version 1.5. This implies that OpenGL does not get updated often. However, the ARB is working hard on a new version of the specifications, one that takes better advantage of the latest technologies.

OpenGL initially was designed to be used in high-end graphics workstations, and until recently, it had the power to take full advantage of consumer graphics hardware. However, with all the recent advances in computer graphics, such as multitexturing and vertex and pixel shaders, the specifications to the API have fallen behind. Because of this, many graphics hardware vendors have developed extensions to the standard to meet the requirements of the latest innovations. However, there has been little consensus over the last few years in regards to extensions among vendors, and this has led to many proprietary extensions that can only be used on specific hardware. The ARB is hard at work on their latest specifications to ensure a more consistent feature set and better cooperation among vendors, ensuring more compatibility with future extensions.

OpenGL offers a collection of several hundred functions, providing easy access to most graphics features offered by your hardware. Internally, OpenGL acts as a simple state machine. Using the API, you can set various parameters that control the state of the machine, including such things as color, lighting, blending, and so on. Using the same API, you can send geometry and rendering commands to the hardware, which will consider the state of the internal machine within OpenGL.

At the center of OpenGL is the rendering pipeline; whether it is software or hardware, it is implemented in much the same way discussed earlier in this chapter. The whole idea is simple, but most of the effort behind OpenGL is to ensure support for current and future hardware, as well as ensuring a cross-platform development environment.

DirectX and Direct3D

A little while after the release of Windows 95, the majority of games were still being developed for the DOS platform. Microsoft decided it was time for game developers to move away from the antiquated DOS platform and towards the Windows platform, thereby increasing the popularity of Windows. Windows, however, did not make a good gaming platform because its internal graphics API had too many abstraction layers and was tuned for user interface development, so it was way too slow! At that point in time, Microsoft decided to create an API aimed more at game development, allowing more direct hardware access and allowing games to run under Windows at reasonable speeds.

Rather than develop its own 3D API from scratch, Microsoft noticed a promising 3D API being developed by a company called RenderMorphics. It was a small project the company developed and was promoting at trade shows. Microsoft decided to take advantage of this API and integrate it as part of what was known at that time as the Game SDK. Eventually, the Game SDK was renamed DirectX 1.0. But at that point, the API did not become widely accepted because it was slow, buggy, and poorly structured.

On the plus side, Microsoft has been known through the years for not abandoning an idea when it didn't work out as they planned. They kept working at it, asking the developer community for suggestions and feedback. In 1998 came the first truly viable version of the SDK, dubbed DirectX 3.0. At that point in time, the API started taking form and getting a broader adoption among developers. As the years went by, Microsoft has released Versions 5, 6, 7, 8, and finally Version 9.0 of the SDK. Each version has performed better and offered more of the features the community wanted. One big step in the evolution of DirectX was Version 8.0, which was the first one to include support for the now famous vertex and pixel shader architectures.

The structure of Direct3D, and DirectX in general, is hugely different from OpenGL. As time goes on, however, DirectX is slowly becoming more and more like OpenGL. Without going into all the details, I'll just say that DirectX is based on the COM object model. What this means is that you create pointers to classes and use those, rather than just calling functions that don't clearly show associations, thus making DirectX better structured than OpenGL.

Which One Is Better?

There has been major debate and battle in deciding which API is better: Direct3D or OpenGL. On one side, Direct3D and DirectX only function on the Windows platform, leaving little choice to cross-platform developers. However, if you are developing only on the Windows platform, it is worth considering the pros and cons of each API.

Both APIs are straightforward to use. However, DirectX usually needs more initialization code to get going. DirectX is updated more often and is better suited to take advantage of the latest technologies than OpenGL. DirectX offers a better object-oriented structure than OpenGL, but on the flipside, OpenGL is generally simpler to use. Most developers have a bias towards one or the other, but new developers can easily be satisfied with either one.

Because this book does not try to focus on any specific API, the answer to this debate will remain unanswered here. Since RenderMonkey currently uses DirectX internally, a few of the development constraints and concepts will come from the DirectX API. If you do choose to develop using OpenGL, though, the lessons learned throughout this book can be easily carried over.

Hardware Architecture

Now that we have a better understanding of how rendering happens and the major APIs involved in the industry, I will briefly go over the common architecture taken by graphics hardware vendors. Figure 2.11 outlines a simple hardware architecture taken by some graphics hardware. Although this diagram is simple when compared to most modern architectures, it serves the purpose of explaining how such hardware is implemented.

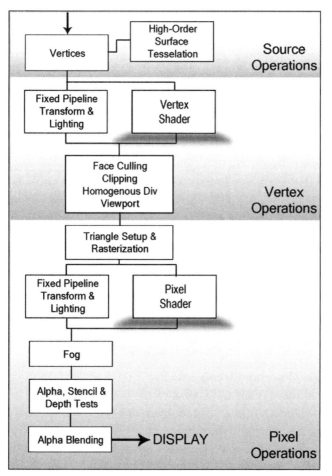

Figure 2.11 Diagram of a possible hardware rendering architecture.

As you can see from Figure 2.11, the whole rendering process can be divided into three distinct categories of operations: source operations, vertex operations, and pixel operations.

The source operations essentially take the incoming vertex data and prepare it for processing. Some hardware architectures allow for high-order surface tessellation, which can take a curved surface description as a geometry source and create polygons on the fly by a tessellation process. Such high-order surfaces have the distinct advantage of allowing more flexibility on the geometric detail based on certain criteria, such as performance and screen size of the mesh.

The next sequence of operations is the vertex operations. This is where vertex shaders come into play. As you can see from Figure 2.11, the incoming vertices from the source operations phase can go either through the vertex shader block or the fixed-pipeline block. The fixed-pipeline is the legacy, backward-compatible implementation, which can take care of transforming and lighting the geometry. Because the fixed-pipeline is there for backward-compatibility, most developers now choose to use vertex shaders. After the vertices have gone through the vertex shader or fixed-pipeline block, they go through the next block, which takes care of the final operations before the actual polygons are formed from the vertex stream. The operations at this point include back face culling, clipping, homogenous space division, and viewport considerations.

Now that your vertices have been massaged and are ready to be drawn, you can move on to the pixel operation phase. The first block in the phase is the triangle setup and rasterization operation. What this does is take the incoming vertex stream, set up polygons from it, and rasterize the triangles into screen pixels. As mentioned earlier, in the rasterization, the screen coverage of the polygons in pixels is determined. After the coverage is determined, it is broken into smaller components, generally horizontal lines of pixels, which are called fragments.

We now have pixels, but they still need to be finalized before they are drawn. This is where our next block comes in. As with the vertex shader, here our pixels can go through either our pixel shader or our fixed-pipeline. Either one of them will take the incoming interpolated pixel information from the rasterization and determine the final pixel color by using texture lookups and other pixel operations. After the final color is determined, it can go through the final set of blocks, which takes care of common rendering operations such as fog, alpha testing, and stencil testing. This leaves us with a final pixel, which can be blended onto the output buffer, ready to be displayed on our screen. One thing to note is that with current hardware architectures, multiple pixels can be processed simultaneously in parallel.

Voilà! Well . . . it's a little more complicated than this in real life with the latest technologies. We've omitted some steps, such as Z-buffering, and new things, such as occlusion testing and compression. However, this should give you a good idea of how our previously discussed rendering algorithm integrates in a hardware architecture. More importantly, it gives you a much better idea as to where vertex and pixel shaders fit into the hardware rendering flow of information. For the scope of this book, we will focus mostly on the vertex and pixel shader operations that have been highlighted in Figure 2.11.

Shaders

You now have an understanding of how rendering happens. But where did shaders come in, and how do they factor into the rendering equation? Computer graphics developers soon discovered that photo realistic rendering has too many variables that cannot be expressed as a simple set of equations or represented by a fixed set of states. In fact, most photo realistic renderings depend partly on equations derived from research and partly on taking real-life observations and trying to reproduce them. Because of this, developers needed a way to fully control the flow of information so they could implement the complex algorithms required for realistic renderings. One of the first incarnations of such architectures, dubbed RenderMan, was developed by Pixar Animation Studios.

RenderMan is actually a standard that was developed a little over 15 years ago. Its purpose was to specify an information exchange scheme to allow compatibility between 3D authoring software and the actual renderer. In addition to specifying the format in which data is exchanged, the standard also defined a programmable approach to materials, allowing developers to specify how surfaces should be rendered. This was accomplished through a simple language, similar to the C language, which allows developers to take the incoming data from the renderer and apply their own algorithms before it is rendered.

RenderMan itself only defines a standard, but Pixar has developed an actual software renderer based on it. Through the use of RenderMan and their own renderer, Pixar proved the use of shaders could produce stunning computer graphics, and RenderMan has now been used in countless CG movies. RenderMan itself was never designed to be used as a real-time shading language and lends itself better to the rendering of movie-grade graphics, which can take a long time to render, but served as the basis from which real-time shading languages were defined.

Because of the success brought about by the flexibility of RenderMan, hardware makers wanted the same flexibility for hardware-accelerated solutions. However, at the time, hardware graphics processor performance wasn't sufficient to allow for programmable shaders, especially per-pixel shaders. Until a few years ago, hardware makers and developers had to live with the limitations of the fixed-pipeline rendering architecture. Finally, with the leaps and bounds of silicon chip-making, hardware could be developed that could finally include programmable shader support.

With the release of the DirectX 8.0 SDK came the first graphics chip capable of rendering with hardware-accelerated shaders. The hardware developed by NVIDIA had limited capabilities but fully implemented the vertex and pixel 1.1 shader standard. This first shader standard had limited functionality and did not include such things as conditional statements and looping support. The pixel shader support also was very limited in terms of instruction count and texture operations. However, this was the first time developers could move away from the constraints of the fixed-pipeline and be allowed to express their own creativity. At the same time, NVIDIA also released their own OpenGL extension fully exposing their vertex and pixel shader architecture to developers.

Because of the fierce competition in the graphics hardware industry, ATI Technologies, the main competition to NVIDIA had to respond to this first release of hardware accelerated shaders. In collaboration with Microsoft, ATI Technologies developed vertex and pixel shader version 1.4, which was released with the DirectX 8.1 SDK. This new version added more flexibility to the pixel shader architecture by allowing more texture operations, more arithmetic operations, and the possibility of interleaving texture operations with arithmetic operations. ATI now had their first generation of hardware-accelerated shader technology. Because of the impending release of the DirectX 9.0 SDK, this incarnation of shaders was short-lived.

Microsoft decided it was time for a little more cooperation among hardware vendors, for the sake of the developers. As they developed DirectX 9.0, Microsoft came up with two new shader standards: version 2.0 and version 3.0. Along with the release of Microsoft's latest SDK, ATI and NVIDIA launched their first iterations of vertex and pixel shader 2.0. This new shader standard finally added all that developers could wish for. The new functionality included more instructions per program, conditional expressions, and loops statements.

This is where we are today. We, the developers, now have the same level of functionality that movie CG developers have, and as we can see in the latest technology demos, the quality of graphics never ceases to increase. So what does the future have in store for us? First of all, version 3.0 of the vertex and pixel shader standard will give developers even more power and flexibility. Secondly, with the ever-increasing speed and power of the graphics hardware, industry leaders predict that within the next few years, real-time graphics will equal or surpass the quality of movie CG. This places a much bigger burden on developers because they have to keep up with the crazy evolution. On the flip side, however, we can finally achieve the graphics we have always dreamed of.

It's Your Turn!

There isn't much to do at this point because we are still going over the basics. If you feel lost with all this matrix math and linear algebra, I strongly suggest you get your hands on an algebra textbook and brush up on your math knowledge. Not that much is needed to understand 3D, but you will still need a good understanding of the basics of matrix and vector math to apply the principles learned throughout this book.

What's Next?

Now that we have a better overhead picture of all that is involved in 3D graphics, it is time to zoom in on our main topic of interest: shaders! I have promised to keep us away as much as possible from non-shader programming and 3D APIs, but we have one more thing to learn before we get our hands dirty . . . RenderMonkey.

This powerful tool, developed by ATI Technologies, allows us to learn and use shaders in an intuitive and flexible way. So fire up your computer, and let's start learning . . .

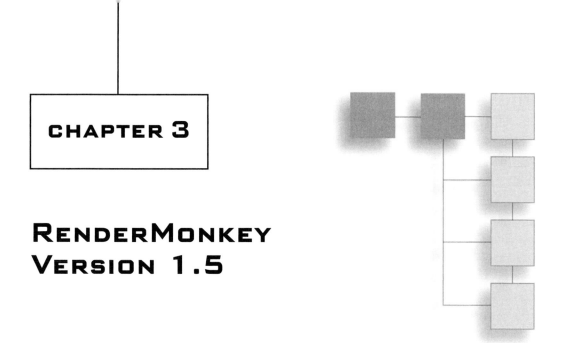

CHAPTER 3

RENDERMONKEY
VERSION 1.5

With the release of the DirectX 9.0 SDK, vertex and pixel shader 2.0 and 3.0 were introduced. These revolutionary new models were great technological breakthroughs and finally made it possible for game developers and artists to consider developing shaders with the use of a high-level language. Because of this, Microsoft has developed the High-Level Shader Language, dubbed HLSL, and included it with their DirectX SDK. However, even to develop and test simple shaders, there is a need to create 3D applications that are dependent on a specific rendering API. Since such an approach needs a fair quantity of code and a basic set of programming skills, it restricts development to intermediate or advanced developers and prevents artists from using their creativity to develop shaders on their own without support from a programmer.

As a response to this issue, ATI Technologies developed a free tool named RenderMonkey. RenderMonkey is a powerful tool that is used throughout this book as a development tool, allowing anybody to develop shaders without any formal programming background. In this chapter you will learn about RenderMonkey and its use. See Appendix B, "Render-Monkey 1.5 User Manual," for a more complete guide to RenderMonkey. The first section of this chapter serves as an overview of RenderMonkey's interface and features. In the second section, you will be guided through the composition of a simple shader within RenderMonkey. As you work your way through this chapter, you will gain a hands-on understanding of how shaders are made using RenderMonkey.

Introduction to RenderMonkey

Recently, ATI Technologies released Version 1.0 of their RenderMonkey tool. This application serves as a simple user interface aimed toward the quick development of shaders and effects. Among its design goals, it considers many factors:

- Shaders are more than just code. They require a framework that takes care of setting up other needed components, such as geometry and textures. Such a tool must handle all this setup and encapsulate it in an easy-to-use way without requiring external code.

- Current methods of shader development are time-consuming and require good quantities of code. This makes the task more difficult and the sharing of technology more restrictive.

- Any shader development tool should help bridge the gap between artists and programmers by removing any API dependencies. Such a tool should also remove the need for programmer intervention in the development of simple or complex shaders.

- The framework for the tool must be flexible enough to allow it to adapt to future technology needs.

Keeping those factors in mind, ATI came up with RenderMonkey, a powerful and efficient tool for shader development. It significantly simplifies and speeds up the shader creation process, making shader development more accessible to any user with a basic understanding of 3D graphics. RenderMonkey Version 1.5 is used throughout this book as the main shader development tool.

Our First Look at RenderMonkey

As you can see in Figure 3.1, there are many subwindows in the main window of RenderMonkey! All of them have straightforward purposes, and I will go over them one by one.

At this point, it is a good idea to have RenderMonkey installed and ready to go. This way you can see for yourself how RenderMonkey works as we explore it. Installation instructions for RenderMonkey are found in Appendix B, "RenderMonkey 1.5 User Manual."

The first and most important window of all is the workspace window, which is located on the left side of the application. This is the staging area where you will compose your shaders by combining various elements in a structured manner. Looking at the zoomed-in version in Figure 3.2, you can see that it contains many different types of elements, which can be categorized into four groups:

- Grouping elements serve the obvious purpose of grouping elements into a hierarchy. Examples are effect groups, effects, and rendering passes.

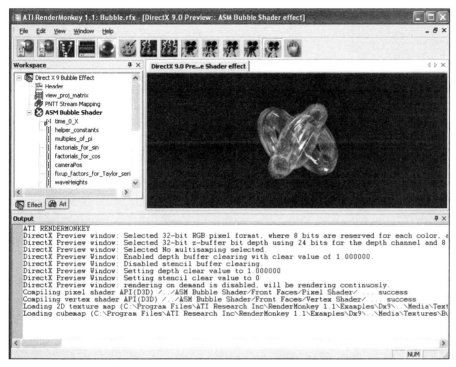

Figure 3.1 RenderMonkey, in action rendering a simple shader.

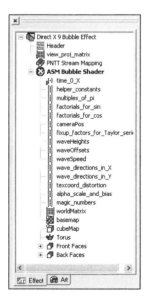

Figure 3.2 Close-up view of RenderMonkey's workspace window.

- Parameters define constants the shader uses such as matrices, vectors, or colors. The artist editor discussed in the following pages can also be used to set such parameters in a user-friendly way.

- States control the behavior of a shader or effect. They consist of shader code, hardware render states, or vertex stream mappings.

- Resources form the data (usually from an external source) used by the shader. Common examples are textures and geometry.

To build a shader, simply to insert the suitable set of elements within the workspace window; RenderMonkey displays the result right away. For the moment, don't worry about what each type of element does; we'll discuss each one individually later in this chapter. All you need to know is that every workspace consists of a set of effect groups. Each effect group, in turn, contains a set of effects, which can then enclose one of many passes. Finally, every rendering pass contains parameters, states, and resource elements for use by the shader.

note

RenderMonkey saves its workspace data in an .RFX file, which is simply an XML file. If you feel comfortable with the XML format, you can open it in a text editor and edit it manually. If you are programming a 3D game or application, you could also support its format natively, significantly reducing your integration time from prototype to final product.

This brings me to the second most important window in RenderMonkey, the preview window, as shown in Figure 3.3. The preview window is where you get to see the fruits of your labor. RenderMonkey draws a final version of your shader in this window based on the elements you specified.

Using the mouse button, you can rotate the camera around your objects, which allows you to see your shader from any angle. With the right mouse button, you can bring up a context menu that allows you to reset the camera into some predefined angles and do other tasks, such as showing object-bounding boxes and resizing the view to fit the object to screen. Also, using buttons in the toolbar at the top of the RenderMonkey application, you can change the mode in which the camera is affected by your mouse movements. Finally, if you don't see what you expect in the preview window, make sure to check the output window for any code errors, and double-check your shader code for any logic errors.

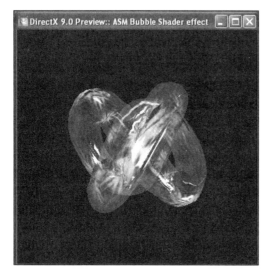

Figure 3.3 Close-up of the preview window showing a simple shader in action.

note

You may have noticed the little tab right above the preview window. When windows such as the preview window are maximized, it may be difficult to navigate from one window to another. These tabs will show you all open windows and give you a quick-and-easy way to access them.

This obviously brings us to the output window. It will come in handy, especially if you are prone to coding errors! In this window, RenderMonkey displays shader compilation errors and other useful warnings it encounters when compiling your shader. Figure 3.4 contains a screen shot of what a sample output looks like.

tip

If you have errors showing up in the output window, you can double-click with your mouse on that line, and RenderMonkey opens the editor window for you with the cursor on the offending line of shader code.

The next window in our RenderMonkey exploration is the editor window, which was not shown in Figure 3.1. This is where you type your shader code. In the current version of RenderMonkey, you can type your code as either HLSL or in vertex and pixel shader assembly language. Throughout this book, we will focus only on the use of the High-Level Shader Language because it is much easier to learn and understand. HLSL is also easier because it allows you to focus more on the actual shader creation process and less on little details like instruction optimization and register allocations.

As you can see in Figure 3.5, the Editor Window actually consists of two parts. The top section consists of general settings and helpers for your shaders, such as target shader version and shader entry point. Finally, the bottom part of the window contains the shader source code in an easy-to-edit, color-highlighted form. You may also notice that the status bar for the editor window gives you statistics on your shader in regards to its instruction count and performance.

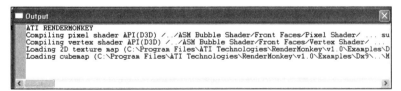

Figure 3.4 Sample output in the output window.

Figure 3.5 A close-up view of RenderMonkey's editor window.

t i p

Take note of the tabs and drop-down list at the top of the editor window; they allow you to quickly switch between all the shaders in your workspace. This is a nice timesaving shortcut!

The last window we need to look at is the artist window. As shown in Figure 3.6, this window simplifies tasks for artists by allowing them to manipulate shader parameters without getting their hands dirty. All parameter elements exposed within the workspace window show up here as a handy set of edit boxes, sliders, and color pickers. You can change any of the parameters and see the new result on the fly. This is a great way for artists to experiment with shader parameters and see the results right away, before they use the shaders in their regular production environment.

Autopsy of a Shader

Now that you have a basic understanding of RenderMonkey's layout, it is time to explore a little deeper by taking a simple shader and performing a little autopsy on it. With this hands-on knowledge, you will have all you need to get started and build your very first shader in Chapter 4, "Getting Started, Your First Shaders."

For the remainder of this chapter, I'll assume RenderMonkey is installed and ready to go. For installation instructions, refer to the user manual in Appendix B.

The first step is to fire up the RenderMonkey application. From the start menu in Windows, select Start: Programs: ATI Technologies: ATI RenderMonkey: RenderMonkey. Figure 3.7 shows an example of where the RenderMonkey program might be found on your computer.

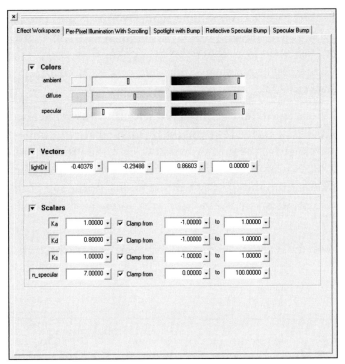

Figure 3.6 A view of the artist window.

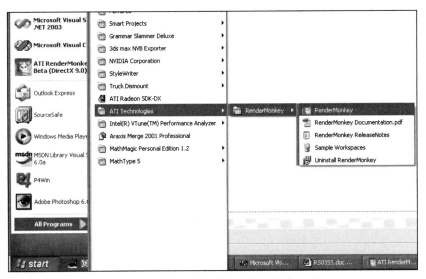

Figure 3.7 How to start RenderMonkey from the Windows Start menu.

After RenderMonkey starts, you need to open the sample shader you will use. For the purpose of this chapter, you will use one of the sample shaders supplied with the tool. To open the workspace, either select File: Open from the menu or click the first icon on the toolbar. You then need to select the `bubble.rfx` shader file. The process used to open the sample shader is illustrated in Figure 3.8.

At this point, the workspace you selected should be displayed within the user interface. You can first look around the object by using your mouse to manipulate the camera within the preview window. If you don't see the preview window, click the Preview toolbar icon at the top of the application. Now, get yourself acquainted with the different camera types by selecting different modes from the right side of the toolbar at the top of the application. As you can see, you can rotate, move around, and even zoom in on the results of the bubble shader.

Now, let's take a look at the skeleton for this shader. Figure 3.9 shows the workspace view for this shader.

Figure 3.8 How to open a sample shader through RenderMonkey.

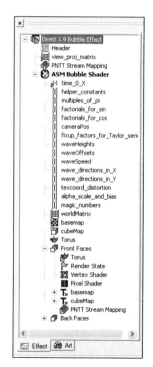

Figure 3.9 Close-up view of the workspace associated with our sample shader.

With the workspace open, you can explore its content element by element. The first node underneath the workspace root is called Header, and this is simply an information node containing some general project comments. The first node of real interest is the next one, named view_proj_matrix. As mentioned in the user manual, this is a stock variable that contains the transformation matrix that is used to do the projection of the vertices from 3D coordinates to 2D screen positions. You will not need to set this variable, because it is filled in automatically by RenderMonkey.

The next item in the workspace is called PNTT Stream Mapping. This node defines how the geometry information is to be sent to the vertex shader. Essentially, this node defines how the information from the geometry will be mapped to the input registers and variables within your shader. If you double-click this item, you will get the dialog box shown in Figure 3.10.

As you can see, the current stream is composed of four elements: position, normal, texture coordinates, and tangent. The mapping defines which piece of information the vertex shader needs, what registers to send it to, and how it should be represented. Now close this dialog box and take a look at the following node. This is an effect group that contains an effect named ASM Bubble Shader. Each effect group essentially represents a different individual shader defined within your workspace. Because you can define multiple shaders within a single RenderMonkey workspace, this is a convenient way to organize your effects.

Under the effect group node, you can see a long list of variables. They serve as constants to be used by the shader to control its behavior. Take a note of the time_0_x variable, which is another built-in constant containing the current time in seconds. This variable is useful when you're developing shaders that are animated over time.

Following the bunch-o-variables are two nodes named basemap and cubemap. They are the textures used by the pixel shader to render the effect. The first one is used to color the bubble, and the second one serves as an environment map to handle reflections.

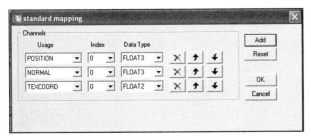

Figure 3.10 Close-up view of the stream mapping window for our sample.

Double-clicking on any texture node brings up a file selection dialog box where you can select a .DDS file (or other standard image file format) to use as a texture.

Now look at the next node, named Torus. This node defines the geometry used by the shader. Currently, RenderMonkey only supports .3DS and .X files. .3DS files require 3DStudio MAX for editing, and .X files are a format developed by Microsoft that can also be edited through 3DSMax. Do not worry, though; RenderMonkey includes a fair number of sample models for you to use. Double-clicking on the geometry node brings up a dialog box that prompts you to choose a model file on your computer.

The next two nodes are render passes named front faces and back faces, the meat of this effect! Shaders can be composed of multiple passes, each of which renders a different version of the geometry. They serve as an easy way to break complex shaders into smaller subsets. Here we will only consider the front faces pass, because the second one is somewhat redundant. Open the render pass, and you will see seven new nodes.

The first node in the render pass is simply a geometry reference node that points back to a model previously loaded in the workspace. The second node is a render state node; if you double-click it, you will see a new dialog box with a list of states with values for those that were modified, as shown in Figure 3.11. For example, you can see that ALPH-ABLENDENABLE has been set to TRUE, telling the hardware to blend the final color of this pass with what is already in the background.

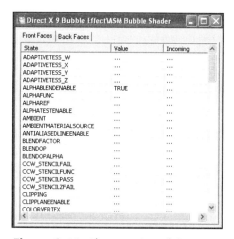

Figure 3.11 Close-up view of the render state window for our sample.

The two following nodes are the core of the effect: the pixel and vertex shaders. This sample shader uses assembly code for its shader code, so we will not look at it. However, for reference and in case you don't have RenderMonkey handy right now, I have included the source code for this shader:

```
vs.1.1

dcl_position v0
dcl_normal   v1
dcl_texcoord v2
dcl_tangent  v3

// c0   - { 0.0,  0.5, 1.0, 2.0}
// c1   - { 4.0, .5pi, pi, 2pi}
// c2   - {1, -1/3!, 1/5!, -1/7!} for sin// c3   - {1/2!, -1/4!, 1/6!, -1/8!} for cos//
```

```
c4-7 - Composite World-View-Projection Matrix
// c8    - Model Space Camera Position
// c10   - {1.02, 0.04, 0, 0} fixup factor for Taylor series imprecision
// c11   - {0.5, 0.5, 0.25, 0.25}
//          waveHeight0, waveHeight1, waveHeight2, waveHeight3
// c12   - {0.0, 0.0, 0.0, 0.0}
//          waveOffset0, waveOffset1, waveOffset2, waveOffset3
// c13   - {0.6, 0.7, 1.2, 1.4}
//          waveSpeed0, waveSpeed1, waveSpeed2, waveSpeed3
// c14   - {0.0, 2.0, 0.0, 4.0}
//          waveDirX0, waveDirX1, waveDirX2, waveDirX3
// c15   - {2.0, 0.0, 4.0, 0.0}
//          waveDirY0, waveDirY1, waveDirY2, waveDirY3
// c16   - { time }
// c17   - {-0.00015, 1.0, 0.0, 0.0} base texcoord distortion x0, y0, x1, y1
// c18   - World Martix

mul r0, c14, v2.x      // use tex coords as inputs to sinusoidal warp
mad r0, c15, v2.y, r0  // use tex coords as inputs to sinusoidal warp

mov r1, c16.x          // time...
mad r0, r1, c13, r0    // add scaled time to move bumps according to frequency
add r0, r0, c12
frc r0.xy, r0          // take frac of all 4 components
frc r1.xy, r0.zwzw
mov r0.zw, r1.xyxy

mul r0, r0, c10.x      // multiply by fixup factor sub r0, r0, c0.y    // subtract
.5
mul r0, r0, c1.w       // mult tex coords by 2pi  coords range from(-pi to pi)

mul r5, r0, r0         // (wave vec)^2
mul r1, r5, r0         // (wave vec)^3
mul r6, r1, r0         // (wave vec)^4
mul r2, r6, r0         // (wave vec)^5
mul r7, r2, r0         // (wave vec)^6
mul r3, r7, r0         // (wave vec)^7
mul r8, r3, r0         // (wave vec)^8

mad r4, r1, c2.y, r0   // (wave vec) - ((wave vec)^3)/3!
mad r4, r2, c2.z, r4   //   + ((wave vec)^5)/5!
mad r4, r3, c2.w, r4   //   - ((wave vec)^7)/7!
```

```
mov r0, c0.z          // 1
mad r5, r5, c3.x ,r0  // -(wave vec)^2/2!
mad r5, r6, c3.y, r5  // +(wave vec)^4/4!
mad r5, r7, c3.z, r5  // -(wave vec)^6/6!
mad r5, r8, c3.w, r5  // +(wave vec)^8/8!


dp4 r0, r4, c11       // multiply wave heights by waves


mul r0, r0, v1        // apply deformation in direction of normal


add r0.xyz, r0, v0    // add to position
mov r0.w, c0.z        // homogenous component


m4x4    oPos, r0, c4  // OutPos = WorldSpacePos * Composite View-Proj Matrix
mov     oT0, v2       // Pass along texture coordinates

;This is where the shader starts to diverge a bit from the Ocean shader.  \;
First the binormal is computed

mov     r3, v1
mul     r4, v3.yzxw, r3.zxyw
mad     r4, v3.zxyw, -r3.yzxw, r4    // cross product to find binormal

;Then the normal is warped based on the tangent space basis vectors
;(tangent and binormal).

mul     r1, r5, c11       // cos * waveheight
dp4     r9.x, -r1, c14    // amount of normal warping in direction of binormal
dp4     r9.y, -r1, c15    // amount of normal warping in direction of tangent
mul     r1, r4, r9.x      // normal warping in direction of binormal
mad     r1, v3, r9.y, r1  // normal warping in direction of tangent
mad     r5, r1, c10.y, v1 // warped normal move nx, ny

;The normal is then renormalized.

mov     r10, r5
m3x3    r5, r10, c18      // transform normal
dp3     r10.x, r5, r5
rsq     r10.y, r10.x
mul     r5, r5, r10.y     // normalize warped normal
```

```
;Next the view vector is computed:
mov      r10, r0
m4x4     r0, r10, c18        // transform vertex position


sub      r2, c8, r0          // view vector
dp3      r10.x, r2, r2
rsq      r10.y, r10.x
mul      r2, r2, r10.y       // normalized view vector

;Then the dot product of the view vector and the warped normal is computed:

dp3      r7, r5, r2          // N.V
mov      oT2, r7             // Pass along N.V

; This is used to compute the reflection vector.

add      r6, r7, r7          // 2N.V
mad      r6, r6, r5, -r2     // 2N(N.V)-V
mov      oT1, r6             // reflection vector
```

Pixel shader code for our sample shader:

```
// c0  - (0.0, 0.5, 1.0, -0.75)
// c1  - (0.6, 0.1, 0.0, 0.0) Alpha Scale and bias
ps.1.4

texld r0, t0
texld r1, t1
texcrd r2.rgb, t2


cmp r2.r, r2.r, r2.r, -r2.r     // abs(V.N)
+mad_x4_sat r1.a, r1.a, r1.a, c0.a // 4 * (a^2 - .75), clamped


mul_x2_sat r2.rgb, r0, r1       //  base * env (may change scale factor later)
+mad r2.a, 1-r2.r, c1.x, c1.y   // alphascale * abs(V.N) + alphabias


lrp r0.rgb, r1.a, r1, r2        // Lerp between Env and Base*Env
+add r0.a, r2.a, r1.a           // Add glow map to Fresnel term for alpha
```

Following the shader code are two texture nodes named basemap and cubemap. They map the texture variables previously set to hardware texture samplers and enable those textures for use within the shader. Double-clicking either of the nodes brings up the dialog box shown in Figure 3.12.

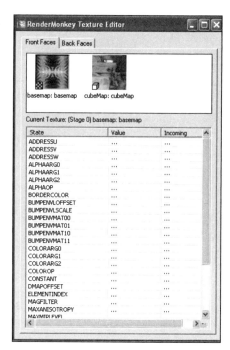

In this dialog box, there is a thumbnail for each texture used in the pass and a set of sampling stage states to tell the graphics hardware how the textures should be sampled. These states can specify things such as whether the texture should be tiled or not, how mipmapping should be handled, and so forth. Many of the states in the dialog box are for the fixed function pipeline and can be disregarded.

The final node to look at is the stream mapping reference named PNTT Stream Mapping. This enables you to specify a reference to a previously defined stream mapping within your workspace, telling RenderMonkey how the geometry information should be sent to the vertex shader of this

Figure 3.12 Close-up view of the texture window for our sample.

particular rendering pass. If you wish to edit a particular stream mapping, you will need to edit the original node because you cannot change references.

It's Your Turn!

Your task is easy for this chapter! Simply play around with this shader, look at it from different angles, and change some render states. If you feel like it, you can even take a look at the shader code and change it. Now is the best time for you to get acquainted with the look and feel of RenderMonkey.

What's Next?

As you have seen, RenderMonkey is a powerful tool when it comes to shader and effect design. With its component-based architecture, it makes shader development a cinch without making you spend much time setting up your scene.

Now that you have a good grip on the layout and functioning of RenderMonkey, you can finally start using it to create your first shader in the next chapter.

CHAPTER 4

GETTING STARTED, YOUR FIRST SHADERS

Now that you have a basic understanding of 3D graphics, the importance of shaders, and how RenderMonkey works, it is finally time to get your hands dirty and write your first set of shaders. We'll start with some basic shaders, which should give you a handle on how everything fits together before you start exploring real algorithms and techniques.

In this chapter, you will create three simple shaders that do simple tasks such as displaying an object and texturing it. The resulting shaders and the data needed for them are included on the CD-ROM and can be used to compare your results with mine. The exercises at the end of the chapter will help you expand the shaders you develop here.

Your First Shader

Your first shader will be as simple as possible. You will draw a little teapot with no texture and a constant color. Then you will add texture and more color to your teapot. To get ready, start up RenderMonkey on your computer. Note that all the assets needed for this shader are found in the source code directory for this chapter on the CD-ROM.

The first thing you need is an effect group to contain your shader. To create one, right-click on the workspace root node and select Add Effect Group: Effect Group w/DirectX Effect. You should see something already being rendered in your Preview Window. This is because RenderMonkey fills the new effect group with a sample effect, as shown in the workspace in Figure 4.1. Because you want to do everything from scratch in this chapter, you should delete all the nodes under the effect group except for the effect node. To do so, select the nodes you want to delete and press the Delete key. Another way to accomplish the same thing is to use the right-click menu and select Add Effect Group: Empty Effect

Group. You might also want to rename the effect group to something more meaningful, like MyEffect, by right-clicking on the Effect Group node and selecting Rename.

Do not worry if you see error messages when deleting nodes from an effect. This is RenderMonkey's way of letting you know some items are missing for it to be able to render a shader. The errors can be ignored for now, because you will be adding these elements.

note

RenderMonkey enables you to create default effect data when you create a new Effect Group or Effect node. This is a great time saver later on. For this chapter, we will create everything from scratch because you want to learn how everything is set up.

To get anything on the screen, you definitely need some geometry to render. So at this point, you will need to add a new model to your shader. Right-click on the Effect node you just added, and select the Add Model option from the context menu that appears. A new model node will be created for you. You can now rename the node MyModel through the right-click menu, and select the proper geometry file by double-clicking the model node. This brings up the Open Model menu, as shown in Figure 4.2. Browse to the chapter's source code directory, select the teapot.3ds file, and click the Open button.

With your geometry set up and ready, you need to tell RenderMonkey how the geometry information will be sent to the vertex shader. This is done by using a Stream Mapping node. This node contains the settings necessary to translate the information from your

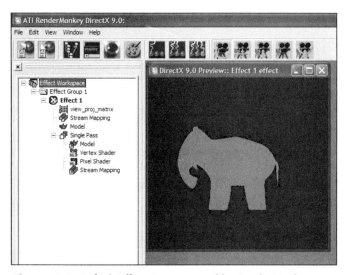

Figure 4.1 Default Effect Group created by RenderMonkey.

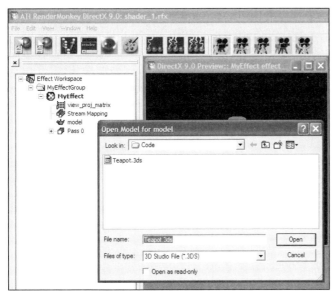

Figure 4.2 Selecting the model file for your shader.

model to something your shader can use. Specifically, this node will map information from the geometry to specific input registers within your vertex shader. To accomplish this, right-click on the Effect node and select the Add Stream Mapping option. As illustrated in Figure 4.3, double-clicking on the new Stream Mapping node will bring up the stream mapping editor. Initially, this editor only contains positional information, but clicking the Add button will allow you to add more stream information, such as normals and texture coordinates, which is enough for this shader. You are done setting up your stream mapping, so you should now close the editor window.

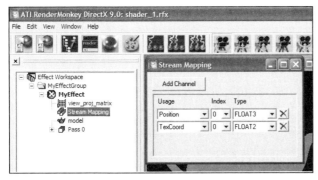

Figure 4.3 Setting up the stream mapping for your teapot model.

Because your shader is going to be basic, at this point you will only need to add a single variable, the view-projection matrix. Although this is a built-in variable supplied by RenderMonkey, it must still be added to the workspace before it can be used in a shader. Right-click on your Effect node and select Add Variable: Matrix: Predefined: view_proj_matrix from the menu. This creates a matrix that will be filled automatically by RenderMonkey with the combined model/view/projection matrix used to display your object, allowing you to transform the incoming vertices from object space into screen space.

At this point, you have all you need in your effect except for the effect rendering pass itself. To add a new rendering pass, right-click on the Effect node and select the Add Pass option. This creates a new effect pass, which is filled with a sample effect. You may now rename your rendering pass My Pass and delete the contents of the effect so you can create it from scratch.

The first two things needed for your rendering pass are a reference to a model and stream mapping. Although you can add models and stream mapping at any point in your effect, you still need to tell RenderMonkey which ones to use for each particular pass. To set up a reference for the model, simply right-click on your Pass node and select Add Model Reference. This creates a model reference holder, but it still needs to point to the right model. To select the actual model reference, right-click on your new Model Reference node and select the Reference Node option, as shown in Figure 4.4. This brings up a list of models that can be selected, from which you can pick MyModel. For the stream mapping reference, simply repeat the same process by picking Add Stream Mapping Reference from the Pass node right-click menu.

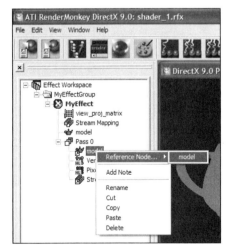

Figure 4.4 Setting up a model reference for your rendering pass.

The last thing needed for your shader is the vertex and pixel shader code. Let's start by adding a new vertex shader to your pass by right-clicking the render Pass node and selecting Add Vertex Shader: DirectX HLSL. The newly created vertex shader will be filled with some default code, but you will replace it with your own. You may now double-click the vertex shader node to pop up the shader editor window.

As you can see in the code editor part of the window shown in Figure 4.5, the view_proj_matrix variable is already preset because most shaders will need it. Generally, to set up this variable, simply add the variable to the shader code as you would declare any other variables. For more information on this, you should refer to the HLSL Reference Manual in Appendix B. The variable declaration for your view-projection matrix looks like this:

```
float4x4 view_proj_matrix;
```

If you had other variables in your shader, you would insert them at this point. But for now, this is all you need, so you should now add the code needed for your vertex shader. The first thing you need to define is the structure used to pass the vertex information from your vertex shader onto your pixel shader. You can define this in a structure called VS_OUTPUT, but you can give any name you wish. Because all you need at this point is the position of the vertex, the structure should be the following (which is the default structure created for you by RenderMonkey):

```
struct VS_OUTPUT
{
    float4 Pos:     POSITION;
};
```

This structure essentially creates a vector variable as part of the structure named Pos and has a semantic of POSITION. The semantic defines the meaning of the variable and how it should be passed along to the pixel shader.

The core of the shader is the entry point function defined in the Entry Point field within the vertex shader editor. Assuming you'll call your function vs_main, you can define an empty function that will serve as the template for your vertex shader. The parameters to the function must also be defined so the stream mapping values needed are passed to your function. For this simple shader, all you need is the vertex position, so the empty function for your vertex shader will look as follows:

```
VS_OUTPUT vs_main( float4 inPos: POSITION )
{
    VS_OUTPUT Out;
    return Out;
}
```

Take note that the input parameter `inPos` is followed by the semantics declaration `POSITION`. This tells the vertex shader how to map the geometry stream information to this input parameter. Also take note that the function defines and returns a variable of type `VS_OUTPUT`. This is the information that will be passed on from your vertex shader to your pixel shader after the vertices are processed. This information is also passed to the pixel shader as a return value to your vertex shader function. Because all this vertex shader needs to do is display your geometry with no special processing, the only thing needed is to transform the incoming vertex positions with the view-projection matrix and return the resulting value. This is done by multiplying the vertex position with your `view_proj_matrix`:

```
Out.Pos = mul(view_proj_matrix, inPos);
```

This shader will take the incoming geometry from your teapot, transform and project it into the screen, and send the final information to the pixel shader. Here is what the final code looks like:

```
float4x4 view_proj_matrix;
struct VS_OUTPUT
{
    float4 Pos:      POSITION;
};

VS_OUTPUT vs_main( float4 inPos: POSITION )
{
    VS_OUTPUT Out;

    // Output a transformed and projected vertex position
    Out.Pos = mul(view_proj_matrix, inPos);

    return Out;
}
```

That does it for your vertex shader; you now need to define the pixel shader for this effect. Close the current shader editor, right-click on the Pass node, and select Add Pixel Shader: DirectX HLSL from the context menu. If you double-click the new Pixel Shader node, you will see the shader editor with a default pixel shader created by RenderMonkey. The default code supplied looks like this:

```
float4 ps_main( float4 inDiffuse: COLOR0 ) : COLOR0
{
    //  Output constant color:
    float4 color;
```

```
   color[0] = color[3] = 1.0;
   color[1] = color[2] = 0.0;
   return color;
}
```

note

Under DirectX and OpenGl, normally you can render using either a vertex shader, pixel shader or both; falling back on the fixed-pipeline for the unused portion. However, since RenderMonkey is intended as a shader development platform, it does require you to create both a pixel and vertex shader before it can render anything on the screen.

Notice that this default shader returns a `float4` value with the semantic `COLOR0`. This defines the return value of the function as the final color to render onto the screen and is generally the only semantic marker you will use in your pixel shaders. The other thing worth mentioning is the input variable `inDiffuse`, which also has the semantic `COLOR0`. This value maps a vertex shader output with the same semantic to the pixel shader input. You do not need the input color because your vertex shader does not supply it, so you can take that input parameter out. Also, you can now change your shader to make your object red. If you apply those two steps, the resulting pixel shader code becomes the following:

```
float4 ps_main() : COLOR0
{
   // Output a constant color
   float4 color = float4(0,0,0,0);
   color.r = 1.0;

  // Set the alpha value to 1.0 to avoid alpha blending
   color.a = 1.0;

   return color;
}
```

note

You may have noticed that in both the vertex and pixel shader editors, your shader target was set to version 1.1. Although most of the shaders you build in this book require you to set the target to version 2.0, the shaders in this chapter are simple enough not to require this change, and we did not bother with it. Generally, if your shader is simple enough to run on a lesser version of pixel and vertex shader, stick with that version number, because the shader may run more efficiently on certain hardware architectures.

There you go, your first shader. Now that everything is complete, you can click the Compile All Shaders in Active Effect toolbar button (or press the F7 key). You should see a red teapot in the preview window, as shown in Figure 4.5. If the preview window does not show up, you may need to click the Preview button on the toolbar. Also, if you do not see a teapot, make sure to check the output window, because you may have made a typo in your shader, preventing it from compiling properly. A functional version of this shader is available as shader_1.rfx on the CD-ROM in the source code directory for this chapter.

Texturing Your Object

Now that you have a red teapot rendering, how about adding a little more color by applying a texture to it? Because you are simply extending your previous shader, you'll use it as a starting point and add on to it. The final shader for this section can be found as shader_2.rfx on the CD-ROM.

Use the shader from the previous section and close any open editor or preview windows. Obviously, the first thing you will need to add to the shader is a texture. To do this, right-click on the effect node and choose the Add Variable option from the context menu. From the variable editor window, pick the TEXTURE type and type in "My Texture" as the name for your texture variable, as shown in Figure 4.6. After this variable is created, double-click it to bring up the file selection dialog box, and pick the fieldstone.tga file from the CD-ROM in the source code folder for this chapter.

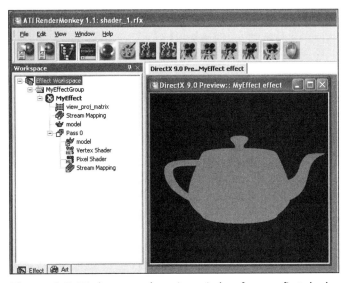

Figure 4.5 Workspace and preview window for your first shader.

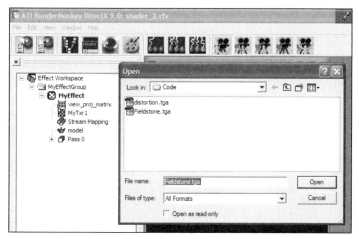

Figure 4.6 Setting up a texture variable and selecting a texture file.

Now that you have a texture in your effect, you have to let the render pass know that it must use this texture. You can do this by adding a texture object to your render Pass node through the right-click menu. To this newly created texture object, you will need to add a texture reference node by right-clicking on the texture object and selecting Add Texture Reference. To point this reference to a specific texture, you will need to right-click on the reference and pick which texture this reference points to, like you did with model or stream mapping references. By double-clicking the texture object node, you will get the texture state editor window. This editor shows you different states that can be set to control how the texture will be accessed by the hardware, along with thumbnails of all your textures in a specific rendering pass. However, for this shader, the default values in the editor will do fine.

With a texture set up and ready, all you need to do at this point is set up the vertex and pixel shaders to make use of it. The first thing you need to do is make the vertex shader aware of the texture mapping coordinates on your object so you can pass them to the pixel shader. To make this happen, you need to create an input parameter to your vertex shader function, one which takes a value from the TEXCOORD0 semantic as defined in your stream mapping node. This is done through the following code added to your vertex shader function parameters:

```
float2 Txr1: TEXCOORD0
```

You will also need an output variable so you can route the texture coordinate through to the pixel shader. This is done by changing your VS_OUTPUT structure to the following:

```
struct VS_OUTPUT
{
    float4 Pos:      POSITION;
    float2 Txr1:     TEXCOORD0;
};
```

Because you will not be doing any special processing on the texture coordinates, all the shader needs to do is route the texture coordinates straight from the input parameter to the output structure. The resulting vertex shader code with all your adjustments is as follows:

```
float4x4 view_proj_matrix;
struct VS_OUTPUT
{
    float4 Pos:      POSITION;
    float2 Txr1:     TEXCOORD0;
};

VS_OUTPUT vs_main(
    float4 inPos: POSITION,
    float2 Txr1: TEXCOORD0
)
{
    VS_OUTPUT Out;

    // Output our transformed and projected vertex
    // position and texture coordinate
    Out.Pos = mul(view_proj_matrix, inPos);
    Out.Txr1 = Txr1;

    return Out;
}
```

You are finished with the vertex shader for now; switch to the pixel shader by clicking the Pixel Shader tab at the top of the shader editor window. The first thing your pixel shader needs is a sampler variable. This variable tells your pixel shader which textures are available for use, in the same way you had to create a variable in your vertex shader for your view_proj_matrix. You can add a sampler by simply adding the variable to the top of your pixel shader of type Sampler and with a name that corresponds to the name of the texture object you want to reference.

This will add the following variable to the constant part of the shader editor:

```
sampler Texture0;
```

To access this texture, you need to adjust the pixel shader slightly. First, set up the texture coordinate input parameter to the shader function. This is done the same way it was done for the vertex shader and requires adding a parameter that points to the TEXCOORD0 semantic. The second thing to do is read pixels from within the shader by using the tex2D function. Reading a texture with a specific sampler and texture coordinate named inTxr1 can be done through the following code:

```
tex2D(MyTexture,inTxr1);
```

With this function call, you can finally put the shader together. The final pixel shader code with all the changes is as follows:

```
sampler Texture0;
float4 ps_main(
   float4 inDiffuse: COLOR0,
   float2 inTxr1: TEXCOORD0
) : COLOR0
{
   // Output the color taken from our texture
   return tex2D(Texture0,inTxr1);
}
```

You are now done and ready to see the fruits of your labor. As you did with your previous shader, close the shader editor and click the Compile All Shaders in Active Effect toolbar button. You should now see a textured teapot, as shown in Figure 4.7.

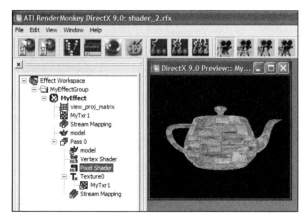

Figure 4.7 Workspace and preview output for your second shader.

Seeing Double

Our first two shaders illustrate some basic ideas in shader building. In real-life applications, you will usually have multiple objects in your scene. In this section, I will show you how to expand your previous shaders to render two teapots instead of one. This can be accomplished easily with RenderMonkey by using multiple render passes, one for each object to be rendered.

To add a second teapot to your scene, add another render pass node by right-clicking on your Effect node and selecting Add Pass from the context menu. This creates a new pass called `Pass 1` and will be filled, as usual, with a simple default shader. For this second object, you will only render a teapot with a simple opaque color, as you did with the first shader in this chapter.

The first steps are then to set up the model and stream mapping references to point to the correct nodes. You can then edit the vertex and pixel shader code to render the new teapot. You can use the same shader code as was used in your first shader earlier in this chapter, so you may want to simply copy and paste the previous code onto the new shader. Select the shader text, press Ctrl+C to copy, and press Ctrl+V to paste it into your new shader.

This seemed too easy, didn't it? But wait, there is a problem with this setup! Both teapots are rendered on top of each other, and you would like them to be rendered next to each other. RenderMonkey does not have a built-in method to set specific positions for a particular object. However, this does not stop us from being able to position your second object. What if you create a new vector variable to be used as a position offset for your second object?

To perform this, right-click on the Effect node, select Add Variable, pick the VECTOR type, and name your variable `teapot_position`. By double-clicking this new variable, you can set an offset value for the second teapot, the one in the second rendering pass. You may set this variable to any value you wish, somewhere around 100 in any components, but make sure the W component of the vector is set to zero because any other value will interfere with the rendering of the object.

You can now edit the vertex shader code to apply this offset to the object's position. To do this, you must first add the variable to your vertex shader code as you did with your other variables, and then add this variable to the incoming vertex positions defined in `inPos`. The resulting vertex shader code for this follows:

```
float4x4 view_proj_matrix;
float4 teapot_position;
struct VS_OUTPUT
{
   float4 Pos:     POSITION;
```

```
};

VS_OUTPUT vs_main( float4 inPos: POSITION )
{
    VS_OUTPUT Out;

    // Output an offset and transformed vertex position
    Out.Pos = mul(view_proj_matrix, inPos+teapot_position);
    return Out;
}
```

You are now ready to compile and display your two sets of teapots, as shown in Figure 4.8. Once the shader is rendering, you can double-click the teapot_position variable to bring up the variable editor dialog box. The results of any changes made to this variable are shown in real-time in the preview window.

The final RenderMonkey shader file for this shader can also be found on the CD-ROM as shader_3.rfx.

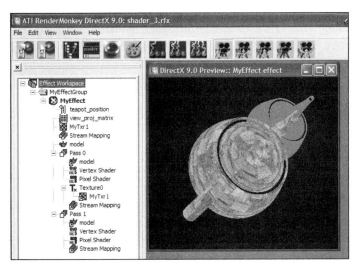

Figure 4.8 Workspace and preview output for your two teapots.

It's Your Turn!

Here are a few exercises that involve changing the shaders you have just created. I will only give you an indication of what you need to do and some hints to get you started, but the creative process is up to you. You can find the solutions to theses exercises in Appendix D.

Exercise 1: ANIMATING A TEXTURE

In this exercise, you add a little animation to the last shader developed. The first part of this exercise is to animate the texture on the first teapot from your previous shader. Take advantage of the `cos_time_0_X` and `sin_time_0_X` built-in SCALAR variables to modify the texture coordinate inputs in your vertex shader. This type of animation may seem simple, but it can come in handy for animating such things as water surfaces.

For the second part of this exercise, use the same `cos_time_0_X` and `sin_time_0_X` variables in the pixel shader of the second teapot, the constant-colored one, to animate its output color.

Exercise 2: BLENDING TWO TEXTURES

Starting with the shader just developed in the previous exercise, add the texture `distortion.tga` (found in the source code directory for this chapter) to the shader of the textured teapot and blend them together. This involves adding a new texture variable and setting up the pixel shader properly. To make your life simpler, reuse the same set of texture coordinates supplied for the first texture, and modulate both textures together. Modulation is done by multiplying the colors of both textures, which are in the range of [0…1].

What's Next?

You now have written your first shaders. Although they are basic and simple, they give you a firsthand look at how shaders are developed in general, and show you the groundwork needed for all shaders and effects. From this point on, I will start teaching you real shader techniques that can be used in real applications and focus less on how the basics of RenderMonkey work. The next part of this book covers screen space effects and explains how great effects can be achieved by simply manipulating the pixels of a final rendered output.

SCREEN EFFECTS

N ow that you know how to write basic shaders, it is time to start developing some shaders based on a simple concept, which I have dubbed screen effects. What are screen effects, you may ask? The idea is simple: render your scene to a temporary texture, and then use a special shader to manipulate the result before presenting it to the user.

Although this may sound simple and boring, such screen manipulation effects are very powerful and advantageous for many reasons. First, because you are simply manipulating pixels from one texture to another, such effects are easy to implement and can work in any application. Second, these effects can produce spectacular results, yet have the major advantage of a constant performance cost, no matter how complex your scene is. This is because you only have to render each screen pixel once, which is attractive for developers doing real-time graphics.

In Chapter 5, "Looking Through a Filter," I will explore the basics needed to render screen-based effects, such as rendering your scene to a temporary texture and manipulating it through a shader. I will initially focus on color manipulation filters and other basic filters, such as blurs and other convolution filters. In Chapters 6, "Blurring Things Up," 7, "It's Getting Hot in Here," and 8, "Making Your Day Brighter," I will explain how to accomplish more powerful effects such as depth of field, heat haze, and high-dynamic range rendering.

Sometimes, stunning effects can be achieved through minimal work. Be prepared, because screen space effects will be easy to develop, yet with them you can create some of the most stunning graphics.

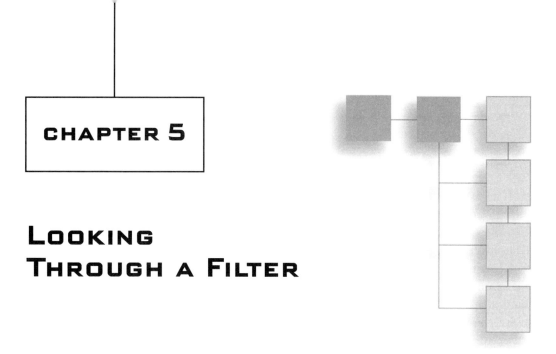

CHAPTER 5

LOOKING THROUGH A FILTER

I n this chapter, I will explore both color manipulation filters and simple pixel manip- ulation filters such as blurs. But before I can get deeper into those effects, I must explain some basic elements needed for all screen effect rendering. First, I will show you how you can render your scene to a temporary texture, and second, how to use this texture and present it to the user.

Rendering to a Sketchpad

The general process used to do screen effects is simple. First of all, the scene is rendered to a temporary texture instead of the regular screen buffer. After this has been done, the temporary texture is processed by the filter of your choice. The result is then put into the screen buffer to be presented to the user. So before you can even consider some of the effects, I need to teach you how to render your scene to a temporary texture. This will also prove valuable later, for other types of effects.

In RenderMonkey, rendering to a temporary texture can be carried out using something called a render target. Render targets are a technique exposed by the different rendering APIs to allow you to redirect the hardware's rendering output to the texture of your choice. Such textures can then be used to accomplish other effects, such as shadowing or motion blur. Generally, this has few implications for the 3D hardware, because normal rendering usually happens to a hidden texture that has been allocated in the background and is presented to the user after the rendering is complete. Using render targets simply tells the 3D hardware to redirect the output to the texture you specify.

n o t e

Because of the nature of render targets, some hardware may impose restrictions on the size and format of such textures. If you do not see any output for one of your render target shaders, check your output window; it may contain error messages pointing out that you have broken such a limit.

I will start off with the basic two-teapot shader that was developed in Chapter 4, "Getting Started, Your First Shaders," which was modified to render both a teapot and an elephant for variety, and expand it to render to a target texture of your choice. After you accomplish this, I will go through the process you can use to render your render target texture back to your regular screen buffer. The actual process under DirectX and OpenGL may be a little more involved, because RenderMonkey takes care of most of the details for us. Note that the teapot shader sample you will be starting with is included as shader_1.rfx in the source code directory for this chapter on the CD-ROM.

Start by loading the two-teapot shader developed in the "Seeing Double" section of Chapter 4. I will be using this shader to show you how to use render targets and how to apply filters to your renderings. After you open the workspace, open the Effect Group node and the Effect node. Within the Effect node, you can add a new render target by right-clicking on the Effect node and selecting the Add Renderable Texture option from the context menu. This adds a new node called RenderTarget, which can be renamed if you wish.

Creating a Render Target node essentially creates a new texture for you. However, this texture is different from regular textures because it is not imported from a file and is managed automatically by RenderMonkey. If you double-click the new Render Target node, a Render Target property dialog box appears. As you can see in Figure 5.1, this dialog box has a few settings that can be used to control the size and format of the render target. This is necessary because the texture is created for you, and you will need some control over its specifications so it can match your needs.

Figure 5.1
RenderMonkey's Render Target setting dialog box.

The first part of the dialog box in Figure 5.1 controls the width and height of the texture. This allows you to manually specify the dimensions for your render target. You may have noticed the Use viewport dimensions checkbox underneath the dimensions for the texture. This tells RenderMonkey to force the size of the render target texture to always match the size of the preview window. This is useful in cases such as the screen effect filters you will develop in this chapter, where each pixel in your render target should match a single pixel in your preview window to avoid losing any precision in your rendering. So make sure this option is turned on. You will generally leave this option on except for some effects where the render target resolution does not need to match the resolution of your render output.

The second part of the Render Target editor is a dropdown list that allows you to pick a texture format. Although this may be useful in some cases, for now you can leave it at the default value, which should be set to match the format used for the preview window. Combining the adaptive render target size and default texture format allows you to ensure that no detail is lost when you move the pixels from your temporary texture onto your frame buffer. This is all you need to do in this dialog box for now, so you can close it.

Now that you have a render target, you need to tell Render-Monkey to use it. To do this, add a Render Target node to each render pass you wish to render to this target. For this shader, you will need to do this for both passes that render your scene objects. To add a Render Target node, right-click on the Pass node and select Add Render Target from the menu. This adds a node named `RenderTarget` to the pass. If you right-click on this node, a Reference Node option appears in the menu that allows you to pick which renderable texture to use; this allows you to use multiple render targets within your effect if needed. After you select the render target reference, double-click the Render Target node you just added. This brings up the dialog box shown in Figure 5.2.

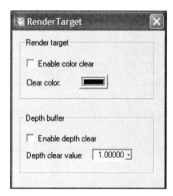

Figure 5.2 RenderTarget Reference setting dialog box.

This dialog box contains two sets of settings, which control whether the color and the depth buffer should be cleared. The settings for the first pass render target should be to clear the color to black and the depth buffer to 1.0, because the render target may still contain previous renders or garbage. For later passes, you must ensure that the render target settings do not clear the depth and color, because you want to keep the rendered results from your previous passes.

After you set up the render target for a pass, you can repeat the same process for the second pass. Notice that the preview window is now blank. This is because all your objects are now being rendered to the render target, instead of to the frame buffer as before. At this point, you can assume all is well; the next step is to set up a new rendering pass that copies the pixels from the render target to the frame buffer.

To render your render target to the screen, you need to trick the hardware to some extent. Because you want to use a pixel shader during the copy, you need to do the process in a 3D world, but essentially using a 2D copy. If you were to take a piece of geometry and place it in the scene so that it fully covers the projection region generated by the camera, you could apply the render target texture to the object and fill the screen. This is essentially like draping your camera with a screen and projecting your texture onto it. The whole process is illustrated in Figure 5.3.

For the process to work, your geometry needs to be a simple rectangle, set up so that its coordinates match the corners of the screen in screen-space: $(-1,-1,0)$, $(1,-1,0)$, $(-1,1,0)$ and $(1,1,0)$. Such a pre-setup piece of geometry has been supplied with RenderMonkey in the file called ScreenAlignedQuad.3ds. Because the coordinates of the geometry are already supplied in screen space with this model, you don't need to apply a projection matrix to the coordinates; you simply need to route them to the pixel shader.

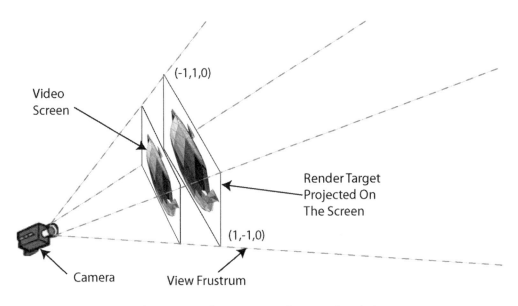

Figure 5.3 Process used in 3D to render a texture so it covers the whole screen.

Texture Coordinates

Because you want to use the full texture, you will need to ensure that the texture coordinates for each corner of the rectangle geometry are as follows: (0,0), (1,0), (1,1) and (0,1). This can be determined by using the vertex positions for the geometry, which I will cover later.

Because you want every pixel on the screen to correspond to a single pixel in your texture, there is one aspect of the rendering hardware that must be considered. If you take a look at Figure 5.4, a specific coordinate when rendering to the screen corresponds to the top left of that pixel. On the other hand, when a texture is read by the hardware, the coordinates actually correspond to the center of the texture pixel. So if you were to simply render as outlined previously, the pixels would be slightly offset and would create some unwanted filtering and aliasing.

To correct this, you need to offset the render target texture slightly so that the pixels overlap correctly. Figure 5.5 shows how the texture can be offset to create a correct overlap of the screen and texture pixels. In essence, you need to offset your texture pixels by half a pixel, which corresponds to 1/Width and 1/Height in texture coordinates.

With all the basics covered, it's now time for me to show you how to do this texture copy operation in RenderMonkey. First, you need to add the geometry needed for the screen projection rectangle. Right-click on the Effect Group node and select Add Model. Double-click the new node and select the ScreenAlignedQuad.3ds file located in the

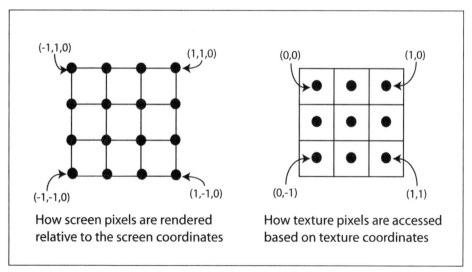

How screen pixels are rendered relative to the screen coordinates

How texture pixels are accessed based on texture coordinates

Figure 5.4 How texture coordinates are accessed and how pixels are rendered.

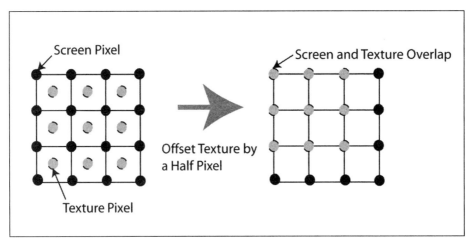

Figure 5.5 How to offset the render target pixels so you get a proper overlap.

CD-ROM source code folder for this chapter. Then add a new render pass to your effect group by selecting Add Pass from the right-click menu for the Effect node.

With this new Pass node created, set up the model reference to point to your ScreenAlignedQuad model, and set up the stream mapping reference to use the common Stream Mapping node for this workspace. The next thing is to set up a texture object that points to your render target texture so it can be used in this pass. To do this, right-click on the Pass node and select Add Texture Object from the context menu. Set up this texture object by right-clicking the Texture Object node. Then select Add Texture Reference and configure this reference to point to your renderable texture.

The next thing you need is the shader code for this pass. The vertex shader must accomplish two tasks. The first is to pass the vertex positions to the pixel shader. Because the geometry you are using is already set up so that the vertex positions are in screen space, you do not need to transform and project the position; you simply need to route it through to the pixel shader. The second step is to set up the texture coordinates for the geometry.

Our geometry does not have proper texture coordinates supplied with it, but this will not stop us. Because the vertex positions in screen space are in the range (−1,−1,0) to (1,1,0), you can simply scale and offset these values so that they match the needed texture coordinate range of (0,0) to (1,1). This scale and offset is simply done through the following code:

```
// Texture coordinates are setup so that the full texture
// is mapped completely onto the screen
Out.texCoord.x = 0.5 * (1 + Pos.x);
Out.texCoord.y = 0.5 * (1 - Pos.y);
```

As discussed earlier, the way pixels are read from texture and the way they are written by the renderer do not match. To correct for this, you need to offset the texture by half a pixel. In this case, because the width and height of the render target matches the size of the preview window, you can take advantage of the built-in variables `viewport_inv_width` and `viewport_inv_height` to properly offset the texture. These built-in variables can be added to your workspace through the right-click menu by selecting Add Variable: Scalar: Predefined and choosing the proper built-in variable from the list. Also remember that you need to add the variable declaration to your shader code before you can use its value. Combining the standard scale and offset with the texture correction offset yields the following code:

```
// Texture coordinates are setup so that the full texture
// is mapped completely onto the screen
Out.texCoord.x = 0.5 * (1 + Pos.x - viewport_inv_width);
Out.texCoord.y = 0.5 * (1 - Pos.y - viewport_inv_height);
```

Don't forget to add the needed variables to the shader editor before you use them in the shader code.

When the texture coordinate code and the vertex position code are combined, you should have the following final vertex shader code:

```
float4x4 view_proj_matrix;
float viewport_inv_width;
float viewport_inv_height;
struct VS_OUTPUT
{
    float4 Pos: POSITION;
    float2 texCoord: TEXCOORD0;
};

VS_OUTPUT vs_main(float4 Pos: POSITION)
{
    VS_OUTPUT Out;

    // Simply output the position without transforming it
    Out.Pos = float4(Pos.xy, 0, 1);

    // Texture coordinates are setup so that the full texture
    // is mapped completely onto the screen
    Out.texCoord.x = 0.5 * (1 + Pos.x - viewport_inv_width);
    Out.texCoord.y = 0.5 * (1 - Pos.y - viewport_inv_height);

    return Out;
}
```

Finally Rendering Your Render Target

It is now time to finish your effect with the pixel shader. The shader should be receiving the proper texture coordinates, so all it needs to do at this point is to copy the texture pixels. To do that, sample the texture at the supplied texture coordinate and output the sampled color. But remember that you need to add a sampler variable to your pixel shader before you can do so. The resulting code for this pixel shader is as follows:

```
sampler Texture0;
float4 ps_main(float2 texCoord: TEXCOORD0) : COLOR
{
    // Simply read the temporary texture and send
    // the color to the output without manipulating it
    return tex2D(Texture0,  texCoord);
}
```

Figure 5.6 shows the resulting workspace and preview window for this effect. The complete shader for this effect can be found as shader_2.rfx on the CD-ROM.

We'll use this shader as a starting point for the following effects. Now that you understand all the basics involved in doing full screen effects, let's do one of the most basic effects, color manipulation filters.

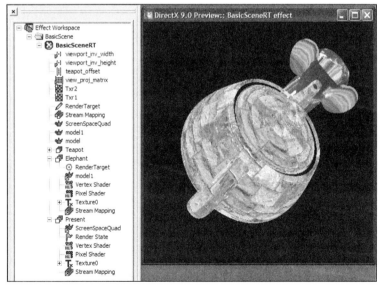

Figure 5.6 Final workspace and preview for your basic screen effect shader.

Don't Adjust Your TV!

As with any new technique you learn, it is always best to start simple and grow from there. When it comes to screen effects, the easiest way to start is to manipulate the colors of your texture pixels as you copy them from your render target to your screen. This may seem too simple and naïve, but the fact is you can do many useful things, such as render in black and white or sepia, do night vision modes, and more.

Black and White, Like in the Old Times

In the spirit of starting with something easy, how about making your renderings in black and white? This is very simple and only requires determining the intensity of a pixel and using that to output a grayscale color. The first step is finding out the intensity of the pixel. A quick and intuitive way would be to say that the intensity is the average of the red, green, and blue components of your texture, defined as: Intensity = (Red+Green+Blue)/3.

Although this will give you a grayscale value, it is not totally correct because it assumes an equal weight for all color components. This is a flawed idea that assumes the human eye makes out all color components equally. The reality is that your eyes see color components differently, being most sensitive to green and least sensitive to the blues. Some researchers have determined estimated weights for the color perception of the human eye and have determined that intensity is determined as: Intensity = 0.299*Red + 0.587*Green + 0.184*Blue.

Starting with the template shader developed in the previous section, which can be loaded from the CD-ROM as shader_1.rfx, you can modify the pixel shader of the render target copy pass to simply take in the incoming texture pixel and modify it to use this equation. With this simple adjustment, you should have the following pixel shader code:

```
sampler Texture0;
float4 ps_main(float2 texCoord: TEXCOORD0) : COLOR
{
   // Read the source color
   float4 col = tex2D(Texture0,  texCoord);
   float Intensity;

   // Make it B&W, intensity defines as being
   // I = 0.299*R + 0.587*G + 0.184*B
   Intensity = 0.299*col.r + 0.587*col.g + 0.184*col.r;

   // Note, can also be done as a dot product such as
   // Intensity = dot(col,float4(0.299,0.587,0.184,0));
```

```
// Return the intensity as a uniform RGB color
return float4(Intensity.xxx,col.a);
}
```

As you can see in the code, I use two techniques for computing the intensity. The first is the obvious one, where you simply apply the intensity equation with the proper weights. The second one performs the same task, but with the use of a dot product. This still works, because the dot product can be expanded into the same equation as shown in Figure 5.7.

The use of the dot product has two major advantages. The first is that most pixel shader architectures have native dot product instructions that are more efficient than performing the full equation operation manually. The second advantage, which you will exploit in the following section, is that a dot product is a sub-operation of a matrix multiplication, allowing us to generalize the color manipulation process to a simple matrix operation.

The result of this shader is shown in Figure 5.8. This complete shader can also be found on the CD-ROM as shader_3.rfx.

$$A = (A_x, A_y, A_z, A_w); B = (B_x, B_y, B_z, B_w)$$
$$dot(A, B) = A_x B_x + A_y B_y + A_z B_z + A_w B_w$$

Figure 5.7 Expanding a dot product operation to its final equation.

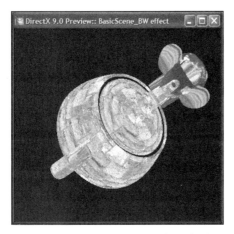

Figure 5.8 Your black and white shader in action.

In the first exercise in the "It's Your Turn" section at the end of this chapter, you will be invited to implement a variation of this black and white shader called Sepia.

note

Because all the figures within this book are in black and white and may not always show an effect at its best, I have included all the figures on the CD-ROM in high-resolution color. Refer to Appendix C for more information on how to access the high-resolution illustrations.

Generalizations Are Good!

It is always nice when you can take a specific effect and generalize it so that it can be used in many different ways. What if you can take the color manipulation approach shown in the previous section and generalize it so any basic color manipulation effect can be expressed with the same shader? In this section, I will go back to your black and white shader and show you how you can modify it and express any color manipulation through a simple yet reusable shader.

Previously, I showed how the grayscale conversion can be expressed with a dot product. I pointed out that a dot product can be seen as a sub-operation of a matrix operation. In fact, if you take a matrix multiplication between a matrix and a vector, the operation can be decomposed into a set of dot product operations applied to each row of the matrix. This decomposition is explained in more detail in Figure 5.9.

$$\begin{pmatrix} r_x & r_y & r_z & r_w \end{pmatrix} = \begin{bmatrix} m_{11} & m_{12} & m_{13} & m_{14} \\ m_{21} & m_{22} & m_{23} & m_{24} \\ m_{31} & m_{32} & m_{33} & m_{34} \\ m_{41} & m_{42} & m_{43} & m_{44} \end{bmatrix} \begin{bmatrix} c_x \\ c_y \\ c_z \\ c_w \end{bmatrix}$$

$$r_x = m_{11}c_x + m_{12}c_y + m_{13}c_z + m_{14}c_w = dot(C, (m_{11}\ m_{12}\ m_{13}\ m_{14}))$$

$$r_y = m_{21}c_x + m_{22}c_y + m_{23}c_z + m_{24}c_w = dot(C, (m_{21}\ m_{22}\ m_{23}\ m_{24}))$$

$$r_z = m_{31}c_x + m_{32}c_y + m_{33}c_z + m_{34}c_w = dot(C, (m_{31}\ m_{32}\ m_{33}\ m_{34}))$$

$$r_w = m_{41}c_x + m_{42}c_y + m_{43}c_z + m_{44}c_w = dot(C, (m_{41}\ m_{42}\ m_{43}\ m_{44}))$$

Figure 5.9 Decomposition of a matrix multiplication into a set of dot product operations.

With your previous grayscale shader example, the red, green, and blue components end up with the same values but can still be represented by a simple matrix operation, as shown in Figure 5.10.

$$\begin{bmatrix} 0.299 & 0.587 & 0.184 & 0 \\ 0.299 & 0.587 & 0.184 & 0 \\ 0.299 & 0.587 & 0.184 & 0 \\ 0 & 0 & 0 & 1 \end{bmatrix}$$

With this in mind, it is now time to generalize your color manipulation shader by taking advantage of a color conversion matrix. The first step is to add a new matrix variable to your Effect Group node by right-clicking on it and selecting Add Variable from the menu. Pick a MATRIX type variable, name it color_filter, and edit it by fill-

Figure 5.10 Our grayscale conversion represented as a matrix operation.

ing the values to the ones needed for your grayscale shader as defined in Figure 5.10.

The last step is to change your pixel shader to do the matrix operation. This is simply accomplished by adding the color_filter variable to your shader code and multiplying the incoming color with your color transform matrix. Following is the final pixel shader code implementing your generalized color manipulation shader:

```
float4x4 color_filter;
sampler Texture0;
float4 ps_main(float2 texCoord: TEXCOORD0) : COLOR
{
    // Read the source color
    float4 col = tex2D(Texture0,  texCoord);

    // Apply the matrix to the incoming color
    return mul(color_filter,col);
}
```

The completed shader is available on the CD-ROM as shader_4.rfx.

Now that you have generalized the color manipulation shader, let's look at another example of how to use it. Let's say you wish to simulate thermal vision, as shown in movies such as *Predator*. In such a mode, blue represents low heat, green represents mid-level heat, and red is for maximum heat. If you assume that heat is based on the color intensity of your initial render target pixel, you can compose a matrix that approximates this effect.

Based on my description, you could come to the conclusion that the final color should be defined as something similar to the following, keeping in mind that the numbers below come from experimentation:

```
Color.r = 0.1495*RT.r + 0.2935*RT.g + 0.057*RT.b + 0.5;
Color.g = 0.1495*RT.r + 0.2935*RT.g + 0.057*RT.b + 0.25;
Color.b = 0.1495*RT.r + 0.2935*RT.g + 0.057*RT.b;
```

After you define the matrix, you can simply edit the values by double-clicking the color matrix and inputting them. After you put in the values, you can see the results right away in the Preview Window, as shown in Figure 5.11. This completed shader can be found as shader_5.rfx on the CD-ROM.

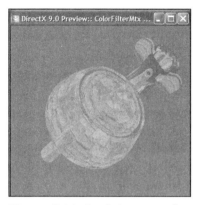

Figure 5.11 Rendering output for your thermal imaging shader.

You may notice that this shader does not resemble thermal imaging on television. This is because the actual color scale used isn't linear and cannot be represented by a simple matrix transformation. In the next section, I will outline a texture lookup technique that can be used in cases where color conversions cannot be represented by simple linear equations.

To conclude this section, let me introduce you to a few other common color manipulation matrices that can be used for standard things such as negative image, contrast control, and mode. Figure 5.12 summarizes those matrices, along with their coefficients and functions.

Things Are Not Always Linear

As you saw in the previous section, your thermal imaging shader didn't look very convincing. This is because the color scale generally used isn't linear and cannot be represented by a simple matrix transformation. You could always try to come up with a set of equations that look better, but one thing to think about when it comes to pixel shaders is that complex equations can turn a simple shader into an expensive one quickly. At this point, I'll introduce lookup textures because they can be a great way to optimize shaders.

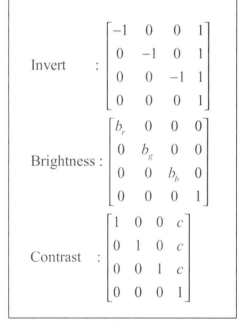

$$\text{Invert} \quad : \quad \begin{bmatrix} -1 & 0 & 0 & 1 \\ 0 & -1 & 0 & 1 \\ 0 & 0 & -1 & 1 \\ 0 & 0 & 0 & 1 \end{bmatrix}$$

$$\text{Brightness} : \quad \begin{bmatrix} b_r & 0 & 0 & 0 \\ 0 & b_g & 0 & 0 \\ 0 & 0 & b_b & 0 \\ 0 & 0 & 0 & 1 \end{bmatrix}$$

$$\text{Contrast} \quad : \quad \begin{bmatrix} 1 & 0 & 0 & c \\ 0 & 1 & 0 & c \\ 0 & 0 & 1 & c \\ 0 & 0 & 0 & 1 \end{bmatrix}$$

Figure 5.12 Miscellaneous color matrices used for standard operation.

Although I will not develop a shader now, this subject is worth approaching because it will be used many times throughout the following chapters.

The basic idea behind the approach is simple. Because your function is known and constant, what if you precomputed it into a texture and used the texture as a lookup table to get your result instead of computing it directly? This has an advantage because you only need to calculate the equation once to build the lookup texture, and then you only pay the processing cost of looking up a texture instead of the full equation for each pixel. This can be much more efficient if your color conversion equation is complex.

In the case of your thermal imaging example, you could use an image editing program to create a one-dimensional texture that represents the output color based on the heat, or intensity, of your render target. The color conversion operation simply becomes a dependent texture read.

Our previous pixel shader, adapted to use a lookup texture, would be the following:

```
float4x4 color_filter;
sampler Texture0;
float4 ps_main(float2 texCoord: TEXCOORD0) : COLOR
{
   // Read the source color
   float4 col = tex2D(Texture0,  texCoord);
   float Intensity;

   // Compute the intensity or heat of the pixel
   // In other words, compute the grayscale value of
   // the pixel.
   Intensity = dot(col,float4(0.299,0.587,0.184,0));

   // Use the intensity to lookup the heat color table
   return tex1D(Texture_Heat,Intensity);
}
```

Dependent texture lookups are a very powerful technique. Keep this approach in mind; it will come in handy in future chapters. This will be all for color manipulation for now. It is time to move on to more complex pixel manipulation shaders.

Blurring Things Up

The first question you may ask is, why do I need to blur my render target? You are right to ask; blurring the render target on its own serves little purpose. However, this serves as a good introduction to pixel manipulation and convolution filters. I also will be using the blurring technique in the next chapter to introduce the depth of field effect.

There are many types of filters, or filter kernels, which can be used to blur a texture. We'll start with what is commonly known as the box filter. In a box filter, as shown in Figure 5.13, a pixel becomes the average of its four neighboring pixels: up, down, left, and right. Within a shader, this can easily be carried out by sampling your render target four times and averaging the values together.

Although this approach can be written in a simple expanded form where you take all your samples individually, I will take advantage of the power of the pixel shader 2.0 standard to write this filter in a more generic and reusable way. Because the pixel shader 2.0 standard allows us to use loop statements, I will write the shader using the added functionality.

Such blurring and convolution filters require you to sample your texture multiple times. Each sample is at some offset from the current position and has some weight applied to it. Because of this, you can store the offsets and weight into a constant array within the shader. For example, the following table shows how the four samples for your box filter can be represented in an array:

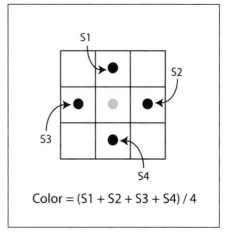

$$Color = (S1 + S2 + S3 + S4) / 4$$

Figure 5.13 Illustration of how a box filter is implemented.

```
const float4 samples[4] = {
    -1.0,     0.0,      0,      0.25,
     1.0,     0.0,      0,      0.25,
     0.0,      .0,      0,      0.25,
     0.0     -1.0,      0,      0.25
};
```

With this representation, you can take advantage of a loop statement that iterates through all the elements of your array to compute the shader. For each iteration of the loop, you must sample the texture at the desired offset, weigh the result by the correct factor, and add the final value to an accumulation variable, repeating the process for every sample in your filter. Implementing such a technique yields the following code:

```
// Sample and output the box averaged colors
for(int i=0;i<4;i++)
   col += samples[i].w*tex2D(Texture0,texCoord+
   float2(samples[i].x*viewport_inv_width,
         samples[i].y*viewport_inv_height));
```

Now that you have all the components, putting this box filter blur shader together is simple. Starting with the basic pixel manipulation shader developed at the beginning of this chapter, you simply need to modify the pixel shader code of the manipulation pass to incorporate the pixel shader code that was just developed. When the changes are implemented, the final pixel shader code should look as follows:

```
float viewport_inv_width;
float viewport_inv_height;
sampler Texture0;
const float4 samples[4] = {
    -1.0,     0.0,      0,       0.25,
     1.0,     0.0,      0,       0.25,
     0.0,     1.0,      0,       0.25,
     0.0,    -1.0,      0,       0.25
};


float4 ps_main(float2 texCoord: TEXCOORD0) : COLOR
{
    float4 col = float4(0,0,0,0);

    // Sample and output the box averaged colors
    for(int i=0;i<4;i++)
        col += samples[i].w*tex2D(Texture0,texCoord+
        float2(samples[i].x*viewport_inv_width,
            samples[i].x*viewport_inv_height));

    return col;
}
```

When the code is compiled, your preview window should show you a blurred version of your scene, as shown in Figure 5.14. You may notice that the blurring might not be as extreme as expected. This is because a box filter only performs its operation by looking at its immediate neighboring pixels. You can also find the complete version of this shader on the CD-ROM as shader_6.rfx.

To blur the image more, two approaches can be taken. In the first approach, you can simply repeat the same blur process several times, using your previously blurred result as input for the next pass. This iterative approach is advantageous because it can be applied as

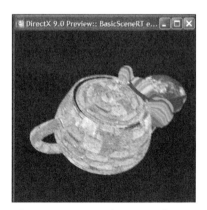

Figure 5.14 Render output for a box filter blurring shader.

many times as needed, but occasionally can lead to aliasing depending on your input. The second approach is to use a more complex filter kernel, which can lead to better result but is generally more expensive. You will have a chance to implement such a kernel in Exercise 2 at the end of this chapter.

Bring on the Filters

Blurring is probably one of the simplest forms of convolution filter that can be implemented. There are many more type of filters that can be implemented through the same techniques. With these filters, you can implement such things as edge detection and image sharpening.

An edge detection filter highlights the edges of an image. The edges are defined as sharp color transitions between pixels. An edge detection filter serves little purpose in most applications beyond teaching you about different filters but will come in handy later on when you're rendering silhouettes. An image sharpening filter, on the other hand, can enhance the contrast on sharp color transitions within an image. This filter may be useful to improve the sharpness of your final renderings.

Both filters are implemented with the same approach used in the box blur filter. Figure 5.15 describes the actual filter kernels for both edge detection and image sharpening that you will implement in this section.

For both filters, you need to start with the blur filter you previously built. Because the approach taken was to use an array of filter components and a loop to sample the textures, all you need to change is the array for it to match the kernel. Looking at the kernel for the edge detection filter in Figure 5.15, you can extract the coefficients and offsets and put them in the array. This gives you the following:

$$\text{Edge Detection} : \begin{bmatrix} 1 & 2 & 1 \\ 0 & 0 & 0 \\ -1 & -2 & -1 \end{bmatrix} / 1$$

$$\text{Sharpening} \quad : \begin{bmatrix} 0 & -2 & 0 \\ -2 & 11 & -2 \\ 0 & -2 & 0 \end{bmatrix} / 3$$

Figure 5.15 Filter kernels for both edge detection and image sharpening.

```
const float4 samples[6] = {
    -1.0,     1.0,     0,     1.0,
     0.0,     1.0,     0,     2.0,
     1.0,     1.0,     0,     1.0,
    -1.0,    -1.0,     0,    -1.0,
     0.0,    -1.0,     0,    -2.0,
     1.0,    -1.0,     0,    -1.0
};
```

With this new array, you need to adjust the loop to do the right number of iterations. You can do the same process with the image sharpening filter. Extracting the filter kernel coefficients from Figure 5.15, you end up with the following array:

```
const float4 samples[5] = {
    0.0,     0.0,     0,      11.0/3.0,
    0.0,     1.0,     0,      -2.0/3.0,
    0.0,    -1.0,     0,      -2.0/3.0,
   -1.0,     0.0,     0,      -2.0/3.0,
    1.0,     0.0,     0,      -2.0/3.0
};
```

Figure 5.16 shows the rendering output for both shaders. As you can see, setting up convolution filters by taking advantage of the pixel shader 2.0 instructions proves a great way to make your shader code flexible and reusable. You can find a complete version of both filters on the CD-ROM under shader_6a.rfx and shader_6b.rfx.

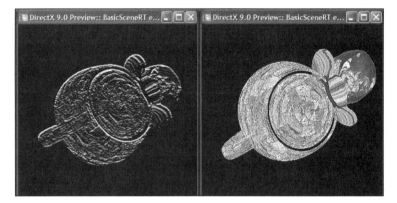

Figure 5.16 Rendering output for both the edge detection and image sharpening filters in action.

Motion Blur

Most of the effects covered in this chapter have little value on their own, but serve as a framework for later effect. Because of this, we will develop a simple screen effect in this chapter that could prove useful. Following is a simple screen effect that can estimate the motion blur effect seen in real-life video.

Have you ever moved your hand in front of your eyes rapidly from left to right? If you do so, you'll notice that you cannot see your hand clearly and it appears mostly as a big blur. The same phenomenon also happens with photo and video cameras. This happens because the human eye and cameras do not take in information at an infinite rate but take snapshots of what they see many times per second. If an object is moving faster than the rate at which images are captured, it will appear to streak across the image.

Knowing how the effect happens in real life can tell us to implement it in our rendering environment. The ideal approach is to determine the movement speed of each pixel in the scene from one frame to another, and use this information to blur the image correctly. This approach is feasible but too complicated at this point in this book. Another approach would be to ignore the speed of movement and take the pixels from the previous frame and blend them with the pixels of the current frame. This approach is a gross estimation because it does not account for actual speed but has been taken in many of today's video games and is the approach I will take in this chapter.

tip

A motion blur screen effect can serve one of two purposes. The first is the obvious: a simple emulation of the real-life motion blur effect. The second is that when the effect is applied slightly to a scene, it can cancel out aliasing effects that can occur in your rendering, effectively serving as an inexpensive alternative when you do not have hardware antialiasing.

My approach may seem like a crude approximation of the real effect, and you may think it would not function. A common misconception in computer graphics is that unless you do it the exact way it appears in real life, it can't look good. As you read this book, you will learn that the essence of computer graphics is not how exactly you do something, but how convincing it is to the human eye. Human vision is a very subjective thing and does not perceive everything equally, just as you can't assume the intensity of a color is the simple average of all its components.

Before you can write a motion blur shader, you should understand the process of how the effect happens using RenderMonkey. In essence, you will need to render your scene to a render target and then blend the current result with the previous output from the previous frame. Figure 5.17 pictures the process in a clearer way. Looking at the diagram, you can see that the whole motion blur process is simply a recursive loop, where the result from the previous frame is used to render the next frame.

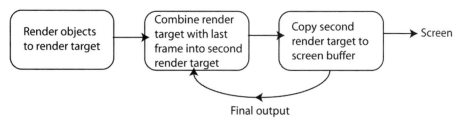

Figure 5.17 The workflow process for your motion blur effect.

Building the Motion Blur Shader

With the information you have so far, it is easy to implement a motion blur effect, starting from your template shader developed at the beginning of this chapter. This shader already takes care of rendering your scene to a render target and gives you a rendering pass to copy a render target to the screen. Based on the diagram in Figure 5.17, the only thing missing is a pass that takes care of blending the result from the previous frame with the current result. To do this, you need to add another Pass node to your effect. You will notice this new pass is added at the end of the effect, but you will need it right before the final pass. To do this, right-click on the new Pass node and select Move Up from the menu. The reason you need to "Move Up" the new pass you have just added is that RenderMonkey actually renders them sequentially in the order they are presented within the workspace. Since your new pass needs to be rendered before the final "Present" pass, it needs to be placed before it in the workspace.

Another thing you will need to add to your effect is a new render target. You may not have thought about it, but because you need to keep the previous frame's render result, you will need a new render target to keep track of this. So add the new render target to the effect by using the right-click menu on the Effect node and renaming it RenterTarget2.

At this point, the objects from the scene are being rendered to RenderTarget, and you have your blending pass almost ready. Because you will be blending the two render targets together, it will be worth adding a variable to the effect to control how the two textures will be combined. Add a VECTOR variable to your effect, name it blend_factor, and set its value to 0.5. Because the blending pass essentially blends two render targets into one, the basic task is essentially the same as the regular render target copy pass. So to start, copy the vertex and pixel shader code from the regular copy pass onto your blending pass, which is the new rendering pass you just created.

Another thing is needed for this to work. Because you will need the results of the rendering for your next frame, this blending pass needs to output its result to RenderTarget2 so you can reuse it next frame. To do this, add a Render Target Reference node to the blending pass and point it to RenderTarget2.

With this basic setup, the vertex shader already does all it needs to do; the only changes needed are to the pixel shader. The two basic setup items needed are to add the second render target sampler and the blend_factor. Add those to the pixel shader as you have done for other shaders before. Remember that you will also need to copy your model and texture references from your regular copy pass to the new blending pass, so that it can render the proper geometry and texture.

The current pixel shader code simply samples the first texture and outputs it to Blur1. But now you want to blend two textures together. For this effect, you can simply sample both textures using the same texture coordinates, and interpolate between the two values based on the blend factor variable. With HLSL, this can easily be done by using the `lerp` function, which will perform a simple linear interpolation between two values. The pixel shader code that interpolates the two render targets is as follows:

```
float4 blur_factor;
sampler Texture0;
sampler Texture1;
float4 ps_main(float2 texCoord: TEXCOORD0) : COLOR
{
    float4 col1 = tex2D(Texture0, texCoord);
    float4 col2 = tex2D(Texture1, texCoord);

    // Interpolate in-between the two render targets
    return lerp(col1,col2,blur_factor);
}
```

This almost does it; the only thing that needs to be changed is your final copy pass. This pass still copies the first render target to the screen. This needs to be changed so that it uses the result contained in `RenderTarget2`. Compile the effect, and there you have it! If you move your objects around, you will see a trail left behind by the effect, as shown in Figure 5.18. You can also play around with the `blur_factor` variable to control the amount of blur that occurs. This shader can be found as `shader_8.rfx` on the CD-ROM.

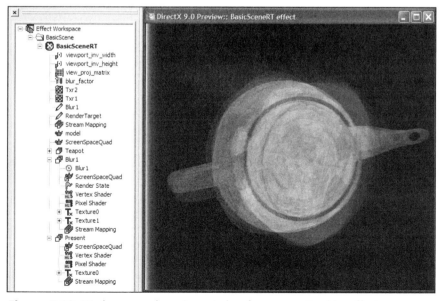

Figure 5.18 Workspace and preview window for your motion blur effect.

It's Your Turn!

There was much content in this chapter for you to understand. Most of it is simple, but it will serve as a foundation for the next few chapters. The following exercises will allow you to explore those screen effects a little further, and explore your own creativity as well. You can find the solutions to these exercises in Appendix D.

Exercise 1: OLD TIME MOVIE

This first exercise is simple because you will be using the generalized color manipulation shader to implement a Sepia shader. Sepia is a color mode that emulates old-time western pictures. In that time of early photography, pigments used in film prevented photography from reproducing correct black and white. In fact, pictures had more of a brownish tint. To reproduce this effect, you will need to determine the grayscale color intensity as with black and white, but apply a tint to the resulting image. To apply the tint, you simply need to add to the color generated by the grayscale conversion. The tint to apply for Sepia rendering is: Red=80/255, Green=43/255 and Blue=−23/255.

Your real task is to discover how this tint can be integrated into the color conversion matrix. Look at Figure 5.9 to determine how the tint can be applied to the matrix.

Exercise 2: GAUSS FILTER

In this chapter, you have learned how to implement a simple box filter. There are many other forms of filters that can be used to blur an image. The most popular one is the Gauss filter. This filter requires reading many more pixels along a 7×7 grid, which would require many samplings of a texture. However, to your advantage, this filter is *separatable*. This means the whole filter can be broken down into distinct horizontal and vertical passes.

For this exercise, you will need to expand the box filter shader to implement a Gauss filter. You will need to add an extra pass to the shader so you can filter both horizontally and vertically. The weight coefficients used for the Gauss filter are: 1/64, 6/64, 15/64, 20/64, 15/64, 6/64 and 1/64.

What's Next?

As you have seen in this chapter, screen-based filters are easy to set up and use. At this point, you may wonder about the usefulness of such filters. This chapter was a basic introduction, showing simple filters so you can get a handle on the basic principles before you tackle more complex effects. On their own, most of the simple effects demonstrated in this chapter have little value, but they do serve as basic components in the effects developed in the following chapters.

In the next chapter, you'll be introduced to your first real-life usable effect. The effect is called depth of field and can simulate the in- and out-of-focus properties that the human eye and video cameras perceive. This new effect takes advantage of the blurring filters I have developed in this chapter to re-create an out-of-focus version of your scene.

CHAPTER 6

BLURRING THINGS UP

O ne important aspect of computer graphics is rendering scenes that look perfect and flawless. This is because of the approaches taken and the precision of the rendering hardware. Of course, this is dependent on the extent of the geometric and texture precision put in them. Although this may be a valuable asset in some fields, such as medical imaging or architecture, it poses some problems in the fields of video games and movie CG. Those perfect-looking graphics lack the usual artifacts and phenomena perceived by either the human eye or a camera, making the graphics look synthetic.

Graphics developers strive to artificially reintroduce those artifacts by using clever rendering techniques. The hope behind this is to re-create visual cues, which appear naturally in photography but are lacking in computer graphics, thus creating a more immersive and realistic environment for the viewer.

In the art of video game making, developers have put time and effort into reproducing those effects. For example, many games feature lens flares, which are artifacts seen with video cameras when bright light is reflected internally by the lens. This effect, although simplistic, was one of the first steps taken toward artificially re-creating the photography effects observed in real life. With the introduction of flexible vertex and pixel shaders, more and more of those effects can now be re-created, giving even more immersive richness to your renderings.

In this chapter, you will learn about a common effect observed with the human eye and through photography called *depth of field*. I will explain how the effect occurs naturally so you can have a better understanding of its behavior. Then I will focus on a few possible implementations of such an effect that can be achieved with today's hardware through the use of shaders, and conclude with considerations for future implementations on upcoming hardware.

What Is Depth of Field?

Depth of field, or DOF, is an effect that occurs naturally in the human eye and in photographic equipment. The first thing worth considering is what DOF actually is and how it occurs. Take a look at the picture in Figure 6.1.

As you can see in the image, the elements closest and farthest from the camera appear blurred. I am sure you have noticed this in- and out-of-focus effect before. For another example, stare into the distance and hold your finger close to your eye; it will also be fuzzy and blurred out. You may ask yourself how this happens. The reason behind the effect can be described easily when you understand a little more about how your eye or a camera captures an image.

In Figure 6.2, you can see a basic setup for a camera with a subject, a lens, and a receiver. The principle described here works with the human eye as well, because cameras were created based on the same principle.

If you look closely at Figure 6.2, the first thing you'll notice is that the camera captures the image of the object by capturing the light that is reflected off the object. This light bounces off the object in all directions and eventually reaches the camera's lens. The purpose of the lens is to control the zoom of the object, while ensuring that the light coming straight into the camera lens converges towards the aperture. The aperture serves as a small entrance that controls the amount of light making it to the receiver. The receiver—the cornea, film, or CCD—receives the energy from the light and converts it into colors. (CCD means *charge-coupled device.*)

Figure 6.1 Outdoor photograph exhibiting the depth of field effect.

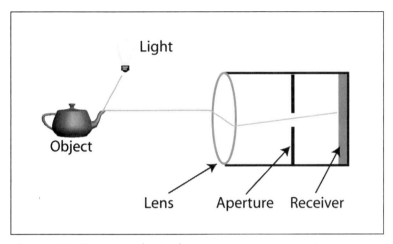

Figure 6.2 Diagram explaining how a camera captures an image.

In theory, if the aperture was infinitely small, only the light that perfectly converged through the aperture would make it to the receiver, and the image would be crisp for all distances. However, in such cases, this also means that very little light energy would make it to the receiver. Most cameras do not have an infinitely small aperture because more light is needed to capture a picture.

This has the side effect of allowing some of the light that is not converging perfectly at the center of the aperture to make it through to the receiver. This excess light then makes it to the receiver and causes unwanted blurring and distortions. You may wonder why such nonconverging light occurs in the first place. Figure 6.3 should shed more "light" on the subject.

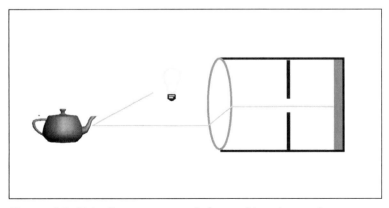

Figure 6.3 Light divergence example for an object close to the camera.

If you look at the object located close to the camera, you will notice something strange. Some of the light that is bouncing off the object, but not heading directly at the camera, can enter the lens. The lens is designed to refract the light rays heading in a perpendicular direction to it, so that they converge at the aperture. However, with the object closer to the lens, a non-perpendicular ray actually makes it to the lens. This ray of light is refracted like any other, but because of its direction, it does not converge exactly at the center of the aperture. If the aperture were really small, the light would be blocked, but in this case it is not.

Because this one intrusive ray made it, millions of others will also make it, causing the object close to the camera to appear blurred and out of focus. This is because light coming from incorrect directions will also contribute to the image, although this light isn't focused properly. I will not go into the details, but a similar phenomenon also occurs for objects far away from the camera.

Because of this flaw in our eyes and cameras, depending on the lens setup and aperture size, there is a region where most rays received will be straight and the image will appear crisp. However, going outside the region leads to an image that is progressively more blurred and distorted. Depth of field, or DOF, refers to the in-focus region. There are many ways to evaluate the focal distances used for DOF. Figure 6.4 outlines an equation that can be used to evaluate the DOF distances for various cameras.

note

The DOF equation given in Figure 6.4 is for reference. Throughout this chapter, I will not use these equations but will use arbitrary values that work well for our specific shader. You may, however, want to use these equations to represent this effect more accurately in more complex scenes.

$$H = \frac{L \times L}{f \times d}$$

Near Focus Limit

$$NF = \frac{H \times D}{(H + (D - L))}$$

Far Focus Limit

$$FF = \frac{H \times D}{(H - (D - L))}$$

Where

H = Hyperfocal distance (Distance of the nearest object which is considered in focus).
L = Lens focal length (35mm, 105mm,...) which is the distance from the center of the lens to the receiver.
f = Lens apreture f-stop (indicates the size of the lens apperture).
d = Diameter of least circle of confusion. This determines the sharpess of the image.
D = Lens focal distance

Figure 6.4 Equations used to calculate the far and near depth of field values for various cameras.

With this basic understanding of how the DOF effect happens within our optical devices, you can start exploring different approaches. The following section will explain how the depth of field can be faked and different techniques that can be used to do so.

It's All About Faking It!

Now that you know how depth of field occurs in real life, it is time to consider the important part: how you can re-create this effect in your 3D environment through the use of shaders. Generally, with such effects you want to create something convincing to the viewer. You should keep in mind when developing effects, however, that re-creating an effect following the equations and theory isn't always the best. Sometimes the cost of doing an effect perfectly is too prohibitive. Other times, an effect is too subtle and needs to be exaggerated so it can catch the viewer's eye.

Because of this, I will not focus on the exact physics behind the depth of field phenomenon, because they would be too expensive to do in real-time. Instead I will focus on creating an approximation that is well suited for use on the current 3D hardware and that looks convincing enough. This is essentially why this section is called "It's All About Faking It."

Based on the explanation in the preceding section, notice that the DOF effect has two major components. The first part to consider is that objects inside a specific depth range are in focus; the rest are out of focus. You will need techniques with which to discover or use the depth of your pixels to determine whether a pixel is in DOF range.

The second component is the blurring of out-of-focus regions. Blurring was covered in Chapter 5, "Looking Through a Filter," and in this chapter, you'll be able to take advantage of what you learned there.

Reproducing the DOF effect is simple. First of all, you need to render the scene to a render target in the same way you did in Chapter 5. This render then needs to be blurred so you can use it later. Following this, as usual, you need to copy this render target to the screen buffer. For every pixel you copy, you need to know its depth and find out if it is in focus or not. Based on this determination, you will either copy the blurred or nonblurred version of your render target to the screen buffer. Although this is a simple process, similar to the ones shown in the previous chapters, here I will cover different approaches that can be taken to implement DOF.

First, we'll take a closer, more detailed look at blurring, which is common to all techniques.

note

Keep in mind that there can be many more approaches to doing DOF than those presented in this chapter. I will cover only the most common approaches that work well on today's hardware, and present some ideas to keep in mind with regards to tomorrow's 3D hardware.

Blurring Things, Take Two

Because the depth of field effect requires you to combine your render target with a blurred version of the same image, it is worth revisiting the blurring techniques discussed in Chapter 5: the box filter and the Gauss filter.

In Figure 6.1, notice that the objects close to the camera are significantly blurred. The box and Gauss filters do not blur that much. Here you will learn how to expand your filters so they perform better for the needs of the DOF effect.

Two basic approaches can be taken to increase the blurring. The first one is to go for a more complex filter with more samples. This creates a smoother blur, but it can be significantly expensive.

The second approach is to do a simpler and less expensive blur, but to repeat the process several times iteratively. I will take this approach throughout this chapter because it has an added benefit. Because you are applying your filter progressively, you can keep intermediate versions of your blur. This will be useful for the depth of field effect, because you can use the intermediate blurs to create a smoother transition from the in-focus to the out-of-focus regions.

Because the box filter is too simple and the Gauss filter needs two passes, we'll try a new blur filter kernel that will do better than a box filter, but will be simple enough to fit in a single pass so it can be repeated several times.

This new filter kernel is essentially a simple 9-samples filter kernel. This filter is simpler than the regular Gauss filter and can be performed in a single pass. As you can see in Figure 6.5, this filter is essentially the expanded form of a 3-by-3 Gauss filter.

1/16	2/16	1/16
2/16	4/16	2/16
1/16	2/16	1/16

Figure 6.5 Kernel for the 9-samples blurring filter.

In Figure 6.5, notice that this filter only considers a single neighbor pixel, leading to minimal blurring. By using multiple iterations of this simple shader, however, you will have more control over the final amount of blurring you wish to apply. Implementing this shader can be done using the same approach used in the previous chapter. You can do this filter as an array of filter positions and weights, which yields the following source code:

```
float viewport_inv_width;
float viewport_inv_height;
sampler Texture0;
const float4 samples[9] = {
    -1.0,    -1.0,    0,    1.0/16.0,
    -1.0,     1.0,    0,    1.0/16.0,
     1.0,    -1.0,    0,    1.0/16.0,
     1.0,     1.0,    0,    1.0/16.0,
```

```
    -1.0,       0.0,      0,       2.0/16.0,
     1.0,       0.0,      0,       2.0/16.0,
     0.0,      -1.0,      0,       2.0/16.0,
     0.0,       1.0,      0,       2.0/16.0,
     0.0,       0.0,      0,       4.0/16.0
};


float4 ps_main(float2 texCoord: TEXCOORD0) : COLOR
{
   float4 col = float4(0,0,0,0);

   // Sample and output the averaged colors
   for(int i=0;i<9;i++)
      col += samples[i].w*tex2D(Texture0,texCoord+
      float2(samples[i].x*viewport_inv_width,
             samples[i].y*viewport_inv_height));
   return col;
}
```

This shader can be found as shader_1.rfx in the CD-ROM source code directory for this chapter.

One variable that still needs to be determined is how much blurring is enough. For this, I have developed a multi-pass version of this shader in which you can control the number of iterations by enabling and disabling render passes. This shader was developed by combining three simple blur iterations with a final Gauss blurring filter. For your convenience and experimentation, I have included this shader as shader_2.rfx on the CD-ROM.

The results for your experiment are shown in Figure 6.6. If you compare Figure 6.6 with Figure 6.1, the 3 iterations with Gauss filter would be enough to achieve a similar level of fuzziness and should be sufficient for the depth of field effect.

This covers one of the two aspects of the depth of field effect. Throughout the rest of this chapter, you will use the 3 iteration with Gauss blurring filter as your basic implementation. For your convenience, I have built a shader that contains the template scene I will be using with the blurring filter. This shader is included as shader_3.rfx on the CD-ROM.

note

By now, you should have noticed the use of a second renderable texture named Blur2 within the previous shader. The reason behind the second texture is that if you want to iterate through multiple filters, you will end up rendering to the same texture that you are using as a source, which can lead to rendering glitches. The way to avoid this is to alternate between two or more renderable textures.

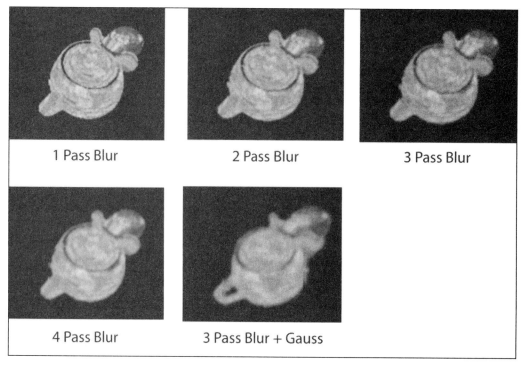

Figure 6.6 Different results for multiple blurring iterations.

Depth Impostors

Under ideal circumstances, you do your depth of field effect by determining a blurring factor for each pixel based on its 3D depth. Such implementation can be expensive, complicated, and even impossible on some hardware implementations, because you may not be able to access the depth information back from the hardware for use in your shader. Because of this, you need a technique that can work on virtually any available hardware and configuration.

In this section, you will learn a technique called *depth impostors*, which allows you to implement DOF without having to manually consider the depth of each pixel. The approach is simple; instead of determining the blurring factor for the depth of each pixel, you can render a full-screen polygon within your scene at an appropriate depth for the near and far focus regions. The polygon serves as an *impostor*, rendering the blurred version of the scene at the appropriate depth. The approach is the same as that of copying a renderable texture to the screen, with the exception that the geometry has a depth value set so that it interacts with the existing scene. Figure 6.7 illustrates the whole process.

Starting with the template from shader_3.rfx, you will need to add many variables. The first two variables to add to the Effect node are two scalar values named Near_Dist and

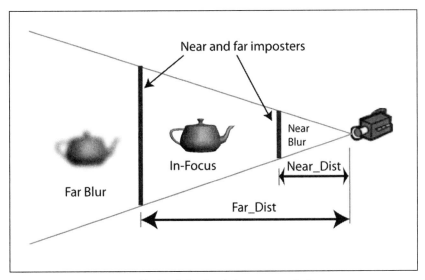

Figure 6.7 Process used behind the depth impostor technique.

`Far_Dist`. Those variables are used to contain the depth at which the near and far out-of-focus regions start. To start, set the `Near_Dist` variable to 0.4 and `Far_Dist` to 0.75.

You will also need a Camera node. This allows you to control the camera more precisely and set parameters, such as the far and near clipping planes. To create a Camera node, right-click on your Effect node and select Add Camera from the context menu. Because you can add multiple cameras to an effect, you will need to select the active one by picking Set Active Camera from the Camera node's right-click menu.

note

Placing manual cameras in the scene allows you to finely control its parameters, such as field of view and far and near clip planes. Cameras also enable you to render a scene from multiple perspectives as needed. Keep in mind that when you do not create a manual camera, a default camera is created for you, but it will not appear within your workspace.

Camera nodes will come in handy later on in this book.

When a scene is rendered, each pass needs to know which camera it must use. In our previous shaders, there was only one camera, the default one. Now, because you have created a manual camera, every pass that requires a projection matrix needs a Camera Reference node telling it which camera to use. In your shader, you need to add this reference node to all of the object-rendering passes. To do this, right-click on the Pass node and select Add Camera Reference. As with other reference nodes, you also need to select which camera to use with the right-click menu.

Before you can take on the rendering of the impostors, you need to make a minor adjustment to the pass nodes for both models. In this shader, I will be using W-Buffering instead of Z-Buffering. I will explain why in the next section, but for now, simply add a Render State node to both model rendering passes and change the ZENABLE state to USEW.

You now have a scene that will render your two models to a render target named RenderTarget, blur this render target using the textures named Blur and Blur2, and present RenderTarget to the user. You have all you need to create your actual impostors. The impostors will be rendered using the same trick you used to do all your render target copies in the past. The vertex shader code that handles the vertex position looks like this:

```
Out.Pos = float4(Pos.xy, 0, 1);
```

Notice that the z component of the position has been set to zero. This essentially means the geometry will be rendered right in front of the camera. Using a z value other than zero, you can control where your impostor will be rendered depth-wise but still guarantee that the polygon will cover the full screen. Changing this code to use the far and near distance variables yields the following:

```
// Set the position of the impostor so that it covers the screen.
// The Z value is set to either Far_Dist or Near_Dist and the W
// component is set to one so that no perspective occurs on the
// geometry.
Out.Pos = float4(Pos.xy, Far_Dist, 1);
// Or for the near plane.
Out.Pos = float4(Pos.xy, Near_Dist, 1);
```

Rendering depth impostors is simply a matter of reusing your standard render target copy pass and modifying its vertex shader code to use the proper depth, instead of forcing it to the front of the camera. Copy two passes from the blurring process by using the right-click menu Copy and Paste options, and rename them Impostor_Near and Impostor_Far. These passes simply apply a full-screen rendering of a renderable texture while blurring the end result, which is almost what you need to render a depth impostor. You will also need to move those passes so they are located between the last blurring pass and the present pass node. You can move them up using the Move Up option from the right-click menu.

Let's start by looking at the Impostor_Far pass. The first thing you need to do is add a Render State node and change its Z-Buffering settings. Because you will want the far impostor to render only when something is located behind it, the impostor must be drawn if its depth is less than what is in the Z-Buffer. You then need to enable Z-Buffering by setting ZENABLE to USEW and setting the ZFUNC to LESSEQUAL. You also need to make sure the impostors do not modify the depth buffer by setting the ZWRITEENABLE render state to FALSE; this is to avoid having the impostor overwrite the depth values from your scene.

The second thing to do with this render pass is to ensure that the texture references are set up properly. You need to make sure the render target reference points to RenderTarget and the texture object points to the Blur texture. With these settings, all that is left to configure is the shader code for this pass.

The vertex shader code is essentially the same as the blur pass from which you copied your shader, with two exceptions. The first is the vertex shader change I discussed a few paragraphs ago, which leads to the following vertex shader code:

```
float4x4 view_proj_matrix: register(c0);
float Near_Dist;
float viewport_inv_width;
float viewport_inv_height;
struct VS_OUTPUT
{
    float4 Pos: POSITION;
    float2 texCoord: TEXCOORD0;
};

VS_OUTPUT vs_main(float4 Pos: POSITION)
{
    VS_OUTPUT Out;

    // Simply output the position without transforming it
    Out.Pos = float4(Pos.xy, Far_Dist, 1);

    // Texture coordinates are set up so that the full texture
    // is mapped completely onto the screen
    Out.texCoord.x = 0.5 * (1 + Pos.x +viewport_inv_width);
    Out.texCoord.y = 0.5 * (1 - Pos.y +viewport_inv_height);

    return Out;
}
```

The second change is to the pixel shader. Because this pass isn't combining multiple samples from a texture, it can be changed to a simple "read and output" form, which gives the following pixel shader code:

```
float viewport_inv_width;
float viewport_inv_height;
sampler Texture0;
float4 ps_main(float2 texCoord: TEXCOORD0) : COLOR
{
    return tex2D(Texture0,texCoord);
}
```

With the `Impostor_Far` pass setup, creating the `Impostor_Near` pass is a matter of applying the same steps I just covered and substituting `Far_Dist` in the vertex shader with `Near_Dist`. The other change needed is to change your Render State Block so that `ZFUNC` is set to `GREATERQUAL`, allowing the portion in front of the impostor to be blurred.

Figure 6.8 shows the final workspace and preview window for the rendered effect. Play around with the camera, and you will see the scene objects going in and out of focus as you change their depth.

This shader can be found on the CD-ROM's source code folder as `shader_4.rfx`.

As you can see, this approach is simple to implement and can be used on most of today's hardware. It does suffer from one major drawback, though. Because you use a simple polygon placed at the proper depth, you can see a distinct separation between the in-focus the out-of-focus regions.

One way to improve on this is to blend in multiple far and near focus polygons with different levels of blending. This would create a more progressive transition to the effect. I invite you to carry out this extension in the first exercise at the end of this chapter. Other approaches that improve the in- and out-of-focus transitions involve finding out the depth and blurring per-pixel. I will be covering a few of these techniques in the following sections.

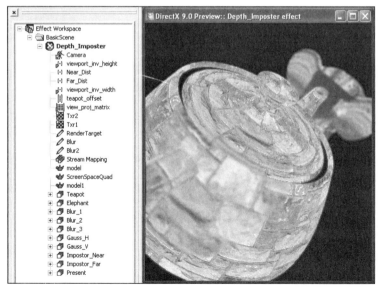

Figure 6.8 Final workspace and rendering result for the depth impostor technique. Notice the sharp transition between in-focus and out-of-focus regions.

A Note About Z-Buffers

You may have noticed during the development of the previous shader that I switched to a different Z-Buffering mode called W-Buffering by using the ZENABLE render state. I did this for a specific reason, which is worth discussing at this point.

Depth buffering on most 3D hardware is done with a Z-Buffer. In this buffer, the depth is stored as 1/z. This is convenient for the hardware because it needs this value to do proper perspective interpolation. However, using 1/z has a negative consequence when the values in the depth buffer are not linear. This means the values inside the depth buffer do not grow proportionally to the actual depth, but follow more of an exponential curve.

In the case of your impostor shader, this would have made it difficult to empirically discover the Near_Dist and Far_Dist values without some extra math. The W-Buffering scheme, on the other hand, uses the w value resulting from the projection matrix, which is linear, and makes it easy to determine correct depth values. With a W-Buffer to determine the proper depth, simply follow this equation: WDepth = Depth / Far_Z_Clip.

Not all 3D hardware supports W-Buffering, and if such is the case, you will get an error message and will need to revert to Z-Buffering.

If you have to do so, one solution to the problem of discovering the right depth values is to manually project a fake position in 3D space and use the resulting z value from the operation. To do so, you can use the built-in view_position and view_direction variables to create and project a fake position in 3D space. The following shader code explains how this could be achieved:

```
VS_OUTPUT vs_main(float4 Pos: POSITION)
{
   VS_OUTPUT Out;

   // Compute a proper z-buffer depth by projecting a fake position
   // in 3D and extracting its final Z value
   Out.Pos = float4(Pos.xy, 0, 1);
   Out.Pos.z = mul(view_proj_matrix,
                   view_position+Near_Dist*view_direction).z;

   // Texture coordinates are setup so that the full texture
   // is mapped completely onto the screen
   Out.texCoord.x = 0.5 * (1 + Pos.x +viewport_inv_width);
   Out.texCoord.y = 0.5 * (1 - Pos.y +viewport_inv_height);

   return Out;
}
```

Using the Alpha Channel

When using a technique like the depth impostors, you must solve the problem of the sharp transition between your in and out-of-focus areas. Adding multiple impostors can help reduce the problem, but can also lead to the added fill rate expense due to the increased number of times you fill the screen. Another way around this problem is to go through the screen once and determine the amount of blurring to apply for each pixel.

As you render your scene initially, you can discover each object's per-vertex depth by passing this depth information from the vertex shader to the pixel shader. Using this information and knowing your near and far focus regions, you can calculate a per-pixel factor that determines how in- or out-of-focus the pixel is.

Because your render target has an alpha channel, which is currently unused, the blurring factors can be put in this channel and used in the final DOF pass to determine how much of the blurred render target to apply. Before you can write this shader, though, you need to decide how to calculate the blurring factor in the first place.

If you assume the near and far focus distances are the point at which the scene is totally out-of-focus, you can define a little subregion right before which the output is progressively blurred. Figure 6.9 explains this process. In your shader, this region, or range, will be stored in variables called Near_Range and Far_Range.

The following shader code estimates the depth of field blurring factor based on Near_Dist, Near_Range, Far_Dist and Far_Range:

```
float Blur = max(clamp(0,1, 1 - (Depth-Near_Dist)/Near_Range),
            clamp(0,1, (Depth-(Far_Dist-Far_Range))/Far_Range));
```

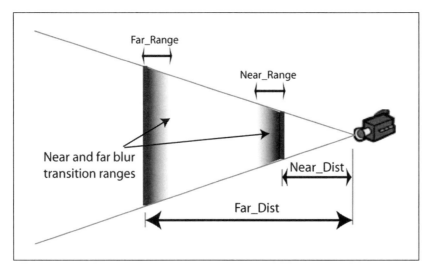

Figure 6.9 How to define an out-of-focus transition region.

The clamp function in the code above is an HLSL function that takes in three parameters and will ensure that the third parameter is within the range defined by the first two parameters.

Armed with this information, you are now ready to develop this new technique. You first need to make a few adjustments to the vertex shader, specifically to the passes that render the scene geometry; in other words, the Teapot and Elephant passes. The first thing you need to do is compute the per-vertex depth and send it to the pixel shader. In reality, this information is already computed for each vertex during the projection process and is stored as Out.Pos.z and Out.Pos.w. By taking the w value resulting from the vertex position projection and dividing it by the far clipping plane distance, you get a depth value in the zero-to-one range. This also means you will need to set up a variable called far_clip that contains the far clipping distance for your camera. To do this in the shader, all you need to do is add an output variable to the vertex shader and pass the depth value to the pixel shader through it. Applying this modification gives you the following vertex shader code:

```
float4x4 view_proj_matrix: register(c0);
float far_clip;
struct VS_OUTPUT
{
   float4 Pos:      POSITION;
   float2 Txr1:     TEXCOORD0;
   float1 Depth:    TEXCOORD1;
};

VS_OUTPUT vs_main(
    float4 inPos: POSITION,
    float2 Txr1: TEXCOORD0
)
{
   VS_OUTPUT Out;
   float4 OutPos;

   // Compute the position of the vertex
   Out.Pos = OutPos = mul(view_proj_matrix, inPos);
   Out.Txr1 = Txr1;

   // Send the depth to the pixel shader for encoding
   Out.Depth = OutPos.w/far_clip;

   return Out;
}
```

With this change to your vertex shader, you need to make matching changes to your pixel shader. You need to add an extra input parameter to the pixel shader, and use the equation determined previously to translate this depth into a blur factor. Remember to add the needed `Near_Dist`, `Near_Range`, `Far_Dist` and `Far_Range` variables to both your Effect node and your pixel shader.

The following pixel shader code takes in the interpolated vertex shader depth and outputs the proper blur factor as the alpha value of your render target:

```
float Near_Range;
float Far_Range;
float Near_Dist;
float Far_Dist;
sampler Texture0;
float4 ps_main(
    float4 inDiffuse: COLOR0,
    float2 inTxr1: TEXCOORD0,
    float1 Depth: TEXCOORD1
) : COLOR0
{
   float Blur = max(clamp(0,1, 1 - (Depth-Near_Dist)/Near_Range),
              clamp(0,1, (Depth-(Far_Dist-Far_Range))/Far_Range));

   //  Output the pixel color along with the blurring factor
   // The blurring factor being stored in the alpha channel of
   // the output color so that it can be reused when doing the
   // final DOF pass.
   return float4(tex2D(Texture0,inTxr1).rgb,Blur);
}
```

note

One drawback to using the alpha channel is that it prevents you from having translucent objects. This is because the alpha value is used to represent blur and not translucency. This means you will not be able to correctly blend objects that are affected by depth of field.

At this point, the alpha channel for your render target contains a blurring factor, which tells you how much blurring to apply to each pixel. Figure 6.10 illustrates the content of the alpha channel after the blurring factors are determined.

All you need to do is adapt your blending pass to take in both the blurred and original render targets as texture, sample both of them, and use the blur factor to combine both textures together. This can be done easily through the HLSL `lerp` function. You can add

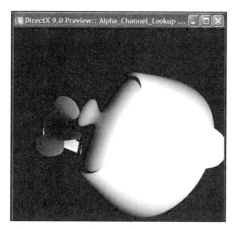

Figure 6.10 Blurring factors generated for your scene as the alpha channel of your render target.

both textures to your rendering pass and change the pixel shader to combine them, which should yield the following shader code:

```
float viewport_inv_width;
float viewport_inv_height;
float Near_Dist;
float Far_Dist;
float Near_Range;
float Far_Range;
sampler Texture0;
sampler Texture1;
sampler Texture2;
float4 ps_main(float2 texCoord: TEXCOORD0) : COLOR
{
    // Sample our regular and blurred scene
    float4 BlurColor = tex2D(Texture1,texCoord);
    float4 SceneColor = tex2D(Texture0,texCoord);

    // Interpolate the two textures based on the
    // DOF blurring factor stored in SceneColor.a
    return lerp(SceneColor,BlurColor,SceneColor.a);
}
```

After you are done, you can compile and run your shader. You should see results similar to those shown in Figure 6.11. Notice how much smoother the transition is between the in- and out-of-focus regions.

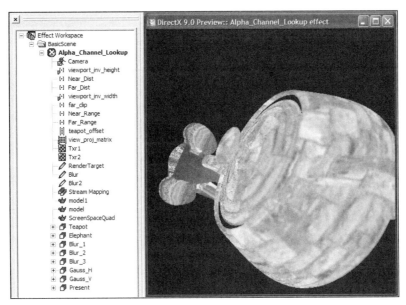

Figure 6.11 Final workspace and rendering result for the Alpha Channel
depth of field technique.

The completed shader for this section can be found on the CD-ROM as shader_5.rfx. In
the second exercise at the end of this chapter, I invite you to simplify this shader by using
a lookup texture that contains the relationship between depth and the blurring factor.

A Note About Multiple Render Targets

Monopolizing the alpha channel for your DOF effect may seem excessive, and you may
wish to use it for other effects, but it's a reasonable compromise under most circumstances. As an alternative to using your alpha channel, I figured that I should mention
what are called multiple render targets.

The latest hardware generations support a feature that allows you to render simultaneously to more than one render target. In essence, this allows you to output more than one
color value during your pixel shader, which will get put into different output textures. For
your depth of field effect, you could output your blurring factors to a different render target instead of being part of the alpha channel of your regular one, thus letting you use
your alpha for such things as translucency.

However, at the time of this writing, multiple render targets are still sparsely supported,
and I will not take advantage of them. In addition to this, multiple render targets are not
supported by RenderMonkey. On the bright side, however, you can expect support for this
feature to become more widespread with the next few 3D hardware generations.

Doing It Twice

The problem with the alpha channel approach is that you must render all your objects with a special shader that sets the alpha channel as well as monopolizing your alpha channel for this task. Personally, as a developer, I dislike such techniques for one big reason: they require that your whole application know that you intend to apply DOF to your scene. In reality, screen effects should be separated enough from regular rendering to be turned on and off without needing major changes in the way your scene is rendered. In addition, until 3D hardware has more support for secondary render targets, monopolizing your alpha channel for depth of field may significantly restrict you from using it to implement other rendering effects.

Another approach, which works in a similar way, is to render your scene, or at least each object you want the effect applied to, twice. Once to fill your Z-buffer and render target, and the second time to fill in another render target with depth information encoded within the RGB components of the render target. You can then decode this depth information within your DOF pass and use it to calculate a blurring factor per-pixel.

The obvious disadvantage of this approach is that it requires you to render your scene twice, which may be too prohibitive in some applications. On the plus side, you can use the depth information you have gathered for other shaders such as the Heat Haze effect, which will be discussed in the next chapter.

Encoding Your Depth as a Rainbow of Colors

I mentioned a few paragraphs ago about encoding depth information as colors in a render target. Your first instinct might be to say: "Well, the depth is in the range of zero to one, and so is a color component. Why can't I just put the depth in a single component?"

This is true but it's also false. Remember that most Z-buffers have 24 bits of precision for their depth values, whereas color components only offer 8 bits. Now, you may ask about those new 16- and 32-bit floating-point texture formats available on the latest hardware. Unfortunately, at the time of this writing, their support is sparse and their performance is even worse. For this generation of hardware, you cannot consider using them in any sort of real-time application, but they are worth keeping in mind as their support and performance improves.

Because you can't yet count on support for floating-point textures, you must take matters into your own hands, which isn't so complicated. Because you want to divide a value that can have up to 24 bits of precision into three components that have 8 bits, you can essentially let each component represent a certain level of precision and let the hardware take care of the little details for you.

For example, consider the full depth value that is contained between zero and one, and simply put it in the red component of the texture. Because the texture is only eight bits' worth of precision, the hardware takes care of rounding out the extra unwanted precision, which is equivalent to doing: `Color.Red = round(Depth*256)`. You see that the hardware takes care of automatically getting the 8 high bits of precision from your depth value. To repeat the same process with the following 8 bits of precision, you simply need to remove the 8 high bits and repeat the same process. This is equivalent to: `Color.Green = round((Depth*256 - Color.Red)*256)`.

This process, in HLSL form, yields some code similar to the following:

```
float4 Depth;
Depth.w = 1.0;
Depth.x = floor(inDepth.x*127)/127;
Depth.y = floor((inDepth.x-Depth.x)*127*127)/127;
Depth.z = 0;
```

In this code example, `inDepth` is the depth of the pixel in a zero to one range. Also notice that I use 127 as a multiplier and only do two-color components. The use of 127 instead of 255 allows you to guard against overflows and allows you to potentially do additional operations, such as adding depth together, which I will use later on in this book. I have also restricted my use of the color components to only the Red, Green, and Blue ones, giving you 21 bits of precision, which is enough for the DOF effect and reduces the processing cost. The reverse process, to convert an encoded depth back to a floating-point depth value, is as follows:

```
float Depth = DepthValue.r + DepthValue.g/127 +
              DepthValue.b/(127*127);
```

Because of this encoding, any interpolation of the depth values in the RGB form will give wrong depth results. This has two consequences for your applications. First of all, you will need to do the conversion from depth to RGB in the pixel shader, because the vertex information interpolation will distort your values before they reach the pixel shader. Second, you must ensure that any filtering on your depth render targets, either bilinear or trilinear, is disabled before you read from the texture because the blending between two neighboring pixels will obviously give a wrong result. Figure 6.12 shows what the encoded depth for your sample scene looks like.

Figure 6.12 Render of a sample scene using the depth encoding technique.

This technique essentially gives you the same abilities the new floating-point texture formats give you, without your having to worry if a particular hardware supports them or not. Armed with this knowledge, you can now attack and develop the two-pass DOF shader.

Creating a Two-Pass DOF Shader

Creating a two-pass shader is straightforward and can be separated into two phases. In the first phase, you will need to render your scene a second time, taking the depth values and encoding them into a new depth render target. In the second phase, you will use your depth texture, decode the depth information, and use it to decide the correct blurring factor.

For the first phase, you will need a new render target for the depth information. Right-click on the Effect node, select Add Render Target, and rename it to Depth. You will also need to create a copy of both the Teapot and Elephant rendering Pass nodes. To do so, use the right-click menu to copy and paste them. You will also need to reposition them so that they are just below the original ones by using the Move Up option from the right-click menu.

With the two new nodes, you will need to ensure that they render to the Depth render target and change their vertex and pixel shaders so they encode the depth values to the texture. The following is the resulting vertex shader code:

```
float4x4 view_proj_matrix;
float far_clip;
struct VS_OUTPUT
{
   float4 Pos:     POSITION;
   float1 Depth:   TEXCOORD0;
};

VS_OUTPUT vs_main(
    float4 inPos: POSITION,
    float2 Txr1: TEXCOORD0
)
{
   VS_OUTPUT Out;
   float4 OutPos;

   // Compute the position of the vertex
   Out.Pos = OutPos = mul(view_proj_matrix, inPos);

   // Send the depth to the pixel shader for encoding
   Out.Depth = OutPos.w/far_clip;
   return Out;
}
The pixel shader code is as follows:
float4 ps_main(
    float4 inDepth: TEXCOORD0
```

```
) : COLOR0
{
   //  Output the depth as computed by
   //  the vertex shader
   float4 Depth;
   Depth.w = 1.0;
   Depth.x = floor(inDepth.x*127)/127;
   Depth.y = floor((inDepth.x-Depth.x)*127*127)/127;
   Depth.z = 0;

   return Depth;
}
```

Looking at the preceding vertex shader, you will notice the following line when the depth is output to the pixel shader.

```
Out.Depth = OutPos.w/far_clip;
```

The reason I divide the w value by far_clip is that the depth value computed during the projection process is in actual scene depth. Because you want to encode a value in the zero to one range, you need to scale the depth down using the value for the far clipping plane, since you know your scene depth will be somewhere in the zero to far_clip range initially. Note that you will need to create this variable and ensure that it is set to the same value as the far clip plane for your camera.

For the second phase of this shader, you need to access the depth information, decode it, compute the blurring factor for the pixel, and render the appropriate blend between the unblurred and blurred versions of the scene. This is the same process done with the Alpha Channel technique, except for the blurring factor being determined during the Present pass instead of during the rendering of the scene objects.

For this second pass, you need to make sure the Present render pass can access all three major render targets: RenderTarget, Blur, and Depth. In addition, you need to make changes to the pixel shader so it will read from the depth texture, decode the values, determine the blurring factor, and render the final output. I will not go into specific details, because each component has already been covered, but you should end up with the following pixel shader:

```
float viewport_inv_width;
float viewport_inv_height;
float Near_Dist;
float Far_Dist;
float Near_Range;
float Far_Range;
sampler Texture0;
```

```
sampler Texture1;
sampler Texture2;
float4 ps_main(float2 texCoord: TEXCOORD0) : COLOR
{
   // Sample and decode our depth value
   float4 DepthValue = tex2D(Texture2,texCoord);
   float Depth = DepthValue.r + DepthValue.g/127
               + DepthValue.b/(127*127);


   // Sample our regular and blurred scene
   float4 BlurColor = tex2D(Texture1,texCoord);
   float4 SceneColor = tex2D(Texture0,texCoord);

   // Use the defined ranges to determine the proper
   // combination of both render targets based on
   // the distance.
   float Blur = max(clamp(0,1, 1 - (Depth-Near_Dist)/Near_Range),
            clamp(0,1, (Depth-(Far_Dist-Far_Range))/Far_Range));

   return lerp(SceneColor,BlurColor,clamp(0,1,Blur));
}
```

Close the editors, compile the shader, and you have your two-pass depth of field shader. Figure 6.13 shows the resulting workspace and render output for this shader. This completed shader can also be found on the CD-ROM as shader_6.rfx.

In the third exercise at the end of this chapter, I will invite you to use intermediate blur textures to create a smoother transition between the focus and out-of-focus regions.

What About the Z-Buffer?

One thing you may have wondered throughout this chapter is, why did I bend over backwards to determine the depth of the scene objects? Cleverly, you may ask, "Well, because we are rendering our scene, and the depth values get put into the Z-Buffer, why can't we just use that?" This is a very valid point, and I must explain why I have not done so.

In theory, the Z-Buffer is essentially a texture that contains encoded depth values for each pixel on the screen. If you could use it as a source texture and decode the depth, you could use those values to do your effect without any special work. But the reality is that most 3D hardware has special implementations of Z-Buffers and will not let you access depth values directly, thus limiting this approach. In addition to this, the 3D rendering APIs do not give obvious means to access and treat the depth buffer as a texture.

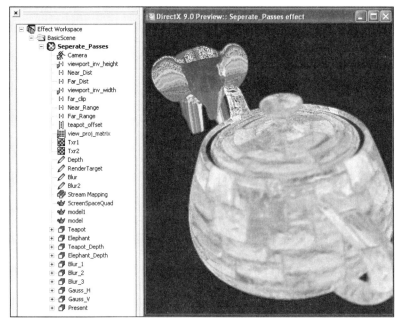

Figure 6.13 Final workspace and rendering result for the two-pass DOF technique.

On the plus side, however, more hardware vendors are supporting extensions, such as shadow mapping, which requires texture access to depth buffers. Current support is still limited and restrictive, but developers have been asking for this feature, and you can expect a more broad support for this in the following generations of 3D hardware and APIs.

Meanwhile, unless you are developing on the Microsoft Xbox, you will have to stick with the basic approaches developed in this chapter.

Special Considerations

A last little thing I have not talked about yet but that is worth considering is the way DOF happens on the transition between in-focus and out-of-focus regions. If you take another peek at Figure 6.1, you will notice that blurriness for the edge of an out-of focus object actually extends onto objects that are in focus.

This phenomenon is fully understandable when you think about the way depth of field happens. In essence, an out-of-focus object appears blurred because many ghost images of it appear offset from its real position. These ghost images come from rays of light that come in at a nonperpendicular angle from the camera.

If you look at the results from all the DOF shader variations developed during this chapter, however, none exhibit this side effect. This is, of course, because you are faking the effect, trying to reproduce something that looks similar to DOF without actually mimicking the physics behind the effect.

If you wish to re-create such "border blurring," it can be accomplished with the use of per-pixel DOF techniques. Although I will not fully develop such shaders in this chapter, I thought it might be useful for you to know how this could be carried out.

The idea is simple because blurring contributions for a particular pixel actually come from many neighboring ones. You may want to sample your depth information at many of the neighbors, and weigh the contributions together. If you think about it, because the blurred texture color comes from a set of neighbors, it makes sense to also determine the DOF factor in a similar fashion. In fact, you can use the same kernels you used with the blurring phase to find out the weighed depth for each pixel. Figure 6.14 illustrates this process in more detail.

Obviously, the complexity and cost of this approach is greater and is generally not needed because it adds little visual quality to the results. However, some applications may benefit from the added realism.

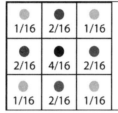

1/16	2/16	1/16
2/16	4/16	2/16
1/16	2/16	1/16

Blurring factor is the weighed sum of all neighboring blur factors. This is essentially the same process and kernel as with our blur.

Figure 6.14 Taking into consideration the boundary blurring by sampling the depth from many neighbors.

It's Your Turn!

As you can see, great effects can be achieved with little work, and your work doesn't have to be perfect to look good. It is now time to exercise your own creativity and expand on what you have learned throughout the chapter. The solutions to these exercises can be found in Appendix D.

Exercise 1: MULTIPLE IMPOSTORS

For this first exercise, I invite you to improve on the depth impostor shader developed in this chapter. One of the major drawbacks of the impostor approach is that it displays a sharp transition between the in and out-of-focus regions. One way to counteract this is to render multiple far and near blurring planes, creating a smoother transition. In this exercise, simply add additional front and near blurring planes, which are slightly offset in depth, and use alpha blending to create a less blurred transition region.

Exercise 2: USING A LOOKUP TEXTURE

In this second exercise, I invite you to improve on the Alpha Channel DOF shader developed in this chapter. One of the issues with this shader is that it requires you to calculate the full depth-to-blur function for each pixel of each object in your scene. This can be cumbersome, especially if you use a complex formula to compute the DOF blurring factor. For this exercise, I invite you to create a lookup texture, using a separate render target that will be filled with your precomputed equation. You will then use this lookup texture within your scene rendering to determine the proper blurring in relation to the pixel depth.

Exercise 3: USING INTERMEDIATE BLUR TEXTURES TO CREATE A SMOOTHER TRANSITION

For the last exercise of this chapter, I invite you to take advantage of the intermediate blurred render targets to create a smoother transition. Adapt the two-pass DOF shader so that it combines both the final blur and an intermediate blur to produce the final DOF result. To accomplish this, you need to add an additional render target to keep the result of the intermediate blur and use this new texture in your final pixel shader by combining the scene render target, the intermediate blur, and the complete blur.

What's Next?

Depth of field is a great yet simple effect. By re-creating natural phenomena that occur in cameras and the human eye, you can create truly stunning and immersive graphics. In addition, you have finally seen how simple screen effects can be combined to produce more complex and impressive ones.

Keep in mind that I reviewed different approaches to the problem, because some may be more suitable to particular applications or hardware. I also reviewed some techniques that may not be applicable on current hardware but are worth keeping in mind for future generations of 3D graphics cards.

In the next chapter, I keep going along the same lines and introduce your to another screen effect called heat haze, or heat shimmer. The heat haze effect re-creates the distortion effect you may have noticed when hot air rises from a surface. I will introduce the fundamentals of the phenomenon and describe to you some techniques that can be used to reproduce this effect.

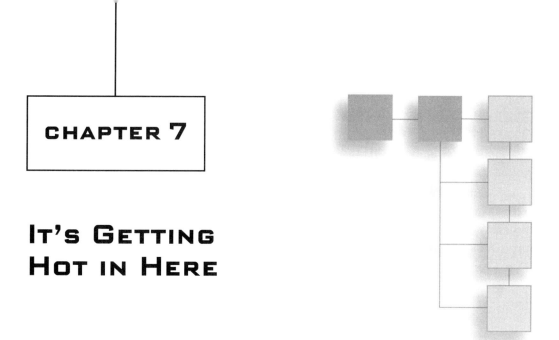

CHAPTER 7

IT'S GETTING
HOT IN HERE

Have you ever looked at the pavement on a hot sunny day? Ever noticed how the image in the distance seems distorted? Ever wonder why? It's due to a natural phenomenon called heat haze, or heat shimmer. In this chapter you will learn where this effect comes from in the real world and how you can reproduce it in a 3D rendering environment.

With this effect, you will be able to re-create the heat distortion seen on hot pavement as well as the same effect observed from a heat source such as an open flame. I will explain how the effect occurs from a physical point of view and then follow up with actual techniques that can be performed through RenderMonkey. So let's start with explaining how heat haze happens in the first place.

What Is Heat Haze?

Heat haze, or heat shimmer, is an effect that occurs naturally in real life where an image seems distorted because of the rising air off a hot surface. This is commonly seen above asphalt pavement on a warm and sunny day. This phenomenon stems from a simple physical concept called refraction.

Although you may think of light as a wave, particle, or both, most people assume that it always travels in a perfectly straight line. This is true most of the time, but there are some cases where light direction actually changes.

Have you ever noticed a particular phenomenon when you put a straw in a glass of water? At the separation point between the water and air, if you look at it sideways, it appears as if the straw is cut in half. In other words, the part of the straw outside the water appears to go in at an angle different from the part in the water. This visual effect is due to a physical phenomenon called refraction. In fact, light changes its direction when it goes from one medium to another with a different density. Figure 7.1 shows how this happens.

Knowing the densities of both materials, you can calculate how a ray of light is redirected to a new direction. To calculate the new direction for rays of light, you can use Snell's law, shown in Figure 7.2. Also note that under HLSL, you can use the built-in function `refract` to compute the new light direction based on the incoming light direction, surface normal, and media densities. In fact, under the right conditions and the right light and surface angles, a medium can become reflective through refraction.

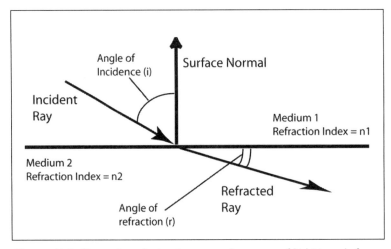

Figure 7.1 Illustration of what happens when a ray of light travels from a medium with one density to another with a different density.

$$\text{Snell's Law}$$

$$n_1 \sin i = n_2 \sin r$$

$$r = \arcsin\left(\frac{n_1}{n_2} \sin i\right)$$

Figure 7.2 Equation you can use to calculate refraction based on the incoming light direction, the surface normal, and media densities. This equation is also known as Snell's Law.

In the first exercise at the end of this chapter, I will invite you to develop a new shader from scratch, one which implements refraction. You will need to use an environment map and the HLSL refract function to perform this. This exercise will probably be the most difficult you have encountered so far and will be your first chance to use all that you have learned thus far.

All this discussion about refraction and media densities is interesting, but it still does not explain how heat shimmer happens. Starting with the hot pavement example. . . . Asphalt has a property that allows it to store heat; under sunlight the surface itself can get very hot. This has the effect of heating up the air close to the surface, which in turn rises above the surface because hot air is lighter than colder air.

The reason hot air rises above colder air stems from one main phenomenon. As air gets hotter, it expands and its density decreases. The cold air of greater density is heavier, and it heads down as the hotter air rises. This hot air, because it is of lesser density, also has a different refraction index than regular air. This causes the pockets of hot air to act as pockets of media with a differing refraction index, causing light to bend when it encounters them. Figure 7.3 shows this process for the hot pavement example.

Because of the pockets of varying air density, it is hard, if not impossible, to model heat shimmer accurately. Because of this, it is important with this effect not to follow the physics behind the phenomenon but to re-create it in a way that is convincing to the human eye. In the following sections, I will introduce you to a basic technique that can be used to simulate this phenomenon and teach you how you can use it to create the phenomenon as it would appear above pavement and over a fire.

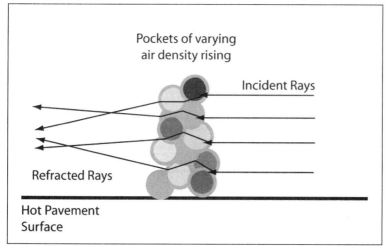

Figure 7.3 Diagram of how heat haze happens above hot pavement.

Uses for Heat Haze

Although the hot pavement example serves as a good illustration for the heat haze effect, it is worth going over a few different situations in which this effect can be used. Starting with the hot pavement scenario, you can see that the effect is similar to the depth of field effect covered in the previous chapter.

In fact, you can apply heat haze distortions in a distance-based way by defining a distance region for which the effect kicks in. Because of this, you can apply the same techniques used with DOF, such as impostors, to render your heat-distorted scene.

In addition to the hot pavement scenario, you can use the same effect to emulate hot gasses coming out of a fire or a jet engine, for example. For those effects, you can apply the same principle for the effect but use a particle system to render your distorted portions of the scene. We will discuss this approach later in this chapter.

In this chapter, you will learn that this basic effect can also be used to emulate effects, such as refraction for wavy water or even some nonrealistic sci–fi-type spatial distortions by using cleverly crafted distortion maps.

It's All About Distortion Maps

The most important thing needed to create a heat haze effect is the ability to distort your render target when you copy it back to your frame buffer. This section will serve as a quick introduction to distortion and bumpmaps.

The process for the heat haze effect is simple. You render your scene to a render target, as you did in Chapter 5, "Looking Through a Filter," and Chapter 6, "Blurring Things Up." However, this time when you copy your render target pixels to the screen, you will distort them from their original state.

Distortion does not mean changing the pixel itself; it means picking a neighboring pixel instead of the one that matches the pixel you are rendering to. In doing this, you are emulating the light ray deviations caused by the refraction within the hot air, as shown in Figure 7.3. The process is accomplished by using distortion maps, which cause pixels to be offset when copying them from the renderable texture to the screen.

One basic approach would be to skew the texture coordinates on your render target copy geometry. This would create an offset on the pixels, but it would be of limited resolution and use because the offset would be constant for the whole screen, and you obviously want a somewhat random distortion throughout the screen.

A better approach is to use a distortion map. Before sampling the actual render target, you will sample the distortion map. The values contained within this map are not actual pixels, but offsets, which can be used to offset how the render target itself is read.

Based on the type of effect, different types of distortion maps can be used. Noisy ones can be well suited for effects such as heat haze, and more smooth ones can be used for effects such as wavy water refraction. Either way, there is one more detail that you must know about before you can use a distortion map.

Because the distortion map is intended to be an offset and not a color, it would be nice if its values were in a −1 to 1 range. However, colors within textures are encoded in a 0 to 1 range. To correct this, you need to scale and offset the values read from the distortion map so that they will map to the correct range. You can accomplish this by scaling down the color values by 2 and subtracting 1 from the result. The following code shows how the values from a distortion map can be properly offset.

```
// Compute the distortion by reading the distortion map
// and bringing it into the -1 to 1 range. The OffsetScale
// is used to give control over final range of the distortion.
float2 offset = tex3D(Distortion,
                float3(texCoord2.xy,0)).xy;
offset = ((offset*2.0)-1.0)*OffsetScale;
```

note

When authoring distortion maps, keep in mind that the values read from the texture will be offset and scaled. This means that a 0 offset is not 0 but 0.5 in terms of colors.

Taking this offset texture, you can use the computed values to do a dependent texture lookup to read your render target in an offset way. The shader code below shows how the whole process works:

```
float OffsetScale;
sampler Texture0;
sampler Texture1;
float4 ps_main(float2 texCoord: TEXCOORD0) : COLOR
{
    // Read and scale the distortion offsets
    float2 offset = tex3D(Texture1,float3(texCoord.x,texCoord.y,0)).xy;
    offset = ((offset*2.0)-1.0)*OffsetScale;

    // Offset texture lookup into our render target
    return tex2D(Texture0,texCoord+offset);
}
```

In the preceding code, you may have noticed the OffsetScale variable. Because the distortion map, once scaled and offset, maps to a −1 to 1 range, you may not wish to use this full range when applying the distortion to the render target. Doing so results in an offset range that equals the whole render target, which is too much for most applications. The `OffsetScale` variable is used to control the range, or amplitude, of your distortion map so that it may be more usable within your application.

---

note

As you may have noticed, using distortion maps to perform heat haze does not follow the rules of refraction. Because heat shimmer is a complex effect, I will focus on making an effect that looks good, although it is not accurate. You will get to use Snell's Law in Chapter 11, "Mirror, Mirror, On the Wall," to create accurate refraction.

I will not cover the topic of bumpmaps in this chapter; I just wanted to mention that bumpmaps essentially follow the same principle as distortion maps but modify the surface normal of an object instead of being used to distort a render target copy. I will talk some more about bumpmaps when I get into the lighting chapters later in this book.

Putting a Background to Your Shader

In your previous shaders, there was not much in the background beyond the two objects. Because the heat haze effect needs a little more than a teapot and an elephant to appear in all its glory, I will show how you can use an environment map to spice your scene up.

Imagine yourself in an outside scene. You would like to use this environment as a background or a source of reflection for your shader. How can you do this?

The basic approach would be to take snapshots from different angles and composite them together to form a full view of your environment. There are many ways to do this, and I will not delve into the explanation of some of the common techniques, such as sphere maps or parabolic maps. Because almost all the latest video cards have built-in support for what are called cube maps, this is the approach I will explore.

Imagine that you want to take a full panoramic snapshot of an environment. The best way to do this would be to take many pictures at different angles and composite them around a virtual sphere. Each point on the sphere would represent the environment from a particular angle. This approach poses some mathematical problems, however, and is generally too complex for implementation on hardware.

To work around this limitation, 3D hardware makers came up with the clever idea of mapping the environment onto a cube instead of a sphere, as shown in Figure 7.4. Although this approach may seem awkward, it has several advantages. First, by assimilating a 3D vector pointing in a specific direction, such as a reflection vector, the hardware can easily deduce which face of the cubemap to look up and at which position to do so. This makes it easy for hardware vendors to implement because it is essentially an extension to the regular approach taken to sample a texture.

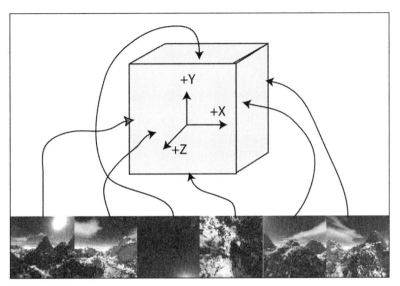

Figure 7.4 Diagram explaining how a cube environment map works.

The second major advantage to a cube environment map is that it is easy to create. Because you compose your environment on a cube, you can simply position a camera at 90-degree increments, rendering each face of the cubemap one by one. This can be easily done on today's hardware using standard render targets.

Notice that the texture coordinates used to access the texture represent the direction vectors for which you wish to sample the texture, which means you will need to pass a three-component vector when sampling such a texture. You also need to tell RenderMonkey to sample a cube texture by using the texCUBE HLSL function.

note

Because cubemaps are essentially a composition of six regular textures, you need to use a texture format that supports such an arrangement. At the time of this writing, only the Microsoft .DDS file format supports cubemaps natively by allowing you to compose six individual textures and save them as a cubemap.

Let's now create a basic shader that uses a sample cubemap to make a shader which shows a teapot against an environmental background. This completed shader can be found as shader_1.rfx on the CD-ROM.

Starting with a basic shader, similar to the shader_1.rfx developed in Chapter 6, you need a blank pass to render the environment map. Create this new pass by using Add Pass from the Effect node right-click menu.

For this node, you need both a model and an environment texture to use. Create a new texture variable and select the file snow.dds by double-clicking your new node. Keep in mind that because this is a cube texture and not a regular texture, you need to make your texture variable of type CUBEMAP. Also remember to properly set up your texture object within your environment pass node.

Now that you have a texture, you need something to render it to. Because you want to cover the whole screen, no matter where the camera is looking, a big sphere centered at the camera position would do the trick. Such a sphere model has been supplied with RenderMonkey as sphere.3ds. Create a new Model node in your Effect node, and point it to the proper model file.

With this setup, all you need is suitable shader code that takes into consideration the rotation of the camera and displays the proper texture coordinates, so you see the correct environment based on where the camera is looking.

Keep in mind that the sphere is of finite size, but you wish to have it treated as if it was of infinite size. To do so, you need to disable the Z-Buffer when rendering this object, by turning off both the ZENABLE and ZWRITEENBALE render states.

The sphere geometry is centered about the origin, but you need to ensure that it is always positioned where the camera is. Simply offset the sphere geometry by the view_position variable, which contains the current camera position.

You must pass to the pixel shader the direction in which you want to sample the cubemap. In other words, you need to determine the eye vector for each vertex of the sphere. For your convenience, because the sphere geometry model supplied with RenderMonkey is a unit sphere and you have centered it about the camera, the eye vector is simply the position of the vertex.

Putting this together yields the following vertex shader code:

```
float4x4 view_proj_matrix;
float4 view_position;
struct VS_OUTPUT
{
    float4 Pos: POSITION;
    float3 dir: TEXCOORD0;
};

VS_OUTPUT vs_main(float4 Pos: POSITION)
{
    VS_OUTPUT Out;

    // Center environment around camera and pass the environment direction
```

```
    // to the pixel shader.
    Out.Pos = mul(view_proj_matrix, float4(Pos.xyz + view_position, 1));
    Out.dir = Pos.xyz;

    return Out;
}
```

On the other hand, the pixel shader code for this environment pass simply needs to sample the texture and output the colors to the frame buffer. Remember that because the texture is a cubemap, you must use the texCUBE function and not the tex2D function to sample the texture. Here is the resulting pixel shader code:

```
sampler Environment;
float4 ps_main(float3 dir: TEXCOORD0) : COLOR
{
    // Sample and output the environment map color
    return texCUBE(Environment, dir);
}
```

Now, all you need is some extra geometry and, of course, a teapot! You can copy and paste a teapot-rendering pass from one of the previous shaders or repeat the same steps taken in the past. With those two passes, you have a simple shader that renders a teapot with a background based on the environment map, as shown in Figure 7.5.

There is one thing missing from this shader. To create heat haze, you need to use a copy of the rendered scene. As you learned in the last two chapters, to do this you need to ensure that your scene is rendered to a render target instead of the frame buffer. For this, you need to create a render target node within your scene and ensure that both the environment and the teapot pass render to this render target.

Figure 7.5 Environment map background and teapot shader in action.

You also need to have the scene rendered to the frame buffer because the heat haze effect is used to enhance the scene and not to construct it in the first place. This means you also need to create, or copy from a previous shader, another pass node, which takes care of copying your render target back to the frame buffer after all objects have been rendered to it.

The final version of this template shader is included on the CD-ROM as shader_2.rfx.

Hitting the Pavement

Now that you have a basic scene with an object and a background, it is time to implement the simplest form of heat haze. Based on the hot pavement scenario explained earlier in this chapter, you can take an approach similar to the one taken for the depth of field effect used in Chapter 6. If you assume that the heat shimmer only appears at a certain distance from the camera, you can use the depth impostor approach to produce a simple yet convincing heat haze effect.

For this shader, you can simply use the base shader developed in the previous section and copy the depth impostor pass from the shader in Chapter 6. As with the depth impostor, you need to add the proper Far_Dist variable to your workspace, which I will call Heat_Dist.

With this depth impostor shader pass, you simply need to adjust the vertex and pixel shaders based on what I described in the last few paragraphs. With the proper changes to vertex shader to use the Heat_Dist variable, you should have the following shader code:

```
float Heat_Dist;
float viewport_inv_width;
float viewport_inv_height;
float4x4 view_proj_matrix;
struct VS_OUTPUT
{
   float4 Pos: POSITION;
   float2 texCoord: TEXCOORD0;
};

VS_OUTPUT vs_main(float4 Pos: POSITION)
{
   VS_OUTPUT Out;

   // Simply output the position without transforming it
   // The Z value contains the depth position of the
   // Heat Impostor
   Out.Pos = float4(Pos.xy, Heat_Dist, 1);

   // Texture coordinates are setup so that the full texture
   // is mapped completely onto the screen
   Out.texCoord.x = 0.5 * (1 + Pos.x + viewport_inv_width);
   Out.texCoord.y = 0.5 * (1 - Pos.y + viewport_inv_height);

   return Out;
}
```

For the pixel shader, instead of simply fetching a blurred render target, you need to apply the distortion code illustrated earlier and apply it to your original render target. With these modifications, you should get the following pixel shader code:

```
float OffsetScale;
float time_0_1;
sampler Texture0;
sampler Texture1;
float4 ps_main(float2 texCoord: TEXCOORD0) : COLOR
{
    // Read and scale the distortion offsets
    float2 offset = tex3D(Texture1,float3(8*texCoord.x,8*texCoord.y,0)).xy;
    offset = ((offset*2.0)-1.0)*OffsetScale;

    // Fetch render target with the texture offset applied
    return tex2D(Texture0,texCoord+offset);
}
```

The texture coordinates for the distortion map are multiplied by 8 in the proposed pixel shader code. This is merely to allow a better noisiness of the texture by repeating the distortion map multiple times throughout the screen. For the purpose of this shader, you can use the texture noisevolume.dds, which has been supplied on the CD-ROM. In addition to this, to allow for the distortion map to be repeated multiple time across the screen, you will need to ensure that the texture object states ADDRESSU and ADDRESSV are set to D3DTADDRESS_WRAP. Figure 7.6 shows the final rendered output for this shader. This shader has also been included on the CD-ROM as shader_3.rfx.

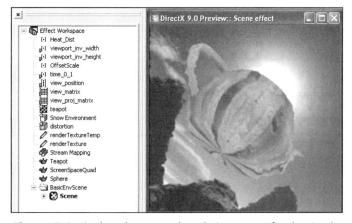

Figure 7.6 Final workspace and rendering output for the simple depth-based heat haze effect.

In the hot pavement example, you may notice that the heat shimmer phenomenon dissipates a few meters above the ground. In this implementation, the effect takes over the whole screen. If you wish to emulate this behavior, you could fade out the impostor in relationship to the *ground height* or simply take advantage of the technique exposed in the next section.

The previous shader, however, is missing something; the distortion is static and does not move relative to the screen. In the hot pavement example, hot gasses rise from the surface, causing the distortion to appear to move upwards. By using the built-in time_0_1 variable, which returns a value that progresses from 0 to 1 over time, you can change the pixel shader to animate the distortion map. Because the distortion map is a volume texture where each slice of the texture is a frame of animation for this texture, you also can apply the time animation to the Z component of the texture to create even more animation. By applying those changes, you get the following pixel shader code:

```
float OffsetScale;
float time_0_1;
sampler Texture0;
sampler Texture1;
float4 ps_main(float2 texCoord: TEXCOORD0) : COLOR
{
    // Read and scale the distortion offsets
    float2 offset = tex3D(Texture1,float3(8*texCoord.x,
                    8*texCoord.y+2*time_0_1,time_0_1)).xy;
    offset = ((offset*2.0)-1.0)*OffsetScale;

    return tex2D(Texture0,texCoord+offset);
}
```

note

Volume texture enables you to store pixels in 3D instead of 2D and to address its texels using not only X and Y coordinates but also using Z. In simpler terms, you can imagine a volume texture as a set of regular textures layered on top of each other. Because volume textures are a special hardware-supported format, they can only be stored using .DDS files.

This animation makes the distortions look more realistic and natural. In the second exercise at the end of this chapter, I will invite you to explore a different approach to animating the distortion map so that it looks even more natural. I have included this shader as shader_4.rfx on the CD-ROM.

Looking Above the Flame

The problem with the depth-based approach is that it only considers cases where the whole environment at a certain distance is composed of heated air. The reality is that the heat haze phenomenon can be more localized for a jet exhaust or an open flame. Because the heat haze effect simply involves taking a copy of your current scene and rendering a distorted version of this same scene where you want to apply the effect, this means the effect can be applied to any type of geometry you wish throughout your scene.

The heat haze effect can be applied not only to depth impostors but also to any piece of geometry in your scene. I will now develop a new shader that takes advantage of the same template scene developed earlier but uses a particle system that emits screen-facing polygons from the spout of the teapot, essentially mimicking what hot gasses emanating from the teapot would look like.

This code is based on the `ParticleSystem.rfx` sample file included with RenderMonkey.

This sample file takes advantage of a model that is composed of a set of individual rectangles which are all set up in the same way with the exception of their Z-coordinate, which increments from 0 to 1 for each polygon. The individual Z value for each polygon allows you to distinguish between each particle so you can animate them individually.

The sample shader that comes with RenderMonkey emits flame-like particles from the spout of a teapot. This is similar to what you want to do with the heat haze effect. The vertex shader for this sample is as follows:

```
float4x4 view_proj_matrix: register(c0);
float4x4 view_matrix: register(c4);
float time_0_X: register(c8);
float4 particleSystemPosition: register(c9);
float particleSystemShape: register(c10);
float particleSpread: register(c11);
float particleSpeed: register(c12);
float particleSystemHeight: register(c13);
float particleSize: register(c14);
// The model for the particle system consists of a hundred quads.
// These quads are simple (-1,-1) to (1,1) quads where each quad
// has a z ranging from 0 to 1. The z will be used to distinguish
// between different particles

struct VS_OUTPUT
{
    float4 Pos: POSITION;
```

```
    float2 texCoord: TEXCOORD0;
    float color: TEXCOORD1;
};


VS_OUTPUT main(float4 Pos: POSITION)
{
    VS_OUTPUT Out;

    // Loop particles
    float t = frac(Pos.z + particleSpeed * time_0_X);
    // Determine the shape of the system
    float s = pow(t, particleSystemShape);

    float3 pos;
    // Spread particles in a semi-random fashion
    pos.x = particleSpread * s * cos(62 * Pos.z);
    pos.z = particleSpread * s * sin(163 * Pos.z);
    // Particles goes up
    pos.y = particleSystemHeight * t;

    // Billboard the quads.
    // The view matrix gives us our right and up vectors.
    pos += particleSize * (Pos.x * view_matrix[0] + Pos.y * view_matrix[1]);
    // And put the system into place
    pos += particleSystemPosition;

    Out.Pos = mul(view_proj_matrix, float4(pos, 1));
    Out.texCoord = Pos.xy;
    Out.color = 1 - t;

    return Out;
}
```

The shader also has the following pixel shader:

```
float particleShape: register(c0);
sampler Flame: register(s0);
float4 main(float2 texCoord: TEXCOORD0, float color: TEXCOORD1) : COLOR
{
    // Fade the particle to a circular shape
    float fade = pow(dot(texCoord, texCoord), particleShape);
    return (1 - fade) * tex1D(Flame, color);
}
```

You can take the particle pass from RenderMonkey's sample shader and copy it to your template shader by using the right-click menu Copy and Paste options. With this shader in place, you need to make some adjustments for it to work properly with the heat haze effect.

First of all, you need to re-create many of the variables that existed in the sample particle shader and that are needed by the particle rendering pass. These variables include particleShape, particleSize, particleSystemHeight, particleSpeed, particleSystemShape, and particleSpread. With these variables in place, you need to make a few more changes to the shader for it to render the heat haze effect.

Besides this, you need to make a few modifications to the vertex shader. The essence of the changes is that the texturing on the particles matches the screen positions of the render target, and not the full texture you would normally use for a particle. To do this, you must calculate the screen x and y positions for each particle vertex and pass that to the pixel shader as a texture coordinate. This can be done with the following code:

```
texCoord.x = ((pPos.x/pPos.w)+1)*0.5;
texCoord.y = ((-pPos.y/pPos.w)+1)*0.5;
```

With this, the only other thing you need to know is the time, or life, of the particle. Knowing this enables you to properly fade in and out the heat haze effect within the pixel shader. This has been done by passing this value through the Z component of the texture coordinate.

The final vertex shader code resulting from these modifications is as follows:

```
float4x4 view_proj_matrix;
float4x4 view_matrix;
float time_0_X;
float4 particleSystemPosition;
float particleSystemShape;
float particleSpread;
float particleSpeed;
float particleSystemHeight;
float particleSize

struct VS_OUTPUT
{
    float4 Pos: POSITION;
    float3 texCoord: TEXCOORD0;
    float2 texCoord2: TEXCOORD1;
};
```

```
VS_OUTPUT main(float4 Pos: POSITION, float2 inTxr:TEXCOORD0)
{
    VS_OUTPUT Out;

    // Loop particles
    float t = frac(Pos.z + particleSpeed * time_0_X);

    // Determine the shape of the system
    float s = pow(t, particleSystemShape);

    float3 pos;
    // Spread particles in a semi-random fashion
    pos.x = particleSpread * s * cos(62 * Pos.z);
    pos.z = particleSpread * s * sin(163 * Pos.z);
    // Particles goes up
    pos.y = particleSystemHeight * t;

    // Billboard the quads.
    // The view matrix gives us our right and up vectors.
    pos += particleSize * (Pos.x * view_matrix[0] + Pos.y * view_matrix[1]);
    // And put the system into place
    pos += particleSystemPosition;

    float4 pPos = mul(view_proj_matrix, float4(pos, 1));
    Out.Pos = pPos;


    Out.texCoord.x = ((pPos.x/pPos.w)+1)*0.5;
    Out.texCoord.y = ((-pPos.y/pPos.w)+1)*0.5;
    Out.texCoord.z = s;
    Out.texCoord2 = Pos.xy;

    return Out;
}
```

You need to do matching adjustments within your pixel shader. All you really need to change is to sample your offset texture before you read pixels from the render target. Making these modifications should yield the following pixel shader code:

```
float OffsetScale;
float particleShape;
sampler RT;
```

```
sampler Distortion;
float4 main(float3 texCoord: TEXCOORD0,float2 texCoord2: TEXCOORD1) : COLOR
{
    float2 offset = tex3D(Distortion,
                        float3(texCoord2.xy,0)).xy;
    offset = ((offset*2.0)-1.0)*OffsetScale;

    float fade = pow(dot(texCoord2, texCoord2), particleShape);
    return float4(tex2D(RT, texCoord.xy+offset).xyz,(1 - fade));
}
```

With all those modifications, you are now ready to see the results. Compile this shader by pressing F7, and your output should resemble the one in Figure 7.7. The final version of this shader can be found on the CD-ROM as shader_5.rfx.

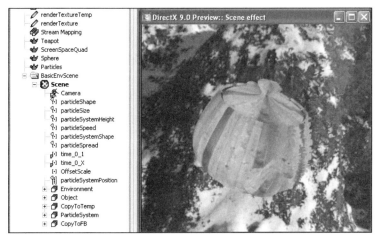

Figure 7.7 Final workspace and rendering output for the particle-based heat haze effect.

It's Your Turn!

Heat haze is a great screen-based effect and can bring much realism to your renderings. In addition, it serves as a great example of how it is not necessary to reproduce an effect perfectly to get good results when you have a basic understanding of how the effect happens in the first place. It is now time to exercise your own creativity and expand on what you have learned throughout the chapter. As always, the solutions to these exercises can be found in Appendix D.

Exercise 1: YOUR OWN REFRACTION SHADER

Here's a way to exercise your creativity and create a full shader on your own. Make a simple scene, rendering both an environment map and a refractive teapot. Set up your scene so that the environment map is rendered in the background. Then render a teapot where you use the `view_position` vector for your camera and the `refract` built-in function to compute a new view direction to look up into the environment map.

It may seem like I am leaving you in the dark about how to implement this effect. This is so you can explore and experiment on your own. If you get stuck, you can consult the solution in Appendix D.

Also remember that the air-to-glass refraction index is 1.33.

Exercise 2: MAKING IT MORE LIVELY

The results of the distance-based heat haze effect developed in this chapter looked too static and nonrealistic. One way to significantly improve on this is to animate your distortion map. For this exercise, take advantage of the built-in time variables in RenderMonkey to animate the texture coordinates to the distortion map you saw earlier in this chapter. To make it even better looking, sample the distortion map twice at two different locations and combine the results. Doing this has the effect of creating a less repetitive distortion texture than using a single sample. Also remember that for it to look good, your distortion map should animate upwards to give the impression that the hot air is rising.

What's Next?

In this chapter, you learned that complex effects such as heat haze can be re-created through simple techniques. By taking a complex idea and observing it closely, you can deduce techniques that can re-create such effects in a convincing yet simple approach.

The heat haze effect you learned in this chapter can serve to represent the image distortions that come from hot air rising from heat sources. However, the same basic technique can also be used to re-create other distortion effects, such as waving water refractions or even some sci-fi special distortion effects such as worm holes or shock waves.

Your bag of tricks now contains techniques to both blur and distort your environment. In the next chapter, we'll explore a new phenomenon where you will learn how to render brightness in your scene. In fact, light from the sun is a thousand times brighter than light from a candle. Although hardware can correctly convey color information, it simply lacks the precision to convey brightness information and the phenomena that can occur from it. Throughout the next chapter, we'll survey and explore techniques to manage high dynamic range and learn how to emulate this on today's and tomorrow's 3D hardware.

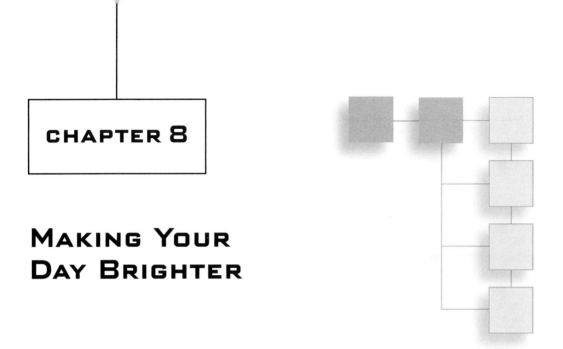

CHAPTER 8

MAKING YOUR DAY BRIGHTER

There have been many debates in the past about whether eight bits of resolution per color component are enough to represent all the colors the human eye can see. Generally speaking, eight bits are plenty, but this does not take into consideration something that is of crucial importance in photography.

Although 256 colors per component is sufficient to represent color, what about light intensity? The difference in intensity between candlelight and sunlight is on the order of thousands to one, which obviously can't be represented with only eight bits worth of resolution. You may think this is of little importance, but here are a few real-life examples of how this makes a difference.

Let's say you are outside in the sunlight looking into a torch-lit cave. From this position, you most likely cannot see anything inside the cave, and it appears dark. If you flip the situation around and you are inside the cave looking out, you can see the inside of the cave fine, but the outside appears overly bright, and you cannot see much of what is out there. The reason behind this phenomenon is that both cameras and the human eye can only see a certain range of brightness, and both have exposure control mechanisms, which control the amount of light energy that can be seen based on the average light of their surroundings.

Another example is putting an object between the viewer and a bright source of light. In this case, it seems as if the object is overcome by the light, even though it should normally block the light out. This is because the bright light tends to oversaturate the light receiver, causing some of the light energy to spread onto anything else in your field of vision.

As you can see from these examples, taking light intensity into account can be a strong factor in creating more realistic and immersive renderings. Because of this, many studies have been done on the phenomenon called *high dynamic range*, or HDR. In this chapter, you will

133

learn about this effect and its implications. You will also learn a few techniques that can be used to re-create this phenomenon on today's and tomorrow's rendering hardware.

What Is High Dynamic Range?

High dynamic range is the science of recognizing the different intensity levels of light. Under normal rendering circumstances, where the average level of lighting is similar throughout the scene, eight bits of color precision are enough to represent the different colors and light intensities. However, in real life, there are many situations where the levels of lighting vary significantly throughout the scene, leading to a scenario where there isn't enough precision to represent all the phenomena that occur from differences in intensities.

The general process used in HDR rendering is simple and involves the use of render targets like the ones used in previous chapters. This is illustrated in Figure 8.1.

Glare

Probably the most common effect that comes out of bright intensity light is the glare effect. A bright source of light exhibits a blooming effect, where it can even take over neighboring regions that stand between the light and the receiver.

This effect is caused by the way the human eye and photography equipment work; excess lighting energy affects not only a particular point on the receiver but also neighboring points. In fact, the excess light energy leaks onto its surroundings, creating a glow-like effect often referred to as glare, or *blooming*.

In the past, this effect was reproduced using billboard polygons on top of the source of light with the clever use of alpha blending. This approach is simple and effective but

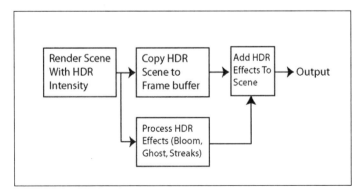

Figure 8.1 Diagram of the general process used to render high dynamic range effects.

suffers from one major shortcoming. It cannot account for the varying intensities that occur when your source of light is partially occluded. Later in this chapter, I will show you how this effect can be accomplished with blur filters and render targets with proper high-dynamic range considerations.

There is another side effect worth mentioning that comes out of this oversaturation of the receiver. Because a bright source of light overexcites the receiver, once the bright light goes away, it takes some time for the receiver to go back to its normal state. This is the phenomenon that occurs when you see a white blob for a while after seeing a bright flash of light. This effect will not be implemented in this chapter, but it is analogous to setting up an intensity-based motion blur filter, where the current image affects subsequent images while the excitation dissipates.

Streaks

You may have noticed when driving in a car that sometimes street lights and headlights seem to have a star-like glow around them. This phenomenon is generally due to internal reflections and refractions caused by microscopic scratches on the glass surface of the camera lens. The same thing happens through your car windshield because it is not a well polished surface.

Later in this chapter, I will explain how you can re-create this effect using specifically designed blur filters. These filters blur the bright portions of the render target in a diagonal manner instead of the standard way it has been done with the regular blur filters.

Lens Flares

Lens flares, or *ghosts*, are commonly seen effects when you see film or photography of a bright source of light such as the sun. This is probably one of the first HDR effects ever used in video games. This phenomenon comes from the fact that the bright light source is reflected between the different lenses of a camera, creating ghost images of the bright lights.

Video games have reproduced this effect by creating fake billboard geometry, placed suitably depending on where the source of light is. In this chapter, you will learn how to generically reproduce this with proper filters.

A Few HDR Basics

Before you get started on discovering how to re-create all the high dynamic range effects discussed earlier, we have to look at a few basic topics that will come in handy. These topics range from the use of floating-point textures to exposure control.

What About Floating-Point Textures?

The main reason behind the introduction of the new floating-point textures is to enable support for features that require a wider range of values and precisions than that offered by regular eight-bit textures. High dynamic range rendering is a prime example of where such high-precision textures can be used.

note

Because floating-point textures are not yet widely supported, it is likely you will have to use the Hardware Emulation Layer (HEL) mode in RenderMonkey to develop the following high dynamic range shader. Later in this chapter, you will learn how to use regular render targets to estimate some of the HDR effects.

Some hardware implementations do not support bilinear filtering when using floating-point textures. If you have such hardware, you might need to switch to software emulation to get proper results from the HDR shaders developed in this chapter.

Floating-point textures come in two flavors. In fact, you can elect to use either a 16- or 32-bit precision texture. Although 32 bits offer great precision, they also require twice the memory and bandwidth. What this means for you is that the color values in a floating-point texture are represented in a way that enables you to represent any numerical value. Because HDR does not require such a great range, 16-bit textures will be used for the render targets throughout this chapter, especially the `A16R16G16B16` format.

Because floating-point textures are ideal for high dynamic range rendering, it makes sense to show you the basic techniques using these high-precision textures. If your hardware does not support them, however, you can use software emulation. Later in this chapter, you'll learn how to use non-floating-point textures to approximate the same effects.

Exposure Control: The First Step

The first thing to consider when dealing with high dynamic range is exposure control. Both the human eye and cameras need to be able to adjust to different lighting conditions. You do not wish to have a bright outdoor scene being washed out and an indoor scene being totally dark. This is why, for example, the iris of the human eye adjusts to different lighting environments.

In rendering high dynamic range scenery, you need a similar mechanism to control the average lighting intensity on your scene. This mechanism is commonly called exposure control. The framework shader introduced here includes a basic scene with a background and teapot object and incorporates the needed components to handle exposure control.

Because we want to develop a simple shader with an environment and an object, we'll start by using the `shader_1.rfx` template developed in Chapter 7. The first step to make this shader HDR-ready is to add some brightness to the scene. For this example, we will be adding HDR information to the environment map.

The ideal solution for this would be to adjust or create the environment as a floating-texture that contains full brightness information for the scene. Although this is doable, few software solutions are available to do such a task at the moment. An easier solution is to take the current environment map and use the alpha channel as a brightness multiplier. A 0 alpha indicates the lowest brightness level, and 1 is the maximum intensity. You would then use this value from the alpha channel in your rendering to multiply with the color intensities, essentially creating a higher range of colors than normally available.

Using image editing software, such as Adobe Photoshop, you can add alpha values to your environment map so that brighter components, such as the sun, have a greater value in their alpha channel. Figure 8.2 shows the snow environment side-by-side with its HDR alpha channel.

note

For more information on how to build high dynamic range environment maps, you can refer to Paul Debevec's high dynamic range imaging website at: http://www.debevec.org.

With a high dynamic range environment map, the first step needed to create an HDR shader is to convert the render targets to use floating-point textures. To do so, simply double-click on every target and change the texture format to `A16R16G16B16F`:

The next step is to use the alpha channel from the environment map to calculate the real HDR values. This is done by multiplying the environment color by the alpha channel when each object is rendered, considering the alpha value as being within the zero to 64 range. This leads to the following pixel shader code snippet:

```
color = color * (1.0+(color.a*64.0));
```

Figure 8.2 Color and alpha channel values for the HDR-ready environment map.

This little piece of shader code takes the alpha value from a zero to one range and converts this value to an integer multiplier in the range of one to 256. This value is then used as a multiplier for the incoming color values from the environment map.

The only aspect missing in this shader is exposure control. For this, you first need a variable to define the exposure value. Create a new variable called Exposure_Level, which is of type SCALAR. This value controls the exposure by serving as a scaling factor for the render target colors when it is copied to the screen buffer.

For this, you need to modify the pixel shader we developed earlier to scale down the values based on the exposure value. This change yields the following code:

```
sampler Texture0;
float4 ps_main(float3 dir: TEXCOORD0) : COLOR
{
    // Read texture and determine HDR color based on alpha
    // channel and exposure level
    float4 color = texCUBE(Environment, dir);
    return color * ((1.0+(color.a*64.0))* Exposure_Level);
}
```

With this shader, you can now see your HDR environment being rendered. Try different values of exposure control and see how the scene changes. Figure 8.3 shows different rendered outputs for different exposure values.

The complete version of this shader is included on the CD-ROM as shader_1.rfx.

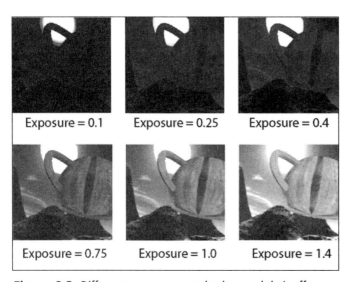

Figure 8.3 Different exposure control values and their effect on a rendered scene.

A Note on Automatic Exposure Control

The human eye adjusts its iris automatically to adapt to the surrounding light. This is a behavior you might want to emulate in your rendering.

Automatic exposure control aims to adjust the average brightness of the scene. The idea is that the average brightness of the scene should be around 0.5 because the displayable intensity range is from zero to one. If the average brightness is known, the exposure value can be determined with

```
Exposure = 0.5 / Average_Brightness;
```

Keep in mind that you wish the exposure to slowly adapt and not change instantaneously. To do this, you could use the following code:

```
Exposure = lerp(Exposure, 0.5 / Average_Brightness, Exposure_Adjust_Speed);
```

You need to determine the average brightness of the scene, which isn't an easy task. One way you can do it within a DirectX or OpenGL application is to lock the texture and calculate the average procedurally by going through all the pixels and manually computing the average. However, on most hardware, this has severe performance implications.

Another approach to approximate the same result is to use render targets to compute the average by taking advantage of the rendering hardware. If you have a successive set of renderable textures, each one being half the size of the preceding one, you can use a simple box filter to copy the initial scene from render target to render target. After you reach a one-by-one render target, the single pixel remaining will be the average value for the initial scene. You can then use this final one-pixel texture as an input to your shader to do your automatic exposure control.

Time for Some High Dynamic Range Effects

Now that you know a few of the important basics required to implement high dynamic range effects, it is time for the meat of this chapter. Over the next few sections, I will teach you how to implement most of the common HDR effects, including glare, lens flare, and streaks.

Your First HDR Shader: The Glare!

One of the most commonly seen high dynamic range effects is the glare, or glow, or even bloom . . . In this section, I will show you how to create a shader to emulate this effect in an easy to use way.

The glare phenomenon is caused by the energy from a bright source of light not only exciting the area it contacts but also leaking onto neighboring areas. Because of this leaking, this phenomenon can easily be simulated using a properly selected sequence of blur filters.

The first aspect to consider is which blur filter to use. Because you will want the blurring to be smooth and consistent, a 9-samples Gauss blur filter will do fine. You'll recall that we used this filter in Chapter 7. The other advantage to using this Gauss filter is that you can control the blurriness of the output by deciding in how many passes you will apply it to your scene.

Because you wish to have the scene sufficiently blurred and to lessen the impact on the graphics processor, all the glare blurs will be done on a 1/4-by-1/4 size render target. When enough blur has been applied to the original render target, the only thing needed is to additively blend this blurred image onto the screen in a way where only the brightest parts show up.

note

Because RenderMonkey does not offer the functionality to select a render target of a size that is proportional to the size of the screen, you can approximate by making an estimation—which should be sufficient—and setting this value manually in RenderMonkey.

Starting with the blur filter, the use of floating-point textures has no real impact, and the pixel shader for a specific blurring pass should be as follows:

```
float viewport_inv_width;
float viewport_inv_height;
sampler Texture0;
const float4 samples[9] = {
    -1.0,      1.0,      0,      1.0/16.0,
    -1.0,      1.0,      0,      1.0/16.0,
     1.0,     -1.0,      0,      1.0/16.0,
     1.0,      1.0,      0,      1.0/16.0,
    -1.0,      0.0,      0,      2.0/16.0,
     1.0,      0.0,      0,      2.0/16.0,
     0.0,     -1.0,      0,      2.0/16.0,
     0.0,      1.0,      0,      2.0/16.0,
     0.0,      0.0,      0,      4.0/16.0
};


float4 ps_main(float2 texCoord: TEXCOORD0) : COLOR
{
    float4 color = float4(0,0,0,0);

    // Sample and output the averaged colors
    for(int i=0;i<9;i++)
```

```
    {
        float4 col = samples[i].w*tex2D(Texture0,texCoord+
                     float2(samples[i].x*viewport_inv_width,
                     samples[i].y*viewport_inv_height));
        color += col;
    }
    return color;
}
```

The next consideration is how many blurring passes are needed to get a good result. This is essentially a trial and error type of task. To save you time, I have included results for different numbers of blur passes in Figure 8.4.

Because a single blur pass isn't enough to get the whole blurring task done, you need to repeat the process multiple times. For this shader, I have done six passes, keeping the blur for the past two blurring passes. These intermediate blurring results will be used within the glare shader a little later. Keep in mind that you need to create multiple render targets to account for this and for the intermediate results needed.

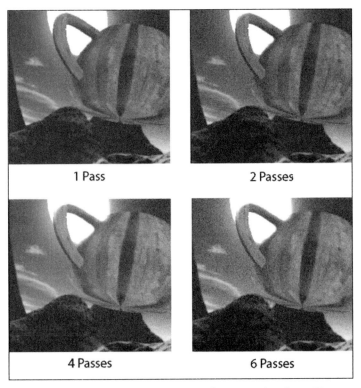

Figure 8.4 Different levels of blurring for use in the glare effect.

The last missing component to this shader is the final pass where the blurred and regular scene render targets are combined. Although this could be done as separate alpha blending passes for each of our source textures, the easiest way to do this under a pixel shader 2.0-compatible configuration is to sample both render targets in a single pass and use the pixel shader code.

To combine the three blurred versions of your HDR render target, you simply need to combine the values within the pixel shader. To do this, you must define three constants named Glow_Factor, Glow_Factor2, and Glow_Factor3. These variables determine the contribution of each blurred render target. The following pixel shader code shows how this can be done:

```
float Glow_Factor;
float Glow_Factor2;
float Glow_Factor3;
sampler Texture0;
sampler Texture1;
sampler Texture2;
float4 ps_main(float2 texCoord: TEXCOORD0) : COLOR
{
    // Sample 3 glow blurring levels and combine them together
    return
      float4((tex2D(Texture0,texCoord).xyz)*Glow_Factor,1.0) +
      float4((tex2D(Texture1,texCoord).xyz)*Glow_Factor2,0) +
      float4((tex2D(Texture2,texCoord).xyz)*Glow_Factor3,0);
}
```

The final rendering results for the shader are shown in Figure 8.5. The final version of this shader is included on the CD-ROM as shader_2.rfx. In the first exercise at the end of this chapter, you will be invited to expand on this shader by using a more complex blur filter than a 9-sample Gauss filter.

Figure 8.5 Final rendering results for the Glare HDR effect.

Time for Some Streaking!

You have probably noticed a star-shaped pattern through your car's windshield that occurs when driving at night. This effect is the result of tiny scratches in the surface of the glass, which cause light to reflect and refract on the surface. The physics behind this phenomenon is fairly complex, but it isn't necessary for our purposes to discuss the underlying cause. We will just develop an approximation, which should produce sufficiently convincing results.

To estimate this effect, you need to create a star pattern. This can be achieved by using a specific blur filter, which acts in a specific direction, causing a streak in that direction. This filter is simple and involves the use of four samples, which are taken along a specific diagonal. Figure 8.6 illustrates how this filter works.

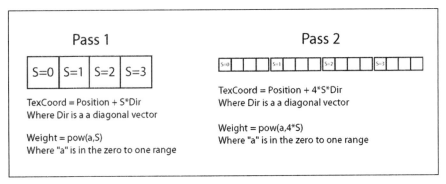

Figure 8.6 Diagonal filter used to perform the streaking effect.

As you can see from the figure, the position of the sample for each pass is taken at an offset that is proportional to the rendering pass and the sample number. Also, each sample has a weight of `blurFactor`, which is raised to a power that is proportional to the sample number and pass. This allows you to attribute less weight to samples that are farther from the pixel you are rendering. This combination allows the creation of a filter that creates a progressively longer streak in a specific direction with each pass. For example, with one pass, the streak would be 4 pixels long, and with two passes, it would be 16 pixels long.

Translating this basic filter into a pixel shader is simple using the basic array-based approach taken with the other blur filters. Keep in mind that you need the `blurFactor` and `offsetFactor` variables to control the filter for each pass. The result should be a pixel shader similar to the following:

```
float viewport_inv_width;
float viewport_inv_height;
sampler Texture0;
const float  blurFactor = 0.96;
```

```
const float   offsetFactor = 1;
const float4 samples[4] = {
    0.0,  -0.0,   0,   0,
    1.0,  -1.0,   0,   1,
    2.0,  -2.0,   0,   2,
    3.0,  -3.0,   0,   3
};


float4 ps_main(float2 texCoord: TEXCOORD0) : COLOR
{
    float4 color = float4(0,0,0,0);

    // Sample and output the averaged colors
    for(int i=0;i<4;i++)
    {
        float4 col = pow(blurFactor,offsetFactor*samples[i].w)*
                     tex2D(Texture0,texCoord+
                     offsetFactor*float2(samples[i].x*viewport_inv_width,
                     samples[i].y*viewport_inv_height));
        color += col;
    }
    return color;
}
```

Figure 8.7 shows the blurred results for a single streak. You need to do the same process for all four directions by changing the signs in the filter table and putting in the suitable offsetFactor. Then you only need to combine the four streaks in a way similar to the Glare shader. Note that this time you will need a single glow factor variable because each streak has the same combination. You may also wish to reduce the alpha blending on the final result so it does not oversaturate the scene. Doing so gives the following shader code:

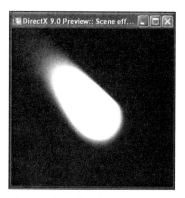

Figure 8.7 Rendering the shader results for a single streak.

```
float Glow_Factor;
sampler Texture0;
sampler Texture1;
sampler Texture2;
sampler Texture3;
float4 ps_main(float2 texCoord: TEXCOORD0) : COLOR
{
    // Combine 4 streak directions
```

```
   return
     min(1.0,
     float4((tex2D(Texture0,texCoord).xyz)*Glow_Factor,0.15) +
     float4((tex2D(Texture1,texCoord).xyz)*Glow_Factor,0.15) +
     float4((tex2D(Texture2,texCoord).xyz)*Glow_Factor,0.15) +
     float4((tex2D(Texture3,texCoord).xyz)*Glow_Factor,0.15)
     );
}
```

The final rendering results for the shader are shown in Figure 8.8. Also note that the final version of this shader is included on the CD-ROM as shader_3.rfx.

Figure 8.8 Rendering the Streak HDR shader.

Lens Flare Free-for-All

The last of the high dynamic range effects worth exploring is the lens flare effect, also called ghost. This effect comes from bright light reflecting between the lenses of the camera, which creates ghost images of the bright components of the image. In this section, I will show how this effect can be re-created with the proper shader code.

Before you write any shader, you need to understand how this effect happens in the first place. Because lens flares originate from reflections between lenses, you need to create mirror images and combine them. The first thing you need to consider is that lenses make rays converge, which has the side effect of creating upside-down mirror images.

With that in mind, you must be able to access render targets in a way that can be scaled and flipped. This can easily be done by changing the way the texture coordinates are passed to the pixel shader. Keeping in mind that a texture is centered around (0.5,0.5), you can scale and flip a texture by using the following vertex shader code:

```
texCoord = (texCoord-0.5)*(Scale) + 0.5;
```

From this code, you can see that the Scale variable controls the scale of the texture. If you wish to flip the texture, you simply need to input a negative scale to this equation.

note

Keep in mind that because scaling the texture can lead to accesses outside of the texture, you need to set the texture addressing state to CLAMP to avoid repeating the render target.

For the effect to look good, you should repeat the same process multiple times. Here, we'll be doing it four times for each pass. You will also need to pick out various scale factors to use. In this example, I have used 2.0, –2.0, 0.6, and –0.6. You may wish to experiment and pick your own values.

Making these adjustments to the vertex shader yields the following code:

```
float4x4 view_proj_matrix;
struct VS_OUTPUT
{
    float4 Pos: POSITION;
    float2 texCoord:  TEXCOORD0;
    float2 texCoord1: TEXCOORD1;
    float2 texCoord2: TEXCOORD2;
    float2 texCoord3: TEXCOORD3;
    float2 texCoord4: TEXCOORD4;
};


VS_OUTPUT vs_main(float4 Pos: POSITION)
{
    VS_OUTPUT Out;

    // Simply output the position without transforming it
    Out.Pos = float4(Pos.xy, 0, 1);

    // Texture coordinates are setup so that the full texture
    // is mapped completely onto the screen
    float2 texCoord;
    texCoord.x = 0.5 * (1 + Pos.x - 1/128);
    texCoord.y = 0.5 * (1 - Pos.y - 1/128);
    Out.texCoord = texCoord;

    // Compute the scaled texture coordinates for the ghost images
    Out.texCoord1 = (texCoord-0.5)*(-2.0) + 0.5;
    Out.texCoord2 = (texCoord-0.5)*(2.0) + 0.5;
    Out.texCoord3 = (texCoord-0.5)*(-0.6) + 0.5;
    Out.texCoord4 = (texCoord-0.5)*(0.6) + 0.5;

    return Out;
}
```

The pixel shader side of this effect is essentially a matter of sampling the texture four times and combining the results. There is one little issue, however, that is a result of the scaling. If you simply sample the texture four times, you end up with hard borders on the edges of the render target. To remove this effect, you must apply a circular mask, like the one shown in Figure 8.9, which masks out the pixels on the edges.

With this, you need to sample four render targets and four mask values. The mask values are modulated by the render target color for each sample, and the final results are added together and scaled by Glow_Factor. This factor helps control the intensity of the glow effect and is determined through experimentation. Applying these changes to the pixel shader yields the following code:

Figure 8.9 Texture used to mask out hard edges on the lens flare effect.

```
float viewport_inv_height;
float viewport_inv_width;
float Glow_Factor;
sampler Texture0;
sampler Texture1;
float4 ps_main(float2 texCoord:  TEXCOORD0,
               float2 texCoord1: TEXCOORD1,
               float2 texCoord2: TEXCOORD2,
               float2 texCoord3: TEXCOORD3,
               float2 texCoord4: TEXCOORD4) : COLOR
{
   // Sample all ghost pictures
   float4 col1 = tex2D(Texture0, texCoord1)*tex2D(Texture1, texCoord1).a;
   float4 col2 = tex2D(Texture0, texCoord2)*tex2D(Texture1, texCoord2).a;
   float4 col3 = tex2D(Texture0, texCoord3)*tex2D(Texture1, texCoord3).a;
   float4 col4 = tex2D(Texture0, texCoord4)*tex2D(Texture1, texCoord4).a;

   // Combine the ghost images together
   return (col1+col2+col3+col4)*Glow_Factor;
}
```

Because you want multiple ghosts, you must repeat this process a second time using the result from the first pass as the source of the following pass. The two passes combined yield 16 ghost images, which should be plenty.

The last step needed is to render the results onto your scene. This can be done through the use of alpha blending and the following pixel shader code:

```
float4 ps_main(float2 texCoord: TEXCOORD0) : COLOR
{
   return float4((tex2D(Texture0,texCoord).xyz),0.8);
}
```

With these changes, you can compile the shaders and see the results. The final rendering results for the shader are shown in Figure 8.10. Also note that the final version of this shader is included on the CD-ROM as shader_4.rfx.

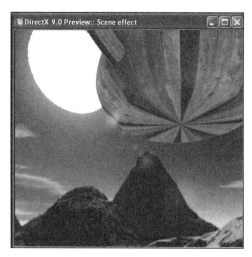

Figure 8.10 Rendering the ghost HDR shader.

Putting It All Together

Putting all the effects together is simply a matter of combining all the render targets and render passes of each individual effect. This can be done with the Copy and Paste options on the right-click menu.

Beyond this, all that is needed is a new final pixel shader that takes the results of each individual effect and combines them. The following pixel shader code shows how this can be done:

```
float Streak_Factor;
float Ghost_Factor;
float Glow_Factor;
float Glow_Factor2;
float Glow_Factor3;
sampler Texture0;
sampler Texture1;
sampler Texture2;
sampler Texture3;
sampler Texture4;
sampler Texture5;
sampler Texture6;
sampler Texture7;
```

```
float4 ps_main(float2 texCoord: TEXCOORD0) : COLOR
{
    float4 col;

    // Glow
    col = float4((tex2D(Texture1,texCoord).xyz)*Glow_Factor,1.0) +
            float4((tex2D(Texture2,texCoord).xyz)*Glow_Factor2,0) +
            float4((tex2D(Texture3,texCoord).xyz)*Glow_Factor3,0);

    // Ghost
    col += float4((tex2D(Texture0,texCoord).xyz),0);

    // Streak
    col +=
      float4((tex2D(Texture4,texCoord).xyz)*Streak_Factor,0) +
      float4((tex2D(Texture5,texCoord).xyz)*Streak_Factor,0) +
      float4((tex2D(Texture6,texCoord).xyz)*Streak_Factor,0) +
      float4((tex2D(Texture7,texCoord).xyz)*Streak_Factor,0);

    return col;
}
```

This is all that is needed to get this working. You may need to adjust the different variables so that all of the effects blend well together. You can see a tuned version of the output in Figure 8.11. This shader is included on the CD-ROM as shader_5.rfx.

Figure 8.11 Rendering the final HDR shader.

Solutions for Today's Hardware

Although the use of floating-point textures and render targets is the ideal way of implementing high dynamic range effects, it is not necessarily well suited to today's hardware. At the time of this writing, support for such features is sparse, and its speed is not so good. Although in the future, floating-point textures will be the way to go, you need a solution that works on most of today's hardware architectures.

Because you cannot use floating-point textures, you need a way to represent light intensity with less precision. If you are willing to make the concession that all the color components are at the same intensity level, you can use the alpha channel of your render targets to carry the overall brightness. In other words, the alpha channel will contain a multiplier to be applied to all the color components. This is similar to the way the brightness information was encoded into the environment map earlier in this chapter.

This approach has still another issue. Because the alpha channel values are represented in a zero to one range, you need to redefine what range these values correspond to. For this example, I will assume the range of alpha values is zero to 64, which should give sufficient intensity range and fractional precision. This is simply a matter of multiplying the values from the alpha channel by 64 before using them.

With this basic knowledge, you can now convert the glare or bloom effect to make use of this new approach. Although it may seem like a complex task, it is easier than it looks. Because the glare blurring filters blur both the alpha and the color components of the render targets, there is no need to take any special consideration for this new approach. In fact, the only changes needed are making sure the render targets are of A8R8G8B8 format and changing the object rendering passes so that the intensity values are scaled down to fit within the alpha channel. The pixel shader code for the object rendering pass becomes the following:

```
float Exposure_Level;
sampler Environment;
float4 ps_main(float3 dir: TEXCOORD0) : COLOR
{
    float4 color = texCUBE(Environment, dir);
    return float4(color.rgb,((1.0+(color.a*64.0))* Exposure_Level)/64.0);
}
```

With this, no other changes are needed to any of the shaders to do the effects. The only exception to this is the final pass where you will need to make modifications to decode the intensity of the pixel. This is done by taking the zero to one alpha value and multiplying it by 64 and using this value to scale the incoming color values. The resulting pixel shader code is as follows:

```
float Glow_Factor;
```

```
float Glow_Factor2;
float Glow_Factor3;
sampler Texture0;
sampler Texture1;
sampler Texture2;
float4 ps_main(float2 texCoord: TEXCOORD0) : COLOR
{
   // Sample 3 glow blurring levels and combine them together
   float4 col1 = tex2D(Texture0,texCoord);
   float4 col2 = tex2D(Texture1,texCoord);
   float4 col3 = tex2D(Texture2,texCoord);

   // Mix the three glows together
   return
     float4(col1.rgb*(col1.a*64.0)*Glow_Factor,1.0) +
     float4(col2.rgb*(col2.a*64.0)*Glow_Factor2,0.0) +
     float4(col3.rgb*(col3.a*64.0)*Glow_Factor3,0.0);
}
```

As you can see in Figure 8.12, the rendering results are similar to the one obtained earlier in this chapter. I have also included this shader on the CD-ROM as shader_6.rfx. You will be invited in the second exercise at the end of this chapter to apply the same process to the streaking shader developed earlier in the chapter.

Figure 8.12 Rendering the final HDR shader using non-floating-point textures.

It's Your Turn!

High dynamic range is one of the effects that can add so much realism to your scene. It is now your turn to learn a little more on the topic of HDR through a couple of exercises. The solutions to these exercises can be found in Appendix D.

Exercise 1: USING A BIG FILTER

For this first exercise, I invite you to improve on the glare filter developed in this chapter. Your task is simple: take the shader and use the 49-samples Gauss filter used in Chapter 7 instead of the 9-samples filter. This will involve changing the glare filter passes and determining the appropriate number of blur passes needed.

Exercise 2: STREAKING ON TODAY'S HARDWARE

Throughout this chapter, I have demonstrated how the glare HDR effect could be accomplished through the use of non-floating-point textures. For this exercise, I invite you to use the same process for the floating-point streaking effect developed earlier.

What's Next?

High dynamic range, or HDR, is a great way to enhance your renderings. Instead of taking into account color only, now you can account for the intensity of light. This enables you to create a richer environment and take into account the wide range of lighting that occurs in real life.

At this point, we have covered many screen-based effects. Such effects are powerful in their ease of use and visual appeal.

In the next chapter, I will be covering the topic of lighting. From the basics to more complex approaches, you will explore how to use light to create a much richer environment for your renderings.

PART III

MAKING IT LOOK REAL

In Part II, "Screen Effects," you learned how simple screen-based effects can be used to achieve stunning graphics and enhance the realism of your renderings. One drawback with these techniques is that they only focus on improving the quality of something that has already been rendered. It is now time to start focusing on making the objects look better as you render them in the first place.

In Part III, you'll learn several techniques that can be used to improve the quality of your objects. Lighting, discussed in Chapters 9, "May There Be Light," 10, "Shiny Little Pixels," and 11, "Mirror, Mirror, On the Wall," is probably one of the most important visual cues and can do wonders for your graphics. In those chapters you will explore many topics, including basic lighting information, per-vertex lighting, per-pixel lighting, and even bumpmapping.

In Chapters 12, "Not All Materials Are the Same," 13, "Building Materials from Scratch," and 14, "Why Does It Always Need to Look Real?," you will explore the topic of materials. Although textures and lighting may look good, some materials have different behaviors, and exploring techniques to reproduce this can yield stunningly realistic results. Here you will learn about techniques such as BRDFs and procedural materials.

Finally, you will learn how fogging and animations can make your scene even livelier.

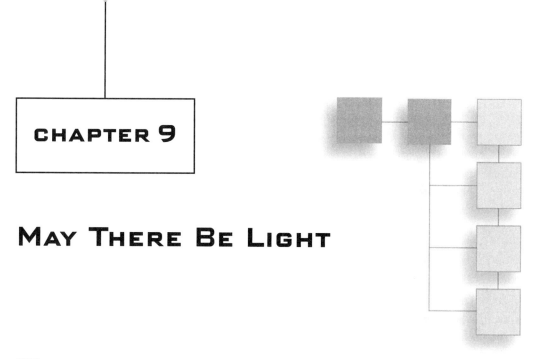

CHAPTER 9

MAY THERE BE LIGHT

In this chapter, you will learn how lighting can be applied to your geometry. You will start with some theory of how lighting works and explore some of the basic types of lights and approaches taken in computer graphics.

Later, you will learn how to take advantage of this knowledge to apply lighting to your object. During this chapter, I will show you how you can light your objects in both a per-vertex and per-pixel way.

Of Light and Magic

People tend to underestimate the importance of lights. As a matter of fact, if there wasn't any light, there would not be any world to see. When you see an object, what you see is not the object itself but the light that is reflected off it. Rendering your scene with proper lighting not only makes your objects visible but ensures a much greater realism.

In this chapter, you will learn the basics and the essentials of lighting, from the physical basics to actual algorithms and implementations. I will focus only on per-vertex lighting in this chapter. In the following chapters, I will show you how these approaches can be expanded to be used with per-pixel lighting and explore even more approaches such as bumpmapping and *Bi-Directional Refractance Distribution Functions* (BRDFs).

What Makes Light in the First Place

Let's examine how you perceive an object's color. The first thing you need is a source of illumination. This source of light has a color, intensity, and position. The light can be from several different sources, such as an area light, sunlight, or even an off-the-shelf light bulb.

This source of light emits some light that will hit your object. But what is light in the first place? For a long time, there was great debate as to whether light was a wave, like sound, or a particle, like an electron. Then Albert Einstein came along and solved the debate. He proved that light was both a particle and a wave at the same time. As you can see from Figure 9.1, light is a particle (a photon) that travels along a wave.

Unlike radio waves, light cannot travel through most opaque solid objects, because the objects actually block the particles. On the other hand, the color of light comes from a wave-like phenomenon, which is determined by the frequency of the light. With this in mind, once the light particle/wave has left the light source, it travels through space until it hits your object, or more precisely its surface.

When light hits a surface of any type, two phenomena happen. The light directly interacts with the surface. There, light is reflected in a way which is specific to the properties of the material of the surface. Each material has specific properties that are related to the structure of the material. For example, a polished metal surface tends to directly reflect the incident light, while a matte finish wall diffuses the light in many directions.

The second phenomenon is what happens to light when it is absorbed, transmitted, and scattered within the surface. For example, glass is mostly translucent and lets most of the

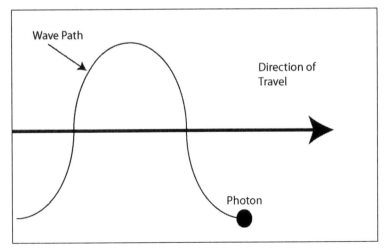

Figure 9.1 Illustration of how light acts as both a particle and a wave.

light through. On the other hand, clouds, which may seem opaque, actually scatter light in many directions as it passes through their vapor surface.

Materials are various, and their behaviors differ from one to another. However, in an attempt to generalize lighting so it could be rendered efficiently, several different lighting phenomena have been identified. Although the following list summarizes them, keep in mind that this is a simple generalization, and I will discuss other techniques later on.

- **Ambient lighting:** This is a gross approximation of the total level of lighting in a scene. In reality, there is no such thing because the ambient lighting level comes from a multitude of discrete lights. However, this serves as a good approximation that can help to significantly reduce the number of lights to consider within a particular scene. Ambient lighting generally manifests itself as a constant-colored light that affects the object uniformly.
- **Diffuse lighting:** Materials with a rough surface exhibit what is called diffuse lighting. The surface's microscopic roughness has the effect of reflecting incoming light uniformly in all directions. This causes the perceived lighting to be the same from any viewing angle.
- **Specular lighting:** When the surface of a material is smooth, you will observe what is called specular lighting. In this case, light reflects off the surface in a nonuniform way. This means that for specular lighting, the light intensity not only depends on the light-to-surface angle but also on the viewing angle.

To put things into perspective, you must understand what happens on the surface when light hits it. Both the surface and the light have a color expressed in terms of red, green, and blue. What your shaders will do is calculate the intensity of the light source at a particular point on the surface and determine the reflected color through modulation. Figure 9.2 illustrates this process.

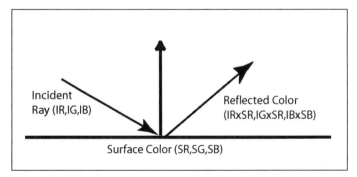

Figure 9.2 How light color and surface color are modulated together.

You need to follow a few basic steps when creating a shader. First of all, you need to determine the overall ambient lighting for a scene. This is usually a constant value that is determined ahead of time, but in more complex scenes, you may want to vary the intensity and color of the ambient lighting in relation to the position of an object.

The second step is to determine the lighting contribution of each of the individual lights in your scene. For each of them, you need to find out its intensity, which is usually based on angle, distance, and color. This value is a combination of a diffuse term and a specular term and is dependent on the surface properties of the material you are rendering. Once you have determined both values, it is simply of matter of adding them together and modulating the resulting color with the color of the surface.

Keep in mind that this is a simplistic representation of materials and lighting. There are other types of surface interactions that are worth considering. For example, a surface that is not perfectly opaque, such as skin, exhibits a scattering phenomenon where some of the incoming light is absorbed and then re-emitted. Another example is a brushed metal surface that is rough on a macroscopic level, and the basic concept of diffuse lighting isn't enough. In such cases, you might need to account for such phenomena by using *Bi-Directional Refractance Distribution Functions* (BRDFs).

Although I will cover some of these topics later on in this book, the following sections survey some of the most common material phenomena. Keep in mind that the following sections are intended as an introduction to the topic, and no shader code will be developed.

Refraction

As you know, not all materials are opaque. Glass, for example, reflects some of the light hitting its surface but also lets a significant number of rays through. As discussed in an earlier chapter, the rays that go through the surface are affected by the difference in density between the surfaces.

The difference of density between the air and the surface of the material causes the rays of light going through the surface to be deviated, as shown in Figure 9.3.

In the previous discussion of refraction, I neglected the color of light in the refraction equation. The reality is that the actual refraction index is influenced by the frequency of the rays of light penetrating the surface. Because the color of the light is dependent on its frequency, light of different colors are refracted differently. This is exactly why prisms create rainbows. Figure 9.4 shows how a refraction factors in the frequency of the light and how the color of a ray of light translates into frequency.

When performing refraction, you may wish to take this into account to improve the result. Because color is determined in terms of red, green, and blue, you need to approximate the result by determining an individual refraction index for each color component.

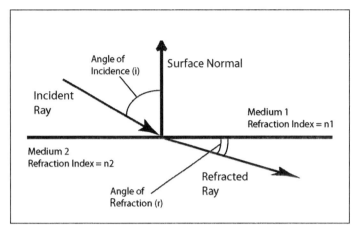

Figure 9.3 Illustration of how rays of light are refracted as they go from the density of air to a surface with a different density.

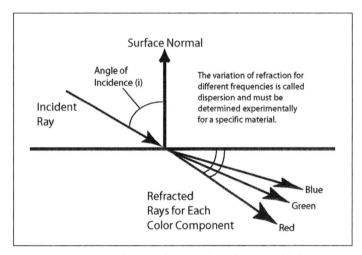

Figure 9.4 How to factor color into the refraction of light.

Sub-Surface Scattering

Most people tend to see the world as either black and white, translucent, or opaque. The reality is that many materials which seem opaque are actually translucent. Probably one of the best examples is skin. Although on the surface it appears opaque, it is not! I'm sure you have at some point put a laser or flashlight on your finger and noticed how you could see a glow on the other side. For this to happen, some of the light must actually make it through your finger to the other side.

Sub-surface scattering stems from this. For a particular material surface, light is reflected off the surface, but some of the rays penetrate the surface. As Figure 9.5 shows, the rays that manage to penetrate the surface either make it through the surface or encounter other particles within the surface and bounce. Those bouncing rays can potentially head back towards the surface and remerge at another point.

In essence, with sub-surface scattering, some of the light hitting the surface can potentially re-emerge at another point on that surface. With the skin example, such rays pass through the first layer of skin and meet some particles of flesh or blood. The rays then are tinted properly for the encountered particles and re-emerge somewhere near their entry point. This explains both the pinkish tone of skin and why lit skin always tends to exhibit a soft glow.

BRDFs

Both the specular and diffuse lighting models assume a predictable distribution of reflected light with the relationship between the incident light angle and the angle of the viewer. Unfortunately, most materials do not follow this pattern. One classic example of materials that break the rules is velvet.

With velvet, light that comes in is not reflected directly. Because the material is composed of a multitude of microscopic brushed hairs, light is not reflected in relationship to the surface normal, but in a way that is dependent on the angle of the hairs, as shown in Figure 9.6.

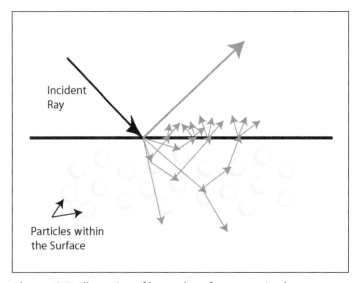

Figure 9.5 Illustration of how sub-surface scattering happens.

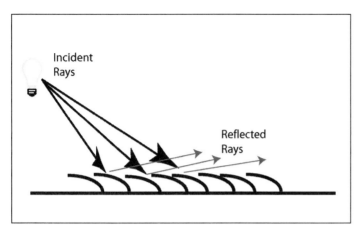

Figure 9.6 How light is reflected off a velvet-like material.

As you can see, there is a direct relationship between the angle of the incoming light and how it is reflected. However, this reflection does not follow the standard paradigms of specular and diffuse lighting. Figure 9.7 shows the distribution of reflected light in relationship to the incident light angle for specular, diffuse, and velvet surfaces.

You can see in Figure 9.7 that BRDFs can be useful in describing the relationship between the incident light angle and the viewing angle. We'll examine this phenomenon further in Chapter 12, "Not All Materials Are the Same."

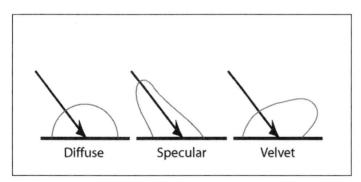

Figure 9.7 Diffuse, specular, and velvet BRDF reflectance distributions.

Types of Lights

Although I have focused a lot so far on how light affects surfaces, you also need to consider that the source of light itself has some properties. Lights, by their shapes and properties, can affect many factors when it comes to rendering. Such factors define how the light attenuates as a function of distance and the direction in which the rays of light will be heading.

In this section, you will learn how the standard types of light work and how you can use them in your shaders. So let's get started with one of the simplest forms of light, the directional light.

Directional Light

Directional lights are the simplest form of lighting out there. They do not have a position and simply assume that all light rays are parallel to each other and heading in the same direction. You may wonder what kind of light actually behaves like this, and in fact, none do. A directional light only has the purpose of estimating the case where a source of light is sufficiently far away. In such a case, you can estimate it by assuming that all rays of light are parallel to one another.

The best example of this is sunlight. Considering that the sun can be treated as a point light and that it is located millions of miles away from Earth, rays that hit the surface of the Earth are almost parallel and can be considered directional light. This concept is shown in Figure 9.8.

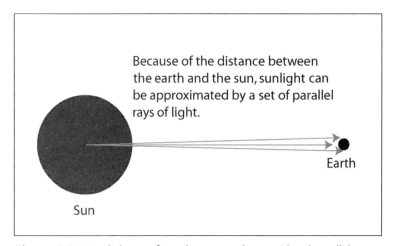

Figure 9.8 How light rays from the sun can be considered parallel because of the sun-to-earth distance.

Another consequence of the fact that a directional light has no position is that it does not attenuate with distance. The only factors to consider in the end are the light ray's direction and the color of the light.

One question that may come to mind is how this light influences the surface. As Figure 9.9 shows, you only need to consider the angle between the light rays and the surface normal.

Knowing this, you can simply find out the intensity of the light on a particular point of the surface by taking the dot product between the light direction and surface normal and factoring in the light color. The surface normal represents the direction, which is perpendicular to the surface at a specific point. This would yield the following shader code:

```
Color = Light_Color * clamp(0, 1, dot( Light_Direction, inNormal ));
```

note

Take a look at the `clamp` function used in the angle-based attenuation code for the directional light. Because the dot product can give a negative result for a surface that faces away from the light, you need to ensure that you do not get any negative light contributions. The `clamp` function ensures that any negative value will be clamped to zero.

This is as simple as it gets! Although no light physically behaves this way in real life, directional lights are an inexpensive way to create a more rich ambient lighting with an approximation. By considering distant sources of light in such a way, you can have multiple lights affecting an object at a lesser cost than using point lights.

Although you will be using point lights throughout the chapter, I will invite you in the first exercise at the end of the chapter to implement a shader making use of directional lights.

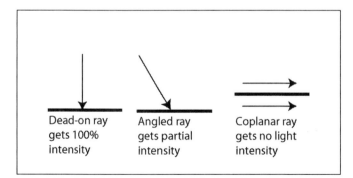

Figure 9.9 How the intensity of light on a surface relates to the angle between the light direction and the surface normal.

Point Lights

Most of the light in a scene comes in the form of a light bulb, torch, or similar lighting element. When you think about it, most of those sources are small, finite, and located at a discrete position within your scene. For simplification, you may consider all of them as being a source of light that is contained as a single discrete point in your scene, therefore, a *point light*.

With such lights, rays emerge in a radial fashion (illustrated in Figure 9.10). This means that any object in any position relative to the light is affected in the same way. Because the intensity of light on a surface is determined by the relationship between the light rays and the surface normal, the only extra step to take is to discover the direction of the rays of light in the first place. This can easily be done by determining the vector from the source of light to the 3D position of the surface point you are considering. Finding out the angle-based attenuation for a point light yields the following code:

```
float3 Light_Direction = normalize( inPos - Light_Position );
float AngleAttn = clamp(0, 1, dot( inNormal, Light_Direction ));
```

The other consideration with point lights is that the light attenuates based on distance. The first step is to determine the distance from the surface to the light. This can be done easily with the following shader code:

```
Float Distance = length( inPos - Light_Position );
```

Generally, because of the nature of a point light, light attenuates proportionally to the square of the distance from the light. However, to allow flexibility within your scene, you should adjust the light based on three different components: the inverse of the distance, the distance, and the distance squared. This added flexibility allows you to have full

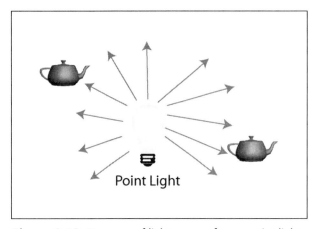

Figure 9.10 How rays of light emerge from a point light.

artistic control and tweak the values as needed by your scene. The reality is that quite often, it is not a matter of rendering accurately but more so of rendering so it looks convincing.

The following code illustrates how this can be done:

```
// Compute distance based attenuation. This is defined as:
// Attenuation = 1 / ( LA.x + LA.y*Dist + LA.z*Distance*Distance )
float DistAttn = clamp(0,1, 1 / (LightAttenuation.x +
                              LightAttenuation.y * Distance +
                              LightAttenuation.z * Distance * Distance ));
```

Because point lights are so common in rendering, I will be using them later on in this chapter to illustrate the differences between ambient, diffuse, and specular lighting.

note

At this point, you may wonder what happens if a source of light is occluded, or blocked, by another object. The reality is that such phenomena are difficult to re-create in real time with simple light primitives and will be explored in Chapter 17, "Advanced Lighting," and Chapter 18, "Shadowing."

Spot Lights

Generally speaking, a flashlight behaves just like a point light. However, the light is restricted to a small cone where light comes out. A spot light is, in essence, a point light where part of the source is blocked, causing light to be emitted only along a specific cone. Figure 9.11 explains how a spot light works.

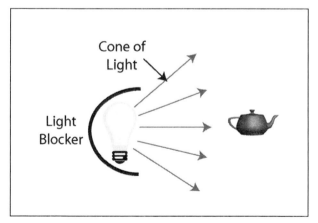

Figure 9.11 How a spot light works (like a point light but with a restricted cone of action).

With this in mind, a spot light behaves in exactly the same way a point light does. You only need to consider the angle of the cone the light comes from. The cone for a spot light is defined by two angles. The first angle represents the inner cone, where the light is at full intensity. The second angle, the outer cone angle, is the point at which the lighting ends. For any angle values between the inner and outer cone, light will fall off with the equation shown in Figure 9.12.

$$Intensity = \left(\frac{\cos\alpha - \cos\phi}{\cos\theta - \cos\phi} \right)^{p}$$

$\alpha =$ Current Lighting Angle
within the cone

$\theta =$ Inner Cone Angle

$\phi =$ Outer Cone Angle

Only valid for $\alpha \geq \theta$

Figure 9.12 Spot light cone fall-off equation.

From this equation, many of the components can be replaced with dot products to improve performance. However, to properly implement this, you need to take advantage of the conditional statements of the vertex shader 2.0 model. The following code illustrates how this can be done:

```
float LightAngle = dot(Light_Direction, Light_Orientation);
float ConeAttn = 1.0;
if ( LightAngle > Light_InnerCone )
    ConeAttn = pow((LightAngle-Light_OuterCone) /
                (Light_InnerCone-Light_OuterCone), Light_ConePower);
```

Spot lights can be useful occasionally, but they can be significantly expensive to compute. There are some techniques that can be used, such as projective lights, to simplify the process.

Area Lights

All the types of lights I have covered depend on the fact that rays of light originate from a single discrete point. The reality is that no light in the universe behaves this way, and we have simply been estimating the results. Even when you consider a light bulb, light comes from a heated filament that glows. This filament isn't a single point in the world and covers some area.

Obviously, this filament is small and can be well approximated as a single point. In reality, however, lighting actually comes from the sum of all the minuscule points that compose the filament. Figure 9.13 shows how this works.

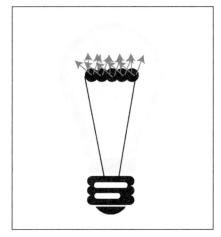

Figure 9.13 Light treated as a set of discrete points to create an area light.

Considering this information, all light in a scene is actually a set of area lights, which emit light from a surface area and not a single point in your world. In essence, this boils down to considering a set of point lights that represent each element that composes the source of light.

Obviously, this is too complex and expensive for real-time rendering. But off-line rendering approaches, such as radiosity, fully take advantage of this lighting approach. The big advantage of area lighting is that it can re-create much more realistic environments because the use of small discrete lights can create a much softer lighting environment and even create soft shadows where needed. For more information on radiosity, you should refer to the Siggraph overview at:

http://www.siggraph.org/education/materials/HyperGraph/radiosity/overview_1.htm

Let's Get Shading

In the following sections, I will implement shaders for ambient, diffuse, and specular lighting. For the purpose of this chapter, you will be using a simple shader with a single teapot. I will not go into great detail on how to set it up, but if you need a refresher, I encourage you to see Chapter 4, "Getting Started, Your First Shaders."

You will need to create a basic one-pass shader that renders a teapot model. The vertex shader for this is standard, simply rendering the teapot object in a regular way. The only difference to consider is that you need to pass color information to the pixel shader because the lighting color is determined in the vertex shader; this implies that you need to add a new variable to the output structure. The basic vertex shader to use is as follows:

```
struct VS_OUTPUT
{
   float4 Pos:      POSITION;
   float2 TexCoord: TEXCOORD0;
   float2 Color:    COLOR0;
};

VS_OUTPUT vs_main(float4 inPos: POSITION, float3 inNormal: NORMAL,
                  float2 inTxr: TEXCOORD0)
{
   VS_OUTPUT Out;

   // Compute the projected position and send out the texture coordinates
   Out.Pos = mul(view_proj_matrix, inPos);
   Out.TexCoord = inTxr;

   // Output the ambient color
```

```
   Out.Color = float4(1,1,1,1);

   return Out;
}
```

The pixel shader simply needs to route the color coming in from the vertex shader to the output of the shader. This gives the following code:

```
float4 ps_main(float4 inColor: COLOR0) : COLOR
{
   // Simply route the vertex color to the output
   return inColor;
}
```

With this basic shader, you will be able to render all the lights. So let's get started with a simple ambient lighting shader.

Ambient Lighting

Ambient light is a simple form of lighting that affects an object uniformly. For you to implement this shader, you simply need to add the color of the ambient light to the shader in the form of a COLOR variable named Light_Ambient. After you add this variable, you simply need to change the vertex shader to output the ambient color to the pixel shader through the output structure's Color variable. This can be done with the following vertex shader code:

```
float4x4 view_proj_matrix;
float4 Light_Ambient;
struct VS_OUTPUT
{
   float4 Pos:      POSITION;
   float2 TexCoord: TEXCOORD0;
   float2 Color:    COLOR0;
};

VS_OUTPUT vs_main(float4 inPos: POSITION, float3 inNormal: NORMAL,
                  float2 inTxr: TEXCOORD0)
{
   VS_OUTPUT Out;

   // Compute the projected position and send out the texture coordinates
   Out.Pos = mul(view_proj_matrix, inPos);
   Out.TexCoord = inTxr;

   // Output the ambient color
```

```
    Out.Color = Light_Ambient;

    return Out;
}
```

Putting it all together and compiling gives the final rendering results shown in Figure 9.14. Also note that the final version of this shader has been included on the CD-ROM as `shader_1.rfx`.

Figure 9.14 Rendering results for the ambient lighting shader.

Diffuse Lighting

Now that you have some ambient lighting in the scene, it is time to add a real point light and calculate its diffuse component. Because a point light has position, color, and distance attenuation factors, you need to create the proper variables named `Light_Position`, `Light_Color`, and `Light_Attenuation`. With these variables, you are now set to create the actual shader.

For this shader, you will put the lighting code in a function called `Light_PointDiffuse`, which takes in the light parameters and returns the resulting color. The function takes in the light position, color, and attenuation, as well as the vertex position and normal. The major advantage of using a function to compute the lighting is that it allows you to calculate multiple lights without the need to replicate code throughout your shader.

Taking the pieces of code developed earlier for a point light and integrating them into the vertex shader will give you the following vertex shader code:

```
float4x4 view_proj_matrix;
float4 Light_Ambient;
float4 Light1_Position;
```

```
float4 Light1_Attenuation;
float4 Light1_Color;
struct VS_OUTPUT
{
    float4 Pos:       POSITION;
    float2 TexCoord: TEXCOORD0;
    float2 Color:     COLOR0;
};


float4 Light_PointDiffuse(float3 VertPos, float3 VertNorm, float3 LightPos,
                          float4 LightColor, float4 LightAttenuation)
{
    // Determine the distance from the light to the vertex and the direction
    float3 LightDir = LightPos - VertPos;
    float  Dist = length(LightDir);
    LightDir = LightDir / Dist;

    // Compute distance based attenuation. This is defined as:
    // Attenuation = 1 / ( LA.x + LA.y*Dist + LA.z*Dist*Dist )
    float DistAttn = clamp(0,1, 1 / ( LightAttenuation.x +
                                      LightAttenuation.y * Dist +
                                      LightAttenuation.z * Dist * Dist ));

    // Compute surface/light angle based attenuation defined as dot(N,L)
    // Note : This must be clamped as it may become negative.
    float AngleAttn = clamp(0, 1, dot(VertNorm, LightDir) );

    // Compute final lighting
    return LightColor * DistAttn * AngleAttn;
}


VS_OUTPUT vs_main(float4 inPos: POSITION, float3 inNormal: NORMAL,
                  float2 inTxr: TEXCOORD0)
{
    VS_OUTPUT Out;

    // Compute the projected position and send out the texture coordinates
    Out.Pos = mul(view_proj_matrix, inPos);
    Out.TexCoord = inTxr;

    float4 Color;

    // Compute light contribution
```

```
Color = Light_PointDiffuse(inPos, inNormal, Light1_Position,
                           Light1_Color, Light1_Attenuation);

// Output Final Color
Out.Color = Color;

return Out;
}
```

With the shader, all you will need to do is set the light attributes, and you should get results similar to the one shown in Figure 9.15. Also note that the final version of this shader is included on the CD-ROM as shader_2.rfx.

Figure 9.15 Rendering results for your diffuse lighting shader.

Specular Lighting

The last component to complete the point lighting shader is the integration of a specular part to the lighting equation. The major difference with specular lighting is that the lighting intensity is not only influenced by the surface-to-light angle but also by the light-to-viewer angle.

A common way this is implemented is with the half vector. This is essentially the halfway vector between the view vector and the incident light vector.

The view vector is determined by taking a view position (in this case we'll assume a vector at 0,0,10, which is sufficiently far away from the object) and transforming it into object space. Since the original vector is relative to the camera, transforming it into object space is simply a matter of applying the inverse of the view matrix, which is contained in the `inv_view_matrix` built-in matrix variable. This object-space view vector can then be added to the vertex position, thus giving you a vector that goes from the light to the surface of the object. The following code illustrates how this is done:

```
EyeVector = -normalize(mul(inv_view_matrix,float4(0,0,10,1))+inPos);
```

With this EyeVector, you can determine the half vector by combining it with the incident light vector and then normalizing the result. Because both vectors are normalized to start with, the result is equivalent to averaging them with (A+B)/2. The following code shows how you can do this:

```
HalfVect = normalize(LightDir-EyeVector);
```

Once you have the half vector, the angle-based light intensity can be determined by computing the dot product between the half vector and the surface normal, and raising the result to the power of *m*. Raising the result to a certain power controls the specular exponent of the light. The higher the value, the smaller and sharper the lighting highlight will be. For this shader, you can use an exponent of 32.

Combining all these elements into a function called `Light_PointSpecular` gives the following vertex shader code:

```
float4x4 view_proj_matrix;
float4 Light_Ambient;
float4 Light1_Position;
float4 Light1_Attenuation;
float4 Light1_Color;
float4 view_position;
float4x4 inv_view_matrix;
float4x4 view_matrix;
struct VS_OUTPUT
{
    float4 Pos:      POSITION;
    float2 TexCoord: TEXCOORD0;
    float2 Color:    COLOR0;
};

float4 Light_PointSpecular(float3 VertPos, float3 VertNorm, float3 LightPos,
                           float4 LightColor, float4 LightAttenuation,
                           float3 EyeDir)
{
    // Determine the distance from the light to the vertex and the direction
    float3 LightDir = LightPos - VertPos;
    float  Dist = length(LightDir);
    LightDir = LightDir / Dist;
```

```
    // Compute half vector
    float3 HalfVect = normalize(LightDir-EyeDir);

    // Compute distance based attenuation. This is defined as:
    // Attenuation = 1 / ( LA.x + LA.y*Dist + LA.z*Dist*Dist )
    float DistAttn = clamp(0,1, 1 / ( LightAttenuation.x +
                                      LightAttenuation.y * Dist +
                                      LightAttenuation.z * Dist * Dist ));

    float SpecularAttn =  pow( clamp(0, 1,dot(VertNorm, HalfVect)),32);

    // Compute final lighting
    return LightColor * DistAttn * SpecularAttn;
}

VS_OUTPUT vs_main(float4 inPos: POSITION, float3 inNormal: NORMAL,
                  float2 inTxr: TEXCOORD0)
{
    VS_OUTPUT Out;

    // Compute the projected position and send out the texture coordinates
    Out.Pos = mul(view_proj_matrix, inPos);
    Out.TexCoord = inTxr;

    float4 Color;

    // Determine the eye vector
    float3 EyeVector = -normalize(mul(inv_view_matrix,float4(0,0,10,1))+inPos);

    // Compute light contribution
    Color = Light_PointSpecular(inPos, inNormal, Light1_Position,
                                Light1_Color, Light1_Attenuation,
                                  EyeVector);

    // Output Final Color
    Out.Color = Color;

    return Out;
}
```

The final rendering results for this shader are shown in Figure 9.16. Also note that the final version of this shader is included on the CD-ROM as shader_3.rfx.

Figure 9.16 Rendering results for your specular lighting shader.

Putting It Together

That's it! Well, not all of it; you still need to put it together into a final shader. This is simply a matter of combining the code for the ambient, diffuse, and specular lighting into a single function called Light_Point. Doing so should give you the following vertex shader:

```
float4x4 view_proj_matrix;
float4 Light_Ambient;
float4 Light1_Position;
float4 Light1_Attenuation;
float4 Light1_Color;
float4 view_position;
float4x4 inv_view_matrix;
float4x4 view_matrix;
struct VS_OUTPUT
{
   float4 Pos:      POSITION;
   float2 TexCoord: TEXCOORD0;
   float2 Color:    COLOR0;
};

float4 Light_Point(float3 VertPos, float3 VertNorm, float3 LightPos,
                   float4 LightColor, float4 LightAttenuation,
                   float3 EyeDir)
```

```
{
    // Determine the distance from the light to the vertex and the direction
    float3 LightDir = LightPos - VertPos;
    float  Dist = length(LightDir);
    LightDir = LightDir / Dist;

    // Compute half vector
    float3 HalfVect = normalize(LightDir-EyeDir);

    // Compute distance based attenuation. This is defined as:
    // Attenuation = 1 / ( LA.x + LA.y*Dist + LA.z*Dist*Dist )
    float DistAttn = clamp(0,1, 1 / ( LightAttenuation.x +
                                      LightAttenuation.y * Dist +
                                      LightAttenuation.z * Dist * Dist ));

    // Specular
    float SpecularAttn =  pow( clamp(0, 1,dot(VertNorm, HalfVect)),32);

    // Diffuse
    float AngleAttn = clamp(0, 1, dot(VertNorm, LightDir) );

    // Compute final lighting
    return LightColor * DistAttn * (SpecularAttn+AngleAttn);
}

VS_OUTPUT vs_main(float4 inPos: POSITION, float3 inNormal: NORMAL,
                  float2 inTxr: TEXCOORD0)
{
    VS_OUTPUT Out;

    // Compute the projected position and send out the texture coordinates
    Out.Pos = mul(view_proj_matrix, inPos);
    Out.TexCoord = inTxr;

    // Output the ambient color
    float4 Color = Light_Ambient;

    // Determine the eye vector
    float3 EyeVector = -normalize(mul(inv_view_matrix,float4(0,0,10,1))+inPos);

    // Compute light contribution
    Color += Light_Point(inPos, inNormal, Light1_Position,
            Light1_Color, Light1_Attenuation, EyeVector);
```

```
    // Output Final Color
    Out.Color = Color;

    return Out;
}
```

The final rendering results for this complete lighting shader are shown in Figure 9.17. The final version of this shader is included on the CD-ROM as shader_4.rfx.

I mentioned earlier how light modulates itself with the color of an object. So far, you have only dealt with the assumption of a white teapot. You can now add a texture to the workspace and change the pixel shader so that it samples the texture and modulates it with the resulting light color. The changes required to the pixel shader are as follows:

```
sampler Texture0;
float4 ps_main(float4 inColor: COLOR0,float2 inTxr: TEXCOORD0) : COLOR
{
    // Simply route the vertex color to the output
    return inColor*tex2D(Texture0,inTxr);
}
```

There you have a final lighting solution with ambient, diffuse, and specular lighting. Figure 9.18 shows you the results for this shader. Also note that the final version of this shader is included on the CD-ROM as shader_5.rfx.

Figure 9.17 Rendering results for your complete lighting shader.

Figure 9.18 Rendering results for your complete lighting shader modulated with a texture.

It's Your Turn!

Now that you have a better understanding of the importance of lighting and know some of the basic approaches taken, it is time to explore your own creativity. In the following exercises, you will expand from shaders developed earlier in this chapter and try out new approaches. You can find the solutions to these exercises in Appendix D.

Exercise 1: DIRECTION LIGHTS

Throughout this chapter, all the lighting shaders you developed took advantage of point lights. As described earlier, directional light can often be used to represent distant sources of light, such as the sun, in a more efficient way than can be achieved with point lights. For this exercise, I invite you to modify the ambient/diffuse/specular shader developed in this chapter to use a directional light instead of a point light.

As you develop this shader, you must remember that directional light does not have position or attenuation. The only thing of importance for a directional light is its direction.

Exercise 2: ANIMATING LIGHTS

For this second exercise, I invite you to expand on the previously developed ambient/diffuse/specular shader to animate one of the lights. Taking advantage of the `time_0_1` built-in HLSL variable, you can animate both the light's position and color.

Keep in mind that because you wish to animate the light around the scene object, you need to do a little math to determine an animating position on a sphere located around the object. I will not provide any hints on how this can be done; I encourage you to come up with something on your own.

What's Next?

In this chapter, you have discovered the importance of lighting. This is something that people usually take for granted, but the fact is that if it weren't for light, you wouldn't see the world in the first place. You learned in this chapter that you should have a good understanding of the basics involved in lighting and some of the approaches taken with today's hardware.

You may have noticed that using per-vertex lighting can give unrealistic results, depending on the resolution of the mesh you are lighting. This is because the color interpolation on vertices is done in a linear way where the lighting color does not change in a linear way because lighting depends mostly on the surface normal and lighting vector. In the next chapter, you will learn how to improve upon this by implementing per-pixel lighting. You will also learn how bumpmaps can be used with lighting to re-create small surface details that can't easily be represented with geometry.

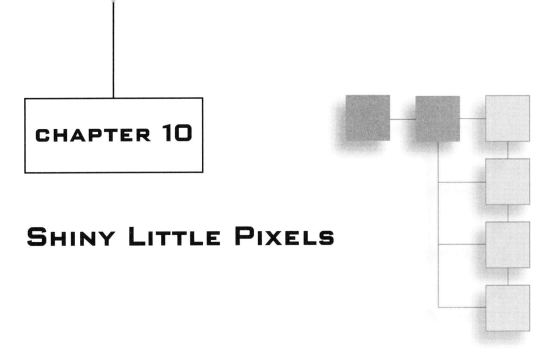

CHAPTER 10

SHINY LITTLE PIXELS

In the previous chapter, you explored the basics of lighting and learned how to apply these techniques to light the vertices of your objects. Such lighting works well for highly tessellated objects because of the way colors are interpolated. When it boils down to lighting your objects precisely, you need to consider lighting them per-pixel.

In this chapter, you will build upon the knowledge you gained in the previous chapter to light your objects per-pixel. You will also learn how to take advantage of per-pixel lighting to add pixel-level details to your objects by using bumpmaps and normal maps.

Although per-pixel lighting can be more expensive to render, it goes a great way toward improving the quality of your graphics. So fasten your seat belts and get ready to light those pixels!

Why Isn't Vertex Lighting Enough?

When considering lighting, most people think that lighting an object per-vertex is sufficient. This is generally true for highly tessellated objects but fails on complex shapes and low detail ones. The reason behind this is the way interpolation of colors between vertices happens.

When you light your object per-vertex, the lighting color is calculated once for each vertex and is then linearly interpolated across the polygon. The reality, however, is that the lighting values are dependent on the incident light angle, the surface normal, and the viewer position (for specular lighting). The interpolation of color resulting from the per-vertex lighting calculations does not give the same results as interpolating each component individually and then computing the result for each pixel.

Imagine the following case where you have one flat surface being lit by a single point light. With per-vertex lighting, the color will be determined for each vertex and then interpolated. With per-pixel lighting, you will interpolate each component needed for lighting and then calculate on a per-pixel basis. Figure 10.1 shows you an example of the difference between vertex- and pixel-based lighting for a simple flat surface.

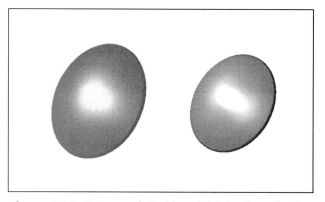

Figure 10.1 Vertex- and pixel-based lighting for a simple flat surface lit by a single point light.

When dealing with high polygon counts, per-vertex lighting can do well because each individual polygon covers little of the screen and each pixel suffers from little interpolation. However, when dealing with lower detail geometry, pixel-based lighting is the way to go!

Another advantage of per-pixel lighting is the ability to add detail that doesn't exist in the original mesh. By using bumpmaps and normal maps, you can add bumpiness to your geometry on a per-pixel level, which doesn't exist on the geometry but which creates the illusion of such detail through the use of proper lighting.

But before you can even consider the more complex uses of pixel-based lighting, you must start by learning how you can light individual pixels. In the next section, you will learn how to extend the lighting techniques from the previous chapter for use with pixel-based lighting.

Basic Pixel Lighting

Now that you know the why behind per-pixel lighting, it is time to discuss the how. Because the reason for the downfall of per-vertex lighting is its linear interpolation, you will need to determine which components of lighting are interpolatable.

Based on those determinations, you will be able to move some of the lighting computing from the vertex shader to the pixel shader to ensure better lighting while keeping the graphics processor work to a minimum.

In regards to ambient lighting, because it is simply a constant color applied over the whole object, the results are the same whether it is done for each vertex or pixel. Therefore, I will not discuss ambient lighting any further in this chapter.

In the next two sections, I will go over both diffuse and specular lighting and help you create the new pixel-based lighting shaders. Note that because you will be doing the same process as done in the previous chapter, you will also use the same base shader.

Diffuse Lighting

Starting with diffuse lighting, you need to decide what lighting components can be interpolated and which ones need to be processed per-pixel. From the end to the beginning, what defines diffuse lighting is the dot product between the surface normal and the light vector.

This dot product defines the intensity of the lighting, but the results of such an operation cannot be interpolated properly. Because of this, the dot product needs to be processed for each pixel and needs to be moved to the pixel shader.

note

> Although normals can be interpolated linearly, such interpolation can yield vectors that are not normalized. To correct this, it is a good idea to renormalize the vector by using the built-in HLSL `normalize` function.
>
> Also keep in mind that throughout this chapter, when I refer to normals, I imply vertex normals, which generally are represented as the average surface normal for all polygons that share a specific vertex.

The two components of this dot product are the surface normal and light vector. Vectors themselves will interpolate correctly when put in on a per-vertex basis. This means you can calculate them ahead of time for each vertex and pass them on to the pixel shader.

For this to happen, you need to add those two components to the vertex shader output structure. They can be passed to the pixel shader using `TEXCOORD1` and `TEXCOORD2`. Applying the modifications yields the following output structure:

```
struct VS_OUTPUT
{
   float4 Pos:      POSITION;
   float2 TexCoord: TEXCOORD0;
   float3 Normal:   TEXCOORD1;
   float3 LightDir: TEXCOORD2;
};
```

You also need to change the vertex shader to pass those values to the output structure. Because you are dealing with a single light, it is easier at this point to remove the lighting function and copy the relevant code in the `vs_main` function.

One thing you may have noticed that was not mentioned is the distance-based attenuation. Although the interpolation of this component is not perfect, lights generally have enough range of action so that small differences in distance don't make a significant difference in the result and hence do not need to be computed on a per-pixel basis.

Because this attenuation factor is a single scalar value, the easiest way to pass it to the pixel shader without wasting another register is to simply make the LightDir vector a float4 and put this result in the W component of this vector.

Applying all those changes should give you the following vertex shader:

```
float4x4 view_proj_matrix;
float4 Light_Ambient;
float4 Light1_Position;
float4 Light1_Attenuation;
float4 Light1_Color;
struct VS_OUTPUT
{
    float4 Pos:      POSITION;
    float2 TexCoord: TEXCOORD0;
    float3 Normal:   TEXCOORD1;
    float4 LightDir: TEXCOORD2;
};

VS_OUTPUT vs_main(float4 inPos: POSITION, float3 inNormal: NORMAL,
                  float2 inTxr: TEXCOORD0)
{
    VS_OUTPUT Out;

    // Compute the projected position and send out the texture coordinates
    Out.Pos = mul(view_proj_matrix, inPos);
    Out.TexCoord = inTxr;

    // Move the normal to the pixel shader
    Out.Normal = inNormal;

    // Compute and move the light direction to the pixel shader
    float4 LightDir;
    LightDir.xyz = Light1_Position - inPos;
    float Dist = length(LightDir.xyz);
    LightDir.xyz = LightDir.xyz / Dist;

    // Compute the distance based attenuation. Distance can be interpolated
    // fairly well so we will precompute it on a per-vertex basis.
```

```
    LightDir.w = clamp(0,1, 1 / ( Light1_Attenuation.x +
                                 Light1_Attenuation.y * Dist +
                                 Light1_Attenuation.z * Dist * Dist ));

    // Output the light direction
    Out.LightDir = LightDir;

    return Out;
}
```

On the pixel shader end, the task is simply a matter of taking the incoming vectors and computing the dot product and the final lighting color. For convenience, the lighting code can be put in a function called Light_PointDiffuse, as was done before in the per-vertex lighting shader. So in essence, the lighting computation code is the same as the vertex shader version.

You also need to add the input parameters to the pixel shader main function, ps_main, so the interpolated normal and light direction can be read. With all those adjustments, you should end up with the following pixel shader:

```
float4 Light1_Color;
float4 Light_PointDiffuse(float4 LightDir,
                          float3 Normal,
                          float4 LightColor)
{
    // Compute suface/light angle based attenuation defined as dot(N,L)
    float AngleAttn = clamp(0, 1, dot(Normal, LightDir.xyz) );

    // Compute final lighting (Color * Distance Attenuation *
    // Angle Attenuation)
    return LightColor * LightDir.w * AngleAttn;
}


float4 ps_main(float3 inNormal:TEXCOORD1,
               float4 inLightDir:TEXCOORD2) : COLOR
{
    // Compute the lighting contribution for this single light
    return Light_PointDiffuse(inLightDir,inNormal,Light1_Color);
}
```

When you are finished with all the changes, you can compile and check out the results. Figure 10.2 shows what the rendering result for this shader will look like. The shader is included on the CD-ROM as shader_1.rfx.

Figure 10.2 Rendering results for the per-pixel diffuse lighting shader.

Specular Lighting

Not too hard yet, huh? Now it is time to tackle the specular lighting shader. The basic process is the same as that for the diffuse lighting shader. The core of this shader is the dot product between the light vector and the half vector. As with the diffuse lighting shader, this computation needs to be done on the pixel shader.

This means that both the light vector and the half vector need to be calculated in the vertex shader and passed to the pixel shader. In the same way as you did with the diffuse lighting shader, you need to add the proper variables to the output structure. With these modifications, the output structure should look as follows:

```
struct VS_OUTPUT
{
   float4 Pos:      POSITION;
   float2 TexCoord: TEXCOORD0;
   float3 Normal:   TEXCOORD1;
   float4 LightDir: TEXCOORD2;
   float3 HalfVect: TEXCOORD3;
};
```

Within the vertex shader code, you need to compute the normal, light vector, half vector, and distance-based attenuation. This is simply a matter of taking the specular lighting shader code developed in the previous chapter and applying a few changes. You should then have the following code:

```
float4x4 view_proj_matrix;
float4 Light_Ambient;
float4 Light1_Position;
float4 Light1_Attenuation;
float4 Light1_Color;
float4 view_position;
float4x4 inv_view_matrix;
float4x4 view_matrix;
struct VS_OUTPUT
{
   float4 Pos:      POSITION;
   float2 TexCoord: TEXCOORD0;
   float3 Normal:   TEXCOORD1;
   float4 LightDir: TEXCOORD2;
   float3 HalfVect: TEXCOORD3;
};

VS_OUTPUT vs_main(float4 inPos: POSITION, float3 inNormal: NORMAL,
                  float2 inTxr: TEXCOORD0)
{
   VS_OUTPUT Out;

   // Compute the projected position and send out the texture coordinates
   Out.Pos = mul(view_proj_matrix, inPos);
   Out.TexCoord = inTxr;

   // Determine the distance from the light to the vertex and the direction
   float4 LightDir;
   LightDir.xyz = Light1_Position - inPos;
   float  Dist = length(LightDir.xyz);
   LightDir.xyz = LightDir.xyz / Dist;

   // Compute the per-vertex distance based attenuation
   LightDir.w = clamp(0,1, 1 / ( Light1_Attenuation.x +
                                 Light1_Attenuation.y * Dist +
                                 Light1_Attenuation.z * Dist * Dist ));

   // Determine the eye vector and the half vector
   float3 EyeVector = -normalize(mul(inv_view_matrix,float4(0,0,10,1))+inPos);
   Out.HalfVect = normalize(LightDir-EyeVector);

   // Output normal and light direction
   Out.Normal = inNormal;
   Out.LightDir = LightDir;
```

```
        return Out;
}
```

On the pixel shader front, it is simply a matter of creating a function called Light_PointSpecular, which will take the input vectors and compute the dot product. With this, you can then consider the lighting color and the distance attenuation. The following pixel shader code implements all these changes:

```
float4 Light1_Color;
float4 Light_PointSpecular(float3 Normal, float3 HalfVect, float4 LightDir,
                           float4 LightColor)
{
   // Compute suface/light angle based attenuation defined as dot(N,L)
   // Note : This must be clamped as it may become negative.
   float SpecularAttn =  pow( clamp(0, 1,dot(Normal, HalfVect)),32);

   // Compute final lighting
   return LightColor * LightDir.w * SpecularAttn;
}


float4 ps_main(float3 inNormal:TEXCOORD1, float4 LightDir:TEXCOORD2,
            float3 HalfVect:TEXCOORD3) : COLOR
{
   // Simply route the vertex color to the output
   return Light_PointSpecular(inNormal,HalfVect,LightDir,Light1_Color);
}
```

After all these changes are finished, you can compile and check the results. Figure 10.3 shows what the rendering result for this shader will look like. The shader is included on the CD-ROM as shader_2.rfx.

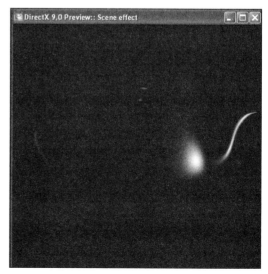

Figure 10.3 Rendering results for the per-pixel specular lighting shader.

Putting It All Together

Now we will put the components together to get a final lighting shader. From the point of view of the vertex shader, the per-pixel specular lighting shader computes all the components required, and no work is needed.

For the pixel shader, you need to create a new function, Light_Point, which calculates both the diffuse and specular dot products and then combines the results to determine the final lighting value. With these simple changes, you should have the following pixel shader:

```
float4 Light1_Color;
float4 Light_Point(float3 Normal, float3 HalfVect, float4 LightDir,
                   float4 LightColor)
{
   // Compute both specular and diffuse factors
   float SpecularAttn =  pow( clamp(0, 1,dot(Normal, HalfVect)),32);
   float DiffuseAttn =  clamp(0, 1,dot(Normal, LightDir));

   // Compute final lighting
   return LightColor * LightDir.w * (SpecularAttn+DiffuseAttn);
}


float4 ps_main(float3 inNormal:TEXCOORD1, float4 LightDir:TEXCOORD2,
               float3 HalfVect:TEXCOORD3) : COLOR
{
   // Simply route the vertex color to the output
   return Light_Point(inNormal,HalfVect,LightDir,Light1_Color);
}
```

With this pixel shader, the rendering result should look like that shown in Figure 10.4. The shader is included on the CD-ROM as shader_3.rfx.

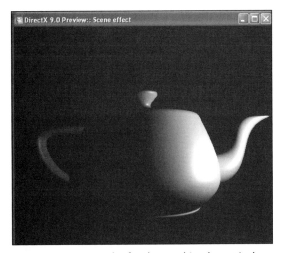

Figure 10.4 Results for the combined per-pixel diffuse and specular shader.

The only thing missing from this shader is a texture. To add one, simply add a new texture variable and reference object in your workspace and change the pixel shader to read in the texture and modulate the result with the lighting color that you just computed. Applying those changes yields the following pixel shader:

```
float4 Light1_Color;
float4 Light_Point(float3 Normal, float3 HalfVect, float4 LightDir,
                   float4 LightColor)
{
   // Compute both specular and diffuse factors
   float SpecularAttn =  pow( clamp(0, 1,dot(Normal, HalfVect)),32);
   float DiffuseAttn =  clamp(0, 1,dot(Normal, LightDir));

   // Compute final lighting
   return LightColor * LightDir.w * (SpecularAttn+DiffuseAttn);
}


float4 ps_main(float2 inTxr:TEXCOORD0,float3 inNormal:TEXCOORD1,
               float4 LightDir:TEXCOORD2,float3 HalfVect:TEXCOORD3) : COLOR
{
   // Simply route the vertex color to the output
   return tex2D(Texture0,inTxr)*
          Light_Point(inNormal,HalfVect,LightDir,Light1_Color);
}
```

The rendering result for this shader should look like that shown in Figure 10.5. The shader is included on the CD-ROM as shader_4.rfx.

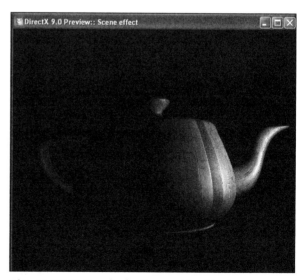

Figure 10.5 Results for the combined textured per-pixel diffuse and specular shader.

Giving You Goose Bumps

Now that you can light each pixel of your object individually, we can explore the topic of bumpmapping and normal mapping. Because you are rendering each pixel individually, what prevents you from adding extra information to each pixel, which can add some extra details to the geometry?

The reality is that real objects are not just bound by polygons and that details go much deeper. Imagine a brick wall. Even though you can represent this wall with a simple planar polygon and texture, bricks have much greater 3D detail, which can't be represented by such geometry. Figure 10.6 illustrates this.

All this extra detail could be represented by geometry, but it would create tremendous numbers of polygons and would be impossible to manage. Another solution to the problem is to consider the impact of the added detail. Because the extra geometry details are small, they do not really affect the shape of the object. However, the impact can mostly be seen on the normal of the surface, as shown in Figure 10.7, which illustrates how normal detail can be represented on a pixel scale.

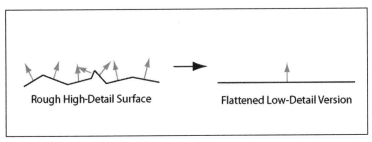

Figure 10.6 Small extra details compared to the flat polygon representation.

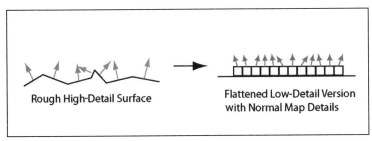

Figure 10.7 How extra details modify the surface normal of the geometry.

Now that you are rendering each pixel individually, nothing prevents you from modifying the normal for each pixel so that it takes into account the added details for this portion of the object. In the next two sections, I will overview two techniques that can be used to re-create such micro-details: bumpmapping and normal mapping.

Bumpmapping

Extra geometric details can be represented in a straightfor-ward manner, which is easily authorable by artists. In this form, you could create a grayscale texture that represents the height of each pixel relative to one another, white pixels being higher than black pixels. Figure 10.8 shows such a height texture for the stone texture used throughout this chapter.

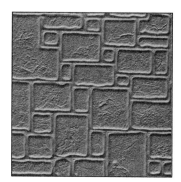

Figure 10.8 Height texture for the stone wall texture.

Although such a texture is easy to create, it is not so useful when rendering. You are interested in the surface normal for a particular pixel and not its height. However, you can preprocess the height texture to extract a U and V offset for each pixel. Because the normal at a particular pixel is sim-ply the slope of the height, you can determine this value through the equation shown in Figure 10.9.

$$\frac{dh}{du} = \text{Variation of height in u texture direction}$$

$$\frac{dh}{dv} = \text{Variation of height in v texture direction}$$

$$Len = \sqrt{(\frac{dh}{du} + \frac{dh}{dv} + 1)}$$

$$BumpMap = \begin{bmatrix} \dfrac{(\frac{dh}{du})}{Len} & \dfrac{(\frac{dh}{dv})}{Len} & \dfrac{1}{Len} \end{bmatrix}$$

Figure 10.9 Equation used to determine the surface normal based on a height map.

Instead of storing the resulting normal with your prepro-
cessing, you can simply discover a U and V offset that represents the difference of the normalized vector, assuming
you are looking at the texture from the top in 2D. Figure
10.10 shows such a bumpmap texture once it has been produced from its height map.

Figure 10.10 Bumpmap
generated from a height
texture.

note

Because of the nature of both bumpmaps and normal maps,
values stored in the textures are signed. Because the textures
are stored in an unsigned value, you will need to process the
pixels when you sample the texture to bring it back to a signed
form. This can be done with the following: Signed = Unsigned
× 2 − 1.

Such an approach may seem unnatural, but it came forth as the first hardware implementation because of its simple use of a dot product. Within a pixel shader, all you need
to do is take the interpolated surface normal and offset it by the bumpmap values. This is
similar to what was done in Chapter 7, "It's Getting Hot in Here," when we implemented
the heat haze screen effect.

This is the old way of doing per-pixel lighting; normal maps are the way of the future.
Therefore, we will move straight on to talking about normal maps. Before you can fully
understand how normal maps work, though, you need to learn about the tangent space
coordinate system.

Tangent Space

When you are dealing with normal maps and bumpmaps, each texel refers to the current
surface normal, which is usually either in object space or world space. However, because
you are texturing your object with a texture or bumpmap that isn't necessarily built for
this object, there is no way for the bumpmap or normal map to specify a new normal
without any knowledge of the surface of the object.

One solution is to ensure that your texture has a relationship with your object and then
to ensure that your normal map or bumpmap refers to the normals in object-space. However, this is impractical because it prevents texture reuse and needs special texture authoring for each bumped object in your scene. The fact that the bump texture has knowledge
of the surface of the objects also prohibits you from animating or deforming the surface,
restricting your use of bumpmapping even further.

A more practical approach is to create a new uniform coordinate system, which is the
same for every pixel on your object and can be built from your bump/normal texture. To

accomplish this, you need to consider that if your object was not bumped, the normal for each point on the surface would be perpendicular to the surface.

When applying a bumpmap or normal map to a surface, you are in essence modifying the normal along the two vectors that go along the U and V texture coordinates. Putting all this together yields a three-vector coordinate system that can be calculated on a per-pixel basis. Figure 10.11 illustrates this coordinate system.

As you can see from Figure 10.11, the vectors along the U and V texture coordinates are called Tangent and Binormal. Those vectors are defined as the 3D spatial direction in which the U and V texture coordinates are headed for a particular point on the surface. Not to worry! RenderMonkey has you covered yet again and can create those vectors for you. If you ever need to calculate them yourself, they can be deduced by taking the variation of the U and V texture coordinates for a vertex by using an average for all the contributing polygons and then generating a 3D vector pointing in the direction of the texture coordinates.

When defining your stream mapping for a model, you can add both the Tangent and Binormal vectors as inputs by selecting Add Stream from the Stream Mapping Editor and picking the right one from the drop-down list.

When doing lighting with tangent space, all you need to do is build a tangent space matrix from the surface normal, tangent vector, and bi-normal vector. This matrix can then be used to transform any of the lighting components into this coordinate system by multiplying it by the tangent space matrix.

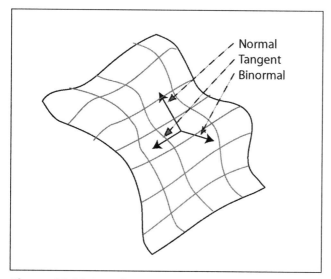

Figure 10.11 How the tangent space coordinate system is generated.

After you complete this operation, all your lighting components are interpolated relative to the local tangent space for each pixel. The following piece of code shows how you can construct a tangent space matrix and use it to convert a vector from object space to tangent space:

```
// Build the tangent space matrix
float3x3 TangentSpace;
TangentSpace[0] = inTangent;
TangentSpace[1] = inBinormal;
TangentSpace[2] = inNormal;

// Transform a vector from object space to tangent space
LightDir = mul(TangentSpace,LightDir);
```

When you're working in tangent space, all lighting vectors become relative to the interpolated surface normal for this pixel. This means that when you do operations such as bumpmapping, you can store the values as simple relative values because you are working with a coordinate system that represents the same thing no matter what point on the surface you are dealing with.

Normal Maps

Now that you understand the usefulness of tangent space, it is time to go ahead and see what can be done with it. The most common use of tangent space when dealing with per-pixel lighting is the use of normal maps to add bump-like details to the surface of an object.

Although the result is similar to the use of a bumpmap, the means used to achieve the results are different. With bumpmapping, the bump texture was used to encode an offset from the interpolated normal using two color components. In the case of a normal map, the texture uses a three-color component which represents the actual normal in tangent space. This representation assumes the blue component, or Z, represents the default normal position in tangent space.

Figure 10.12 Normal map texture created for the stone texture used in this chapter.

Such textures are difficult to author manually because it is a matter of painting vectors using colors. However, tools such as the NVIDIA Photoshop plug-in can generate such normal map textures from a grayscale height texture. Figure 10.12 shows such a normal map texture for the stone texture used throughout this chapter.

With this knowledge, it is now time to take our per-pixel diffuse/specular shader and use a normal map to enhance the lighting on the object. The first step to accomplish this is to add the normal map texture to both the workspace and the rendering pass. The generated normal map texture can be found on the CD-ROM as `FieldstoneBumpDOT3.tga`. Remember to make sure that filtering is enabled on this new texture by setting the `MINFILTER`, `MAGFILTER`, and `MIPFILTER` to `LINEAR` in the texture object settings. This filter setting ensures that the normal map texels are interpolating, reducing the block artifacts in your rendering.

With this set of changes, it is now time to attack the vertex shader. The changes here are fairly simple. The first step is to introduce the tangent space matrix code developed in the previous section. Then, you need to transform both the half vector and light vector into tangent space before passing them to the pixel shader.

Keep in mind that, because you are working in tangent space, the orientation of the surface normal is implicit and its deviations will be read from the normal map. Because of this, it does not need to be passed to the pixel shader, and you can remove this from the output structure.

With this set of adjustments, you should obtain the following vertex shader code:

```
float4 Light1_Attenuation;
float4 view_position;
float4x4 view_proj_matrix;
float4x4 inv_view_matrix;
float4x4 view_matrix;
float4 Light1_Color;
float4 Light_Ambient;
struct VS_OUTPUT
{
    float4 Pos:      POSITION;
    float2 TexCoord: TEXCOORD0;
    float4 LightDir: TEXCOORD1;
    float3 HalfVect: TEXCOORD2;
};

VS_OUTPUT vs_main(float4 inPos: POSITION, float3 inNormal: NORMAL,
              float3 inTangent:TANGENT, float3 inBinormal:BINORMAL,
              float2 inTxr: TEXCOORD0)
{
    VS_OUTPUT Out;

    // Compute the projected position and send out the texture coordinates
    Out.Pos = mul(view_proj_matrix, inPos);
    Out.TexCoord = inTxr;
```

```
// Determine the distance from the light to the vertex and the direction
float4 LightDir;
LightDir.xyz = mul(inv_view_matrix,float3(80,00,-80)) - inPos;
float  Dist = length(LightDir.xyz);
LightDir.xyz = LightDir.xyz / Dist;

// Compute the per-vertex distance based attenuation
LightDir.w = clamp(0,1, 1 / ( Light1_Attenuation.x +
                              Light1_Attenuation.y * Dist +
                              Light1_Attenuation.z * Dist * Dist ));


// Determine the eye vector
float3 EyeVector = normalize(view_position-inPos);

// Transform to tangent space and output
// half vector and light direction
float3x3 TangentSpace;
TangentSpace[0] = inTangent;
TangentSpace[1] = inBinormal;
TangentSpace[2] = inNormal;
Out.HalfVect = mul(TangentSpace,normalize(LightDir.xyz+EyeVector));
Out.LightDir = float4(mul(TangentSpace,LightDir.xyz),LightDir.w);

return Out;
}
```

On the pixel shader's end, the only change needed is in relation to the surface normal. Because all the lighting components are passed to the pixel shader in tangent space, this means that they are already relative to the interpolated vertex surface normal, which is implicit through the definition of tangent space. The actual normal on any point of the surface will then come from the normal map.

To do this, you need to sample the normal map texture and convert it from an unsigned value to a signed one. This value will then be the pixel-specific normal and can be substituted to the vertex-interpolated normal from the previous shader implementations.

The final pixel shader code for this bumped lighting shader is as follows:

```
float4 Light1_Color;
sampler Texture0;
sampler Bump;
float4 Light_Point(float3 Normal, float3 HalfVect, float4 LightDir,
                   float4 LightColor)
```

```
{
    // Compute both specular and diffuse factors
    float SpecularAttn =  pow( clamp(0, 1,dot(Normal, HalfVect)),16);
    float DiffuseAttn =  clamp(0, 1,dot(Normal, LightDir));

    // Compute final lighting
    return LightColor * LightDir.w * (SpecularAttn+DiffuseAttn);
}

float4 ps_main(float2 inTxr:TEXCOORD0,float4 LightDir:TEXCOORD1,
               float3 HalfVect:TEXCOORD2) : COLOR
{
    // Read bump and influence the normal
    float3 normal = tex2D(Bump,inTxr) * 2 - 1;

    // Simply route the vertex color to the output
    return tex2D(Texture0,inTxr)*
           (0.15+Light_Point(normal,HalfVect,LightDir,Light1_Color));
}
```

The rendering result for this normal mapped shader is shown in Figure 10.13. The shader is included on the CD-ROM as shader_5.rfx.

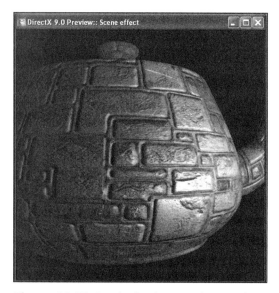

Figure 10.13 Results for the normal mapped per-pixel specular and diffuse lighting shader.

It's Your Turn!

With what I have shown you in this chapter, you should have a real understanding of how powerful per-pixel lighting can be. The following exercises will enable you to expand upon this knowledge by exploring your own creativity. You can also find the solutions to these exercises in Appendix D.

Exercise 1: DIRECTION LIGHTS

As with the previous chapter, you are invited to implement a direction lighting shader, basing your work on the shaders developed throughout this chapter. To complete this shader, start off with the bumpmapped shader developed earlier and change the light to support a directional light.

Exercise 2: MULTIPLE LIGHTS

Starting with the bumpmapped per-pixel lighting shader developed earlier in this chapter, you are invited to add a second point light to it. Doing this requires you to calculate lighting information for multiple lights, and to pass multiple tangent space vectors for each light to the pixel shader for evaluation.

What's Next?

Per-pixel lighting, although more expensive, can go a long way toward improving the realism of your graphics. Initially, by decomposing components that do not interpolate well, you were able to remove the lighting artifacts that can result, especially from low-tessellation meshes.

Stemming from this, you could transform this per-pixel information from object space to tangent space. Tangent space represents the coordinate system, which is local for each pixel on the surface and is the perfect coordinate system to represent surface level details in a way where the representation does not have to be object-dependent.

Through this tangent space coordinate system, you can take advantage of normal maps to add surface details by representing the variations on the surface normals of the objects.

As you have seen, proper object lighting can make significant improvement in your scene. I will cover a few more advanced lighting topics later on in this book. In the next chapter, I'll discuss the topic of reflections.

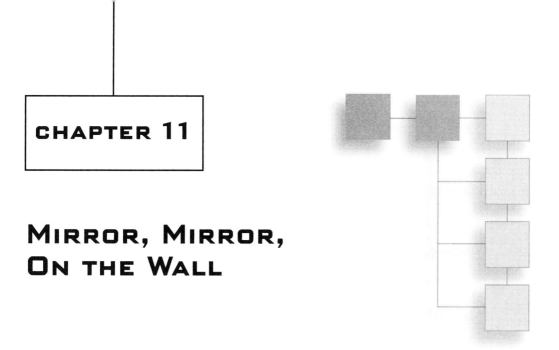

CHAPTER 11

MIRROR, MIRROR, ON THE WALL

In the last few chapters, you learned how lighting is an important component in making realistic graphics. You may remember that not all materials behave the same way or have specific properties. This chapter is the first in a series that addresses how different materials interact with their environment.

In this chapter, you will learn about the essentials you need to know when dealing with materials that are translucent and reflective. I will be covering the topics of reflection and refraction and how they interact. By the end of this chapter, you will be able to render materials that exhibit both translucency and reflectivity.

Although there may be different approaches to doing both reflections and refractions, we will concentrate on using cube environment maps. This method is a great way of representing the captured environment from a specific point within your scene and is easy to use for reflections and refractions.

From Reflections to Refractions

Many materials, as you know, have properties that allow them to either reflect or refract light. Probably the most obvious example is glass, which presents both phenomena at the same time. On the other hand, other materials that have glossy surfaces, such as car paint, also show reflections under the right lighting conditions.

Before we examine the details of how reflection and refraction can be reproduced, I must address two topics. First, I need to explain why cubemap environments are so well suited for such effects. Second, you must build the basic shader that you'll use throughout this chapter.

So why cubemaps? Cubemaps were covered in Chapter 6, "Blurring Things Up," but they are worth revisiting.

A cubemap is a set of six textures grouped together forming a cube centered on a single point in space, with each face being a snapshot of the scene along a specific axis as shown in Figure 11.1. Although this may not seem like a natural way of representing an environment from a single point in space, it is a very efficient way for your hardware to do so.

Because of the way a cubemap is formed, looking up the environment map is easily done when given a direction vector to look at. The major axis of the vector is used to find out which face of the cube will be sampled; the remaining two components of the vector are used to access the cubemap face as if it were a regular texture.

note

Because of the nature of cubemaps and environment maps, there is an aspect you will need to keep in mind. Because the environment map represents a snapshot of your environment from a particular point in space, this implies that everything within it is considered to be at an infinite distance from that point; in simpler terms, because the environment is pre-cooked, it will not contain any perspective.

Accessing a cubemap is simply a matter of determining which face to access and then accessing it as a regular texture. This makes the cubemap a natural and easy feature to implement with existing hardware architectures. Another added benefit is how easy a cubemap is to build.

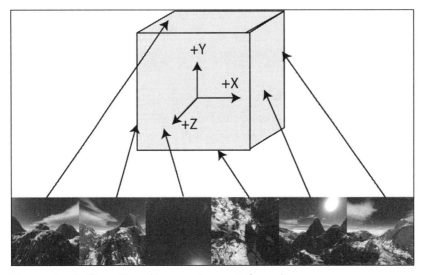

Figure 11.1 Illustration of how a cubemap is formed.

Building a cubemap from scratch is simply a matter of setting up six cameras with a 90 degree field of view facing all three major axes in both directions. At the end of this chapter, I will show you how you can dynamically construct a cubemap for use in a reflection and refraction shader. The process for building static environment maps, such as Snow.dds, generally involves authoring each face separately and using a specialized tool such as the Microsoft Texture Tool to composite them together.

Enough about cubemaps for now, though. Let's set up the basic shader that we will use throughout this chapter.

The basic shader you will use in this chapter is similar to the one developed for the heat haze and depth of field effects. The scene is composed of two passes. The first pass renders the environment cubemap you will use for this chapter to a sphere to create a background environment for the scene. (I recommend using Snow.dds, which is included on the CD-ROM source code directory for this chapter.)

The second rendering pass renders a standard teapot object to the scene. For now, you will simply render the teapot using a wood texture, but you will add reflection and refraction to this object later on. See Chapter 6 to learn how the workspace is set up. Right now, let's go back to the first pass and see how the shader code is formed.

When rendering an environment to a sphere in this way, you must take a few things into account. First of all, the sphere model you have is a unit-sized sphere centered on the origin. However, because you will be using this sphere to map an environment onto the camera, this sphere needs to be re-centered around the camera that is rendering it. This can easily be done by offsetting the sphere vertex positions by the camera's position, as defined by the built-in variable, before transforming it.

In addition to centering the sphere at the center of the camera, the environment map represents visual information that is located at infinity, relative to where the camera is located. This has the consequence that the environment will need to be rendered first, and the ZWRITE render state must be set to D3D_FALSE to avoid writing any depth information to the Z-buffer.

The other item that is needed by this shader is the view direction so the environment map can be sampled properly. Because the 3D sphere we are using is an origin-centered unit sphere, the view direction simply becomes the position of the sphere vertex. The vertex shader code that renders the environment cubemap to a sphere is as follows:

```
float4x4 view_proj_matrix;
float4 view_position;
struct VS_OUTPUT
{
    float4 Pos: POSITION;
    float3 dir: TEXCOORD0;
```

```
};

VS_OUTPUT vs_main(float4 Pos: POSITION)
{
    VS_OUTPUT Out;

    // Center environment around camera
    Out.Pos = mul(view_proj_matrix, float4(Pos.xyz + view_position, 1));
    Out.dir = Pos.xyz;

    return Out;
}
```

Within the pixel shader for this pass, all you have to do is read in the view direction passed in from the vertex shader and use it as a texture coordinate to look up the environment map. Doing so yields the following pixel shader code:

```
sampler Environment;
float4 ps_main(float3 dir: TEXCOORD0) : COLOR
{
    return texCUBE(Environment, dir);
}
```

The second pass needed for this basic shader simply renders a model with a texture applied to it. No point in describing shader code here because this is as simple as it gets.

With this shader compiled and running, you should get results similar to the one shown in Figure 11.2. This template shader has been included on the CD-ROM as `shader_1.rfx` in the directory for this chapter and is in fact very similar to the template shader developed in Chapter 7, "It's Getting Hot in Here."

You are now all set up and ready to start shading. So let's start with the first topic at hand: reflections.

Figure 11.2 Rendering output for this chapter's template shader.

Reflections

You may recall our discussion on specular lighting in Chapter 10, "Shiny Little Pixels." Light from a source bounces off a polished surface onto the viewer. Although this may seem different from reflection, it is the same process. The specular lighting equation emulates the same phenomenon but from the point of view of a single light. The reality is that all visible objects in a scene can be seen as a source of light and treated in the same way, especially when you are dealing with highly glossy surfaces.

The most obvious example of a reflective material is a mirror, which reflects every ray of light it encounters almost perfectly. But some more subtle examples, such as water or glass, also exhibit reflections under the right set of circumstances.

Reflections occur when a ray of light emanating from a source of light (or another lit object) hits the surface of the reflective material and is bounced towards the viewer. As Figure 11.3 shows, the basic concept behind reflection is simple. The angle between the incident light angle and the surface normal is the same as the angle between the reflected ray and the surface normal. Figure 11.3 also shows how the reflected vector can be calculated from the incident light vector and surface normal.

note

Remember that HLSL has built-in functions for both reflection and refraction. Unless you have specific needs, you should use those built-in functions because it gives the compiler a better understanding of what you are trying to accomplish and results in more optimized code.

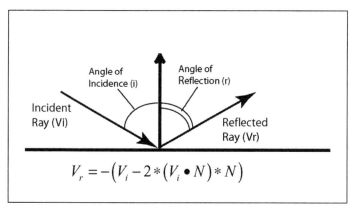

$$V_r = -\left(V_i - 2 * \left(V_i \bullet N\right) * N\right)$$

Figure 11.3 How rays of light reflect off a surface towards the viewer and the standard reflection equation.

With this information, rendering the scene with reflection on your teapot should be fairly straightforward. However, there is one aspect you must consider. In the preceding paragraphs, I discussed how light comes from a source, such as a scene object, bounces off your reflective surface, and heads toward the viewer. Actually, when rendering such a scene, you need to do this process upside-down. Because you cannot practically consider all sources of light in your scene, which would mean all pixels of your environment map, you need to start from your camera and trace the reflection in its reverse path to see what gets reflected.

To do this in a shader is simply a matter of determining the camera-to-object vector, and performing the reflection from this vector to get the source of the reflection from which to look up the environment map. The camera-to-object vector can be defined as the difference between the vertex position and the camera position (through the use of the built-in view_position variable).

For this shader, you only need to do the reflection calculations on the vertex shader to maximize shader efficiency. You will be asked to repeat the same process per-pixel in the exercises at the end of the chapter. After you calculate the reflection vector, it simply needs to be passed to the pixel shader, where it will be used to read from the environment map. Doing so yields the following vertex shader code:

```
float4x4 view_proj_matrix;
float4 view_position;
struct VS_OUTPUT
{
   float4 Pos:      POSITION;
   float2 TexCoord: TEXCOORD0;
   float3 Reflect:  TEXCOORD1;
};

VS_OUTPUT vs_main(float4 inPos: POSITION, float3 inNormal: NORMAL,
                  float2 inTxr: TEXCOORD0)
{
   VS_OUTPUT Out;

   // Compute the projected position and send out the texture coordinates
   Out.Pos = mul(view_proj_matrix, inPos);
   Out.TexCoord = inTxr;

   // Compute the reflection vector
```

```
    Out.Reflect = -reflect(view_position-inPos,inNormal);

    return Out;
}
```

Notice the negative sign in front of the `reflect` function call. Because you are tracing the reflection from its destination to its source, you need to invert the resulting vector from the `reflect` function so that it points in the right direction within the environment cube-map. The pixel shader code simply needs to take in the reflection direction vector and sample the environment map by using the `texCUBE` function. Taking this environment value, proper reflection can be done by adding it to the object's texture to create glossiness on it. Following is an example of how this can be done, assuming a material with 40 percent reflectivity:

```
sampler Wood;
sampler EnvMap;
float4 ps_main(float2 inTxr: TEXCOORD0,float3 inReflect: TEXCOORD1) : COLOR
{
    // Output texture color with reflection map
    return 0.6*tex2D(Wood,inTxr)+0.4*texCUBE(EnvMap,inReflect);
}
```

With this shader compiled and running, your output should look similar to that shown in Figure 11.4. The complete version of this shader is included on the CD-ROM as `shader_2.rfx`.

Figure 11.4 Screenshot of the reflection shader in action.

Refraction

On the other end of the spectrum is the refraction effect. Translucent materials, such as glass, let rays of light through their surface. However, as I mentioned in Chapter 7, these rays of light are affected by the differences in density between the two media they cross, causing the rays of light to be deviated. This deviation is defined by Snell's Law, described through illustration and equation in Figure 11.5.

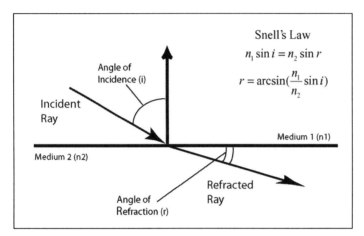

Figure 11.5 How refraction happens, and a description of the Snell's Law equation.

As you can see from the equation in Figure 11.5, the relationship between entering and exiting angles is dependent on the ratio of the index of refraction between the two media involved. The index of refraction is defined as the ratio between the two surface densities, that is, IOR = n1/n2. Table 11.1 summarizes the IOR (index of refraction) for many common materials.

Keep in mind that the IOR generally varies slightly in relationship to the color of light. The values given in Table 11.1 assume a midrange yellow-colored light. In the second exercise at the end of this chapter, I will ask you to expand on the refraction shader to consider the color of light in the refraction equation.

Table 11.1 Refraction Indexes for Various Materials

Material	Refraction Index
Air	1.00
Ice	1.31
Alcohol	1.32
Water	1.33
Plastic	1.46
Plexiglass	1.51
Glass	1.52
Emerald	1.58
Mercury	1.62
Ruby	1.76
Diamond	2.42

With this, writing a refraction shader should be a simple matter of taking our previous shader and substituting the `reflect` function call with the `refract` one. However, at the time of this writing, the `refract` function does not always work as expected. Because of this, we will take the long way to solving the problem.

The first step in determining the refraction is to take the view vector and apply a dot product with the surface normal. As you may remember, the dot product of two vectors essentially gives you the cosine of the angle between the two vectors. However, to solve Snell's equation, you need the sine and not the cosine of the angle. This can be resolved by using the following identity: **sine = sqrt(1 – cosine*cosine)**.

With this result, you can use your refraction indices to deduce the angle of the exiting ray. However, this angle only gives us a direction, not a vector! Because the refracted ray will be in the same plane as that formed by the surface normal and the incident ray of light, you can determine a 3D basis from the two vectors and then use the sine/cosine of the refracted ray angle to define the refracted ray vector.

The following code shows how this can be done:

```
float4x4 view_proj_matrix;
float4 view_position;
struct VS_OUTPUT
{
    float4 Pos:      POSITION;
    float2 TexCoord: TEXCOORD0;
    float3 Refract:  TEXCOORD1;
};

VS_OUTPUT vs_main(float4 inPos: POSITION, float3 inNormal: NORMAL,
                  float2 inTxr: TEXCOORD0)
{
    VS_OUTPUT Out;

    // Compute the projected position and send out the texture coordinates
    Out.Pos = mul(view_proj_matrix, inPos);
    Out.TexCoord = inTxr;

    float3 viewVec = normalize(view_position - inPos);

    // Compute the reflection vector using Snell's Law
    // the refract HLSL function does not always work properly
    // n_i * sin(theta_i) = n_r  * sin(theta_r)

    // sin(theta_i) : Determine the sine of the incident vector
```

```
    float cosine = dot(viewVec, inNormal);
    float sine = sqrt(1 - cosine * cosine);

    // sin(theta_r) : Determine cosine of the refracted vector
    // Note that the saturate(x) function is equivalent to
    // using clamp(0,1,x). Also, 1.14 is the IOR for this
    // shader.
    float sine2 = saturate(1.14 * sine);
    float cosine2 = sqrt(1 - sine2 * sine2);

    // Determine the refraction vector be using the normal and tangent
    // vectors as basis to determine the refraction direction
    float3 x = -inNormal;
    float3 y = normalize(cross(cross(viewVec, inNormal), inNormal));
    Out.Refract = x * cosine2 + y * sine2;

    return Out;
}
```

On the pixel shader side, all you need to do is sample the environment map and output the color as the following code does:

```
sampler Wood;
sampler EnvMap;
float4 ps_main(float2 inTxr: TEXCOORD0,float3 inRefract: TEXCOORD1) : COLOR
{
    // Output texture color with reflection map
    return texCUBE(EnvMap,inRefract);
}
```

With this shader compiled and running, your output should look similar to the one shown in Figure 11.6. The complete version of this shader is included on the CD-ROM as shader_3.rfx in the directory for this chapter. You may have noticed the gray border on the sides of the object. This is a natural phenomenon that I will address in the next section.

Figure 11.6 Rendering output for the final refraction shader.

Walking Hand in Hand

As you have seen from the rendering for the refraction shader, there are regions where no refraction occurs, and the result is a grayish color. The reason behind this result is not a coding error or similar glitch, but a natural phenomenon that occurs when dealing with refraction.

If you look at a container of water, such as an aquarium, dead-on, you will see through the water without any difficulty. However, if you look at the same container from a shallow angle, it will not be transparent anymore and will start behaving more like a mirror.

This phenomenon happens because refraction will stop happening past a certain angle, called the *critical angle*. At this angle, the refraction angle is equal to 90 degrees, and any incident rays past this angle exhibit a phenomenon called *total internal reflection* (or TIR), which in essence means that the surface will then behave as a mirror instead of being transparent. Figure 11.7 shows the transition of a refractive material towards TIR.

As you can see, because of total internal reflection, reflection and refraction actually go hand in hand, and this is exactly the next shader you will be writing. But before you can do so, you need to find out how the reflection and refraction combine.

We know that refraction will stop happening when the critical angle is, hit or in other words, when the refraction angle is equal to 90 degrees. Because you already have the sine and cosine of the exiting angle, you can use this value to determine the correct ratio of reflected and refracted environment. Because the sine of this angle is already in the zero to one range, it makes a great candidate to be used as a blending factor.

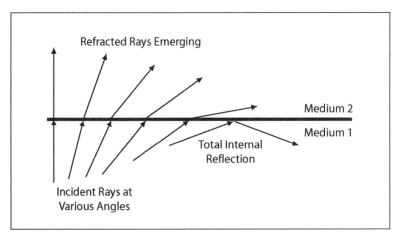

Figure 11.7 Illustration of how the total internal reflection phenomenon happens and the relationship between reflected and refracted light.

After you determine the blending factors for both reflection and refraction, which will also be passed to the pixel shader through one of the TEXCOORD variables, combining the two effects is simply a matter of putting the two code bases together and passing the blend factors, the reflection vectors, and the refraction vectors on to the pixel shader. Once the changes are done, you should end up with the following vertex shader code:

```
float4x4 view_proj_matrix;
float4 view_position;
struct VS_OUTPUT
{
    float4 Pos:      POSITION;
    float2 TexCoord: TEXCOORD0;
    float3 Refract:  TEXCOORD1;
    float3 Reflect:  TEXCOORD2;
    float2 Factors:  TEXCOORD3;
};

VS_OUTPUT vs_main(float4 inPos: POSITION, float3 inNormal: NORMAL,
                  float2 inTxr: TEXCOORD0)
{
    VS_OUTPUT Out;

    // Compute the projected position and send out the texture coordinates
    Out.Pos = mul(view_proj_matrix, inPos);
    Out.TexCoord = inTxr;

    float3 viewVec = normalize(view_position - inPos);

    // Compute reflection
    Out.Reflect = reflect(-viewVec,inNormal);

    // Compute the reflection vector using Snell's Law
    // the refract HLSL function does not always work properly
    // n_i * sin(theta_i) = n_r  * sin(theta_r)

    // sin(theta_i)
    float cosine = dot(viewVec, inNormal);
    float sine = sqrt(1 - cosine * cosine);

    // sin(theta_r)
    float sine2 = saturate(1.14 * sine);
    float cosine2 = sqrt(1 - sine2 * sine2);
```

```
// Determine the refraction vector be using the normal and tangent
// vectors as basis to determine the refraction direction
float3 x = -inNormal;
float3 y = normalize(cross(cross(viewVec, inNormal), inNormal));
Out.Refract = x * cosine2 + y * sine2;

// Determine proper reflection and refraction factors through
// a Fresnel approximation. (x = reflect, y = refract)
Out.Factors.x = sine2;
Out.Factors.y = (1 - sine2);

return Out;
}
```

The pixel shader for this combined reflection/refraction shader needs to take in three values. The first two are the lookup vectors for the environment cubemap lookup for the reflection and refraction, and the last value is the blending factors to use. Once you have looked up both environment values, combining them is a straightforward process.

Keep in mind that if you are applying a texture to your object, the refraction environment map value for refraction needs to be modulated with the object texture value because the texture has the effect of tinting the rays of light as they traverse the object. The following is an example pixel shader code detailing how the refraction and reflection can be combined:

```
sampler Wood;
sampler EnvMap;
float4 ps_main(float2 inTxr: TEXCOORD0,float3 inRefract: TEXCOORD1,
               float3 inReflect: TEXCOORD2,float2 inFct: TEXCOORD3) : COLOR
{
   // Output texture color with reflection map
   // Note the addition of 0.4 to the reflection/refraction
   // results to ensure a certain amount of ambient lighting
   return inFct.x * texCUBE(EnvMap,inReflect) +
       (inFct.y * texCUBE(EnvMap,inRefract) + 0.4)
               * tex2D(Wood,inTxr);
}
```

With this shader compiled and running, your output should look similar to the one shown in Figure 11.8. The complete version of this shader is included on the CD-ROM as shader_4.rfx in the directory for this chapter.

Figure 11.8 Rendering for the combined reflection and refraction shader.

Building Dynamic Environment Maps

All these reflection and refraction shenanigans are nice for static scenes with one object, but when your scene gets more dynamic or contains many objects, our current scheme falls short. Because the environment map contains only a static, prebuilt scene, any reflections or refractions done with it will not contain any other objects in your scene. Doesn't make much sense to do refraction on a teapot if you will not see the elephant right behind it, right?

The common solution to this problem is to use a dynamic cubemap instead of a static one. In this section I will briefly review how this can be achieved. Unfortunately, at the time of this writing, RenderMonkey does not support using cubemaps as render targets, so you will not be able to implement a shader with this technique.

Because a cubemap is essentially a collection of six textures, building a cubemap dynamically requires filling those textures one-by-one. When rendering with DirectX, each face of a cubemap can be accessed as an individual texture, which, in turn, can also be used as a render target. So the overall process is to render your scene six times, once for each face of the cube, setting up the camera so that it matches the point of view from that particular cubemap face.

note

At the time of this writing, cubemap textures are a special texture format that can only be read from .DDS files. This means that you cannot directly render to these textures, or you will need to use specialized tools such as the DirectX Texture Tool to author such textures. Also note that these textures can only be accessed through the use of the `texCUBE HLSL` functions because you need to tell the hardware you want to use a cubemap.

Because of the nature of a cubemap, rendering a face is a simple process. The camera needs to be positioned at the point in space where you want to build your environment map and must face the direction that matches the particular face you are rendering. You may want to refer to Figure 11.1 to see how cubemap faces correspond to a specific axis direction in world space.

The only other setting required for your camera to render cubemap faces is the field of view angle. The field of view defines the angle of the viewing frustum cone that the camera defines in space. Because all cubemap faces are of equal size, you need to set the FOV for your camera to 90 degrees. Doing so ensures that the edges for each cubemap face properly correspond and that the resulting environment appears seamless.

One last consideration when creating dynamic environment maps is performance. Because you must render each face individually, your scene needs to be rendered six times every time you update the cubemap. This may become a performance issue for some applications, and you may need to avoid updating the environment map every frame and try to spread the cost over time as much as possible.

It's Your Turn!

There you have it, your very own reflection and refraction shaders. The following exercises will ask you to expand on those shaders to try out your own shading skills. And as always, the solutions to these exercises are in Appendix D.

Exercise 1: DOING IT ALL PER-PIXEL

Starting with the combined reflection/refraction shader developed a few pages ago, modify it to do all of its operations on a per-pixel basis. This task should be simple and familiar by now, especially considering that per-pixel lighting was the topic of Chapter 10, so no hints will be given on how to perform this.

Exercise 2: COLOR-BASED REFRACTION

As mentioned earlier, the index of refraction, or IOR, for a particular material varies in function based on the color of the light that passes through the object. So far, you have assumed a constant IOR and have ignored this fact.

For this exercise, you are asked to implement a refraction shader which considers the color dispersion due to the variation of the IOR based on the color of light. To do this, start off with the per-pixel shader developed in the previous exercise and adapt it so that a different refraction vector will be calculated for each color component (red, green, and blue) and sample the environment once for each color component. Do not focus on trying to correctly determine an IOR for each color; simply use three nearby values.

What's Next?

As you learned in this chapter, the interaction of light with translucent materials has many aspects for you to consider, the main two being reflection and refraction. Although the concepts behind those two effects are simple, they require you to render components of your scene that are not necessarily easy to access.

This is where environment maps save the day! By estimating a full environment from a specific point in your scene, you can take advantage of those powerful effects and significantly enrich your renderings. However, when dealing with more dynamic environments, you will have to take advantage of the nature of cubemaps and dynamically build an environment map by rendering your scene to each face of the cubemap.

Now that you are on the topic of the interaction of light with surface materials, the next chapter will discuss the topic of *Bi-Directional Refractance Functions*, or BDRFs. These functions help define the properties for materials such as velvet, where the relationship between the lighting and viewing angle cannot be described in terms of simple diffuse and specular lighting.

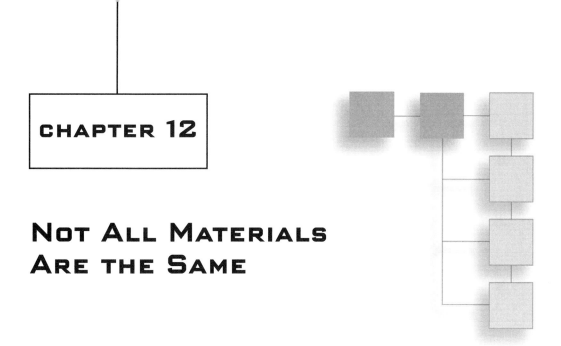

CHAPTER 12

NOT ALL MATERIALS ARE THE SAME

As you know by now, Part 3 mainly focuses on different materials and their behaviors when they are lit. So far, I have discussed simple lighting models, such as diffuse and specular, as well as reflection and refraction.

Although these models work well for many objects and materials, when it comes to lighting, no material actually follows the models I have described. They are merely simplifications and approximations that were created to enable us to light objects in a realistic manner while keeping in mind the performance limitations that 3D rendering hardware imposes.

This works fine for many cases, but every once in a while, you want to render a material that seems to defy the laws of physics when it comes to lighting. Don't worry, the material isn't really breaking any laws of nature; it's simply behaving in a manner that isn't consistent with our simplified models. Probably one of the most significant examples of this is velvet.

As you may have noticed from looking at velvet, although it seems to have a diffuse lighting property, the intensity of lighting is not only dependent on the incident light angle, but also on the viewer's angle. Although this may sound like a specular behavior, the material does not display sharp highlights as a specular material does. Figure 12.1 illustrates the lighting distribution based on a specific incoming light angle. The lobe represents the proportional amount of light that is reflected relative to the viewing direction for a specific incoming light direction.

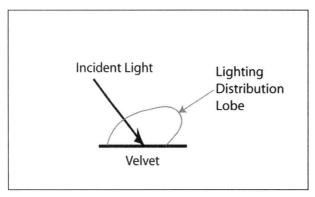

Figure 12.1 The lighting distribution lobe for a velvet-like material.

As you can see in Figure 12.1, the lighting distribution lobe for a velvet-like material follows neither the specular nor the diffuse model. The shape of the lobe resembles more a flattened diffuse lobe, where more of the light is re-emitted at sharp angles.

As discussed in Chapter 9, "May There Be Light," this is because the minuscule hairs on the surface of the velvet material tend to reflect the rays in a semi-random way at angles sharper than the normal reflection angle. Figure 12.2 illustrates how the light actually interacts with a velvet surface.

This being said, how can we light such materials? The answer comes from taking into account the angles of both the light and the viewer. One such way of representing this type of lighting is by using a *Bi-Directional Refractance Distribution Function*, commonly referred to as BRDF.

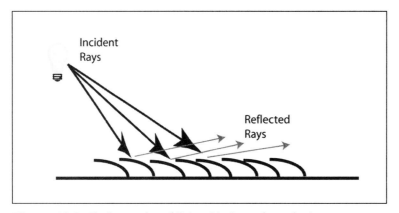

Figure 12.2 The interaction of light with the surface of velvet.

BRDFs Are Your Friends

BRDFs are one of many ways to represent lighting in a more correct way. One thing you have to remember when dealing with an algorithm such as a BRDF is that it does not provide a "fits-all" equation to solve all your problems, but is more of a framework on which you can build.

There are a few assumptions with BRDFs that you must know before you get started. The most important one comes from the *Bi-Directional* part of its name. In essence, this means that if you have a set of lighting and viewing vectors, switching them around has no impact on the lighting result. This restricts the factors you must consider when lighting an object with a BRDF. The only things you need to consider when rendering lighting with Bi-Directional Refractance Distribution Functions are the angles, which are defined by the light vector, eye vector, and angles on the plane of the surface. This is illustrated in Figure 12.3.

In Figure 12.3, notice the light (incident) and view vector (reflected) angles. These are the same vectors you dealt with in regular diffuse and specular lighting. However, the basic BRDF equation also refers to the angles of the view vector along the plane of the material's surface, which is defined by the surface's tangent space. Some materials have lighting that is not only dependent on the angles in the light/view plane, but also on the angle along the plane of the surface. These materials, such as brushed metal, are called *anisotropic*. On the other hand, many materials, such as velvet, have a uniform distribution and do not depend on this angle, and will light the same no matter which direction the material is viewed from; they are called *isotropic*. Because a great majority of materials are isotropic, I will focus on them in this chapter. Just remember that what you learn here can easily be applied to anisotropic materials also.

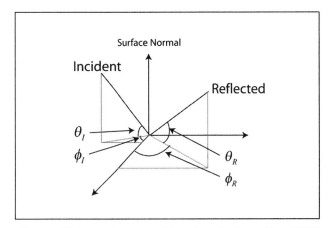

Figure 12.3 Angles to consider when dealing with a BRDF.

Now, looking at the equation in Figure 12.3, you see that a BRDF is defined by this set of angles and a function, but no equation is given. This is because the idea behind Bi-Directional Refractance Distribution Functions only gives you a function that establishes the relationship between lighting and a set of parameters, but the function itself can be defined on a per-material basis.

Unfortunately, there is no "fits-all" equation, nor is there a standard way of discovering the BRDF function for a specific material. All the results come from observation and measurement. Because we have discussed the case of lighting a velvet-like material in Chapter 9, it seems like a natural place to start.

Soft and Velvety

As mentioned earlier, velvet is one of those materials that seem to defy the rules of physics when it comes to lighting. Because of this, standard models like diffuse and specular lighting just won't do. This is one of those cases where a BRDF can be used to represent more accurately the lighting for such a material. Before you can consider defining a function to represent the lighting of velvet, however, you need to determine why it is lit so differently.

For this, you need to consider what composes the surface of a velvet-like material. The surface of velvet is composed of a multitude of tiny little hairs. Those hairs cause the incident light to be reflected at an angle greater than normally occurs with specular lighting. However, because of the random distribution of the hairs on the surface, velvet lighting also has a softer component than specular lighting. Figure 12.2 shows how light interacts with the surface of a velvet-like material.

Looking at the interaction of light with the surface of the velvet material, in addition to looking at the lighting distribution lobe shown in Figure 12.1, gives you a good idea of how light interacts with the surface of the material. Because you are working on the assumption that velvet is an isotropic material, all you need to consider is the incident and view angle about the surface normal.

At this point, you understand the behavior that governs the lighting of velvet, but you still need to define a BRDF function that will approximate velvet closely enough. One approach would be to take lighting measurements at different angle combinations and somehow find a function that matches the samplings as closely as possible. We'll get into that a bit later in this chapter.

Because the behavior of velvet is somewhat simpler than many other materials, easier approaches can be taken. In 1941, a researcher named Minneart came up with a lighting equation for the subtle lighting of anisotropic surfaces and darkening at the edges of objects. As it turns out, his lighting model can be easily adapted to the lighting of velvet. Figure 12.4 illustrates this simplified equation, which will be used to shade our velvet materials. The figure also shows the estimated lighting distribution lobe for the Minneart equation. The k factor in the equation is a constant that will be defined for a specific material to control its softness.

$$I = \cos(\theta_I)^k \cos(\theta_R)^{-k}$$
$$\theta_I = \text{Incident Angle}$$
$$\theta_R = \text{Viewer Angle}$$

Figure 12.4 Minneart lighting equation and sample lighting distribution lobe.

To implement velvet lighting in the form of a shader, you can simply take the Minneart equation from Figure 12.4 and apply it to a shader. To start, all you need is a simple workspace that renders a simple object. Because you are doing the lighting on a per-pixel basis, the vertex shader needs to send in the appropriate information to the pixel shader, which consists of the incident and view angle relative to the surface normal. This is similar to the diffuse and specular lighting shader developed previously. Because velvet is considered an isotropic material, all you need to send to the pixel shader is the surface normal, light direction, and eye vector. The vertex shader code to accomplish this is as follows:

```
struct VS_OUTPUT
{
    float4 Pos:      POSITION;
    float3 Normal:   TEXCOORD0;
    float3 LightDir: TEXCOORD1;
    float3 EyeVect:  TEXCOORD2;
};

VS_OUTPUT vs_main(float4 inPos: POSITION, float3 inNormal: NORMAL)
{
    VS_OUTPUT Out;

    // Compute the projected position for this vertex and the
    // object space normal
    Out.Pos = mul(view_proj_matrix, inPos);
    Out.Normal = inNormal;

    // Determine the light direction vector. This assumes that the vector
    // is constant relative to the camera.
    Out.LightDir.xyz = mul(inv_view_matrix,
                       normalize(Light1_Position - inPos));

    // Determine the eye vector for the light
    // The value of (0,0,100,1) is an arbitrary
    // position for our light.
```

```
    Out.EyeVect = -normalize(mul(inv_view_matrix,float4(0,0,100,1))
                    +inPos);

    return Out;
}
```

On the pixel shader side, you will need to take in the three vectors and determine the light angle and view angle through the use of dot product. You also need to raise the result to the power defined by the Minneart equation, which is stored in the variable Velvet_Exponent. Once you have determined these values, all that is needed to determine the lighting intensity is to multiply both values together. This yields the following pixel shader code. Note that the Minneart lighting function has been put in a function called Light_Velvet:

```
float4x4 view_proj_matrix;
float4 Light1_Position;
float4x4 inv_view_matrix;
float4x4 view_matrix;
float4 Light_Velvet(float3 Normal, float3 EyeVect, float3 LightDir,
                    float4 LightColor)
{
    // Compute both the light and eye angle about the surface
    // normal for the surface
    float l = pow( clamp(dot(Normal, LightDir),0,1),
            Velvet_Exponent );
    float e = pow( clamp(dot(Normal, EyeVect),0,1),
            -Velvet_Exponent );

    // Compute final lighting. Which is defined as the product
    // of the cosine of both the light and eye vectors. We clamp
    // the lighting with a minimum of 0.2 to ensure a minimal level
    // of ambient lighting.
    return LightColor * clamp(l*e,0.2,1);
}


float4 Light1_Color;
float Velvet_Exponent;
float4 ps_main(float3 inNormal:TEXCOORD0, float3 LightDir:TEXCOORD1,
            float3 EyeVect:TEXCOORD2) : COLOR
{
    // Call the lighting function and return the result
    return Light_Velvet(inNormal,-normalize(EyeVect),
                    normalize(LightDir),Light1_Color);
}
```

In regards to the Velvet_Exponent variable, a good exponent value to use for simulating velvet is 0.225. But you may wish to experiment with different values to see how the exponent affects the lighting of your object.

Once compiled, the result should be similar to that shown in Figure 12.5. You can see in the illustration how soft and velvety the shader makes the surface look. You can find the complete and compiled version of this shader on the CD-ROM as shader_1.rfx.

You may have noticed that although the equation is fairly simple, you will pay the costs of calculating the angles and powers for every pixel on your object. In addition, such equations cannot be evaluated on the per-2.0 pixel shader models. When dealing with isotropic BRDF models, you only need to take two variables into account, both of which are in the zero-to-one range, making it ideal for the use of a 2D lookup texture. In the first exercise at the end of this chapter, you will be invited to implement the same Minneart-based velvet shader by using a lookup texture instead of computing the full equation.

When doing an isotropic BRDF with a lookup texture, you will have two input variables, which correspond to the light and viewer angles. Making those inputs correspond to the U and V axes of the texture makes the process easy. You need to pre-compute the results of the lighting equation into a texture and then simply use the input parameters to perform a regular texture lookup. Although this may seem convoluted, it can be much more efficient than computing complex functions in real-time inside your pixel shader.

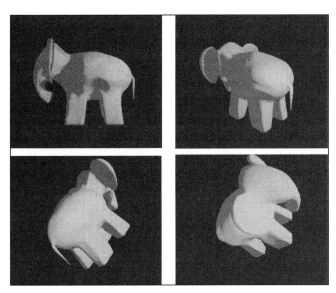

Figure 12.5 Minneart velvet shader shown in action at different lighting angles.

Determining BRDFs

The velvet shader you just developed was based on a lighting equation developed by Minneart. This equation and coefficients come mostly from observation and experimentation, and although it wasn't initially conceived for velvet lighting, it can be used to approximate the look of a velvet-like material. But what can you do when dealing with other, more complex materials? How can you determine an appropriate approximation?

The reality is that it can be hard to determine an exact model to estimate a material. The simplest approach is to develop a general form of the BRDF function, which can be adapted to match the characteristics of different materials. The best way to perform this is to take several measurements of a material and then use a general curve matching function to adapt its coefficients to match the characteristics of the material as closely as possible.

Researchers at Columbia University and Utrecht University have collaborated in a joint effort to explore the visual appearance of real-world surfaces. Their research has yielded a database of BRDF measurements for over 60 common, real-world materials. In addition to these BRDF samples, they have created best-matching functions of those materials for use with the Oren-Nayer or Koenderink lighting models. The database can be found online at http://www1.cs.columbia.edu/CAVE/curet/.

The simplest form of curve matching the Curet team has employed was to use the Oren-Nayer lighting model. This model uses three coefficients to represent a variety of mostly diffuse materials. Figure 12.6 shows the equation used by the Oren-Nayer model.

As you can see by the equation, the model itself is fairly hefty for only three coefficients. This is why I will use this model instead of the even more complex 5 and 55 coefficient models. Table 12.1 gives the Oren-Nayer coefficients for some of the most interesting models.

The interesting aspect of such an approach to BRDF is that after you sample the material and determine the proper curve matching function parameters, most materials can be represented with a single function. For more information on how you can accomplish this, please refer to the Curet Web site.

$$I = R(\cos\theta_I)(A + B \max[0_R \cos(\phi - \phi_I)][\sin\alpha][\sin\beta])$$

Where:

$$R = \frac{\rho}{\pi} E \quad A = 1 - 0.5\left(\frac{\sigma^2}{\sigma^2 + 0.33}\right) \quad B = 0.45\left(\frac{\sigma^2}{\sigma^2 + 0.09}\right)$$

$$\alpha = \max(\theta_R, \theta_I) \quad \beta = \min(\theta_R, \theta_I) \quad \sigma = \text{Surface Roughness}$$

Figure 12.6 The Oren-Nayer lighting equation exposed.

Table 12.1 Oren-Nayer Coefficients for Common Materials

Material	Rho [rho]	Sigma	Kd
Artificial grass	0.026120	1.378872	0.993315
Brick	0.132886	0.893379	0.991720
Concrete	0.668533	0.600672	0.994044
Corduroy	0.439532	0.699112	0.972717
Cork	0.249295	0.659956	0.960105
Cotton	0.484087	0.482679	0.947116
Felt	0.386790	0.414686	0.944892
Foil	0.581514	0.252702	0.891302
Frosted glass	0.142109	0.416384	0.907097
Human skin	0.198588	0.579386	0.956055
Insulation	0.556606	0.136013	0.884576
Lambswool	0.325133	0.978133	0.966085
Leather	0.579367	0.179776	0.926559
Limestone	0.292841	0.413544	0.972684
Linen	0.251781	0.514593	0.958734
Loofah	0.527886	0.300436	0.973872
Moss	0.006588	0.542447	0.996590
Orange peel	0.526023	0.235808	0.876384
Plant	0.141438	0.758465	0.986035
Plaster	0.834116	0.362825	0.997624
Polyester	0.379962	0.576862	0.959845
Rabbit fur	0.457542	0.933632	0.973208
Roof shingle	0.195128	0.819147	0.997328
Rough plastic	0.480943	0.278057	0.969021
Rug	0.444769	0.566478	0.961640
Sandpaper	0.422396	0.513084	0.980324
Slate	0.030252	0.356822	0.974449
Sponge	0.301070	0.872413	0.967614
Stones	0.561534	1.107168	0.996424
Straw	0.282849	0.717587	0.978161
Styrofoam	0.477248	0.509725	0.956598
Terrycloth	0.619111	0.458514	0.973167
Velvet	0.171323	0.751002	0.990415
Wood	0.132031	0.598438	0.965061

Now that we have a more general approach to determining and rendering BRDFs, let's take the Oren-Nayer approach to reimplement the velvet shader previously developed. The Minneart lighting equation served as a specific purpose lighting function which represented velvet well. On the other hand, the Oren-Nayer function was developed to represent a broader class of BRDF functions.

Oren-Nayer Velvet

To implement an Oren–Nayer-based shader, you need to understand its equation. The first thing to notice is that the equation needs the surface normal, eye vector, light direction, and both of the tangent space angles. However, you do not need to worry about the tangent space angles because they can be determined with the use of the eye vector, surface normal, and light direction vectors. In essence, assuming you compute the Oren-Nayer equation on a per-pixel basis, all you need to pass the pixel shader is the surface normal, eye vector, and light direction vector. Doing so will give you the following vertex shader code:

```
float4x4 view_proj_matrix;
float4 Light1_Position;
float4x4 inv_view_matrix;
float4x4 view_matrix;
struct VS_OUTPUT
{
   float4 Pos:      POSITION;
   float3 Normal:   TEXCOORD0;
   float3 LightDir: TEXCOORD1;
   float3 EyeVect:  TEXCOORD2;
};

VS_OUTPUT vs_main(float4 inPos: POSITION, float3 inNormal: NORMAL)
{
   VS_OUTPUT Out;

   // Compute the projected position for this vertex and the
   // object space normal
   Out.Pos = mul(view_proj_matrix, inPos);
   Out.Normal = inNormal;

   // Determine the light direction vector. This assumes that the vector
   // is constant relative to the camera.
   Out.LightDir.xyz = mul(inv_view_matrix,
                      normalize(Light1_Position - inPos));
```

```
// Determine the eye vector for the light
Out.EyeVect = -normalize(mul(inv_view_matrix,float4(0,0,100,1))
                +inPos);

    return Out;
}
```

The pixel shader is where things get a little more complicated; the first things you need to determine are the angles corresponding to the light and eye vectors. This can easily be done with a dot product and will give you the following code:

```
float NdotL = dot(Normal, LightDir);
float NdotE = dot(Normal, EyeVect);
```

Beyond this, you will also need to determine the sine, cosine, and tangent of each vector. The cosine is given to you explicitly through the use of the dot product. The sine itself can be determined by computing the length of the cross product between the vectors. The following code shows how:

```
float sinTheta_r = length(cross(EyeVect,Normal));
float sinTheta_i = length(cross(LightDir,Normal));
```

The tangent is simply defined by sine/cosine and is easy to calculate from the sine and cosine values you have already determined.

The next step is to determine the *azimuth* angle, which is the angle defined by the projection of our vectors into the plane of the surface. The azimuth angle is equivalent to the phi angles illustrated in Figure 12.3 . This is a little more complicated but can be determined by projecting the eye and light vectors onto the surface plane, using the surface normal, and computing the dot product of the two vectors. This gives the following code:

```
float3 E_p = normalize(EyeVect-NdotE*Normal);
float3 L_p = normalize(LightDir-NdotL*Normal);
float cosAzimuth = dot(E_p, L_p);
```

This is all you need to compute the Oren-Nayer lighting component. Take the calculated values and plug them into the equation. The pixel shader code to do this is as follows:

```
float inten = rho_pi * cosTheta_i *
    (A + B * max(0, cosAzimuth) *
    max(sinTheta_r, sinTheta_i) * min(tanTheta_i, tanTheta_r));
```

The only thing missing to complete this shader is determining the proper values for A, B, and ρ_π (rho_pi) within the Oren-Nayer shader. If you take the coefficients from Table 12.1 and input them into the factored equations in Figure 12.6, you will arrive at the conclusion that A = 0.68, B = 0.38, and ρ_π = 0.054.

note

You may notice the low value on ρ_π for the velvet shader. Taking a look at the equation in Figure 12.6, you may notice that ρ_π actually translates into the maximum lighting intensity for the shader. Because of the low value, you may need to manually skew this number or introduce a global intensity multiplier to enable you to adjust the scale of this value.

Putting all the little bits of shader code together gives you the following shader:

```
float4 Light1_Color;
float Velvet_Exponent;
float PI;
float rho_pi;
float A;
float B;
float4 Light_Velvet(float3 Normal, float3 EyeVect, float3 LightDir,
                    float4 LightColor)
{
   // calculate all the dot products
   float NdotL = dot(Normal, LightDir);
   float NdotE = dot(Normal, EyeVect);

   // calculate the zenith angles
   float sinTheta_r = length(cross(EyeVect,Normal));
   float cosTheta_r = max(NdotE,0.001);
   float sinTheta_i = length(cross(LightDir,Normal));
   float cosTheta_i = max(NdotL,0.001);
   float tanTheta_i = sinTheta_i / cosTheta_i;
   float tanTheta_r = sinTheta_r / cosTheta_r;

   // calculate the azimuth angles
   float3 E_p = normalize(EyeVect-NdotE*Normal);
   float3 L_p = normalize(LightDir-NdotL*Normal);
   float cosAzimuth = dot(E_p, L_p);

   // Compute final lighting
   float inten = rho_pi * cosTheta_i *
        (A + B * max(0, cosAzimuth) *
        max(sinTheta_r, sinTheta_i) * min(tanTheta_i, tanTheta_r));

   return LightColor * clamp(inten,0,1);
}
```

```
float4 ps_main(float3 inNormal:TEXCOORD0, float3 LightDir:TEXCOORD1,
               float3 EyeVect:TEXCOORD2) : COLOR
{
    // Simply call the lighting function and return the result
    return Light_Velvet(inNormal,-normalize(EyeVect),
                        normalize(LightDir),Light1_Color);
}
```

Once you have compiled this shader and input the proper coefficients, the result should be similar to what is shown in Figure 12.8. You can find the complete and compiled version of this shader on the CD-ROM as shader_2.rfx. In the second exercise at the end of this chapter, you will be asked to implement a few other BRDF shaders by using the Oren-Nayer model.

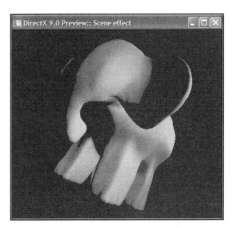

As you can see from the results of the shader, the Oren-Nayer approach yields a reasonable estimation to rendering velvet through a BRDF. Unfortunately, as you can see from the shader code and its execution speed, even a three-coefficient model is prohibitive, performance-wise. Because of this, anything more than a simple Oren-Nayer implementation cannot be considered for anything in real-time.

Figure 12.7 Rendering results for the Oren–Nayer-based velvet shader.

On the bright side, data from a BRDF observation database, such as the Curet database, can be used in combination with lookup textures to reproduce a BRDF with minimal computational costs. The trickier part when dealing with lookup textures is building them in the first place. However, this is outside the scope of this chapter and will not be explained further. For more information, refer to the Curet Web site.

It's Your Turn!

BRDFs are a great way for you to represent lighting on somewhat unusual materials. The following exercises will ask you to expand on those shaders and try out your own shading skills. As always, the solutions to these exercises are in Appendix D.

Exercise 1: USING LOOKUP TEXTURES

In this chapter, you developed a velvet shader by using the Minneart equation. However, computing this equation on a per-pixel basis can be prohibitive. One solution to work around this is to precompute the result of the equation in a texture and then use this texture as a lookup table for the results based on the light and view angles about the surface normal.

Implementing this shader is relatively simple, but you need to find a way to bake the results of the Minneart equation into a texture; this is the major challenge for this exercise.

For this shader, start with the Minneart equation and not the Curet database data. Using the Minneart equation and logic, you should be able to determine how to build the lookup texture with ease.

Exercise 2: MULTIPLE BRDFs

For this exercise, you simply need to take the Oren-Nayer BRDF shader developed in this chapter to implement various materials using data from the Curet database. This exercise is simply a matter of taking the Bi-Directional Refractance Distribution Function parameters for the Oren-Nayer implementation and calculating the A, B, and ρ_π coefficients for the shader. For this exercise, you are asked to implement the BRDF shader for felt, skin, and corduroy.

What's Next?

Bi-Directional Refractance Distribution Functions, or BRDFs, are a great approach for determining and rendering the true lighting characteristics of materials. However, because there is no general method for determining the lighting function for a specific material, empirical approaches must be taken.

By using experimentation, sampling, and observation, estimating functions can be determined which reasonably approximate the lighting of a material, such as the Minneart equation for a velvet-like material. However, some materials cannot be represented so easily with a specific equation. For such cases, the ideal approach is the one taken by the Curet group and involves taking many lighting samples at different angles and using a curve matching function such as the Oren-Nayer lighting model.

Even with such approaches, the cost of execution can make such models prohibitive and almost impossible for real-time renderings. In such cases, it is generally a good idea to take advantage of the rendering hardware architectures to represent the results of those complex equations as textures. Such textures can then be used as lookup textures within your shader, making the whole lighting process more efficient and generic.

As you have seen, the use of BRDFs can go a long way in making complex materials look more realistic when rendered. In combination with more basic lighting models, you can create much more realistic scenes through better representation of the lighting in your scene.

Now that you know more about lighting models, how about creating materials from scratch? What if you could render a wood material without applying a wood texture to the object? In the next chapter, I will show you how you can leverage the power of the shader architectures to create new materials procedurally from scratch.

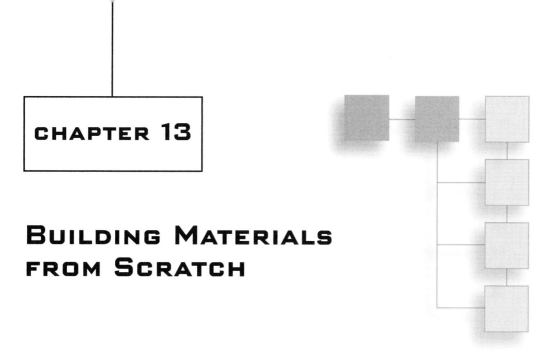

CHAPTER 13

BUILDING MATERIALS FROM SCRATCH

So far throughout this book, we have examined many different forms of materials. All of the preceding chapters concentrated on the texture or the lighting attributes of the materials. But all of them had one thing in common. The looks and texturing of the material were defined ahead of time.

Nature itself has an inherent randomness, which most computer rendered graphics do not capture. This is one reason computer graphics often look artificial. When you think of materials such as wood or marble, the randomness within the material is what makes it unique. Yes, you can have a texture that looks like wood, but then all of your wood looks the same, and the randomness factor goes away.

Wouldn't it be interesting to take advantage of this randomness to render such materials procedurally instead of relying on a prebuilt texture? In this chapter, I will show you a few techniques you can use to render materials in a procedural way where you do not need prebaked textures.

There are several techniques that can be used to achieve this. One of the most common techniques is using *Perlin* noise. This simple technique can be used to generate noise procedurally, and can be used to produce textures, such as clouds or wood. I will also take you through other techniques that can be used to render other noisy materials such as marble.

Later, we will explore how procedural techniques can be used to generate more complex materials, such as animating water. We'll start with the core of procedural materials, Perlin noise.

Turning Up the Noise!

Many materials and objects in nature have inherent random attributes. For example, trees and plants have well known shapes and randomness, which can be well approximated by *fractals*, mathematical functions combining both randomness and pattern repetition. On the other hand, some materials, such as wood or marble, have attributes that can be re-created through the clever use of simple noise functions such as Perlin noise.

---

note

Fractals are defined as non-regular geometric shapes that have the same degree of non-regularity on all scales. From a non-mathematical point of view, they are mathematical formulations that can describe how a stone at the base of a foothill can resemble the mountain from which it came.

Generally, when rendering those types of noisy materials, you depend on artist-built assets. However, this means that if you want some variety within your scene, you will be dependent on getting multiple versions of similar assets. On the other hand, it would be nice to be able to have a self-generating material for which you can adjust parameters and automatically get a countless number of variations with a single shader.

This is where noise generation shaders can come in handy. By determining the random attributes of materials such as marble, you can use a general purpose noise shader to create textures for your material, which will be random based on the parameters you supply. But before you can attack those parameters, let's look at how noise can be generated. There are several methods that can be used to produce useful noise. So let's start by checking out some of the fundamentals when dealing with noise.

In Figure 13.1, you can see a noise texture that has been generated with Adobe Photoshop. The noise in this texture was created with a general random number generation function. This essentially means the noise has a Gaussian distribution, which in turn means that the noise has a perfectly random distribution and is unpredictable.

Figure 13.1 Noise texture created through the use of a general function.

Although such a noise function can have some applications, it is not well suited for use in the generation of procedural materials for several reasons. First of all, if you are to make materials from scratch, you want to have a noise function that can be re-created on demand. Imagine the case where an artist sets up a procedural wood texture within your scene: now if the texture were to look different every single time the material was regenerated, it would be frustrating because you would have no control over the appearance of the scene.

The second thing to consider when deciding what makes a noise function practical is its smoothness. Because you will be using the generated noise in a rendering environment where the precision is unknown, the noise itself has to be sufficiently smooth and interpolatable. Imagine looking at a piece of marble from 100 meters away and then zooming in on a little part of the same piece. You want your noise function to not be discrete but continuous so you can have infinite detail when needed.

In regards to the first property of noise, this means that you need to define it, not in terms of a general random function, but a pseudo-random function, $R(x)$, which yields values that seem random but are the same for each x value.

Regarding the second property, we can get off a little easier here because of some properties of the rendering hardware. Imagine the same kind of noise texture shown in Figure 13.1 but in a one-dimensional space. You will have a discrete function, as shown in Figure 13.2, which defines specific values at integer intervals. As I said earlier, the function must be smooth or interpolatable so that any detail level can be rendered. In fact, the rendering hardware performs bilinear interpolation for free; that is, if you use lookup textures for your noise, the smoothing of the noise function is done automatically for you, as shown in Figure 13.2b. However, to limit blockiness artifacts resulting from the rendering hardware's interpolation, it is good practice to slightly blur the noise ahead of time to allow for better interpolation.

Remember when I said that the noise function in Figure 13.1 was useless. Well, it isn't completely useless. When using a technique such as Perlin noise, such a texture can be used as a base function to define a more complex final noise.

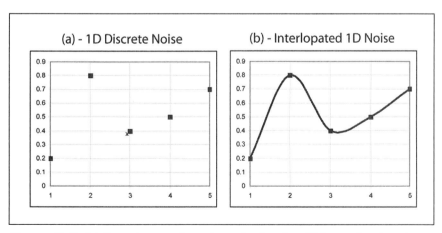

Figure 13.2 (a) Piecewise one-dimension noise function. (b) Interpolated version of the same noise function.

note

Perlin noise was created by Ken Perlin in the early 1980s as a way to create a noise texture primitive. This noise texture, or a combination of them, could be combined at different level of frequency to create various procedural materials. Because these noise textures could be generated on the fly, such texturing could be done without storing any offline textures. However, at this time, due to the performance requirements for generating Perlin noise functions, they are still created offline and joined together in real-time.

The approach behind Perlin noise is simple. By combining a set of simple noise functions of different frequencies, you can achieve a more complex noise function. Each noise function of varying frequency is called an octave and can be either a different noise function or the same noise function at a different scale. A one-dimensional example of this operation has been provided in Figure 13.3.

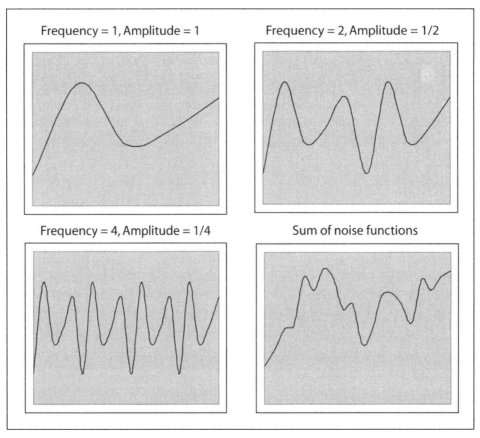

Figure 13.3 One-dimensional example of how several octaves of noise are combined to form some Perlin noise.

One note in regards to the way Perlin noise works. Because you will be combining several noise functions of different frequencies, if all textures are of the same resolution, higher frequency noise functions will be repeated. This has the consequence that the noise function, or texture, will need to be *tillable*, which means that the texture can be repeated without anyone noticing a seam between the repetitions.

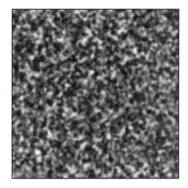

You may have noticed from Figure 13.3 that each octave was twice the frequency of the previous octave. This defines the persistence of the noise and does not need to be set to a value of two. Using different values can, in fact, yield interesting noise results.

Having focused only on one-dimensional noise, let's start looking at more useful noise functions in either two or three dimensions. By using a two-dimensional noise function, you can create several different textures, such as clouds or even marble. Figure 13.4 shows how 2D noise can be combined to generate a cloud-like texture. Don't worry about the details for now, I will address how clouds can be rendered in the next section.

Figure 13.4 Two-dimensional Perlin noise used to generate a cloud-like texture.

Three-dimensional noise function can be even handier. By taking advantage of your hardware's volume texture support, you can build 3D noise textures that can be used to render solid textures, such as wood. On the plus side, you can even use the third dimension as the time axis to create animated 2D textures, such as animated clouds.

I hope by now you have a better understanding of the basics of Perlin noise and its usefulness. I don't want to spend too much time on all the boring details but simply want to show you the basics. Now it is time to show you how to make Perlin noise come true.

To demonstrate Perlin noise, the vertex shader used is a simple screen space rendering one. Using the ScreenAlignedQuad.3ds object, you can render a full-screen polygon that contains a screen full of noise. You can rip this shader from any previous screen space shader. To refresh your memory, here is the vertex shader code:

```
float4x4 view_proj_matrix;
float viewport_inv_width;
```

```
float viewport_inv_height;
struct VS_OUTPUT
{
   float4 Pos:      POSITION;
   float2 texCoord: TEXCOORD0;
};


VS_OUTPUT vs_main(float4 Pos: POSITION)
{
   VS_OUTPUT Out;

   // Simply output the position without transforming it
   Out.Pos = float4(Pos.xy, 0, 1);

   // Texture coordinates are setup so that the full texture
   // is mapped completely onto the screen
   Out.texCoord.x = 0.5 * (1 + Pos.x - viewport_inv_width);
   Out.texCoord.y = 0.5 * (1 - Pos.y - viewport_inv_height);

   return Out;
}
```

The pixel shader is where most of the action happens. The first point of concern is which noise texture to use. You could build one yourself using an image editing tool such as Adobe Photoshop, but for the purpose of this shader, you will be using the `NoiseVolume.dds` texture supplied with Render Monkey. Keep in mind that this texture is a 3D volume noise texture and needs to be set up properly by using a volume texture variable to contain it. Also, because you only need a 2D noise texture for this example, simply specify a Z texture coordinate of zero and use the `tex3D` function to sample it.

To simplify the Perlin noise rendering process even more, you will use the same noise texture for all octaves of the process. If you look back at Figure 13.3, you will see that each octave has a different value for frequency and amplitude. When dealing with texture coordinates, the frequency simply translates into a multiplier. With this in mind, the code to sample the noise for a single octave is as follows:

```
Noise = (1.0/pow(persist,i))*tex3D(Texture0, txr*pow(2,i));
```

The `persist` value defines the persistence of the noise and is generally defined as 2.0. The `i` variable defines the current octave and is a zero-based value. In simpler terms, for a persistence of two, the amplitudes for each octave would be 1,0.5,0.25, . . . and the texture coordinate multiplier would be 1,2,4, . . .

Another thing to keep in mind is that the noise within the volume texture is meant to be signed but is stored in an unsigned form. You need to change the preceding code to scale and offset the noise values to be signed. This yields the following code:

```
Noise = (1.0/pow(persist,i))*tex3D(Texture0, txr*pow(2,i)*2-1);
```

To combine multiple octaves of noise, you simply need to sample the noise texture multiple times and add the result together. Because you want to be flexible and allow for any number of octaves, this can be coded using a for loop. This yields the following final pixel shader code:

```
float time_0_1;
float persistance;
sampler Texture0;
float4 ps_main(float2 texCoord: TEXCOORD0) : COLOR
{
    // Sample only the first slice of the noise texture
    float3 txr = float3(texCoord,0);

    // Combine 4 octaves of noise together
    // Note: that the noise is considered signed but read from
    // an unsigned texture so it must be renormalized
    float final_noise = 0;
    for(int i=0;i<4;i++)
        final_noise +=(1.0/pow(persistance,i))*
                    (tex3D(Texture0, txr*pow(2,i))*2-1);

    // Remove the sign from the noise
    return (final_noise+1)/2;
}
```

After it's compiled, this shader should give you a noise function similar to the one shown in Figure 13.5. The final version of the shader is included on the companion CD-ROM as shader_1.rfx.

Keep in mind that the previous shader only generates basic Perlin noise. Over the next few sections, I will show you how you can use such noise in more creative ways, such as rendering wood and marble materials. But let's start with a more simple shader, using Perlin noise to render clouds.

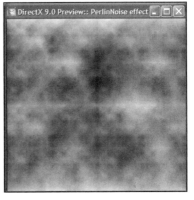

Figure 13.5 Rendering result for a basic Perlin noise shader.

Clouds, Clouds in the Sky

Now that you know more about noise and how Perlin noise can be created, I can demonstrate its use through a simple example. One rendering item that is well suited for the use of noise is the generation of cloud-like textures.

For this example, we will assume that we are looking at the clouds as if we were seeing them from the ground. Cloud rendering gets more complicated as you get closer to the clouds. But with this assumption, clouds are seen as a clump of white puffy balls moving across the sky.

Although it may seems awkward, similar effects can also be achieved through the proper use of Perlin noise. Before you write a shader, let's take a look at how you can take the output from a Perlin noise generator to render a set of clouds.

If you look at the noise generated with the shader in Figure 13.5, you can see that this basic Perlin noise itself has cloud-like qualities, but the cover is too dense to be realistic. In the initial shader, the noise was in a zero to one range, allowing us to see all of it. To make the cloud cover more patchy, you want to expand the range of the noise values so that only a portion of the noise can be seen. The following code shows an example of how this can be done:

```
Cloud = (final_noise+0.15)*2;
```

This code takes a value from -1 to 1 and rescales it so that only a portion of the noise value is displayed, creating sporadic clouds. In addition, the increase in range of the cloud noise causes saturated areas of cover, which is more consistent with the natural look of clouds.

The other aspect to consider when creating the pixel shader for cloud rendering is the persistence and number of octaves needed for the noise. The persistence value for cloud noise should be set to 2.0 because that produces a smoother noise. On the other end, the best approach to determine the needed octaves is to experiment. From my experimentation, two octaves proves to be sufficient.

With all this, the final pixel shader for the cloud rendering should be as follows:

```
float persistance;
sampler Texture0;
float4 ps_main(float2 texCoord: TEXCOORD0) : COLOR
{
    // Sample only the first slice of the noise texture
    float3 txr = float3(texCoord,0);

    // Combine 2 octaves of noise together.
    // Two octaves is sufficient for cloud rendering
    float final_noise = 0;
    for(int i=0;i<2;i++)
```

```
final_noise +=(1.0/pow(persistance,i))*
              (tex3D(Texture0, txr*pow(2,i))*2-1);

// Remove the sign from the noise and prep
// it for cloud rendering
return ((final_noise+0.15)*2);
}
```

After it's compiled, this shader should give you a rendering that looks like clouds, as shown in Figure 13.6. The final version of the shader has also been included on the companion CD-ROM as shader_2.rfx.

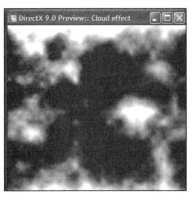

Figure 13.6 Rendering result for Perlin noise-based cloud rendering shader.

Wood and Marble

Now that you have a better understanding of how noise can be used to render simple material such as clouds, you are ready to tackle more complex materials. Both wood and marble have similar attributes when they are rendered. Over the next few paragraphs, I will show you how to take advantage of those attributes to render them in a procedural fashion.

Marble is generally a solid color material with turbulent veins of different colors. When rendering the veins, the proper use of Perlin noise comes in handy. However, from our previous cloud shader, the turbulence needed to render the veins is less dense. For this, you need to adapt the vertex shader slightly to reduce the frequency of the noise. This can easily be done by scaling down the texture coordinates by a factor of 50. Because you also want your marble to be generated as a 3D material from which your object is carved, your texture coordinates need to be a three-vector component derived from the object vertex coordinates. The following piece of vertex shader code shows how this can be done:

```
Out.TexCoord = inPos/50;
```

Now that you have defined the texture coordinates needed to fetch the noise, you need to determine how you can use the noise within the pixel shader to represent marble. The first thing you need is a color. Although you could use a texture, marble is a somewhat constant color, so you can define a constant color variable called marble_color, which you can use in the pixel shader.

Marble is a constant-colored material with colored veins running through it. The noise can be used as a way to modulate the base color so that the veins are of a darker color. However, with the standard behavior of Perlin noise, about 50 percent of the material would be dark for the negative portions of the noise. Because you want narrow veins within your material, you need to address this.

The simplest way to correct for this is to simply use the absolute value of the noise, which can be accomplished in HLSL by using the abs function. Applying this approach and scaling the noise slightly to get a decent result yields a decent looking marble material. The following pixel shader code illustrates the result:

```
float persistance;
float4 marble_color;
sampler Texture0;
float4 ps_main(float3 txr: TEXCOORD0) : COLOR
{
    // Combine 2 octaves of noise together.
    // Two octaves is sufficient for cloud rendering
    float final_noise = 0;
    for(int i=0;i<2;i++)
        final_noise += ((1.0/pow(persistance,i))*
                    ((tex3D(Texture0, txr*pow(2,i))*2)-1));

    // Remove the sign from the noise and prep
    // it for cloud rendering. The 0.2 and 1.2 factors
    // in the equation are manual adjustments to make
    // the rendering look better.
    return marble_color * 0.2+(1.2*abs(final_noise));
}
```

After it's compiled, this shader should give you a marble shaded elephant similar to the one shown in Figure 13.7. The final version of the shader is included on the companion CD-ROM as shader_3.rfx.

Wood is similar to marble in the sense that it has a basic color with veins traversing the material. However, the veins in wood are caused by growth rings in the tree and are periodic. This means they must be constructed differently than when dealing with marble. The first step is to adjust the noise frequency in the shader. Wood needs a slightly higher frequency than marble and can be accomplishing by dividing the noise texture coordinates by 10, thus yielding the following vertex shader code:

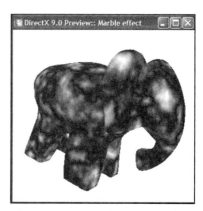

Figure 13.7 Rendering result for your procedural marble shader.

```
Out.TexCoord = inPos/10;
```

Because you want the veins, or the rings in the wood, to be periodic, you can use a function such as a sine or cosine wave to create such veins. The cosine function itself is too smooth, but this can be solved by raising the cosine to a higher power, making the transitions of the function sharper, as shown in Figure 13.8.

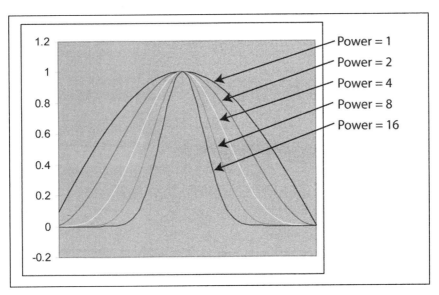

Figure 13.8 How raising the power of a sine/cosine function makes the transitions sharper.

There is still one important aspect missing from the rings in wood. Those rings are concentric, circling around the center of the tree trunk, meaning the function needs to give a circular value along a specific plane. This can be done with the following code, which takes the dot product of two axes along a plane, creating a circular value on that plane. The following code shows how:

```
Circle = dot(noisetxr.xy,noisetxr.xy);
```

It is now time to talk about where the noise comes into play. Because all we want to do is make the rings less regular, the noise can be used to offset the ring. This can easily be done by adding a scaled version of the noise value to the cosine factor calculated through the dot product I described previously. Doing so yields the following final pixel shader code:

```
float persistance;
float4 wood_color;
sampler Texture0;
float4 ps_main(float3 txr: TEXCOORD0) : COLOR
{
    // Determine two sets of coordinates, one for the noise
    // and one for the wood rings which is scaled by a factor
    // of eight to reduce its frequency relative to the noise.
    float3 noisetxr = txr;
    txr = txr/8;
```

```
// Combine 3 octaves of noise together.
float final_noise = 0;
for(int i=0;i<2;i++)
    final_noise += ((1.0/pow(persistance,i))*
                    ((tex3D(Texture0, txr*pow(2,i))*2)-1));

// The wood is defined by a set of concentric rings in the XY
// plane. Those rings are pertubated by the computed noise multiplied
// by four to increase its amplitude
final_noise = abs(final_noise);
float grain = cos(dot(noisetxr.xy,noisetxr.xy) + final_noise*4);
return wood_color - pow(grain,8)/2;
}
```

After it's completed, this shader should give you a wood texture similar to the one shown in Figure 13.9. The final version of the shader is included on the companion CD-ROM as shader_4.rfx.

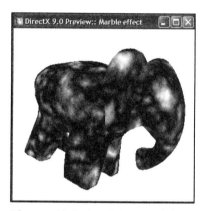

As you can see from the two shaders you just developed, working with procedural materials isn't an exact science. It involves a good amount of trial and error to determine the basic attributes of the materials and how the noise affects them. Although it may seem like a lot of work and effort to get a simple texture on an elephant, such techniques have several added advantages which are worth considering. First of all, procedurally generated materials, with the proper type of noise, can be zoomed in closer with fewer texture

Figure 13.9 Rendering result for your procedural wood texture.

requirements to keep the same amount of detail. Probably the most important advantage of noise-based texturing is that you can have a totally different material by only changing a few constants within your shader; this allows you to add variety to your scene with little or no added texture cost.

With this in mind, there are other uses for noise beyond making procedural materials or textures. It can be used to procedurally animate objects, as I will overview in the next few paragraphs.

Using Noise to Move Things Around

Although the main topic of this chapter is the use of noise to render procedural materials, I want to touch on another topic of importance when dealing with noise: procedural animations. So far, when using shaders, you have dealt with objects that were static in your scene. However, what prevents you from taking advantage of your vertex shader to also manipulate the position of vertices?

In the spirit of using noise within shaders, why can't you use a function such as Perlin noise, not just to create a procedural material, but also to animate the surface of an object? One of the most obvious uses for something like this is the animation of a water surface.

Unfortunately, with current generations of hardware and the 2.0 vertex shader model, you cannot do texture lookups within your vertex shader. You can expect this functionality to appear in future generations of hardware, but for now, you need to do something else to generate your noise. One approach is to combine several sine waves of different frequencies. Although this leads to smoother noise, it suffices to animate the surface of an object.

Take one sine wave from each axis of an object and combine them. Taking the dot product of the components along the axis for each of the sine waves, you get a circular sine wave along this plane. The following code illustrates how this can be done:

```
Wave = sin( dot(inPos.xy,inPos.xy) + time_0_2PI);
```

Combining several sine waves for each plane for each major axis yields a sufficiently noisy function. The following vertex shader shows how you can combine multiple waves to create a somewhat noisy function:

```
float4x4 view_proj_matrix;
float viewport_inv_width;
float viewport_inv_height;
float time_0_2PI;
struct VS_OUTPUT
{
    float4 Pos:     POSITION;
};


VS_OUTPUT vs_main(float4 inPos: POSITION)
{
    VS_OUTPUT Out;

    // Define a noisy function based on a sequence
    // of sine waves and manipulate the surface based
    // on the result. The 0.05 factor is used to control
    // the amplitude of the sine wave so they are proportional
    // to the size of the used object.
    inPos = inPos +
            0.05*sin( dot(inPos.xy,inPos.xy) + time_0_2PI) +
            0.05*sin( dot(inPos.xz,inPos.xz) + time_0_2PI) +
            0.05*sin( dot(inPos.yz,inPos.yz) + time_0_2PI );
```

```
    // Compute the object position.
    Out.Pos = mul(view_proj_matrix, inPos);
    return Out;
}
```

If you compile this shader, the surface of your object is distorted in a way similar to the one shown in Figure 13.10. The final version of the shader is included on the companion CD-ROM as shader_5.rfx.

Now, keep in mind that this example is simplistic and somewhat pointless, but similar techniques can be used to create interesting effects. For example, you could take an expanding sphere with a fiery texture and, by applying noise to the sphere, create an explosion that animates and varies every time. This is a sure way to create truly organic and dynamic animations within your scene.

Figure 13.10 Rendering result for noise-animated geometry shader.

It's Your Turn!

Procedural materials are a great way to detach yourself from prebuilt assets and give you full control over the look and appearance of your objects. The following exercises will let you explore procedural materials on your own. The solutions to these exercises can be found in Appendix D.

Exercise 1: ANIMATING CLOUDS

For this first exercise, you are asked to take the Perlin noise cloud shader developed earlier in this chapter and extend it to animate the clouds in function of time. For this task, you need to take advantage of the three dimensions of the noise texture used for this shader. You can use the built-in time_0_1 variable to access the third dimension of the noise texture so that it animates with time.

Exercise 2: RENDERING STRATA

Because we are on the topic of procedural materials, it makes sense to have you create your own material from scratch. For this exercise, you are asked to develop a material based on a rock material called strata. In this material, rocks of different colors are layered together. To render such a material, you need to use a one-dimensional texture containing the colors for each layer. This texture can be found as StrataSpline.dds on the CD-ROM.

Using this texture, you need to access it based on one of the special coordinates of your object, as was done with wood or marble. Obviously, you do not want the layers to be fully straight and uniform; this is where you will use a Perlin noise function to add turbulence to the material.

What's Next?

Perlin noise can be a powerful tool when rendering. By using the latest shader technologies, you can not only render objects based on predefined materials, but also detach yourself from prebuilt assets and render your own materials from scratch.

Whether you are rendering wood, marble, or any other noisy materials in nature, procedural materials can add a new richness to your scene. In addition to this enhanced realism, you are given full control over the parameters of the material. This gives you full control over its appearance and the ability to create an unprecedented level of variety, which can make such procedural textures a powerful scene design tool.

In addition to rendering procedural materials such as wood, the same techniques can be applied to other tasks, such as the procedural animation of semi-random materials like the waves on the surface of water.

This brings up another topic of importance. Why is there a requirement that materials always look realistic? Some types of applications may require that you adopt different rendering styles. The next chapter focuses on such non-realistic rendering techniques and how you can use them within your applications.

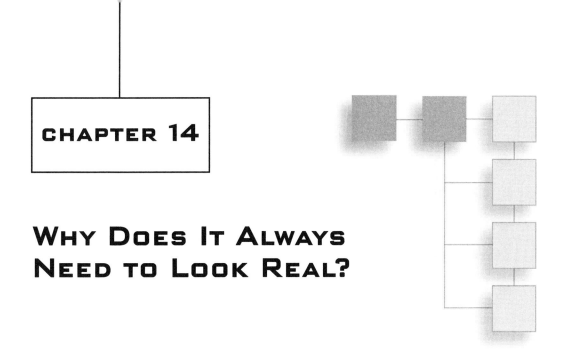

CHAPTER 14

WHY DOES IT ALWAYS NEED TO LOOK REAL?

Throughout this book, you have striven to create realistic renderings, taking advantage of the rendering hardware architectures to make your graphics appear less synthetic. This is what we want for most of our graphics, and when you think about it, it makes sense. Computer graphics are meant to be immersive, and there is no better way to do so than fooling the human eye and brain into thinking that what is on your monitor is the real deal.

There are cases, however, where style is more important than realism. Imagine that you are creating a game based on a television cartoon character. Making your graphics look real does not increase the illusion; rather, it breaks it. For this particular case, you want the user to be immersed in the cartoon itself, so it is more than natural to try to re-create a cartoonish style for your renderings.

In this chapter, I will discuss the topic of non-photorealistic rendering. As the name implies, this topic is wider than just rendering cartoonish graphics but refers to the general art of adapting your graphics to various non-realistic styles. In the first part of this chapter, I mostly focus on toon rendering techniques, which are the most used *non-photorealistic rendering*, or NPR, techniques. In the second half of the chapter, I will discuss the topic of *hatching*, which allows you to take advantage of the rendering hardware to render geometry in a such way that it looks as if it has been pencil-sketched.

Just Like a Television Cartoon

Sometimes you just want to render a scene in a non-realistic way to adapt yourself to a particular style. Cartoon rendering is probably one of the most common forms of non-photorealistic rendering that are used in computer graphics. Before you can learn how to render in this way, you need to know what composes such graphics. Take a look at Figure 14.1.

From the picture in Figure 14.1, you can see a couple of distinct attributes. The first thing is the low number of colors used in both the texturing and lighting; this is something I will address later. But the second point of interest is that most objects have an outline.

At first glance, it may not be obvious why such outlines are there, but if you think about it, it makes sense. Because not many colors are used with toon style graphics, it may become difficult to distinguish objects because adjacent objects may end up using the same colors. Giving objects an outline ensures that the human eye can easily distinguish all the objects.

With this in mind, I will start by introducing to you several common approaches taken to render outlines in a 3D environment.

Figure 14.1 Image taken from a cartoon.

Outline Rendering

Rendering object outlines in a 3D environment may seem difficult or awkward, but it is a simple process, and many different techniques exist, all of them with pros and cons. In this section, I will discuss several techniques but will only lead you through the implementation of the first one. You will be asked to implement a second technique as your first exercise at the end of the chapter.

Although there are many ways to perform the same task, outline rendering is simply a matter of determining where the object begins and ends. This may seem like a complicated process, especially in a 3D environment, but that's where a little cleverness comes in.

Because the rendered result of your scene will be on a flat 2D surface, as a drawing would be, why not do the outline of the object in screen-space, taking away all the considerations of 3D rendering?

In this approach, you will use a render target to render your object in a solid color, such as white against a black background. Although this does not give you the outline, you can use this texture and run an edge detection filter to deduce the outline of your object. But before talking about the edge detection algorithms, let's render the object to the render target.

For this shader, you need to create a first pass that takes an object and renders it to a render target. Refer to Chapter 5, "Looking Through a Filter," if you need to brush up on this process. Just remember that the render target size should be set to match the viewport size, or you may experience aliasing in the final rendering.

With this in mind, all your shaders need to do is render the object in a simple, static color. The vertex shader to accomplish this is straightforward and simply needs to transform the incoming vertex position to screen space. The shader code for this is

```
float4x4 view_proj_matrix;
struct VS_OUTPUT
{
    float4 Pos: POSITION;
};

VS_OUTPUT vs_main( float4 Pos: POSITION )
{
    VS_OUTPUT Out;

    // Simply project and output the vertex position
    Out.Pos = mul( view_proj_matrix, Pos );
    return Out;
}
```

The simplicity of this shader is that the object only needs to be rendered in a single opaque color, such as white. If your scene has multiple objects, you may need to assign each object a different color so the edge detection algorithm can discern between them. For this particular shader, all that is needed is to render the object in white. The following pixel shader code accomplishes this:

```
float4 ps_main( float4 Diff: COLOR0 ) : COLOR
{
    return 1;
}
```

This render pass renders your object in a single opaque color, as shown in Figure 14.2. This unique color version in your render target is then used in the next rendering pass to render the outline of the object.

To render the outline of an object with this shader, you essentially need to take the render target and detect the edges between the solid color object and the background. In Chapter 5, we explored the topic of screen space filters and talked about edge detection filters. Believe it or not, this filter finally comes in handy!

Figure 14.2 Object rendered in a single color to be used for edge detection.

For this particular task, you will use a *Sobel* filter, which detects edges both horizontally and vertically. Figure 14.3 illustrates the Sobel filter that is used for the edge detection.

Implementing this filter is a straightforward matter, similar to the edge detection filter that was discussed in Chapter 5. To perform the filtering, you need to set up a new render pass, which takes the render target, passes the filter on it, and renders the outline of the object.

$$\text{Horizontal Edge}: \begin{bmatrix} 1 & 2 & 1 \\ 0 & 0 & 0 \\ -1 & -2 & 1 \end{bmatrix} / 1$$

$$\text{Vertical Edge}: \begin{bmatrix} 1 & 0 & -1 \\ 2 & 0 & -2 \\ 1 & 0 & -1 \end{bmatrix} / 1$$

Figure 14.3 Sobel edge detection filter used to render the object outline.

On the vertex shader end, all you need is to do a full screen render pass using the ScreenAlign-Quad.3ds model. You have done this several times, but for reference, the needed vertex shader code is:

```
float4x4 view_proj_matrix;
struct VS_OUTPUT
{
    float4 Pos      : POSITION;
    float2 TexCoord : TEXCOORD0;
};


VS_OUTPUT vs_main( float4 inPos: POSITION, float2 inTexCoord: TEXCOORD0)
{
    VS_OUTPUT Out;

    // Draw screen-space quad
    In.Pos.xy    = sign(In.Pos.xy);
    Out.Pos      = float4(In.Pos.xy, 0.0, 1.0);
```

```
    Out.TexCoord.x = 0.5 * (1 + In.Pos.x);
    Out.TexCoord.y = 0.5 * (1 - In.Pos.y);

    return Out;
}
```

The pixel shader used for the edge detection is also simple. First of all, you need to sample all the samples required for the Sobel filter, as shown in Figure 14.3. Once you have computed the X and Y component of the edge filter, this gives you a 2D vector representing the direction of the edge for this particular pixel.

For this shader, we have no interest in the edge direction, but we do have an interest in the intensity of the edge detected. With this vector, you can determine its length and compare it against a fixed threshold, determining the presence of an edge sufficiently strong to justify rendering an outline.

That's all you need to do. The following pixel shader is the complete version of the Sobel edge detection filter. Notice the edge detection results are purposely inverted to ensure that outlines are rendered as white:

```
sampler RT;

// Size of a one texel offset, this is hardcoded to 256
// for simplicity and since RenderMonkey cannot allow you
// to know the size of a texture,
const float off = 1.0 / 256.0;

float4 ps_main( float2 TexCoord : TEXCOORD0 ) : COLOR
{
    // Sample the neighbor pixels
    float s00 = tex2D(RT, TexCoord + float2(-off, -off));
    float s01 = tex2D(RT, TexCoord + float2( 0,   -off));
    float s02 = tex2D(RT, TexCoord + float2( off, -off));

    float s10 = tex2D(RT, TexCoord + float2(-off,  0));
    float s12 = tex2D(RT, TexCoord + float2( off,  0));

    float s20 = tex2D(RT, TexCoord + float2(-off,  off));
    float s21 = tex2D(RT, TexCoord + float2( 0,    off));
    float s22 = tex2D(RT, TexCoord + float2( off,  off));

    // Sobel filter in X and Y directions
    float sobelX = s00 + 2 * s10 + s20 - s02 - 2 * s12 - s22;
```

```
float sobelY = s00 + 2 * s01 + s02 - s20 - 2 * s21 - s22;

// Find edge using a threshold of 0.07 which is sufficient
// to detect most edges.
float edgeSqr = (sobelX * sobelX + sobelY * sobelY);
return 1.0-(edgeSqr > (0.07 * 0.07));
}
```

After it is compiled and running, this shader should render an outline of your object similar to the one shown in Figure 14.4. The final version of the shader is included on the companion CD-ROM as shader_1.rfx.

The preceding is one method of rendering outlines for your cartoonish shader. There are several other methods that can be used. The following section reviews some of the other common approaches used to render outlines.

Figure 14.4 Rendering the outline of an object using the edge detection method.

Other Outlining Ideas

Rendering the outlines of objects isn't a cut-and-dried task where there is one single right way of approaching the problem. Several approaches can be taken, and all of them have advantages and drawbacks. The intent of this section is to explain several methods so you may expand your own library of choices and choose which one is most appropriate to your situation.

Because I just mentioned the advantages and shortcomings of outlining methods, it makes sense to address this point for the outlining method discussed in the previous section. On the plus side, this method is easy to implement, and by clever use of varying colors for each object, you can outline your whole scene in one pass. On the downside, you need to do a three-pass scheme where you render your object to a render target, render it again to your screen buffer, and then use the render target to determine the outline of your objects. This additional cost may become prohibitive in the case of complex scenes.

Another shortfall of this method, depending on your situation, is that the method only renders the outer outline of the object. This makes sense because the whole object is rendered in a single opaque color, and then an edge detection algorithm is run on the result. Imagine your teapot being oriented so the spout faces the camera. In this case, you would only get an outline for the teapot itself, not the spout.

One way to work around this problem is to take a similar approach, but instead of using a unique opaque color, you may want to use the depth of the object when building your render target. It may not seem obvious at first, but take a look at Figure 14.5. As you can see, any object boundary is generally accompanied by an abrupt change in the object's depth values.

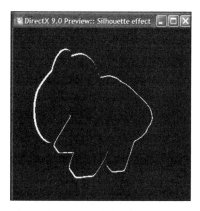

Taking advantage of this property, you can render your object's relative depth into a render target and then run a similar edge detection algorithm to determine the object's outline from the depth discontinuities. This is exactly what you will be asked to implement in the first exercise at the end of this chapter.

Figure 14.5 Depth render target showing the discontinuities at the object's borders.

Sometimes, doing screen space-based approaches can be cumbersome, and you may wish to use a technique that operates straight in 3D space. One approach often taken is to take advantage of the surface normal of an object to determine its outline. Knowing the surface normal of the object and the view vector of the camera, you know you are reaching the boundary of the object when its normal and view vectors are becoming perpendicular. Because of this, you can use the dot product in a similar fashion to determine how much outline to render:

```
float edge = 1 - (dot(Normal,ViewVec)>0.07);
```

Keep in mind that this approach requires good precision normals and will not work well on low-polygon-count geometry. Also, because of interpolation issues, as with lighting, such an approach yields better results when done per pixel instead of on a per-vertex basis.

Another approach to this same problem is to render an object twice in your scene. The first time, use a black opaque color with the object slightly scaled up from its original size. Then on the second pass, simply render your object as you normally would. The scaled version of the object has the effect of creating a halo, or outline, around the extremities of the object. Figure 14.6 shows how this process looks for a simple object. This technique is probably the simplest to integrate and gives you outlines on both the outside and inside boundaries. However, because your scale is done in 3D space, you cannot guarantee the thickness of the border and may suffer from occasional aliasing.

Figure 14.6 Sample object boundary resulting from the object scaling technique.

There are several ways in which outlines can be rendered, and I can assure you I did not present all of them here. When it is time to choose one, you will have to look at several of them and make a decision on which one to use based on performance and feature considerations. It generally becomes a matter of choosing the one that matches the desired style and fits well within your rendering architecture. But for now, let's move on to what is inside the outline: the actual object!

Toon Shading

Rendering the outlines of your object was the first phase of rendering it in a cartoonish manner. The second step is rendering the object itself in a way that is consistent with the style. Toon shading itself can be divided into two separate tasks: texturing and lighting the object.

For the topic of texturing, cartoon shading requires you to use fewer colors. This can be accomplished in two ways.

The first approach involves not using any textures at all and assigning constant colors to vertices or polygons. This may seem simplistic but, depending on the circumstances, can get the job done. The second approach involves using regular textures but changing them so they use less colors.

Take, for example, the `fieldstone.dds` texture you have used several times so far. This texture has too many colors to use in a cartoonish environment. However, using an image editing program, such as Adobe Photoshop, you can stylize and reduce the number of colors on the texture. Figure 14.7 illustrates the `fieldstone.dds` texture after it has been manipulated to fit more of a cartoonish style.

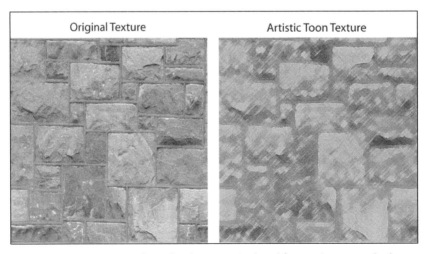

Figure 14.7 A texture after it has been manipulated for use in a toon shader.

To render your object with this new texture, which is included on the CD-ROM as fieldstone_art.dds, you need to add a new render pass after the outline pass to render the object. At this point, all you want is to render the textured object, so a simple projection vertex shader will do the trick:

```
float4x4 view_proj_matrix;
struct VS_OUTPUT
{
    float4 Pos: POSITION;
    float2 Tex: TEXCOORD0;
};


VS_OUTPUT vs_main( float4 inPos: POSITION,float2 inTex: TEXCOORD )
{
    VS_OUTPUT Out;

    // Simply project and output the vertex position
    Out.Pos = mul( view_proj_matrix, inPos );
    Out.Tex = inTex;
    return Out;
}
```

The pixel shader simply needs to sample the texture and return the color. The resulting shader code is as follows:

```
sampler Texture0;
float4 ps_main( float2 Tex: TEXCOORD0 ) : COLOR
{
    return tex2D(Texture0, Tex);
}
```

After it's compiled, this will give you a cartoonish textured object, with outline, such as the one shown in Figure 14.8. The final version of the shader is included on the companion CD-ROM as shader_2.rfx.

Just a simple texture on your object may not be enough to do the trick. Remember that lighting is an important visual cue when rendering, and the same is true when you render cartoonish scenes. The same approach applies to lighting as with textures; because of the nature of cartoonish rendering, you need to reduce your lighting to a discrete set of shades. The easiest way to control the number of shades is scaling

Figure 14.8 Rendering result for the basic textured toon shader.

your light value up and then taking only the integer part of the value; the scaling factor determines the number of discrete shades. The following code snippet does this task:

```
Diffuse = (int)(Diffuse * 4) / 4.0;
```

To render the object with cartoonish lighting, you need to modify the vertex shader code to render some lighting and reduce the number of shades in the final result. For this example, you can calculate the lighting on a per-vertex basis because the style allows for poor interpolation. In addition, we will stick to diffuse lighting for the moment. Applying those changes yields the following vertex shader code:

```
float4x4 view_proj_matrix;
float4 Light1_Position;
float4 Light1_Attenuation;
float4 Light1_Color;
struct VS_OUTPUT
{
    float4 Pos:      POSITION;
    float2 TexCoord: TEXCOORD0;
    float2 Color:    COLOR0;
};


float4 Light_PointDiffuse(float3 VertPos, float3 VertNorm, float3 LightPos,
                          float4 LightColor, float4 LightAttenuation)
{
    // Determine the distance from the light to the vertex and the direction
    float3 LightDir = LightPos - VertPos;
    float  Dist = length(LightDir);
    LightDir = LightDir / Dist;

    // Compute distance based attenuation. This is defined as:
    // Attenuation = 1 / ( LA.x + LA.y*Dist + LA.z*Dist*Dist )
    float DistAttn = clamp(0,1, 1 / ( LightAttenuation.x +
                                      LightAttenuation.y * Dist +
                                      LightAttenuation.z * Dist * Dist ));

    // Compute suface/light angle based attenuation defined as dot(N,L)
    // Note : This must be clamped as it may become negative.
    float AngleAttn = clamp(0, 1, dot(VertNorm, LightDir) );

    // Compute final lighting
    return LightColor * DistAttn * AngleAttn;
}
```

```
VS_OUTPUT vs_main(float4 inPos: POSITION, float3 inNormal: NORMAL,float2 inTxr: TEXCOORD0)
{
    VS_OUTPUT Out;

    // Compute the projected position and send out the texture coordinates
    Out.Pos = mul(view_proj_matrix, inPos);
    Out.TexCoord = inTxr;

    // Output the ambient color
    float4 Color = float4(0.4,0.4,0.4,1);

    // Compute light contribution
    Color += Light_PointDiffuse(inPos, inNormal, Light1_Position,
                                Light1_Color, Light1_Attenuation);

    // Output Final Color
    Out.Color = Color;

    return Out;
}
```

On the pixel shader side, you already have the color of the final lighting. You need to reduce it to a discrete set of shades, as discussed earlier, and then modulate the result with the object's texture. Doing so yields the following pixel shader code:

```
sampler Texture0;
float4 ps_main( float2 Tex: TEXCOORD0, float4 Diffuse:COLOR0) : COLOR
{
    // Clamp diffuse to a fixed set of values and modulate with
    // the texture color
    Diffuse = (int)(Diffuse * 4) / 4.0;
    return Diffuse*tex2D(Texture0, Tex);
}
```

This shader should give you a result similar to the one shown in Figure 14.9. Notice how the banding occurs within the lighting. The final version of the shader is included on the companion CD-ROM as shader_3.rfx.

Figure 14.9 Rendering result for a textured and lit toon shader.

Real-Time Hatching

So far I have focused only on rendering objects in a cartoonish manner; however, there is more to non-photorealistic rendering. Although toon shading is the most common form, it is worth exploring some different approaches. In this section, I will introduce to you an approach that can simulate the shading accomplished when objects are hand-drawn. This shader, called real-time hatching, takes lighting information to render an object in a way that makes its lighting appear as if it were hand-shaded.

The approach behind this shader is simple; you render and light your object as you normally would. However, instead of using the object's texture, you will use the lighting information to blend in a combination of two out of six prebuilt hatch patterns. The six pattern textures represent hatching as it would be rendered at different levels of lighting intensity. Figure 14.10 shows you the six textures you will be using for this shader.

The tricky part with this shader is determining which two textures to use out of the set of six. For this to happen, you need to take advantage of the vertex shader 2.0 architecture. After discovering the diffuse lighting for your object, you can multiply this value by the number of textures you are using, six for this shader. This will then enable you to use the integer part of the lighting to determine which set of textures to use. In addition to this, the fractional part of the texture gives you the interpolation factor between the two textures.

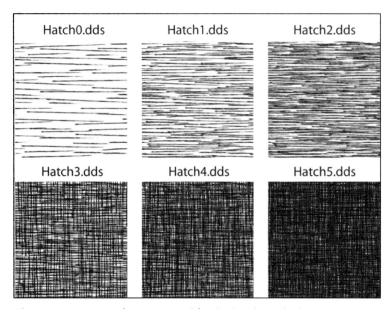

Figure 14.10 Set of textures used for the hatching shader.

Through the clever use of conditional statements, you can write vertex shader code that determines which textures and at which factor to blend them in. However, because all this is happening in the vertex shader, you have no control over which textures the pixel shader will sample. To work around this, pass a factor for each of the six textures and let the pixel shader blend them appropriately. Doing so yields the following vertex shader code:

```
float4 Light_Direction;
float4x4 view_matrix;
float4x4 view_proj_matrix;
struct VS_OUTPUT
{
    float4 Pos            : POSITION0;
    float2 TexCoord       : TEXCOORD0;
    float3 HatchWeights0  : TEXCOORD1;
    float3 HatchWeights1  : TEXCOORD2;
};

VS_OUTPUT vs_main( float4 inPos: POSITION0, float3 inNormal: NORMAL0,
                   float2 inTexCoord : TEXCOORD0 )
{
    VS_OUTPUT Out;

    // Compute projected position and transfer texture
    // coordinates for the object
    Out.Pos = mul( view_proj_matrix, inPos );
    Out.TexCoord = inTexCoord;

    // Determine a simple diffuse lighting component based
    // on a directional light in view space
    float3 pos_world    = mul( view_matrix, inPos );
    float3 normal_world = normalize(mul( (float3x3)view_matrix,
                          inNormal ));
    float  diffuse = min(1.0,max(0,dot(-Light_Direction,normal_world)));
    diffuse = pow(diffuse,4) ;

    float  hatchFactor = diffuse * 6.0;
    float3 weight0 = 0.0;
    float3 weight1 = 0.0;

    // Determine the weights for the hatch textures based on the
    // hatch factor which is simply proportional to the diffuse
    // lighting. In other words, the more lit the object, the less
    // dense the hatching will be.
```

```
if (hatchFactor>5.0) { weight0.x = 1.0; }
else if (hatchFactor>4.0)
{
    weight0.x = 1.0 - (5.0 - hatchFactor);
    weight0.y = 1.0 - weight0.x;
}
else if (hatchFactor>3.0)
{
    weight0.y = 1.0 - (4.0 - hatchFactor);
    weight0.z = 1.0 - weight0.y;
}
else if (hatchFactor>2.0)
{
    weight0.z = 1.0 - (3.0 - hatchFactor);
    weight1.x = 1.0 - weight0.z;
}
else if (hatchFactor>1.0)
{
    weight1.x = 1.0 - (2.0 - hatchFactor);
    weight1.y = 1.0 - weight1.x;
}
else if (hatchFactor>0.0)
{
    weight1.y = 1.0 - (1.0 - hatchFactor);
    weight1.z = 1.0 - weight1.y;
}
Out.HatchWeights0 = weight0;
Out.HatchWeights1 = weight1;

return Out;
}
```

In the pixel shader, take the six factors passed in the two sets of texture coordinates to sample all six textures. Because only two of the textures have a nonzero weight, the appropriate two textures will have a value when they are sampled and weighed. Once you sample all six textures, the result is achieved by adding all the samples together. The following pixel shader accomplishes this:

```
sampler Hatch0;
sampler Hatch1;
sampler Hatch2;
sampler Hatch3;
sampler Hatch4;
```

```
sampler Hatch5;
sampler Base;
float4 ps_main( float2 TexCoord: TEXCOORD0,
                float3 HatchWeights0: TEXCOORD1,
                float3 HatchWeights1 : TEXCOORD2) : COLOR
{
    // Sample eatch hatch texture based on the object's texture
    // coordinates and weight the pattern based on the factor
    // determined from the lighting.
    float4 hatchTex0 = tex2D(Hatch0,TexCoord) * HatchWeights0.x;
    float4 hatchTex1 = tex2D(Hatch1,TexCoord) * HatchWeights0.y;
    float4 hatchTex2 = tex2D(Hatch2,TexCoord) * HatchWeights0.z;
    float4 hatchTex3 = tex2D(Hatch3,TexCoord) * HatchWeights1.x;
    float4 hatchTex4 = tex2D(Hatch4,TexCoord) * HatchWeights1.y;
    float4 hatchTex5 = tex2D(Hatch5,TexCoord) * HatchWeights1.z;

    // Combine all patterns, the final color is simply the sum
    // of all hatch patterns.
    float4 hatchColor = hatchTex0 +
                        hatchTex1 +
                        hatchTex2 +
                        hatchTex3 +
                        hatchTex4 +
                        hatchTex5;
    return hatchColor;
}
```

Figure 14.11 Rendering result for the real-time hatching shader.

After it's compiled, this shader gives you a teapot shaded with appropriate hatching in proportion to the lighting on the object. Your result should be similar to the one shown in Figure 14.11. The complete version of this shader is on the CD-ROM as shader_4.rfx.

It's Your Turn!

It's now your turn to take the wheel! The following exercises will let you explore the topic of non-photorealistic rendering on your own. The solutions to these exercises can be found in Appendix D.

Exercise 1: DEPTH-BASED OUTLINE

In this chapter, I discussed several approaches that can be taken to render object outlines when dealing with non-photorealistic rendering. We have only implemented the image-space-edge detection technique. For this example, you are asked to complete a new silhouette rendering technique using depth information to render the objects outline.

The idea behind this outline technique is similar to the one used in the shader you developed. The difference is that you will initially render the depth of the object to a render target, instead of a solid color, and use an edge detection filter to create an outline. The advantage of this approach is that it enables you to render edges on the visual border of the object and allow for any sharp variation of depth.

When rendering the final outline, you may also wish to use an anti-aliasing, or blur, filter to increase the smoothness of the outline. You may wish to experiment with different types of blur filters as you complete this shader.

Exercise 2: SILHOUETTE AND TOON SHADING

So far, you have implemented both outline rendering and toon shading techniques. For this exercise, you are being asked to combine them. Start with the outline shader developed in the previous exercise and combine it with simple toon shading. The task itself is simple but will require you to deduce a proper set of rendering states so that both the toon shaded object and outline combine properly together.

What's Next?

When rendering a scene, most of the time you will strive to create an output that looks as realistic as possible. This makes sense because you want to produce an environment that is immersive and draws the user in. However, this principle does not apply to all cases. Sometimes you need to adapt to a specific style that is required. In such a case, style often becomes more important than the techniques employed.

Probably one of the most obvious cases is when you want to render a cartoonish scene. In this case, it isn't about realism anymore but about creating a style that closely matches what you want to mimic.

In this chapter, I have shown you how to render the outline of an object, in addition to some of the basic principles involved in toon shading. All those concepts are simple and can easily be applied to any type of object. In the second half of the chapter, I showed you how to apply similar techniques to render your objects in a hatching style, re-creating the look of hand-drawn images. These techniques can go a long way to give your graphics a unique style of their own.

In the next chapter, I will be introducing a basic atmospheric effect that can be used by everyone in many circumstances: Fog. I will cover both simple global scene fog and more advanced topics such as volumetric fog.

So far throughout this book, I have discussed specific topics in very distinct categories. By now, your understanding of shaders should be sufficient to allow you to create all sorts of effects. In this section, I will overview many different topics. Although this section is named "Advanced Topics," it could have been named "Miscellaneous Topics." Some of the chapters cover more advanced topics, while others cover topics that didn't fit in anywhere else.

In Part IV, I will cover various topics, ranging from animations to shadows. Combined with your current knowledge of shaders, by the time you reach the end of Part IV, you will have a complete library of techniques and skills required to excel in the art of shader writing.

One thing you will need to know is that some of the techniques exposed in the following chapters cannot currently be implemented on RenderMonkey. Future versions of this tool will likely give you the functionality needed to do so, but I wanted to cover certain topics anyway for your general knowledge.

CHAPTER 15

WATCH OUT FOR THAT MORNING FOG

Many factors come into play when rendering a scene. When dealing with specific objects, lighting and materials are very important. However, most of the effects discussed so far in this book do not take into account the scene as a whole. When rendering a complex scene, you need to consider global factors that may affect your objects.

Fog is an important aspect of rendering that is often neglected. In addition, it has often been used in the past as a way to optimize performance by restricting how far you can see. This use has given fog a bad name over the years because of its incorrect overuse. The reality is that fog does exist in real life and can contribute a great deal in enhancing the realism of a rendered scene.

Throughout this chapter, I will introduce you to the basic concepts of fog and how such phenomena occur in real life. Armed with this knowledge, you will understand various fogging techniques, ranging from hardware-accelerated fog to a volumetric fogging technique.

We'll start with a few of the fundamentals behind fog. The next section surveys the basic concepts behind fog and its existence.

The Basics of Fog

The existence of fog and haziness is something we all take for granted without understanding the physics behind these natural effects. The reality is that although fog seems to appear out of thin air, its existence is much more complex. We'll save the math behind the principles for later in this chapter when I discuss the topic of estimating real atmospherics.

All atmospheric effects, whether fog or haziness, come from the same basic concept. Although air itself is transparent, many particles actually float around in it. These particles have an effect on the incoming light through one simple effect, scattering. As shown in Figure 15.1, light traversing the air hits some of those floating particles and gets redirected.

In Figure 15.1, you can see that this interaction has two consequences. First, some of the light coming at the viewer straight from the light is deflected away, thus reducing the perceived light intensity. The second effect is that light not oriented at the viewer is deflected back towards the viewer.

Ever noticed how the clouds appear orange at sunset? This is because of this exact effect. As Figure 15.2 shows, light from the sun makes it to the clouds and then is scattered internally until it gets retransmitted to the viewer. The result is that the clouds get an orange tint as if they were glowing. The orange color at sunset coming from the angle of the sun as it sets.

Of course, this effect depends on two major factors. The type and density of the particles in the air make a difference; water reacts with light differently than dust does. The other factor that influences the fogging effect is the thickness of the material. Thicker material deflects more light.

This information should give you a basic understanding of the principle behind scattering and how particles in the air can create fog. As with most effects we have done so far, our concern is more about approximating the result than re-creating it perfectly.

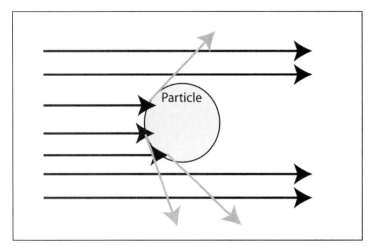

Figure 15.1 The interaction of light with particles floating in the air.

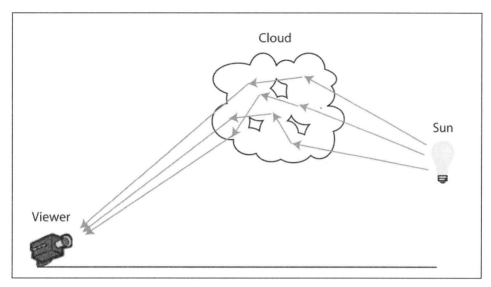

Figure 15.2 Why the scattering of light makes clouds orange at sunset.

This is even more important when dealing with atmospheric scattering, which can yield very complex equations. I will discuss better mathematical guesses for outdoor atmospheric effects at the end of this chapter, but for now, let's focus on emulating simple fog using your rendering hardware.

Hardware Fog

Most 3D video cards have built-in hardware support for fog. It would be ridiculous not to take advantage of it to add atmospherics to your scene at near-zero cost. In fact, the only cost to you is the computation of the fogging intensity; the calculation as to how this fog is applied to the end result is done automatically by the rendering hardware. The hardware, depending on its level of support, allows several forms of basic fogging to be applied to your geometry.

Based on current specifications, hardware can support both per-vertex and per-pixel fogging models. Keep in mind that per-vertex means that the fog intensity is determined for each vertex but is still interpolated for each pixel. Per-pixel implies that the fog value is determined on a per-pixel level based on the perspective interpolated distance value. This can be more expensive because you must determine the fogging intensity for each pixel in your scene instead of taking advantage of the vertex interpolation.

The fogging hardware can be controlled through a set of render states defining many parameters. The first parameters are to enable the fogging hardware and control the start and end of the fog region. They are named D3DRS_FOGENABLE, D3DRS_FOGSTART, and D3DRS_FOGEND. This region, defined by the start and end render states, establishes where the fog effect starts becoming visible and at which point it is at full intensity.

Notice that the start and end values defined through the render state are defined as camera space distances, not world space distances. Figure 15.3(a) illustrates how the depth is determined relative to the camera. Notice that the fog value is determined as the projected depth on the screen, leading to a planar fog start and end plane. The reality is the fog is proportional to the distance from the camera and should yield a circular fog start and end plane, such as that shown in Figure 15.3(b). If the hardware supports it, you can turn on such a *radial* mode with the D3DRS_RANGEFOGENABLE render state.

note

RenderMonkey does not tell you if your hardware supports radial fog. You must either refer to your rendering hardware specifications or simply give radial fog a try. If it doesn't work, it probably isn't supported.

One thing missing from our discussion so far is how the fog gets colored. The hardware enables you to control the color by using the D3DRS_FOGCOLOR render state, which can be set to any valid color. Keep in mind that this is the color to be used when full fog is present. As fog creeps in, this value is blended with your object's color in a way proportionate to the fog ratio determined by the hardware.

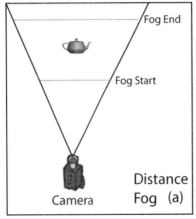
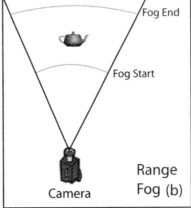

Figure 15.3 How hardware fog is determined based on the distance from the camera. (a) Camera space fog. (b) Range-based fog.

One assumption about the hardware fog so far is that its progression is linear. This is, in fact, the default behavior of the rendering hardware. However, the D3DRS_FOGTABLEMODE allows you to adjust the fog progression to be either linear or exponential. Although exponential fog generally looks more realistic, it can have some additional costs associated with it. Figure 15.4 illustrates the different fogging modes available on most hardware.

The last thing I should mention is how this fog actually gets applied to your scene. Because fog essentially affects the light coming in to the viewer, it is computed based on the fog thickness between the object and the viewer. After you determine the regular rendering result of the object, the fog thickness is determined and used to blend the object color with the fog color based on the fog progression mode chosen.

Under normal circumstances, the use of hardware fog is simply a matter of setting a few render states and letting the hardware take care of the rest. However, the situation is somewhat different when dealing with a vertex shader.

Because of the programmable nature of vertex shaders, you cannot simply set render states and have the fog render. Because the hardware has no control over the rendering of the geometry, an output register with the semantics of FOG has been created. It is your responsibility to set this value to the appropriate fog level. This has the effect of overriding the following render states: D3DRS_FOGSTART, D3DRS_FOGEND, and D3DRS_FOGTABLEMODE. When using vertex shaders, you need to determine the proper fogging value yourself. It may mean a little more work, but in the end, it gives you much more flexibility. After you set a value for your FOG output variable, the hardware automatically blends in the appropriate amount of fogging.

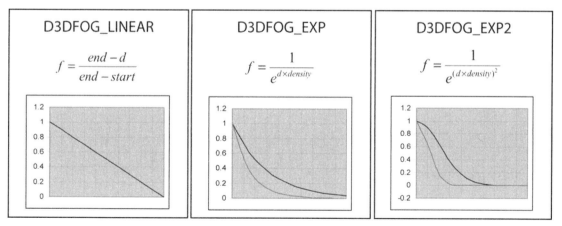

Figure 15.4 The various fog progression modes available on current hardware.

Note that the FOG output variable works upside down, the opposite of what you expect. A value of 1 means no fog, and a value of 0 means full fog. This FOG output value is interpolated, and the final blending with the fog color is done automatically by the hardware.

With this in mind, a simple linear fog can be determined with the following code:

```
Fog = 1.0 - ((Pos.z-Fog_Start)/(Fog_End-Fog_Start));
```

With all this information, you are now set to start writing your shader. The first step is to create a new workspace with the basics you need to render one or two objects.

After you create your basic shader, you should have your object rendering on the screen. To add fog, you need to change a few of the render states associated with your effect. To do this, you will need to add a render state node and set up the following render states: D3DRS_FOGENABLE and D3DRS_FOGCOLOR.

All you need to do now is set the FOG output variable to the proper fog level. The first step in doing this is to add the FOG variable to the output structure. The following code illustrates this updated structure:

```
struct VS_OUTPUT
{
    float4 Pos:      POSITION;
    float2 Txr1:     TEXCOORD0;
    float1 Fog:      FOG;
};
```

To set the FOG variable, you can either create a fog start and end variable or simply choose a simplified equation to determine the fogging level, which I have done for this particular shader. Doing so yields the final vertex shader code:

```
float4x4 view_proj_matrix;
struct VS_OUTPUT
{
    float4 Pos:      POSITION;
    float2 Txr1:     TEXCOORD0;
    float1 Fog:      FOG;
};

VS_OUTPUT vs_main(
    float4 inPos: POSITION,
    float2 Txr1: TEXCOORD0
)
{
    VS_OUTPUT Out;
```

```
    float4 Pos = mul(view_proj_matrix, inPos);
    Out.Pos = Pos;
    Out.Txr1 = Txr1;

    // Set the fog based on a zero fog start and
    // fixed end distance
    Out.Fog = pow(1-((Pos.z)/650),4);

    return Out;
}
```

Because the fogging is actually handled by the hardware, the pixel shader code does not need to do anything special beyond sampling the object's texture and outputting its color. Compiling and running your new shader should give results similar to the one shown in Figure 15.5. The final version of the shader is included on the companion CD-ROM as shader_1.rfx.

Figure 15.5 Rendering the hardware-accelerated fog shader.

Not Just Your Everyday Fog

The use of hardware fog when dealing with vertex shaders is more complicated than performing the same process using the fixed pipeline. Although this extra work may seem involved, it has several advantages.

Because you are the one supplying the fog factor to hardware, you have control over the equation used to determine how much to blend in. In the previous section, you used this in combination with the object's depth to determine the fog, but the system itself is totally flexible.

Using the FOG output variable, what restricts you to using depth as the criteria for determining the fogging intensity? For example, morning or evening dew leaves fog that dissipates as you get higher from the ground. Using the height from a certain point, you can decide the appropriate fog level. The following snippet explains how you can do this:

```
Fog = 1 - (Pos.y-Height_Start)/(Height_End-Height_Start);
```

Taking this into consideration, you can easily write a shader that fogs objects based on their relative height. The following vertex shader illustrates how this can be done:

```
float4x4 view_proj_matrix;
struct VS_OUTPUT
{
    float4 Pos:        POSITION;
```

```
      float2 Txr1:    TEXCOORD0;
      float1 Fog:     FOG;
};


VS_OUTPUT vs_main(
   float4 inPos: POSITION,
   float2 Txr1: TEXCOORD0
)
{
   VS_OUTPUT Out;

   float4 Pos = mul(view_proj_matrix, inPos);
   Out.Pos = Pos;
   Out.Txr1 = Txr1;

   // Set the fog proportional to the Y height.
   // With a vertex shader, the fog can be set to
   // any value you wish. Because you wish a screen
   // height in the proper range, you must divide the
   // Y component by the W component to take perspective
   // into account.
   Out.Fog = (2*Pos.y/Pos.w)+1;

   return Out;
}
```

Applying this new shader code to the shader you previously developed yields a height-based fog similar to the one shown in Figure 15.6. The final version of the shader is included on the companion CD-ROM as shader_2.rfx.

As you can see, this added flexibility may require a little more work but can go a long way toward giving you total control over how you render fog. In the first exercise at the end of the book, you will be asked to use a vertex shader to develop another fogging variation.

Figure 15.6 Rendering our height-based fog shader.

Now that you know how the hardware creates its fog and how you can take advantage of it, how about doing your own volume-based fog from scratch? The next section explains a technique that can render a volume-based fog.

Giving Your Fog a Little Depth

So far, all our fog calculations have been based on the assumption that the density of the air particles was constant. We also assumed that the fog was constant across the whole scene. Although this may make sense when dealing with a global atmospheric effect, sometimes when dealing with other effects, such as clouds or shafts of light, you want to have better control over the fog's location, shape, and density.

To achieve something like this, you need to be able to create your fog in a volumetric way. Unfortunately, for something like this, you cannot count on support from the hardware and will need to generate it yourself.

Because you want the fog to be volumetric, you can simply give it shape by using regular geometry to define its outline and render it. The process to do this is simple; as Figure 15.7 shows, you need to determine the thickness of the fog at any point of the geometry. The real question becomes how you accomplish this.

Taking the depth of the mesh at each point when rendering, you can discover the thickness by determining the difference between the depth of the polygons of the front and the back of the model. If you are dealing with a non-convex object, as in the Figure 15.8 example, you need to consider the fact that there may be multiple entry and exit points to the mesh. To accommodate for this, you need to take the sum of the depths of each back and front face, thus adding up all the depths for each entry/exit. Taking the difference of these front and back depth values will then yield you the total thickness at any point for your mesh.

With this basic knowledge, how do you go about rendering such a fog volume? The answer lies in using render targets to store the depth of the fog object. By using two render targets, one for the depth of the front-facing faces and one for the back-facing ones, you can render your object twice and save the depths.

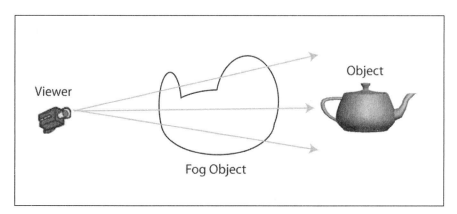

Figure 15.7 How to render volumetric fog using geometry.

To render those two render passes, you need to store the depth of the object in the render target; this is simply a matter of using the depth stored in the Z-coordinate of the projected vertex position as a color to put into the render target. Another thing you need to do is set up an additive blending mode so that multiple depths for concave objects add together correctly. This is done by setting the following render states:

```
D3DRS_ALPHABLENDENABLE = TRUE
D3DRS_BLENDOP = ADD
D3DRS_SRCBLEND = ONE
D3DRS_DESTBLEND = ONE
```

This combination of render states causes the different layers to be added together. For instance, the new value for the render target is the sum of the old value in the render target added to the newly calculated depth value.

Also remember that each pass needs to render either the front or back faces of your object. This can be controlled by D3DRS_CULLMODE. The vertex shader for the depth render passes simply need to transform the position of the vertices and pass the depth on to the pixel shader. The following vertex shader does just that:

```
float4x4 view_proj_matrix;
struct VS_OUTPUT
{
    float4 Pos:     POSITION;
    float Depth:    TEXCOORD0;
};

VS_OUTPUT vs_main(float4 inPos: POSITION)
{
    VS_OUTPUT Out;

    float4 Pos = mul(view_proj_matrix, inPos);
    Out.Pos = Pos;

    // Output the depth value by dividing it by a large
    // enough constant to ensure it is in the zero-to-one
    // range.
    Out.Depth= (Pos.z/800);

    return Out;
}
```

The pixel shader simply needs to take this depth and output it as a color. The following pixel shader code performs this:

```
sampler Texture0;
float4 ps_main( float Depth: TEXCOORD0 ) : COLOR0
{
    return Depth;
}
```

So far, you have the front and back depth for your fog volume object. To determine the fogging factor, you need to find out the actual thickness of the object. This can be accomplished by a third render pass; calculate the difference between the depth of the back polygons and front polygons for both depth render targets. When you've determined this thickness, you can determine the fog factor for a particular pixel by multiplying the thickness by a factor that controls the thickness-to-fog ratio. You might also want to use a lookup texture if you want to use a nonlinear thickness-to-fog ratio.

The vertex shader for this pass is a simple screen-space rendering pass. The pixel shader, on the other hand, samples both the front and back depth, calculates the difference, and outputs a color based on the fog intensity. The pixel shader code for this operation is

```
sampler Front;
sampler Back;
const float off = 1.0 / 128.0;
float4 ps_main( float2 TexCoord : TEXCOORD0 ) : COLOR
{
    float4 F = tex2D(Front,TexCoord);
    float4 B = tex2D(Back,TexCoord);

    // The thickness is defined as the front depth minus
    // the back depth. We multiply by 16 to increate the
    // contrast so the thickness can be seen better.
    return (F-B)*16;
}
```

After it's compiled and running, this shader should give you a fogged-up version of your volume object, as shown in Figure 15.8. The final version of the shader is included on the companion CD-ROM as shader_3.rfx.

Notice in Figure 15.8 and from your rendering output that the fog generated in the previous exercise exhibits a lot of banding. Because the depth is computed in a single component and output to the texture color, this gives you only eight bits of precision, which is usually less than adequate for such a task. You need to find a way to work around this problem and increase your depth precision, but wait. . . .

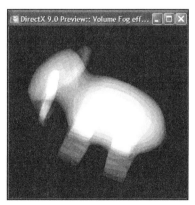

Figure 15.8 Rendering a volumetric fog object.

Didn't we use a technique to do just this in Chapter 6, "Blurring Things Up"? By taking advantage of the different color components to store different levels of precision for your depth, you can increase your total precision. The following code can be used to encode your depth into several components:

```
Depth.x = floor(Depth*32.0)/32.0;
Depth.y = floor((Depth-OutDepth.x)*32.0*32.0)/32.0;
Depth.z = floor((Depth-OutDepth.x-OutDepth.y/32.0)*32.0*32.0*32.0)/32.0;
```

In the preceding code, you will notice that we only use 32 values for each component, thus only using five bits of precision. Doing so enables you to support the addition of several depth values together. You can do this as long as the values within any color component do not overflow. Using only five bits of precision allows for up to 8 depth values to overlap without risking overflows. The decoding process, shown in the following code, takes care of compensating for the addition of multiple depth values:

```
float Depth = DepthTxr.x + DepthTxr.y/32.0 + DepthTxr.z/(32.0*32.0);
```

Applying this to the previous shader requires you to change the pixel shader for your depth rendering passes to encode the depth received from the vertex shader into the different color components. The following code shows the resulting pixel shader:

```
sampler Texture0;
float4 ps_main( float Depth: TEXCOORD0 ) : COLOR0
{
    float4 OutDepth;
    OutDepth.x = floor(Depth*32.0)/32.0;
    OutDepth.y = floor((Depth-OutDepth.x)*32.0*32.0)/32.0;
    OutDepth.z = floor((Depth-OutDepth.x-OutDepth.y/32.0)*32.0*32.0*32.0)/32.0;
    OutDepth.w = 1;
    return OutDepth;
}
```

The other change that you need to apply is to the final pass so that it decodes the depth values to determine the thickness of the volume object. The following pixel shader does just this:

```
sampler Front;
sampler Back;
const float off = 1.0 / 128.0;

float4 ps_main( float2 TexCoord : TEXCOORD0 ) : COLOR
{
    float4 F = tex2D(Front,TexCoord);
```

```
    float4 B = tex2D(Back,TexCoord);

    float DepthF = F.x + F.y/32.0 + F.z/(32.0*32.0);
    float DepthB = B.x + B.y/32.0 + B.z/(32.0*32.0);
    return (DepthF-DepthB)*16;
}
```

The compiled version of this shader gives a result similar to that shown in Figure 15.9. The final version of the shader is included on the companion CD-ROM as shader_4.rfx. As you can see from the output, the generated fog is much more precise than with the previous shader, and all this with little extra work.

So far you have only rendered volume fog as an individual object, but in reality, your fog needs to interact with other geometry. The technique overviewed, does not take care of this situation but fortunately, there is a simple solution to the problem.

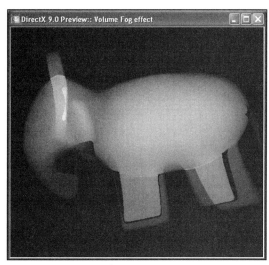

Figure 15.9 Rendering output for the increased resolution volumetric fog shader.

When rendering the scene, you need to render the depth of your solid objects to a separate render target in addition to the scene. The process for this is the same as that taken for the actual fog depth rendered in the previous shaders. With this information, you can adapt the fog depth shaders to consider the depth of the scene.

With the scene depth, you can determine the proper fog depth by comparing the depth of the fog object with the precomputed depth of the scene. If the depth of the fog is greater than the scene depth, you will store the scene depth. If the depth of the fog is less, you will use the fog.

On the vertex shader end, you need to modify your code so that screen space coordinates are passed to the pixel shader. The reason for this is that you need those coordinates to sample the scene depth texture previously calculated. This vertex shader is

```
float4x4 view_proj_matrix;
struct VS_OUTPUT
{
    float4 Pos:      POSITION;
    float  Depth:    TEXCOORD0;
```

```
      float2 TexCoord:    TEXCOORD1;
};

VS_OUTPUT vs_main(float4 inPos: POSITION)
{
   VS_OUTPUT Out;

   // Position the second object with a slight offset
   // so the no not fully overlap.
   inPos.x -= 10.5;

   float4 Pos = mul(view_proj_matrix, inPos);
   Out.Pos = Pos;
   Out.Depth = (Pos.z/1000);
   Out.TexCoord.x = 0.5 * (1 + (Out.Pos.x/Out.Pos.w));
   Out.TexCoord.y = 0.5 * (1 - (Out.Pos.y/Out.Pos.w));
   return Out;
}
```

The pixel shader also needs to be modified to receive the new texture coordinate and sample the scene depth map. After you have the depth for the scene, you need to decode it and compare it with the current fog depth. Because you are using a 2.0 pixel shader, this can easily be done with a conditional statement, such as if or expr?true_val:false_val. The following pixel shader does just that:

```
sampler Texture0;
float4 ps_main(
   float Depth: TEXCOORD0,
   float2 Txr: TEXCOORD1
) : COLOR0
{
   float4 OutDepth;
   float4 SolidDepthTxr = tex2D(Texture0,Txr);
   float SolidDepth = SolidDepthTxr.x +
                      SolidDepthTxr.y/32.0+
                      SolidDepthTxr.z/(32.0*32.0);
   OutDepth.x = floor(Depth*32.0)/32.0;
   OutDepth.y = floor((Depth-OutDepth.x)*32.0*32.0)/32.0;
   OutDepth.z = floor((Depth-OutDepth.x-OutDepth.y/32.0)*32.0*32.0*32.0)/32.0;
   OutDepth.w = 1;
   return (Depth>SolidDepth)?SolidDepthTxr:OutDepth;
}
```

After it's compiled and running, this shader should render an object with a fog volume intersecting it, similar to the one shown in Figure 15.10. The final version of the shader is included on the companion CD-ROM as shader_5.rfx.

As you can see, volumetric fog can be a powerful tool that enables you to create patchy fog or clouds within your scene. So far, I have discussed atmospheric effects without going into any specifics. The next section presents those topics in a bit more detail.

Rendering the Atmosphere

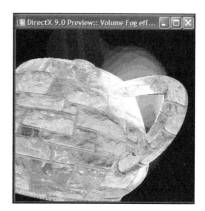

Figure 15.10 Rendering the volumetric fog shader interacting with a solid object.

The focus of this chapter is the rendering of atmospheric effects. So far, we have only concentrated on gross approximations, making use of hardware and volumetric fog. In this section, I will discuss briefly some techniques that can be used to render real outdoor atmospherics using better approximations. Even the estimation of outdoor atmospherics is a complex topic, and I will not go too deeply into details, but I do want to introduce you to some of the basic concepts so that you will have a better understanding of all their implications. For this section, I will not implement a full shader for the approaches discussed because it is not a trivial task to perform with RenderMonkey.

Different atmospherics come from the scattering of light when it encounters particles, either water vapor or dust, in the ambient air. As Figure 15.11 shows, this scattering can be categorized as either primary or secondary. Primary scattering occurs when light gets scattered once before reaching the viewer. Secondary scattering occurs when the light is deflected more than once before reaching the viewer.

Accurately considering all the scattering components is impossible in real-time . Such calculations imply the use of continuous integration to calculate the interaction of light with the atmosphere. Because of this, some assumptions must be taken to simplify the calculations.

There are several different approximations and models, which could be used to represent atmospherics. Because of this, I could write a whole separate book on this specific topic. Instead, I will just discuss a simple, commonly used model to give you a good idea. Pokrowski proposed a simple model to represent the sky's luminescence model, known as the CIE Clear Sky Luminescence Model. This model does a good job of approximating the sky color for a clear day. The equation for the model is illustrated in Figure 15.12. This model is simple to evaluate but requires you to determine many angles relating to the viewer and the sun.

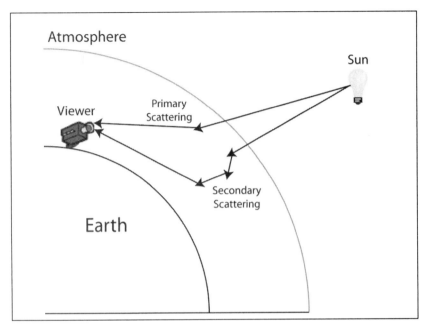

Figure 15.11 The primary and secondary scattering of light in the atmosphere.

$$Y_C = Y_z \frac{(0.91 + 10e^{-3\gamma} + 0.45\cos^2\gamma)(1 - e^{\frac{-0.32}{\cos\theta}})}{(0.91 + 10e^{-3\theta_s} + 0.45\cos^2\theta_s)(1 - e^{-0.32})}$$

Where Y_z is the zenith luminance, γ is the angle between the sun and viewer, θ is the angle of the viewer from vertical, and θ_s is the angle between the sun and a vertical vector.

Figure 15.12 Illustration of the CIE atmospheric model and its equations.

There are a wide range of different models that can be used to render outdoor atmospherics, all varying in realism and complexity. The CIE model is simple and gives good results for the sky atmospherics in a clear sky environment.

The topic of rendering atmospherics is a complex one, and an in-depth discussion is beyond the scope of this book. With the material covered in this chapter, however, you should have sufficient basic knowledge to extend your research if the need is there. For more information on the topics reviewed in this chapter, I invite you to read the Siggraph paper at: http://www.ati.com/developer/SIGGRAPH03/PreethamSig2003CourseNotes.pdf.

It's Your Turn!

The following exercise will let you explore the topic of atmospheric rendering on your own. The solutions to this exercise can be found in Appendix D.

Exercise 1: ROUND FOG

For this exercise, you are asked to expand the hardware-accelerated fog shader developed earlier in this chapter. You need to render your object in a way so that the fog is in a circular pattern around the center of the object. To do so, you need to take the distance of the object from the center of the screen, using its screen space position and scaling appropriately to ensure you have enough fogging.

What's Next?

As you can see from this chapter, rendering proper atmospheric effects goes a long way in making your scene renderings look more realistic. The current rendering hardware is set up to make your life easy by automating the process. Using vertex shaders helps you even more by giving you full control over the fogging factor used by the hardware.

Although hardware fogging is flexible, it cannot represent everything, especially patchy fog or clouds. To render such effects, you can use volumetric fog objects to give you full control over the position and shape of your fog. Taking advantage of the vertex and pixel shader version 2.0 architecture, along with the use of render targets, makes the process relatively simple.

When rendering outdoor scenes, it might be nice to be able to capture the effects of atmospheric scattering. Considering real atmospheric effects can be nearly impossible in real-time. However, using a proper approximation such as the CIE illumination model can give sufficient results for use at real-time speeds.

So far, all of our scenes have been mostly static where nothing moved or animated. In the next chapter, we will address this and introduce you to several animation techniques that you can use in your shaders.

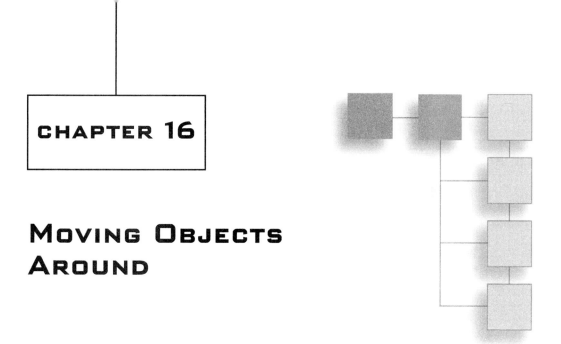

CHAPTER 16

MOVING OBJECTS AROUND

S o far, all the previous chapters focused on the looks of an object, ranging from materials to atmospheric effects. All these shaders give you nice graphics but leave you with a static, nonmoving scene. In this chapter, I will introduce to you some animation techniques that are commonly used in computer graphics and can be optimized by taking advantage of the hardware acceleration of vertex shaders.

Although I have touched upon the topic of vertex animation when introducing procedural materials and noise functions, this chapter will introduce techniques that can be used to animate the mesh as a whole.

Unfortunately, at the time of the writing of this book, RenderMonkey has no built-in support for animation. Because the situation is likely to change with future releases of the tool, I still want to introduce you to the topic of animations and give you code snippets that may come in handy later on.

Light, Camera, Action!

Because the topic of this chapter is animation, it makes sense to start with a simple form of animation. Remember that we previously discussed procedural vertex animations in Chapter 13, "Building Materials from Scratch"? Let me refresh your memory.

Using a Perlin noise function and a time-based variable such as time_0_1, you can offset vertices of an object at run-time. Although this particular example had little significance, such techniques could be used to create procedural explosions or animate objects that distort as they move, such as a water balloon. For reference, here is the vertex shader code used in the previous chapter:

```
struct VS_OUTPUT
{
```

```
        float4 Pos:     POSITION;
};

VS_OUTPUT vs_main(float4 inPos: POSITION)
{
    VS_OUTPUT Out;

    // Define a noisy function based on a sequence
    // of sine waves and manipulate the surface based
    // on the result
    inPos = inPos +
            0.05*sin( dot(inPos.xy,inPos.xy) + time_0_2PI) +
            0.05*sin( dot(inPos.xz,inPos.xz) + time_0_2PI) +
            0.05*sin( dot(inPos.yz,inPos.yz) + time_0_2PI );

    // Compute the object position.
    Out.Pos = mul(view_proj_matrix, inPos);
    return Out;
}
```

Keep in mind that a sine-based noise function was used for this particular shader. How-ever, nothing prevents you from using a function with more significance or even from using a set of shader constants that are set by the processor to control the distortion applied to your mesh.

Another simple procedural animation that could be applied to an object is to use a func-tion to control the actual position of the object. Let's say you are rendering a solar system; you could manually animate each planet, but because they all follow a simple circular path, why not let the shader handle it?

Using a built-in variable such as time_0_2PI, you can input this offset time value into a sine/cosine function to determine the position along a circular path. The following vertex shader code illustrates how this can be done:

```
struct VS_OUTPUT
{
    float4 Pos:     POSITION;
};

VS_OUTPUT vs_main(float4 inPos: POSITION)
{
    VS_OUTPUT Out;

    float4 center_offset = float4(0,0,0,0);
    float radial = time_0_2PI + time_offset;
```

```
// Determine the position on the circle based
// on the time value. This assumes the circle
// is along the X/Y plane.
center_offset.x = radius * sin(radial);
center_offset.y = radius * cos(radial);

// Offset all vertices by the same circle constant.
inPos = inPos + center_offset;

// Compute the object position.
Out.Pos = mul(view_proj_matrix, inPos);
return Out;
}
```

As you can see, even simple hardware-accelerated animations can do a lot for a scene, not only in making it dynamic but also in taking work off the main CPU. This may not seem like much, but when developing video games, any ounce of CPU power you can spare can be used for important tasks such as artificial intelligence or game physics.

Now let's move on from this simple form of animation to something that is more useful. Not everything is composed of randomly deforming meshes or rotating planets. The reality is that you may want to animate characters on your screen. The bad news is that you need to do much more work to animate them because of their complexity. On the good side, there are several good techniques available that can be used in collaboration with hardware acceleration. The next two sections overview two of the most common techniques: keyframing and skinning.

Object Metamorphosis

Although there are countless ways to animate geometry, you must strive to use techniques that can easily be optimized to work well on the rendering hardware. One of the most natural techniques for this is keyframing.

Keyframing is similar to the way still frame animations are done. Under ideal circumstances, you store the mesh for each position, or frame, within your animation. When it is time to replay your animation, you simply pick which mesh corresponds to the frame you want and render it. But this ideal case is less than ideal for hardware optimization.

Imagine a 1,000-vertices mesh that you want to animate for 10 seconds at 20 frames per second. If all the information for a vertex requires 16 bytes, which should be enough for a position, normal, and color, the total size of the animation would be approximately 3MB. And that's only for a simple 10-second animation!

Because most animations are fluid, there is one way to improve this situation. Instead of storing all the frames of the animation, you may want to take advantage of the fluidity of the animation and only store the important, or significant, frames of the animation. These significant frames, commonly called keyframes, give you a snapshot of the mesh at a certain point of the animation. Because of the fluidity of the animation, you may only need to store, say, two keyframes for every second of animation, significantly reducing the memory requirements for the animated mesh. Figure 16.1 explains the keyframing process.

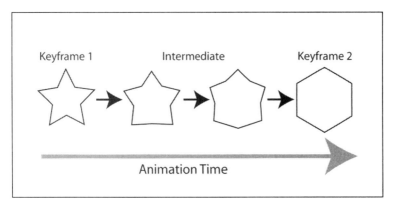

Figure 16.1 How keyframing animations work.

When the time comes to render the animation, based on the current animation time, you need to determine the two keyframes which the animation falls between. The idea is that the vertex shader needs to take those two frames and interpolate between them, based on a ratio determined by the animation time. For this to happen, the geometry for both frames needs to be passed to the vertex shader, which will then interpolate between the two. The easiest, but not necessarily the best looking, form of interpolation is a simple linear interpolation. To do this, you can take advantage of the HLSL built-in lerp function. The following vertex shader code illustrates how the positions of two keyframes can be interpolated:

```
struct VS_OUTPUT
{
    float4 Pos:    POSITION;
};

VS_OUTPUT vs_main(float4 inPos_1: POSITION,
                  float4 inPos_2: POSITION)
{
    VS_OUTPUT Out;

    // Blend the two animation frames together
    float4 inPos = lerp(inPos_1,inPos_2,animation_blend);
```

```
    // Compute the object position.
    Out.Pos = mul(view_proj_matrix, inPos);
    return Out;
}
```

As I have said, there are multiple ways to interpolate animation data from the animation. Using linear interpolation is the simplest way but can lead to discontinuities at keyframes. Figure 16.2 illustrates this problem and how a nonlinear interpolation technique can help improve keyframe transition.

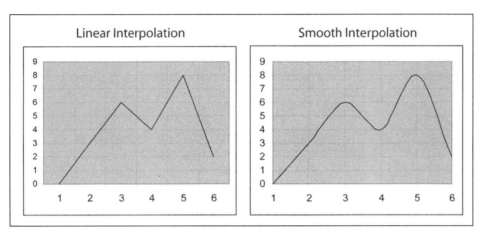

Figure 16.2 Linear versus nonlinear animation interpolation.

note

Under Direct3D, the best way to send data to the vertex shader for two keyframes is to take advantage of multiple streams. Streams enable you to specify vertex information from different sources. Taking advantage of this functionality makes it easy to combine multiple keyframes together.

One solution is to use a spline interpolation technique. This technique yields much better interpolation across keyframes but has a few consequences. The first side effect is that keyframes need to be equally spaced in time for the interpolation to work properly. In addition, you need the information of four keyframes to complete the task, two previous vertices and the two following ones. The following vertex shader code shows you the equation for the Hermite spline interpolation and how it can be used:

```
struct VS_OUTPUT
{
    float4 Pos:    POSITION;
};
```

```
VS_OUTPUT vs_main(float4 inPos_m1: POSITION,
                  float4 inPos_0: POSITION,
                  float4 inPos_1: POSITION,
                  float4 inPos_2: POSITION)
{
   VS_OUTPUT Out;

   // Precompute the spline basis functions
   float h0,h1,h2,h3;
   {
      // h0 = 2t^3 - 3t^2 + 1
      h0 = 2*pow(time,3) - 3*pow(time,2) + 1;

      // h1= -2t^3 + 3t^2
      h1 = -2*pow(time,3) + 3*pow(time,2);

      // h2 = t^3 - 2t^2 + t
      h2 = pow(time,3) - 2*pow(time,2) + time;

      // h3 = t^3 - t^2
      h3 = pow(time,3) - pow(time,2);
   }

   // Blend the keyframes with the Hermite spline equation
   float4 inPos = h0*inPos_0 +
                  h1*(inPos_1 - inPos_m1) +
                  h2*(inPos_2 - inPos_0) +
                  h3*inPos_1;

   // Compute the object position.
   Out.Pos = mul(view_proj_matrix, inPos);
   return Out;
}
```

The cool thing with keyframe interpolation-based animation is that you can animate more than just the position of your object. Any component that can be interpolated can be animated. Because each keyframe can have a full set of vertex information, such as color, you can interpolate it as well. However, you need to be cautious when interpolating vertex normals. Because a normal is meant to be normalized, the linear interpolation of a normal can yield a vector that isn't normalized. You generally need to renormalize your vectors after they have been interpolated. The following code snippet shows you how:

```
float3 normal = normalize(lerp(inNormal1,inNormal2,animation_blend));
```

Although this animation technique gives you a great amount of flexibility, even with proper keyframing it can consume large amounts of memory. This is especially true in today's rendering environment where meshes are getting denser. Because of this, other techniques are needed to animate meshes in a way that requires fewer resources.

In the next section, I will discuss a commonly used technique called skinning. This technique can be somewhat more restrictive but works well when animating characters and is much more memory efficient.

Of Skin and Bones

Although keyframing is a great and flexible animation technique, it can be very memory consuming and prohibitive. Say you want to animate a humanoid character in your scene; you may need something more efficient. Because a humanoid character is actually skin and muscle on top of skeletal structure, wouldn't it make sense to mimic this to animate your character?

Say you have a mesh of your character; you could construct an imaginary skeletal structure underneath it that supports it. You can then attach the vertices of your mesh to this set of bones. Once the vertices are attached, instead of animating the mesh, you can animate the bone instead. The attachment process takes care of animating the mesh automatically. Figure 16.3 shows how this works.

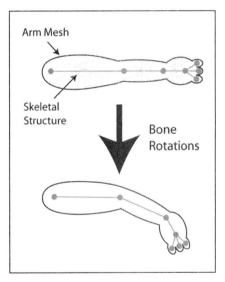

Because you are animating the skeleton instead of the mesh itself, the memory requirements are much less than they would be to represent the animation on the whole mesh. Another significant advantage of this technique is that for a generic skeletal structure, you can animate a multitude of meshes. For example, if you were to define an animation skeletal structure for a human character, you can wrap any humanlike mesh on top of this

Figure 16.3 How a mesh is attached to a skeletal structure and animated.

skeleton. This is a great advantage because it enables you to reuse common animations, such as walking and running, with a multitude of different characters.

On the downside, skinning has some disadvantages. The first is obvious: You can only animate objects for which you can define a skeletal structure. The second inconvenience is that for complex meshes, the number of bones required in your skeleton might be prohibitive, and sometimes, reducing the number of bones can yield unwanted results, such as pinching of the mesh in some joints.

One thing I have not discussed so far is how the mesh actually gets wrapped over the skeletal structure. To get good animation results, especially at joints, you want vertices to be influenced by potentially multiple bones. So let's say a particular vertex can be influenced by up to four bones. You need to store an index and a weight for the influence of the four bones. Keep in mind that the total weights for a vertex should add up to one.

I will not go into the details of how to author such meshes, but most common 3D packages, such as 3DSMax by Discreet, support skinning and offer tools to construct skeletal structures, animate them, and assign weights to the vertices on your mesh.

note

Because bone animations are represented as matrices stored in vertex shader constants, you are limited in the number of bones you can use. If you reach such a restriction, you need to break your mesh into submeshes with smaller bone counts.

Assuming you have a mesh that has been constructed using such a tool and has been exported, the weights and indices to the bone structure would be stored as two input vectors in your vertex data. The bones themselves would be represented as matrices stored as constants within your vertex shader. To animate the vertices, take the initial vertex position and apply the transformation imposed by all four bone influences proportionally to their weights. Doing so yield the following vertex shader code:

```
struct VS_OUTPUT
{
    float4 Pos:     POSITION;
};

VS_OUTPUT vs_main(float4 inPos: POSITION,
                  float4 inIndex: BLENDINDEX,
                  float4 inWeight: BLENDWEIGHT)
{
    VS_OUTPUT Out;

    // Compute in the weight of four bones
    float4 Pos = float4(0,0,0,0);
    Pos += inWeight.x * mul(Bones[inIndex.x],inPos);
    Pos += inWeight.y * mul(Bones[inIndex.y],inPos);
    Pos += inWeight.z * mul(Bones[inIndex.z],inPos);
    Pos += inWeight.w * mul(Bones[inIndex.w],inPos);

    // Compute the object position.
    Out.Pos = mul(view_proj_matrix, inPos);
    return Out;
}
```

When skinning a mesh, you might also want to animate the vertex normals because they are essential to determine proper lighting. Mathematically speaking, to animate a normal using the bone matrices, you need to calculate the inverse of the transpose of the bone animation matrix. This is prohibitive to do in real-time, but there is a saving grace. If your animation matrices only contain rotations and translations, it turns out that the inverse of the matrix is the same as its transpose; this means that you can use the regular bone matrix to animate the matrix in the same way you animate the vertex position. You just need to remember to renormalize your vector after you are done. The following vertex shader code does just that:

```
struct VS_OUTPUT
{
    float4 Pos:      POSITION;
    float3 Normal:   TEXCOORD0;
};

VS_OUTPUT vs_main(float4 inPos: POSITION,
                  float3 inNormal: NORMAL,
                  float4 inIndex: BLENDINDEX,
                  float4 inWeight: BLENDWEIGHT)
{
    VS_OUTPUT Out;

    // Compute in the weight of four bones
    float4 Pos = float4(0,0,0,0);
    Pos += inWeight.x * mul(Bones[inIndex.x],inPos);
    Pos += inWeight.y * mul(Bones[inIndex.y],inPos);
    Pos += inWeight.z * mul(Bones[inIndex.z],inPos);
    Pos += inWeight.w * mul(Bones[inIndex.w],inPos);

    // Compute in the weight of four bones for the normal
    float4 Normal = float4(0,0,0,0);
    Normal += inWeight.x * mul(Bones[inIndex.x],inNormal);
    Normal += inWeight.y * mul(Bones[inIndex.y],inNormal);
    Normal += inWeight.z * mul(Bones[inIndex.z],inNormal);
    Normal += inWeight.w * mul(Bones[inIndex.w],inNormal);
    Normal = normalize(Normal); // Renormalize the normal

    // Compute the object position.
    Out.Pos = mul(view_proj_matrix, inPos);
    Out.Normal = Normal;
    return Out;
}
```

Skinning is a very efficient technique to animate characters within your scene. It does require more initial setup and art work but will pay off in the memory savings. In addition, you can potentially use the skeletal structure of your character and procedurally animate it by combining several animations or by applying some form of inverse kinematics. Skinning might seem more expensive by looking at the vertex shader code, but a four-bone skinning shader can be implemented on the vertex shader 1.1 architecture.

It's Your Turn!

Because most of the topics covered in this chapter cannot currently be implemented under RenderMonkey, there is no homework for this chapter. Enjoy!!

What's Next?

When developing 3D applications, most of the time you need your scene to be dynamic, and animations are the key to making this come true. You might be able to settle for simple procedural animation when dealing with simple objects, such as a solar system, or even procedurally deformed objects, such as a water balloon. However, most of the time, this will not suffice, and you will need something more powerful, especially when rendering characters.

One approach that can be taken is to pre-animate your mesh at certain points in time, or keyframes, from which your vertex shader will be used to procedurally interpolate between two particular keyframes. This technique can need a substantial amount of memory because of the mesh data required by all the keyframes. On the other hand, this technique can be used to create complex deformation as long as the topology of the mesh stays the same from one keyframe to another.

Another approach that can be taken is to use skinning. With this technique, you create a skeletal support structure for your mesh and animate this structure instead of the mesh itself. Each vertex is then assigned a set of weights corresponding to the contribution of each bone-to-vertex position. This technique has some limitations that constrain the number of bones which can be put into play and also restricts the amount of deformation that can be applied. However, this technique is generally well suited for the animation of living beings because it mimics their skeletal structure.

Because RenderMonkey does not support animations at the moment, it is not worth it to focus more on animations for now. In the next chapter, I will take up the topic of lighting again from a more advanced point of view by introducing some of the latest lighting techniques, such as spherical harmonics.

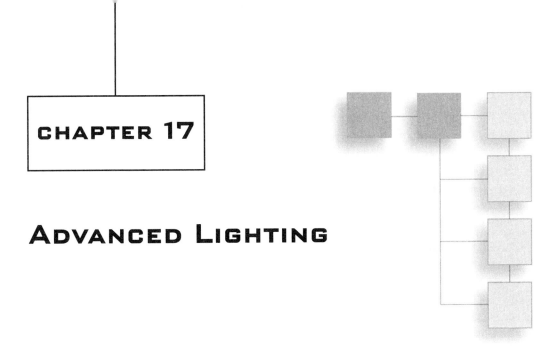

CHAPTER 17

ADVANCED LIGHTING

Lighting is probably one of the most important visual cues. The techniques illustrated earlier in this book cover the most basic and commonly used lighting techniques. However, there are many more approaches that can be applied to the lighting of your rendered scenes. The goal of this chapter is to introduce you to some of these techniques and how they can be used in current and future rendering architectures.

Keep in mind that the techniques overviewed in this chapter are new and emerging approaches to lighting. This means that these techniques can be complex and have not been thoroughly used in real-time rendering environments. This has the consequence that many of the tools needed to use such techniques are not yet available. However, as they gain more widespread use, more tools and support will become available for them to be implemented in real-time production environments.

In the following section, I will discuss how you can create your own custom lighting model by describing how you can use a hemisphere to represent the lighting of an environment. In the next section, I will discuss polynomial textures. They can be used as an alternative to bumpmaps and have the added ability to capture self-shadowing information. Finally, in the last section, I will discuss how you can capture the diffuse environment lighting of a scene and represent it in a simple form that can be computed in real-time.

Let's move on and start by exploring a simple custom-built lighting model that can work well for both outside and indoor scenes.

Outdoor Scene Lighting

All the lighting models we have outlined so far stem from approximations based on real-life lighting models. Quite often, however, by taking a look at an environment, you can come up with your own approximation that will work well for the circumstances you are in. This is essentially what I will show you in this section. We can create a new lighting model that estimates lighting better for an outdoor scene.

Rendering objects in an outdoor environment can be tricky. Because of the interreflections of the objects in your scene, the lighting in the environment comes from all directions. To render accurate lighting on an object, you need to consider numerous amounts of lights, which is, of course, prohibitive for real-time applications. To perform such lighting in real-time, however, you need to find an estimation that runs quickly enough to be feasible in real-time.

Some General Approaches

One solution is to model your environment as a set of discrete directional lights and select a set of lights that does a good job of approximating the global lighting for this environment. The problem with this approach is determining the number, positions, and colors of those lights in the first place. Although there are ways to accomplish this, it is generally a less than convenient technique.

A better approach is to make use of environment mapping techniques to light your object. If your environment is already a cubemap, all is easy. If it is not, you can easily build one on-the-fly as I discussed in Chapter 11, "Mirror, Mirror, On the Wall." However, the question becomes, how can you represent diffuse and specular lighting through an environment map?

The cubemap itself can be used to represent a pure reflection, but when dealing with simple specular and diffuse lighting, you have to change your approach slightly. Specular lighting is almost like reflection, but it is slightly more diffused, or fuzzy. To achieve this perfectly, you need to run a partial integration on your cubemap to extract the specular component. The integration process would, for each texel in your cubemap, traverse all the other texels and add their contributions together proportionately to their contribution to the lighting.

Although this is doable, it can be prohibitively expensive. A simple solution to this is to blur your environment map instead of integrating it; this doesn't give you exactly the same results but is close enough for lighting purposes. When dealing with diffuse lighting, you need a full integration of your lighting environment, which can be achieved with a more significant blur of your cubemap. Figure 17.1 illustrates the results for a cubemap, along with its specular and diffuse version.

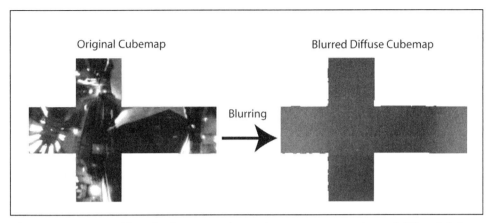

Figure 17.1 How a blurred cubemap can be used to represent specular and diffuse lighting.

With those environment maps, rendering lighting is straightforward. For the specular lighting component, you use the reflection vector as a lookup into the specular blurred environment map. To render diffuse lighting, the process is the same with the exception that you will be using the surface normal instead of the reflection vector to look up into the lighting texture.

Although this technique is simple and effective, the amount of blurring required can be prohibitive, especially when dealing with diffuse lighting maps which could potentially need hundreds of blurring passes to achieve realistic lighting results. Because of this, we need to take a look at better estimations for diffuse lighting in our outdoor environment. But before we consider a new approach, let's take a look at how diffuse lighting happens on the surface of an object for a lighting environment.

Consider a specific point on a surface; you can assume that this particular microfacet is a planar area with a position in space and a constant surface normal. Because of this, the lighting that affects this particular point is defined by a simple hemisphere centered on these microfacets. This has been illustrated in Figure 17.2.

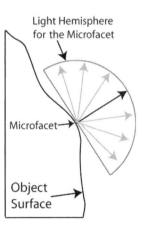

Figure 17.2 How a particular microfacet of your object gets light as the summation of the light coming into the hemisphere and centered on the surface normal at that point.

If you were to consider lighting from an environment at this point, the lighting could be summarized by the integration of the lighting coming at this microfacet from every direction within the hemisphere, as shown in Figure 17.2. The approximation done in our blurred cubemap was to assume that every point within the cubemap is the integration of all lights within the hemisphere defined by the lookup direction within the environment map. Although the blurring process does not give the same result as a real integration, it does factor in the lighting contribution from neighboring pixels.

Hemisphere Lighting Model

When dealing with an outdoor environment, you can simplify the process even more because the most important components of the lighting are the sky and ground reflection colors. Going with this assumption, the process of finding out the total lighting for a particular microfacet of your object becomes a matter of determining the appropriate blend of both the sky and ground colors. This process is illustrated in Figure 17.3. Note that this approach can work well for any circumstance when lighting can be simplified by the representation of two sources of light, one coming from the ground and the other from above, and is not restricted to only outdoor scenes, although it is the most obvious example.

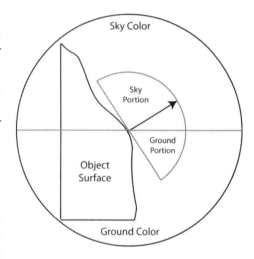

Figure 17.3 Determining lighting by using two hemispheres, which represent the sky and reflected ground colors.

To achieve the appropriate blend, you need to determine the proportion of the microfacet hemisphere that corresponds to the sky and ground portions. Without getting into the mathematical details, such integration is simply a matter of interpolating the sky and ground color in relationship to the dot product of surface normal and a vector pointing towards the sky. Doing so yields the following vertex shader code:

```
blendFactor = (dot(inNormal, float3(0,-1,0)) + 1.0)/2.0;
```

To develop a shader using this technique, you need a one-pass effect that renders an object, taking in both the position and the normals for the object vertices. In addition to the standard components, you need two extra variables to store the color of the ground and sky. With this, your vertex shader simply needs to take in the vertex normal, compute the blending factor, and use the lerp function to blend both colors. The following is the resulting vertex shader:

```
float4x4 view_proj_matrix;
float4 sky_color;
float4 ground_color;
struct VS_OUTPUT
{
   float4 Pos:     POSITION;
   float4 Diff:    COLOR;
   float4 Tex:     TEXCOORD;
};

VS_OUTPUT vs_main(
   float4 inPosition: POSITION,
   float4 inNormal:    NORMAL,
   float4 inTex:       TEXCOORD )
{
   VS_OUTPUT Out;

   // Transform the position and output the texture coordinate
   Out.Pos = mul( view_proj_matrix, inPosition);
   Out.Tex = inTex;

   // Determine the sky/ground factor
   float factor = (dot(inNormal, float3(0,-1,0)) + 1.0)/2.0;

   // Determine final lighting color
   Out.Diff = lerp(sky_color,ground_color,factor);
   Out.Diff.a = 1.0;

   return Out;
}
```

The pixel shader simply needs to take in the determined lighting color and modulate this interpolated value with the texture color of your object, yielding the following pixel shader code:

```
sampler color_map;
float4 ps_main(
   float4    inDiff: COLOR,
   float4    inTex:  TEXCOORD ) : COLOR
{
   // Return the hemisphere color modulated
   // with the color of the base texture
   return inDiff * tex2D(color_map, inTex);
}
```

Keep in mind that this particular shader does its operations on a per-vertex basis but can easily be adapted to do the same in a per-pixel manner. Compiling and running your new shader should give results similar to the one shown in Figure 17.4. The final version of the shader is included on the companion CD-ROM as shader_1.rfx.

Figure 17.4 Rendering result for the hemisphere shader.

Why is this technique so awesome? There are a few reasons worth mentioning; the first is the quality of the rendering results versus its ease of implementation. It is essentially a great, low-cost way of representing ambient lighting.

Another interesting point of this approach is that you can use it to represent *self-occlusion*, or self-shadowing. If you determine a self-shadowing factor for each vertex, you can use this value to attenuate the lighting coming in from the ambient hemisphere lighting. You may not think much of self-shadowing, but when dealing with convex meshes, it is a reality that nooks within your object are less exposed and will get less lighting, thus creating shadows within your object. Being able to add such details to your rendering can make your graphics much richer because you will learn over the next few paragraphs.

To do such self-shadowing, you need to determine the occlusion factor for each vertex on your mesh. This is generally done by casting multiple rays from the vertex along its lighting hemisphere. Based on the ray's intersection with the surrounding geometry, you can build an occlusion ratio, which can be used to scale down the lighting on this particular vertex.

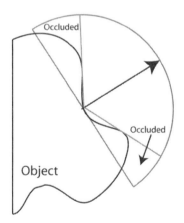

The whole process is illustrated in Figure 17.5, along with a sample of a mesh rendered with and without a self-occlusion term. Take note that the self-shadowing value can easily be stored as part of the alpha channel of the vertex color for your mesh. I will not explain exactly how to determine the shadowing factors because that is outside the scope of this book, but you do need to remember that such a technique only works well for a solid mesh, which does not animate or deform over time.

Figure 17.5 Occlusion determination by ray-tracing and sample of a mesh with and without an occlusion factor.

Polynomial Texture Maps

When doing lighting in previous chapters, you saw how important bumpmaps can be in increasing the amount of detail perceived on your object. As you know, this detail does not exist for real on your mesh, but you manage to fool the human eye by taking advantage of those pixel-level details when performing lighting on your objects.

Even so, bumpmapping assumes that your object is of a constant texture and only represents the variations of elevation on the microstructure of the object through the normal map itself. Because of this, bumpmapping cannot be used to represent such things as varying object texture or self-shadowing.

Combining BRDF and Bumpmapping

In this section, I will introduce a new texture mapping technique called polynomial texture maps. They are a new form of texture representation that enables you not only to consider micro-details, such as the elevations on a surface, but also to take into account self-shadowing and some BRFD-like properties of your object's material. Before you can write a polynomial texture map, or PTM shader, let's look at how this all works.

Lighting for a particular point on a surface comes from the combination of all the incoming light to the hemisphere of this microfacet on the surface of the object. By taking an object made of the material you want to reproduce, you could set up a rig that can take an image of your object with different lighting angles. This is illustrated in Figure 17.6. Because you want to reproduce diffuse lighting only, the position of the viewer, or camera, can remain constant, and you can set up your rig to only capture lighting from different angles with a constant camera position.

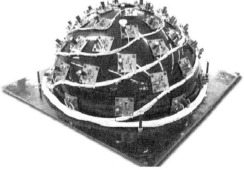

The result of this experiment is a set of images of your surface, lit from various angles. This in itself may seem of little use without a way of representing or compressing this information into a more useful form. Taking the lighting for a particular light on the hemisphere, you can simplify

Figure 17.6 How you can set up a rig to capture lighting properties of an object for various lighting angles and a fixed camera.

this vector by projecting it on the plane of the microfacet. This gives you a U and V vector along the plane of the surface, corresponding to the tangent and binormal vectors. This enables you to represent a full vector with only two components, which will come in handy later. This has been illustrated in Figure 17.7.

note

You will need to keep in mind that building such a rig is probably impractical for most uses but serves to show how such values can be determined. At the time of this writing, there are no tools that can be used to generate polynomial textures. However, as use of this technique grows more widespread, such tools are bound to start showing up.

At this point, you have a set of lighting textures and two variables to represent the direction of the lighting. You need to find a way to combine those two in a simple but meaningful way. The inventors of polynomial textures at Hewlett-Packard decided to take a second order polynomial equation to represent the textures so that the U and V vector components can be used to re-create proper lighting. The equation is in Figure 17.8.

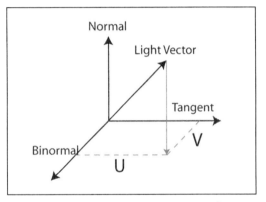

Figure 17.7 How the lighting direction for a microfacet can be represented by two components projected onto the plane of the microfacet.

This leaves you with six coefficients, which can be determined by passing a set of lighting values through a curve-matching algorithm. By applying this curve-matching to the set of lighting images you determined earlier, you can determine a set of coefficients per-pixel. Those coefficients enable you to approximate the lighting in relationship to the lighting angle for each of the pixels in your texture map.

$$Intensity = Au^2 + Bv^2 + Cuv + Du + Ev + F$$

Figure 17.8 Polynomial equation used for polynomial texture mapping.

Because some materials have varying lighting interactions based on the surface color, you need to determine a set of coefficients for each of the color components, which would cause PTMs to require 18 coefficients, one set of six for each color component. But for general use, and because the eye is more sensitive to slight variation in light intensity than to color, you can average the coefficients so that only a single polynomial is needed.

With six coefficients to represent, you can use two textures to store this side information. Samples are provided with RenderMonkey and are named `tablet_a012.tga` and `tablet_a345.tga`. Also keep in mind that because the polynomial coefficients can be signed, proper scale and bias will need to be applied to the texture.

Building the Shader

Developing a shader for polynomial texturing is straightforward. Because the polynomial information is stored in a texture, the bulk of the work needs to be done on the pixel shader. The only thing the vertex shader needs to do is to transform the lighting vector into tangent space so that we may discover a per-pixel U and V coefficient for you to evaluate the polynomial.

To accomplish this, you need to transform the light vector into tangent space. This means you need to set up your stream mapping so that it returns the normal, tangent, and binormal for the vertex. The following is the resulting vertex shader code:

```
float4x4 view_proj_matrix;
float4x4 inv_view_matrix;
float4 light;
struct VS_OUTPUT
{
    float4 Pos:     POSITION;
    float4 Tex:     TEXCOORD0;
    float3 Light:   TEXCOORD1;
};

VS_OUTPUT vs_main(
    float4 inPosition: POSITION,
    float4 inNormal:   NORMAL,
    float4 inTex:      TEXCOORD,
    float4 inTangent:  TANGENT,
    float4 inBinormal: BINORMAL )
{
    VS_OUTPUT Out;

    // Transform the vertex and output its texture coordinate
    Out.Pos = mul(view_proj_matrix, inPosition);
    Out.Tex = inTex;

    // Determine the light vector
    float3 lightVect = normalize(mul(inv_view_matrix, light) - Out.Pos);

    // Transform the light into tangent space
    Out.Light.x = dot(lightVect, inTangent.xyz);
    Out.Light.y = dot(lightVect, inBinormal.xyz);
```

```
    Out.Light.z = dot(lightVect, inNormal.xyz);

    return Out;
}
```

The pixel shader for PTM is significantly more complex. Access to the polynomial textures is simple, but you need to prepare the lighting vector to be useful. The first step is to normalize the lighting vector and extract the U and V components. Because our vector is in tangent space, we are blessed that the U and V components simply correspond to the X and Y components of the vector. However, you need to renormalize them appropriately by scaling the resulting values by the inverse of the Z component, ensuring that the U/V vector has a length of 1. The following code does just this:

```
inLight.xy = normalize(inLight.xy);
inLight.xy *= (1.0 - inLight.z);
```

With this, you only need to evaluate the polynomial using the right combinations of U and V. Remember that the PTM values must be biased and scaled because they are signed. The following is how you can perform this:

```
lu2_lv2_lulv = inLight.xyx * inLight.xyy;
col = dot(lu2_lv2_lulv, a012) +
      dot(float3(inLight.xy,1), a345);
```

At this point, `col` contains the color intensity for the particular pixel. Determining the final color is simply a matter of reading in the surface texture and modulating it with the polynomial texture map lighting intensity you just determined, yielding the following pixel shader code:

```
float mode;
sampler color_map;
sampler Poly1;
sampler Poly2;
float4 ps_main(
    float4 inTex: TEXCOORD0,
    float3 inLight:TEXCOORD1 ) : COLOR
{
    float3 lu2_lv2_lulv;
    float4 col;
    float3 a012;
    float3 a345;

    // Normalize light direction
    inLight = normalize(inLight);

    // z-extrapolation
```

```
    inLight.xy = normalize(inLight.xy);
    inLight.xy *= (1.0 - inLight.z);
    inLight.z = 1.0;

    // Prepare higher-order terms
    lu2_lv2_lulv = inLight.xyx * inLight.xyy;

    // read terms and bias
    a012 = tex2D(Poly1,inTex) * 2.0 - 1.0;
    a345 = tex2D(Poly2,inTex) * 2.0 - 1.0;
    a345.z += 1.0;

    // Evaluate polynomial
    col = dot(lu2_lv2_lulv, a012) + dot(inLight, a345);

    // Multiply by rgb factor
    return col * tex2D(color_map, inTex);
}
```

Compiling and running your new shader should give results similar to the one shown in Figure 17.9. The final version of the shader is included on the companion CD-ROM as shader_2.rfx.

As you can see in Figure 17.9, the image from different angles takes into account not only the bumpiness but also more subtle details, such as self-shadowing. More work is involved, and double the texture is needed to represent the PTM coefficients, but with increasing hardware speeds and texture bandwidth, it is likely that PTMs will be an even more commonly used technique in the future and will likely replace bumpmapping.

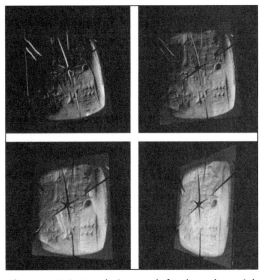

Figure 17.9 Rendering result for the polynomial texture map shader for various lighting directions.

Spherical Harmonics

Earlier when I was talking about hemisphere lighting, I presented it as a primitive way of approximating lighting for an environment. In this section, I will present another technique called *spherical harmonics*. These allow you to represent the lighting from a single environment as seen from a single point.

The Basic Idea

The idea behind spherical harmonics is relatively simple. Instead of thinking of lighting in terms of color, think of it in terms of frequency. A simple frequency representation on its own does not give us much to play with. Instead of going with this approach, what if we take all the light coming in to this point from all directions and wrap it around a sphere? With this representation, you can take the frequency spectrum of not the color but the variation of lighting around the sphere. Think of it as the spatial spectrum.

Because you only use your lighting as a source of ambient diffuse lighting, one major simplification can be done. Diffuse lighting means smooth transitions of the colors and no sharp discontinuities. In the spatial frequency domain, this translates into a spectrum that only requires the lower frequency components.

In simpler words, by representing the diffuse lighting of an environment seen from a point in space by a few low frequency harmonics, you can get a very good approximation. Experimentation has shown that taking 9 to 16 harmonics at low frequency is enough to give good results. Figure 17.10 shows the spherical harmonics for six coefficients.

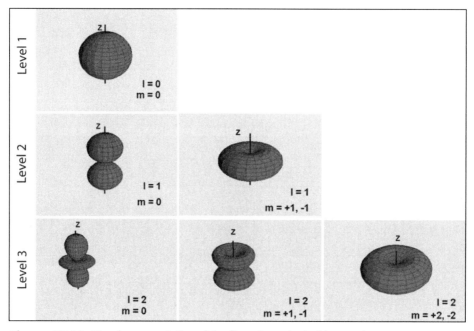

Figure 17.10 Visual representation of the first nine spherical harmonics.

Evaluating a spherical harmonic can be somewhat complex and involves the use of complex numbers. However, the equations can be boiled down to the reconstruction function shown in Figure 17.11.

$$f^{-1}(s) = \sum_{l=0}^{n-1} \sum_{m=-l}^{l} f_l^m y_l^m(s)$$

Figure 17.11 Equation used to reconstruct lighting from a set of spherical harmonics.

Looking at this equation, notice the double sum involved. This can be approximated by the combination of a matrix operation and a dot product. Because you are lighting from a single direction represented by the normal, the y value is simply the vector represented by the normal. The lighting operation becomes a matter of projecting the spherical harmonic coefficients represented in matrix form to the lighting normal based on the vertex normal.

Keep in mind that the following operation applies to a single color component. You will need to repeat the same operation for each of the red, green, and blue color components; this means you need three coefficient matrices in the end. Now, keep in mind that my explanation of spherical harmonics is significantly simplified. The math involved is much more complex, but for the purpose of this book, I just want to stick to the basic implementation of such a technique. But before I can show you how to implement such a shader, you need to know a little about how the spherical harmonic coefficients are determined.

Evaluating the spherical harmonic coefficient matrix in the first place is a more daunting task. In essence, you need to integrate the product of the orientation, along with its color value along the whole sphere, to determine the coefficient. You need to do the same for each of your harmonic coefficients. If you are acquainted with calculus, you know now why determining spherical harmonic coefficients in real-time can prove to be challenging.

For this chapter, we will not create our own coefficients, but will use a predetermined set from an environment map of a cathedral. The coefficients have been extracted from this environment map and are presented in matrix form in Figure 17.12. Using this set of coefficients on an object yields lighting that would simulate the lighting of an object within this environment.

$$red = \begin{bmatrix} 0.09010 & -0.04719 & 0.24026 & -0.14838 \\ -0.04719 & -0.09010 & -0.11155 & 0.19955 \\ 0.24026 & -0.11155 & -0.11890 & -0.17397 \\ -0.14838 & 0.19950 & -0.17397 & -0.07239 \end{bmatrix} \quad green = \begin{bmatrix} -0.02145 & -0.02145 & 0.09010 & -0.03070 \\ -0.02145 & 0.02145 & -0.09439 & 0.17908 \\ 0.09010 & -0.09439 & -0.06688 & -0.09210 \\ -0.03070 & 0.17908 & -0.09210 & -0.01280 \end{bmatrix}$$

$$blue = \begin{bmatrix} -0.12871 & -0.05149 & 0.06007 & 0.00512 \\ -0.05149 & 0.12871 & -0.20165 & 0.30700 \\ 0.06007 & -0.20165 & -0.11147 & -0.13815 \\ 0.00512 & 0.30700 & -0.13815 & -0.03463 \end{bmatrix}$$

Figure 17.12 Spherical harmonic coefficients for our shader.

Lighting with Spherical Harmonics

The workspace for implementing a spherical harmonic shader is simple and requires a basic pass along with a texture for your model. For this shader, I recommend using the teapot model and the `fieldstone.tga` as texture. For this shader, you also need to set your stream mapping to export the vertex normal; it will be useful for lighting. And before I forget, you also need the proper variables within your environment to contain the spherical harmonic matrices.

In this particular shader, we will accomplish the lighting on a per-vertex basis. In the exercise at the end of this chapter, you will be asked to do the same task on a per-pixel basis.

The first step in rendering your object is simply to project the vertex position and output it along with the texture coordinate, as you have done for most shaders in this book. Following this step, you need to prepare yourself for lighting. Because you want your light to stay static and your object to rotate in this light, you need to consider your light as being in view space. To do this, you need to transform your vertex normal into view space. This can be done with the following code:

```
normal = mul(view_matrix, normal);
```

Then all you need to do is take the transformed normal and apply the spherical harmonics to it. This is done by rotating the normal into the space of the harmonic for the proper color component and then projecting it back onto the normal with the use of a dot product. The following shows how this can be done in HLSL:

```
Color.r = dot(mul(r_matrix, normal), normal);
```

Putting all the components together yields the following vertex shader code:

```
float4x4 view_proj_matrix;
float4x4 view_matrix;
float4x4 r_matrix;
float4x4 g_matrix;
float4x4 b_matrix;
struct VS_OUTPUT
{
   float4 Pos:     POSITION;
   float4 Diff:    COLOR;
   float4 Tex:     TEXCOORD;
};
```

```
VS_OUTPUT vs_main(
    float4 inPosition: POSITION,
    float4 inNormal:   NORMAL,
    float4 inTex:      TEXCOORD )
{
    VS_OUTPUT Out;

    // Transform the position and output the texture coordinate
    Out.Pos = mul( view_proj_matrix, inPosition);
    Out.Tex = inTex;

    // Rotate normal into view space since the lighting information
    // is in that space
    float4 normal = float4(inNormal.x, inNormal.y, inNormal.z, 0.0);
    normal = mul(view_matrix, normal);
    normal.w = 1.0;

    // Evaluate spherical harmonic
    Out.Diff.r = dot(mul(r_matrix, normal), normal);
    Out.Diff.g = dot(mul(g_matrix, normal), normal);
    Out.Diff.b = dot(mul(b_matrix, normal), normal);
    Out.Diff.a = 1.0;

    return Out;
}
```

The pixel shader required for this effect simply needs to take the incoming spherical harmonics lighting color and modulate it by the texture color, giving the following code:

```
sampler color_map;
float4 ps_main(
    float4    inDiff: COLOR,
    float4    inTex:  TEXCOORD ) : COLOR
{
    // Return the spherical harmonic color modulated
    // with the color of the base texture
    return inDiff * tex2D(color_map, inTex);
}
```

Compiling and running your new shader should give results similar to the one shown in Figure 17.13. The final version of the shader is included on the companion CD-ROM as `shader_3.rfx`.

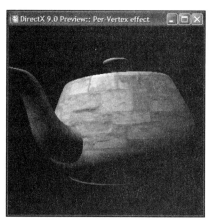

As you can see from the above shader, you can compute very interesting lighting at a relatively low cost. One major drawback with spherical harmonics is that the computation process for the coefficients is relatively expensive and is most likely too prohibitive to be done in real-time. On the plus side, spherical harmonics can be interpolated linearly, which means that you can precompute several sets of coefficients and interpolate from one to another.

Figure 17.13 Rendering result for the spherical harmonic shader.

If you want to push things even further, there are additional uses for spherical harmonics. For example, they can be used to represent self-shadowing coefficients, as well as self-reflections on a mesh. Spherical harmonics are an interesting approach to lighting and with the increase of rendering power will most likely become a more common approach in the future.

It's Your Turn!

The following exercise will let you explore the topic of advanced lighting on your own. The solution to this exercise can be found in Appendix D.

Exercise 1: PER-PIXEL SPHERICAL HARMONICS

For this exercise, you are asked to take the spherical harmonics shader developed earlier in this chapter and expand it to do its operations per-pixel. To do so, you simply need to move some of the variables from the vertex shader to the pixel shader and compute your lighting for each pixel.

What's Next?

In previous chapters, I discussed the topic of lighting by covering the basic aspects and commonly used techniques, such as diffuse and specular lighting and bumpmapping. This chapter was dedicated to the exploration of alternative techniques that can be applied to your renderings. Considering the rate at which the rendering hardware progresses, it is safe to assume that techniques similar to the ones explained in this chapter will soon become more prevalent.

The first way to approach lighting is to derive your own approximation that takes into account your current rendering context. The example presented in this chapter was hemisphere lighting, which works well for an outdoor environment where the two prevalent sources of light are the sky and the ground. By taking such an approach, you can make your ambient lighting for outdoor scenes much more realistic at a relatively low cost. In addition, this technique can be expanded to take into account local mesh phenomena such as self-shadowing.

In the second part of this chapter, I introduced the concept of polynomial texture maps, or PTMs, which serve as a sophisticated replacement for traditional bumpmapping when dealing with diffuse lighting. The advantage of PTMs is that, by taking lighting samples for different angles, you can formulate the lighting of each pixel in terms of a polynomial equation, which can then be evaluated at run-time, allowing more surface detail to be present, such as BRDF characteristics and self-shadowing.

Finally, I discussed the more complex topic of spherical harmonics. By taking advantage of the low frequency characteristics of diffuse lighting, you can represent environmental lighting for a single point in space through a small set of frequency harmonics wrapped around a sphere. Because of their nature, spherical harmonics can be evaluated on current graphics hardware through the use of a simple matrix operation and can even be performed on a per-pixel basis. The major advantage of spherical harmonics is that they can be used not only to represent lighting from a scene, but per-vertex to store surface details such as intra-reflections and self-shadowing.

One thing you are bound to have noticed by now is the importance of lighting when rendering geometry. So far, I have talked about the lights themselves and how they interact with objects and materials. I have left out an important side effect of lighting that can have significant contributions to the look of a scene. The next chapter covers the topic of shadows and how they can be reproduced in your 3D environment.

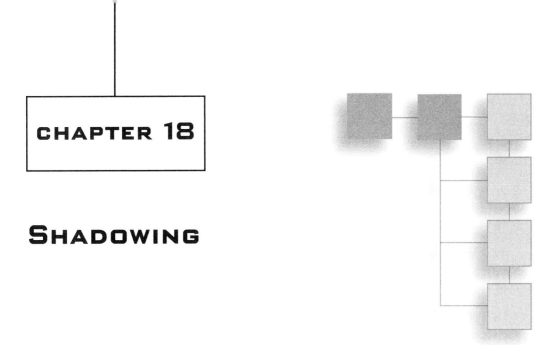

CHAPTER 18

SHADOWING

Lighting is one of the most important visual cues to make a scene more realistic and appealing. No matter how high quality your texture or your meshes are, if you render them with a constant lighting value, your scene does not look natural. Lighting is the reason you can see the world in the first place, and the more you consider the little subtleties of lighting, the more realistic your scene will look.

I have focused a lot on lighting itself throughout this book, but I have yet to discuss an important byproduct of lighting, which can be even more important than lighting itself: shadows. All the lighting approaches so far in this book consider only the angle, distance, and color of the light but fail to consider whether the light can reach an object in the first place. The reality is that lights are occluded by some objects, thus producing shadows within your scene. However, without the use of expensive, non-real–time techniques, such as ray tracing, it is almost impossible to determine accurate shadowing while rendering your initial lighting.

In addition to making renderings more realistic, the use of shadows can be of great importance in some contexts. Imagine a video game where you have to jump from platform to platform. Depending on the camera angle, it may be hard to discern where you are when jumping in the air and to know whether you will reach the next platform. However, if you add a shadow to your character, you add an important visual cue, which can give the user a good idea where they are when in the air.

Throughout this chapter, I will introduce the basic concepts of shadowing so you can have a good idea of how the phenomenon happens and some of the legacy techniques used to represent shadows. Following this, I will introduce the two techniques most commonly used today: shadow mapping and shadow volumes. For now, let's get started with an introduction to the basics of shadowing.

The Basics of Shadows

Shadows are a byproduct of lighting and, under some circumstances, can be an even more important visual cue than the lighting itself. In this section, I will show you how shadows happen so you can have a better understanding of the techniques used to re-create them.

Now, you may have heard before that there is no such thing as warm and cold, just warmth and a lack of warmth. The fact is that people tend to see things as black and white, when in reality it's just different levels of gray. Lack of heat energy causes something to feel cold; add some heat, and it will get warmer. The same principle applies to shadows. There are no such things as shadows; they only come from a lack of lighting. In nature, when some object blocks a source of light, a shadow is left behind because the light-receiving object does not get any lighting because it is occluded. Figure 18.1 shows this phenomenon.

In Figure 18.1, you may have noticed two parts to the shadow. The umbra is the portion of the shadow that is fully covered, and the penumbra is the portion that is partially in shadow. The umbra results from there being no such thing as a real point light. Lights are emitted not from a single position but from an area, which causes the regions on the boundary where the light is not fully occluded to be partially in shadow. Figure 18.2 shows you how a penumbra happens for a non-point light.

When rendering a scene with lighting, you and the hardware have no knowledge of whether a source of light is occluded by another object. Because of this, shadowing does not happen naturally and must be artificially re-created. Because you can't know about light occlusions, you cannot do shadowing as part of your regular lighting process and

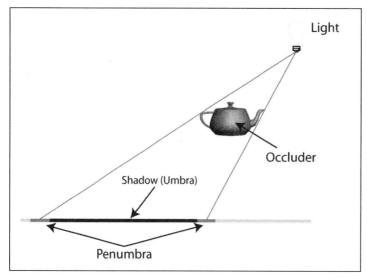

Figure 18.1 How shadows happen when an object blocks a source of light from another object.

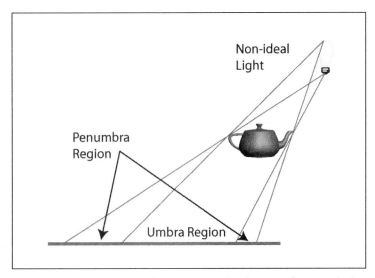

Figure 18.2 Illustration of how a penumbra happens for non-ideal sources of light.

must render shadows as a secondary process. Although it would be nice for them to be part of the lighting process itself, occlusions cannot be easily determined at run-time and are generally kept for more advanced rendering techniques, such as ray tracing.

With this in mind, this chapter will show you techniques that you can use to add shadows as part of your scene so that you can add back the realism that was lost when you did your lighting. Before I talk about these techniques, let's brush up on the more basic techniques that were used in the past.

The first and simplest technique is to render a simple circular shadow on the receiving geometry. Such a shadow is done as a simple polygonal circle or as a projective texture. Although it does not capture the shape of the shadow casting object, it can at least give the user a rough visual cue for the shadow. Remember that platform-jumping game I mentioned earlier? Such a shadow has often been used in this situation so the user would get a rough idea of where he is located when jumping.

The second commonly used technique in the past is known as geometry flattening. With this technique, you take your object geometry and set up a transformation matrix, which takes the geometry from the point of view of the light and projects it flat onto the plane of the receiving shadow geometry. The process essentially flattens, or squashes, the mesh into a flat surface, which is rendered as geometry on top of the shadow receiver.

The major problem with both of those techniques is that they create a shadow by creating a piece of geometry and rendering it on top of the receiver. If the receiver is a plane such as a floor, all goes well. However, if the receiving geometry has a shape that is non-planar, your shadow will not follow the shape of the receiving geometry, and in some cases, it may be even more difficult to determine for which plane the shadow must be created.

Because the old-style techniques work well for flat receiving surfaces, they worked well back when the geometry for the game worlds was simple enough. But with today's complex environments, these techniques just can't cut it; they lead to serious visual problems. Because of this, new techniques needed to be developed to take advantage of the latest hardware and to ensure that the shadows themselves can conform to any kind of receiver within your scene.

In the next two sections, I will talk about two of the most commonly used shadowing techniques today. In the first section, I will discuss shadow mapping, which takes advantage of render targets to determine accurate per-pixel shadows on your geometry. In the second section, I will discuss shadow volumes, which take advantage of some properties of shadows and hardware support of stencil buffers.

Shadow Mapping

The major flaw with the geometry flattening technique was that because it was rendered as geometry, it would not interface well with the shadow receiver because it is not necessarily a flat surface. The question is, how can you take the basic idea of this technique and adapt it so that it works for any type of receiver?

For this to happen, you have to consider an aspect of shadowing. If you take a look at your scene from the point of view of the light, shadowed regions correspond to the portions of the scene that are behind the object occluding the light. In rendering terms, any object whose depth is greater than the occluder's from the point of view of the light will be in shadow.

note

When dealing with shadows in your scene, you must take into consideration the complexity of the scene. The interaction of a light with its environment can cause the creation of many shadows, which can have a negative performance impact on your application. Because of this, you need to ensure that you properly determine which objects in your scene should cast shadows. This helps to maximize your performance and ensures that you get the most out of your shadows.

The key point with shadow mapping is to take advantage of this fact. If you know the depth of the occluders from the point of view of the light, you can potentially use that information to determine whether any pixels of your receiving objects are within the shadow. To do this, when rendering objects in your scene, you can use some math to determine the depth of a particular pixel from the point of view of the light. By comparing this value to the pre-computed depth of the occluders, you can discover whether a specific pixel is shadowed from the source of light. The whole process has been illustrated in Figure 18.3.

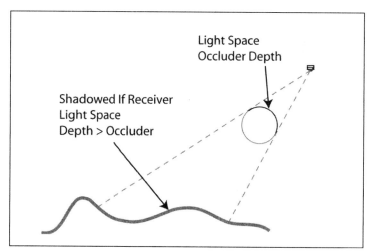

Figure 18.3 Using shadow mapping to determine if a pixel is shadowed by a particular occluder.

To build a shader using this technique, you first need to discover the depth of the occluder from the point of view of the light. To do so, you need to define a camera from the point of view of the light and render your object using this transformation matrix. Instead of storing the color of the object, you will use the shader to store the depth of the pixel from the light's viewpoint. For this particular shader, I have elected to use a floating-point render target to store the depth values, meaning that it may not work on every hardware platform, but it was convenient for simplicity. If you want, you could use a fixed-point texture combined with the depth encoding technique used in previous chapters.

For the purpose of this shader and to better illustrate the shadow, I have opted for an animating source of light. The light is set up to rotate in a circle, based on time, slightly above the shadow casting object. The code used to animate the position of the light is as follows:

```
lightPos.x = cos(1.321 * time_0_X);
lightPos.z = sin(0.923 * time_0_X);
lightPos.xz = 100 * normalize(lightPos.xz);
lightPos.y = 100;
```

The second step to this shader is to determine the view matrix from the point of view of the light. Because the light's position is known and we are assuming that the light is looking at the origin, the matrix can be determined by evaluating the x, y and z-axis, which the light is pointing at. This can be done with the following code:

```
float3 dirZ = -normalize(lightPos);
float3 up = float3(0,0,1);
float3 dirX = cross(up, dirZ);
float3 dirY = cross(dirZ, dirX);
```

With this information, you can transform your object's position into the light-space and project it so you can render it to your depth render target. Putting all the pieces together yields the following vertex shader code:

```
float time_0_X;
float4x4 proj_matrix;
float4x4 view_proj_matrix;
float distanceScale;
struct VS_OUTPUT
{
    float4 Pos:      POSITION;
    float3 lightVec: TEXCOORD0;
};

VS_OUTPUT vs_main(float4 inPos: POSITION)
{
    VS_OUTPUT Out;

    // Animate the light position.
    float3 lightPos;
    lightPos.x = cos(1.321 * time_0_X);
    lightPos.z = sin(0.923 * time_0_X);
    lightPos.xz = 100 * normalize(lightPos.xz);
    lightPos.y = 100;

    // Create view vectors for the light, looking at (0,0,0)
    float3 dirZ = -normalize(lightPos);
    float3 up = float3(0,0,1);
    float3 dirX = cross(up, dirZ);
    float3 dirY = cross(dirZ, dirX);

    // Transform into light's view space.
    float4 pos;
    inPos.xyz -= lightPos;
    pos.x = dot(dirX, inPos);
    pos.y = dot(dirY, inPos);
    pos.z = dot(dirZ, inPos);
    pos.w = 1;

    // Project the object into the light's view
    Out.Pos = mul(proj_matrix, pos);
    Out.lightVec = distanceScale * inPos;

    return Out;
}
```

You may have noticed that the output variable lightVec from the vertex shader is simply the vertex position in light-space. Because we want to be precise, we need to find out the exact radial distance from the light's viewpoint. To do so, we use the interpolated light-space vertex position and determine its length using the length function. This gives you the following pixel shader code:

```
float4 ps_main(float3 lightVec: TEXCOORD0) : COLOR
{
    // Output radial distance
    return length(lightVec);
}
```

Keep in mind that the preceding pixel shader assumes that you are rendering your depth to a floating-point render target. If you were to render it to a fixed-point texture, you will need to adapt the pixel shader to appropriately encode the depth into a set of red, green, and blue components.

Now that you have your occluder depth encoded, how can you take advantage of it to render accurate shadows? When rendering your shadow receiver, you need to determine two things. First of all, you need to find out the light-space position of your vertex so you can get the depth value from the occluder depth texture. To do this, you need to find out the light-space vertex position and project this value; the code for this is the same as the one used when building your depth map. However, you need to determine the texture coordinates for your depth texture lookup; this can be calculated with the following code:

```
// Evaluate the light space coordinates for the render target
// where sPos is the vertex position transformed in light-space
// Note that the Z component is offset by 10 as a bias to prevent
// unwanted self-shadowing
sPos.z += 10;
Out.shadowCrd.x = 0.5 * (sPos.z + sPos.x);
Out.shadowCrd.y = 0.5 * (sPos.z - sPos.y);
Out.shadowCrd.z = 0;
Out.shadowCrd.w = sPos.z;
```

The second thing you need is the depth of this pixel in light-space. Because you have already determined the light-space position for the vertex, you can use the same process used for the depth map pass and send the light-space vector to the pixel shader for it to determine its length with the length function. Also, because you are lighting the object, you need to pass the view vector to the pixel shader so that it can discover the proper lighting and apply shadows where needed. Putting all the pieces together yields the following vertex shader code:

```
float distanceScale;
float4 lightPos;
```

```
float4 view_position;
float4x4 view_proj_matrix;
float4x4 proj_matrix;
float time_0_X;
struct VS_OUTPUT
{
   float4 Pos:       POSITION;
   float3 normal:    TEXCOORD0;
   float3 lightVec : TEXCOORD1;
   float3 viewVec:   TEXCOORD2;
   float4 shadowCrd: TEXCOORD3;
};

VS_OUTPUT vs_main(
   float4 inPos: POSITION,
   float3 inNormal: NORMAL)
{

   VS_OUTPUT Out;

   // Animate the light position.
   float3 lightPos;
   lightPos.x = cos(1.321 * time_0_X);
   lightPos.z = sin(0.923 * time_0_X);
   lightPos.xz = 100 * normalize(lightPos.xz);
   lightPos.y = 100;

   // Project the object's position
   Out.Pos = mul(view_proj_matrix, inPos);

   // World-space lighting
   // Note: distanceScale serves as a scaling factor to ensure
   // that the depth stored in light-space is in the zero-to-one range.
   // It should generally be set to 1 / FarZClip
   Out.normal = inNormal;
   Out.lightVec = distanceScale * (lightPos - inPos.xyz);
   Out.viewVec = view_position - inPos.xyz;

   // Create view vectors for the light, looking at (0,0,0)
   float3 dirZ = -normalize(lightPos);
   float3 up = float3(0,0,1);
   float3 dirX = cross(up, dirZ);
   float3 dirY = cross(dirZ, dirX);
```

```
// Transform into light's view space.
float4 pos;
inPos.xyz -= lightPos;
pos.x = dot(dirX, inPos);
pos.y = dot(dirY, inPos);
pos.z = dot(dirZ, inPos);
pos.w = 1;

// Project it into light space to determine she shadow
// map position
float4 sPos = mul(proj_matrix, pos);

// Use projective texturing to map the position of each fragment
// to its corresponding texel in the shadow map.
sPos.z += 10;
Out.shadowCrd.x = 0.5 * (sPos.z + sPos.x);
Out.shadowCrd.y = 0.5 * (sPos.z - sPos.y);
Out.shadowCrd.z = 0;
Out.shadowCrd.w = sPos.z;

return Out;
}
```

The pixel shader for this pass does most of the hard work. First of all, it determines the light-space depth by finding out the length of the light vector. This is the same code as used for the previous pass. In addition, the shader determines lighting for your object. This is done as a simple specular and diffuse lighting using the following code:

```
diffuse  = saturate(dot(lightVec, inNormal));
specular = pow(saturate(dot(
           reflect(-normalize(viewVec), inNormal), lightVec)),16);
```

The tough part of this shader is determining whether this pixel is in shadow or not. To do so, you simply sample the shadow map and compare it to the pixel depth. The following code does just that:

```
float shadowMap = tex2Dproj(ShadowMap, shadowCrd);
float shadow = (depth < shadowMap + shadowBias);

// Compute the final color as the lighting being canceled out by the
// shadow if any. The Ka, Kd and Ks coefs. Control the ambient, diffuse
// and specular lighting contributions.
return Ka * modelColor +
     (Kd * diffuse * modelColor + Ks * specular) * shadow;
```

There are two things to note about this piece of code. The first one is the shadowBias variable; because you do not want small imprecisions to cause the occluder to be shadowed on its lit side, the ShadowBias ensures a small offset to the depth values to guarantee that anything close to the occluder depth does not get shadowed.

The second item worth mentioning is the shadow variable. This value is set using a conditional test, which means the variable contains either 0 or 1. The result is then used in the final lighting equation to modulate with the lighting color so that the light is canceled out for in-shadow regions. Putting all the pieces of the puzzle together gives you the following pixel shader code:

```
float shadowBias;
float backProjectionCut;
float Ka;
float Kd;
float Ks;
float4 modelColor;
sampler ShadowMap;
sampler SpotLight;
float4 ps_main(
    float3 inNormal:  TEXCOORD0,
    float3 lightVec:  TEXCOORD1,
    float3 viewVec:   TEXCOORD2,
    float4 shadowCrd: TEXCOORD3) : COLOR
{
    // Normalize the normal
    inNormal = normalize(inNormal);

    // Radial distance and normalize light vector
    float depth = length(lightVec);
    lightVec /= depth;

    // Standard lighting
    float diffuse = saturate(dot(lightVec, inNormal));
    float specular = pow(saturate(
                    dot(reflect(-normalize(viewVec), inNormal), lightVec)),
                    16);

    // The depth of the fragment closest to the light
    float shadowMap = tex2Dproj(ShadowMap, shadowCrd);

    // A spot image of the spotlight
```

```
float spotLight = tex2Dproj(SpotLight, shadowCrd);

// If the depth is larger than the stored depth, this fragment
// is not the closest to the light, that is we are in shadow.
// Otherwise, we're lit. Add a bias to avoid precision issues.
float shadow = (depth < shadowMap + shadowBias);

// Cut back-projection, that is, make sure we don't lit
// anything behind the light.
shadow *= (shadowCrd.w > backProjectionCut);

// Modulate with spotlight image
shadow *= spotLight;

// Shadow any light contribution except ambient
return Ka * modelColor +
       (Kd * diffuse * modelColor + Ks * specular) * shadow;
}
```

This process can be applied to any receiver objects within your scene. For the purpose of this shader, it has been applied both to the occluder and a floor object that has been put within the scene. Keep in mind that you generally need to include the occluder object as part of the receivers because the back side of the object will be in shadow, and you should take into account self-shadowing.

Compiling and running your new shader should give results similar to the one shown in Figure 18.4. The final version of the shader has also been included on the companion CD-ROM as shader_1.rfx.

I should mention a few more things regarding the use of shadow mapping. The first one involves hardware support. Some of the current hardware has built-in hardware support for shadow mapping and will take care of the light-space depth test for you automatically. However, at the time of this writing, support is sparse, and there is not any standard as to how it is expressed. Because of this, I have opted for a *software only* version of the algorithm because it can only be implemented on any 2.0 compatible hardware.

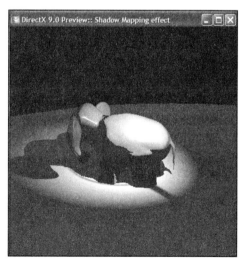

Figure 18.4 Rendering result for various light positions of the shadow mapping shader.

The second point I need to discuss is that shadow mapping leaves you with a hard shadow. In fact, this algorithm leaves you with a sharp shadow edge without any penumbra. If you remember our discussion earlier, most lights are not perfect point lights; you may want to take that into account so that your shadows have soft edges.

Although there isn't an exact implementation with shadow mapping to produce it, a decent approximation can be implemented. If you sample your shadow map several times at slight offsets, you can determine whether the shadow pixel you are rendering is on the boundary of the shadow. The easiest way to accomplish this is to sample neighboring texels within the shadow map and weigh the fraction of in-shadow and out-of-shadow pixels. I will not give you any code on how to do this; it will be your task to accomplish at the end of this chapter.

Shadow mapping is definitely a dandy way of implementing shadows within your hardware. However, it does suffer from some drawbacks. The most obvious one is the fact that you will need to determine your occluders and receivers ahead of time. Also, this technique requires you to render receivers multiple times if you want to account for multiple shadows.

A less obvious drawback is that the depth of your occluder is rendered to a texture. Because of this, you generally need a high precision texture to have sufficient precision. With the math involved, you will likely start getting rendering artifacts when the light and the viewer's position get perpendicular to each other. These artifacts are aliasing issues, which can occur at certain angles when the shadow map is being sampled at a lower resolution. The following technique, shadow volumes, takes care of some of these drawbacks by taking advantage of the stencil buffer and the volumetric properties of shadows.

Shadow Volumes

Although shadow mapping has some definitive advantages, its inconvenience can make it impractical for some applications. Because of this, we need to find another technique that can work well under most circumstances. That's when shadow volumes come into play.

I need to warn you about one thing beforehand. Because of the nature of shadow volume, they currently cannot be implemented under RenderMonkey. Because of this, I will discuss the technique and give pieces of code where appropriate, but no actual shader will be developed.

Imagine a light and an occluder; a portion of the occluder will be lit, and the other part will be in shadows. The fact that there are two regions on the object allows you to define a boundary along the object where the in- and out-of-shadow portions happen. If you project this outline away from the light, you define in 3D the region where any receiver will be shadowed. This has been illustrated in Figure 18.5.

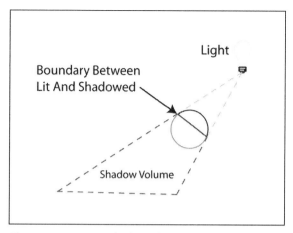

Figure 18.5 How the boundary between in- and out-of-shadow for an occluder defines a volume for which every receiver is shadowed.

Where things get tricky is to determining what the boundary is in the first place. Because we are dealing with a mesh, it is generally most convenient to consider individual polygons. By taking a look at every edge from which the mesh is constructed, you can discover whether any edge is in-shadow, out-of-shadow, or part of the boundary. To determine this, you need to look at each face that makes up the edge. Using the face normal, you can discover whether a particular face is shadowed or not. If, for a particular edge, one face is shadowed and the other isn't, then this particular edge defines the boundary for the shadow volume.

This brings up one important consideration in regards to the mesh of an occluder. Because you want to determine whether each edge is part of the shadow boundary, this will require your mesh to be *n-manifold*. What does this mean? In practical terms, it means that the mesh itself needs to be closed and that each edge of your mesh belongs to two, and only two, faces. If this condition isn't met, determining a proper boundary for the shadow volume likely will fail and lead to visual artifacts. This is because, for the volume shadow algorithm to work properly, the volume that is generated needs to be fully closed; it needs a full boundary without any gaps.

Now that you have determined which set of edges belongs to the shadow boundary, the issue becomes how you can take advantage of this. The boundary of the shadow, if projected away from the light, forms a 3D area where receivers are shadowed. Using the edge information you generated previously, you can use the vertices from those edges to create the volume geometry.

At this point, you have determined the shadow boundary on your occluder and figured out how to generate a volume from it. It's now time to use this geometry to render your shadow. Because of the properties of the shadow volume, you can render it from any 3D position and get your shadow. The trick to getting a shadow out of your volume is to take advantage of both the z-buffer and the stencil buffer that is offered by the rendering hardware. The approach to this is very similar to the one taken earlier to render volumetric fog.

note

The stencil buffer is a hardware feature which allows you to have a few extra bits of information with every pixel in your rendered scene. These bits can be manipulated at your discretion and can even be used to mask out certain potions of the screen.

As shown in Figure 18.6, if you render your shadow volume using the stencil buffer, you can determine the in-shadow regions. By adding to the stencil buffer for every back-facing shadow volume and subtracting for every front-facing face, you normally end up with a zero value in your stencil buffer because the shadow volume is closed. Nothing too interesting yet, but things get more intriguing when you throw the z-buffer into the mix.

If you initially render your scene before rendering the shadow volume into the stencil, the buffer is already populated with the depth values of all your geometry. By testing your shadow volume against the z-buffer, regions of your shadow volume intersecting geometry will leave nonzero values within the stencil buffer.

After you render all your shadow volumes, you can simply do a full-screen pass of a darkening color, which checks for nonzero values. This leaves darkening values where receivers intersect with the shadow volumes.

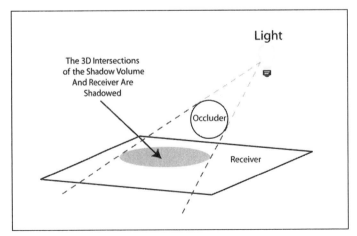

Figure 18.6 How a shadow volume can be used to determine the shadowed regions.

This is a simple as it gets. The whole process is pretty simple, but there are a few caveats that you will need to keep in mind. The first problem arises when the shadow volume intersects the front clipping plane of the camera. This clipping plane prevents the whole volume from being displayed, leading to an incorrect stencil buffer count, which in turn leads to wrong shadowing.

The last major problem is that the shadow volume needs to be determined on the CPU, one of the main reasons why we could not create a shader under RenderMonkey. On the bright side, with a little cleverness, there is a way to avoid building the silhouette on the CPU, which is the topic of this next section.

Taking Advantage of the Hardware

Extracting the shadow volume silhouette may not seem to be a big deal, but if you want to render multiple shadows, you may start to notice that the process is stealing away important clock cycles from other, possibly important tasks. If you are writing a game, wouldn't you rather use the CPU to do things such as AI or physics? Because of this, you may wonder if there is a way to do this whole process on the graphics processor instead of the main processor. Well, you are in luck!

The process itself isn't totally free and you will need to preprocess your meshes, but you can, in fact, do the silhouette extraction. In essence, with shadow volumes, you want to determine the silhouette of where the in-shadow and out-of-shadow regions meet. If you could push the part of your mesh that is shadowed, and project it away from the light, you would have a fully closed volume as long as you have some way of ensuring that there is geometry between the two parts at the silhouette. Figure 18.7 illustrates this.

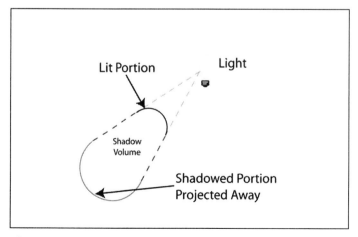

Figure 18.7 How projecting the shadowed part of a mesh away from the light can create a fully closed shadow volume.

For this to happen, there are a few things which need to be taken care of. The first aspect is determining within the vertex shader which part of the mesh is shadowed. This may seem easy, but it is something that needs to be determined for each face, even though you are writing a vertex shader and have no knowledge of the mesh topology.

The solution to this problem is to separate each face as a separate polygon, with its own set of vertices. This enables you not only to avoid sharing issues which may occur, but also to store the triangle normal as part of the vertices so you can perform the silhouette calculations within your vertex shader.

This leaves a second issue. Although you may be able to detect which faces are in shadow and project them away, it creates two mesh segments that are detached from each other. On the CPU, you would simply create new polygons to cover the gap. However, within the vertex shader, you cannot create new geometry and need a way to have this done for you. The solution to this problem lies in the creation of this geometry ahead of time in a way that does not interfere with the original mesh.

Because we have already separated the polygons so that none of the vertices from your mesh are shared, you can create new polygons, which actually attach the polygons together. Under normal conditions these polygons would not show up because they use coincidental vertices, but when part of the silhouette, they stretch out like a rubber band to form a complete volume. The construction of such geometry is illustrated in Figure 18.8.

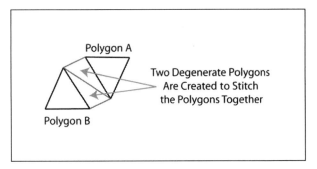

Figure 18.8 How geometry can be added to a mesh to allow the creation of a fully closed shadow volume.

As you may have noticed, this process requires you to change your mesh ahead of time. By detaching the vertices and adding "stitching" polygons ahead of time, you can do a one-time process on the CPU that enables you to construct your silhouette at run-time on the graphics processor.

This brings us to how you determine the silhouette on the graphics processor. With the proper mesh and information, the task is simple. You need to find out if the face normal, which is stored on each vertex, is in shadow. This is done simply by computing a dot product of the normal with the light direction vector. If the vertex itself is in shadow, simply offset its position in the direction of the light by some sufficient amount. The following code illustrates how this can be performed:

```
void vs_main(
    float3    inPos      : POSITION,
    float3    inNormal   : NORMAL)
{
    // Determine vert/light vector
    float3 LightDir = normalize(inPos - lightPosition);

    // If face is facing away from light, offset it
    if (dot(LightDir,inNormal)>0)
        inPos.xyz = inPos.xyz + LightDir*100;

    // Transform the vertex position
    Out.Pos = mul(view_proj_matrix,inPos);
}
```

Even though this technique requires a little more work ahead of time, it can move most of the costs to the graphics processor. This leaves you much more processing time for more important tasks. Although this technique was explained with a static mesh in mind, such techniques can also be adapted to animated meshes also.

On the downside, keep in mind that this technique also has its disadvantages. It requires you to preprocess your geometry before it can be used to cast shadows, adding a substantial number of vertices and triangles to the mesh being rendered. Whether this technique is useful for you mostly depends on where your shadow rendering bottleneck is located.

It's Your Turn!

The following exercise will help you explore the subject of shadow mapping. The solution to this exercise can be found in Appendix D.

Exercise 1: SOFT SHADOW MAPPING

Recent algorithms such as shadow mapping and volume shadows can produce stuffing shadows. However, they all have the side effect of considering lights as being perfect point lights and do not create a soft penumbra region. In this exercise, you are asked to take the shadow mapping shader developed in this chapter and extend it to support soft shadows. You can accomplish this by sampling several adjacent shadow map values and weighing in the proportion of lit and unlit pixels.

What's Next?

Lighting is one of the most important visual cues when rendering. We had so far neglected a crucial fact when rendering lights: Objects occlude light and produce shadows. The intent of this chapter was to introduce to you the main principles driving shadows and teach you some of the techniques used to render shadows on today's hardware.

Old-style techniques, such as geometry flattening, were convenient when hardware severely limited the geometry you could render. Such techniques work well when dealing with shadow receivers, which can be represented as a single plane. These techniques, however, start breaking down when the complexity of your geometry increases. Because of this, newer solutions were needed for this increased scene complexity and to take advantage of the latest hardware advances.

Shadow mapping is a convenient technique to render shadows in today's hardware. By determining the depth of both the occluders and receivers from the light's point of view, you can determine for any pixel rendered whether it is in shadow or not. Although there is some sporadic hardware support for this technique, visual problems at some angles, because of aliasing and the texture requirements, can become overwhelming.

A different solution to the problem is to use shadow volumes. By determining the silhouette for the in- and out-of-shadow regions for an occluder, you can construct a volume that represents the 3D space for which this occluder's shadow exists. Using this volume and taking advantage of the hardware's support for stencil buffering, you can determine the areas on the screen for which shadow must exist and then appropriately darken those areas. The major advantages of this method are that it can be implemented on nearly all available hardware and that with its nature, you only need to know about the occluders, and not the receivers.

It is time to move away from the topic of lighting and move on to something different. In the last chapter of this book, I discuss advanced topics relating to geometry. I discuss topics such as the use of bumpmapping to create a geometric level of detail. I also discuss such topics such as displacement mapping.

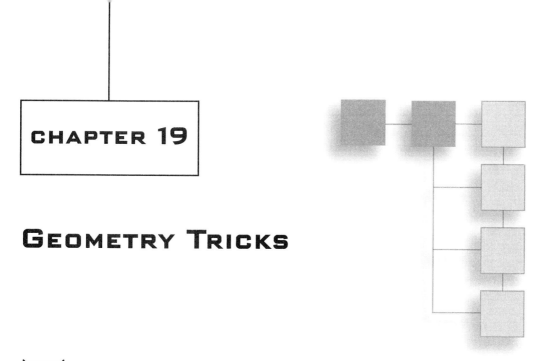

CHAPTER 19

GEOMETRY TRICKS

Throughout this book, I have focused mostly on rendering topics that have hovered around lighting and materials. These approaches are critical in creating more realistic and stunning graphics, but with the advances in rendering technologies, meshes and scenes are becoming more and more complex and dense.

Even though the hardware can handle more complex meshes, you want to maximize your scene complexity by using a minimum of geometry. Although it may seem contradictory at first, it makes total sense. If you were rendering an outdoor scene for a game, would you rather be able to render 10 meshes of 20,000 polygons each or 2,000 meshes of 100 polygons? The answer to this question might vary based on your situation, but the essence is that you want to strike a good balance that gives each of your objects sufficient visual quality yet doesn't hinder you in the quantity of objects you can put in your scene.

In addition to this, in dynamic worlds, this balance might be even harder to achieve because you are not able to predict ahead of time the number of objects onscreen, which can, in turn, lead to performance issues. Because of this, you might need techniques that enable you to control the quantity of objects in your mesh. In this chapter, I will introduce to you a variety of level of detail, or LOD, techniques that can be used to dynamically control the quality and detail of your geometry. Although this section strays away from the topic of shaders, it is something that I believe is an important part of rendering because you will eventually encounter situations where you need to balance your rendering between quality and performance.

In addition to introducing you to LOD techniques, I will spend a little time revisiting the topic of procedural geometry. In this chapter I will especially focus on displacement mapping, which allows you to get geometry data not only from a vertex buffer but from other sources, such as textures. I will teach you how these techniques will be applicable through the use of shaders.

Level of Detail

Geometry, in all its glory, is not necessarily intended to be presented at a specific detail level. The reality is that an object 100 meters away covers much less of the screen than an object 1 meter away. The natural reaction to this is that you do not need as much detail in your mesh to achieve similar detail when a mesh is farther away. So why waste all this graphics processor time rendering a mesh with 20,000 polygons when the average size of a polygon is less than a single pixel?

Another situation that might occur when you are dealing with dynamic scenes is performance-related. If all your players end up in the same room, performance problems may start to occur. In such cases, you may prefer sacrificing the visual quality of your scene to allow for better performance.

Whatever the situation, there is sometimes a need to have the same mesh represented at different quality levels for you to have more control over the balance between performance and quality. These different versions of the same mesh, commonly called levels of detail, are essentially the same mesh represented at different levels of geometric detail.

Although the idea of using different levels of detail, or LOD, may seem simple, several techniques can be used to represent those meshes and determine how they should be displayed. The following sections introduce you to some of the common techniques used in today's video games.

Keep in mind that because we are mostly dealing with geometric details of meshes and not with shaders themselves in the next few sections, no RenderMonkey implementation will be created.

Static LOD

The simplest approach to using levels of detail is to use a set of predefined versions of your geometry. The issue then becomes how to determine the level of details, and even more importantly, how to decide when a specific version of a piece of geometry must be used.

In this section, I will outline a few simple techniques that can be used to select the proper geometry, but because you must first have a set of LODs to work from, let's discuss this a little.

Level of detail geometry generally originates from one of two sources. The first of these techniques is to let the artists prebuild a set of various detail versions for a specific mesh. For this to be done, most advanced 3D software tools enable you to simplify a mesh with a wide variety of settings to control the quality of your mesh.

The advantage of the manual approach is that it gives artists full control over the simplification process, not only allowing them to control the quality of the rendering, but also ensuring that no bad texture mapping or other artifacts will appear from the simplification process. On the other hand, the manual process requires more time to actually generate all your levels of detail.

The second approach usually taken is to use one of those simplification tools, or a specialized one, and automate the process. Using scripts, you can create an automated tool that takes your high resolution mesh and converts it to LODs, each of them, for example, with 20 percent fewer polygons than the previous one. However with this approach, when dealing with skinned characters, you may encounter difficulties because you will need to manually re-skin all of your LODs.

Whichever approach is taken, one question arises as to how you determine which polygons to throw out and which ones you need to keep. There are several metrics that can be used to determine this, but here are a few common ones.

First of all, the idea behind geometry simplification is to reduce the number of polygons. Because you wish to do so for rendering, you need to do it in a way that minimizes the reduction in visual quality of the mesh. So the prime concept behind any metric is to keep the errors introduced by the removal of polygons to a minimum.

The first simple metric is to use the size of a polygon. Keeping in mind that LOD meshes are used when a model is at a certain distance from the camera, smaller polygons have less of a visual impact and can be removed. This can easily be accomplished by determining the area of the polygon and using this value to discover which polygons will be removed first.

However, such a metric is not enough on its own. The size of a polygon isn't the only major criterion in the importance of the polygon. Some polygons, even if tiny, serve as major building blocks within the geometry of a mesh and cannot simply be removed. Although there may be many cases of this type of situation, one way which usually works well to detect this is to look at the angles between the adjacent polygons. Polygons with soft angles between their neighbors are generally small detail, and removing such polygons has a generally low impact on the overall silhouette of the mesh. However, removing geometry with sharp angles causes the overall shape of the object to degrade, and such geometry should not be considered first for removal. The overall idea behind this metric is explained in Figure 19.1.

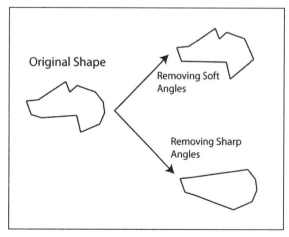

Figure 19.1 How the angle of a face contributes to the overall shape of an object's silhouette.

No matter which approach is taken, you need to ensure that the quality of each level of detail is sufficient to ensure good rendering quality. Even so, you need to determine at which time any particular LOD needs to be displayed. There are two factors that come into play when trying to determine this: visual needs and performance.

When discussing visual needs, you need to determine at which distance from the camera it is appropriate to switch from one LOD to another. There are metrics that look at the visual error between two LODs and find out at which distance this error is noticeable, but they tend to be complex and beyond the scope of this book. However, using a set of fixed camera distances determined by experimentation can yield good results.

The second factor to consider when determining which LOD to use is the performance of your graphics. Because performance is generally directly tied to the number of polygons within your scene, determining the proper LOD is a straightforward task. If your performance falls below a certain threshold, you will then start reducing the quality of your geometry. Say, if you are 10 percent below your target performance, reducing your geometry levels by about 10 percent would bring you back on mark. I know this is a rough metric, but there is no fits-all solution for you to use, and you need to experiment with a more proper metric based on your circumstances.

One little detail to keep in mind when dealing with performance is that you want to be cautious when picking your LODs so as not to make a decision too quickly. Doing so can cause two problems. First of all, if you decide on a per-frame basis, some frames might be slower because of other events in your game, say, an explosion. You may not wish to adapt right away because performance will recover after the event is finished. It is generally a good idea to average your performance calculations over several frames before making a decision.

The other factor to consider is the impact of an LOD change in the first place. Taking the previous example, where you are 10 percent below your target performance, reducing the LOD causes your performance to go back up. If your algorithm is based on an exact breaking point, you might end up ping-ponging between two levels of detail. To avoid such issues, it is generally a good idea to keep the performance regions fuzzy so that a small change in performance does not cause you to oscillate between different levels of detail.

Keeping all this in mind, static LOD techniques are simple and easy to implement. Because there is no fits-all metric, you may need to experiment some to find the best balance in your application One of the biggest drawbacks to static LODs, however, isn't the different levels of geometry but the transition from one to another. Because you need to change from one mesh to another at a specific point in time, even though both meshes are of good quality, it is likely the user will notice the transition.

To reduce such artifacts, you could potentially use dynamic transitions between different meshes, such as fading from one to another, but even such techniques yield some visual problems. To reduce such problems and simplify the authoring of LOD meshes, there are progressive LOD techniques that can be used to construct meshes of any level of detail on-the-fly. These techniques are covered in the next section.

Progressive LOD

As mentioned, the use of static LODs, although simple, can lead to artifacts due to the instantaneous switch from one mesh to another. In addition to these visual artifacts, such techniques require you to create a set of various LOD meshes for each of your models. Even though it gives you good control, it requires more art time to author these models, time which you may not have.

To work around these issues, wouldn't it be nice if you had one single start mesh and were able to create a new LOD on-the-fly based on your rendering criteria? You might remember that real-time mesh simplification is prohibitive. This is true, but there are techniques that can be used to alleviate this problem.

The idea behind progressive meshes is simple. Determine offline which faces need to be removed for simplification. Instead of building a mesh with the simplified geometry, though, keep the original mesh, store the information from which you can take the mesh, and simplify it at run-time.

There are several techniques you can use to accomplish this. For this chapter, we will explore one of the most commonly used techniques developed by Hugues Hoppe of Microsoft, simply called progressive meshes.

The representation offered by the progressive mesh, or PM, technique is useful for on-the-fly LOD determination. In fact, this technique can also be used to do mesh simplification, progressive geometry transmission, and even geometric compression.

The basic idea behind the PM algorithm is as follows: Take a mesh at its lowest level and instead of representing different levels of detail, store such progressive information as how to reconstruct the higher level of detail from this original mesh. The progressive information is stored as a simple transformation called a VERTEX SPLIT, which essentially takes the current mesh and adds a new vertex, thus taking an existing face and splitting it into three new ones by adding a polygon somewhere inside the face.

By repeating the same VERTEX SPLIT process over and over, you are taking the initial coarse LOD mesh and adding detail to it in a progressive way. Knowing the final number of polygons you need in your mesh, you can find out the number of operations you need to perform to move from the low LOD to the target polygon count.

The process itself is composed of two steps. In the first step, you need to take your original mesh and apply a simplification to generate your progressive mesh representation, which is done once at authoring time. Although there are several simplification algorithms out there, the technique describes its own technique, which uses a visual quality metric. The second step defines how you can take the progressively represented mesh and construct any LOD using the representation. In this chapter, we will briefly cover both of these aspects.

Before we talk about simplification, it is easier to talk about the progressive mesh representation and how to reconstruct a mesh. When dealing with progressive meshes, the basic reconstruction operation is called a VERTEX SPLIT. On the opposite side, the reverse operation is called an EDGE COLLAPSE. This operation essentially takes an edge and collapses its two vertices together to create a simplified version of the geometry. This operation has been illustrated in Figure 19.2.

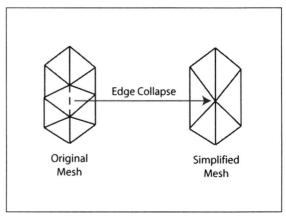

Figure 19.2 Illustration of the edge collapse operation in progressive meshes.

After you determine a sequence of edge collapses leading from your original mesh to the coarsest level you want, you can simply reverse the flow of information, thus converting your transformations to VERTREX SPLITS. This essentially takes an existing vertex and splits it in two, re-creating the edge which was destroyed during the simplification process.

One detail remains in regards to the properties of vertices and how they are treated. These properties include the vertex position but also other properties, such as the vertex colors or normals. Because you are collapsing and re-creating vertices, you need to store information on the vertex as part of the progressive mesh representation. The technique used to store such information can be application-dependent and can depend on whether you want to achieve some compression. For simple purposes, you can store the attributes of the collapsed vertices as part of the progressive mesh data.

As you can see, the whole process is simple and can easily be implemented. Because the hard work of simplification is done ahead of time, reconstruction of a mesh simply becomes a matter of traversing the reconstruction information and adding geometry to the original LOD as you go. Speaking of simplification, let's now look at how you can simplify a mesh's geometry to construct a progressive mesh stream.

note

For more information on progressive meshes, I recommend you visit Hugues Hoppe's Web site at: http://research.microsoft.com/~hoppe/.

The second important part of the process is the mesh simplification. Reconstructing a mesh from a progressive representation is one thing, but you need the progressive mesh to start with. Although this can be a complex mathematical process, I will briefly introduce it to you so you have a better understanding.

As with any simplification process, you strive to reduce the number of polygons inside a mesh but cannot simply do an arbitrary simplification. The process must define a metric that can be used to determine, in a quantitative way, the cost of a particular simplification. The overall goal is to reduce the total number of polygons while ensuring that introduced errors are kept to a minimum.

To complete this process, you need to define a metric that can be used to quantify the energy within a mesh. The equations for such a metric have been illustrated in Figure 19.3.

$$E(M) = E_{dist}(M) + E_{spring}(M) + E_{scalar}(M) + E_{disc}(M)$$

$$E_{dist}(M) = \sum_i d^2(x_i, \phi_v(|K|))$$

$$E_{spring}(M) = \sum_{\{j,k\} \in K} k\|v_j - v_k\|^2$$

$$E_{scalar}(M) = (C_{scalar})^2 \sum_i \|x_i - \phi_v(b_i)\|^2$$

Figure 19.3 Equations used for the mesh simplification energy conservation metric.

As you can see from Figure 19.3, the final metric is a sum of various metrics. The first component, E_{dist}, minimizes the change in the shape of the mesh. This metric is simple because it simply uses the squared geometric distance of the original mesh versus the new mesh. Keep in mind that for simplicity, this value is defined as the geometric distance of all vertices from their original position for a specific simplification in the mesh, not only the one you directly modified.

The second term of the metric, E_{spring}, regularizes the optimization process. In essence, it ensures that simplified vertices are taken uniformly from all around the mesh and are not concentrated on a single area of the mesh.

The final two terms, E_{scalar} and E_{disc}, ensure the continuity of the mesh attributes. Because a mesh is not only defined by its vertex positions, we also need to define metrics to validate the other attributes of the mesh. The first of the two terms defines a way of ensuring that the error on the vertex attributes is minimized, similarly to the metric employed to measure the geometric distance of the vertex positions. The second and final term is to minimize errors on mesh discontinuities, because some attributes, such as texture coordinates, may not be continuous across the mesh. You need to avoid simplifying the mesh at those points because they will likely create big visual errors.

After the metrics are defined, the actual process is straightforward and involves two loops. The outer loop repeats itself for the number of vertices you want to remove from your original mesh. The second loop goes through all the vertices of the current mesh, at the current simplification level, and evaluates the error metric for each of them. Once the metric is evaluated, the vertex with the least error is chosen as the simplification candidate for this pass and is removed. At this point, proper progressive reconstruction information for the vertex and its attributes is generated and stored in the output.

From the preceding explanation, you can understand why the simplification process cannot be done at run-time. The advantage of the progressive mesh technique is that the simplification can be done ahead of time, and you can then use the results in real-time through the edge split information to generate the proper level of detail in your geometry. As you can see, the whole progressive mesh process may seem daunting and complex. But it can make great differences in the run-time performance and quality of an application.

A little note: This technique has been implemented as part of the DirectX 9.0 SDK and is ready for you to use through the `ID3DX9MESH` interfaces.

Re-Creating Lost Details

The advantage of LOD is that it enables you to better control the visual quality and performance of your application. However, whichever approach you take, you still lose some visual detail. So you may wonder if there is any way to compensate for this lost detail. The fact is that there is!

In Chapter 10, "Shiny Little Pixels," I discussed the topic of bumpmapping and how it can be used to create non-existent detail. When simplifying a mesh, you can use this information to re-create the lost detail. Keep in mind that the geometry still stays simplified, but the lost detail can be re-created and used for lighting purposes.

The process to re-create this lost detail involves your original mesh and the simplified one. By mapping the simplified LOD mesh for bumpmapping, you can determine where each pixel is in space. With this position, you can find out, by using ray-tracing techniques, which face of the original mesh the pixel corresponds to.

By discovering this information, you can deduce in which direction the normal of the surface points on the original mesh and thus determine the proper bumpmap values to represent this information. This process is illustrated in Figure 19.4.

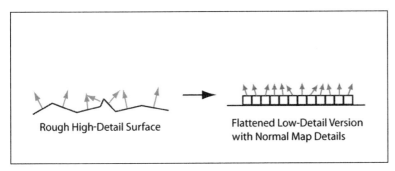

Rough High-Detail Surface

Flattened Low-Detail Version
with Normal Map Details

Figure 19.4 Process used to generate a bumpmap that re-creates lost simplification detail by the use of two LODs.

The process of determining a bumpmap from a high resolution geometry and a lesser level of detail is complex and expensive. Details on the exact process are beyond the scope of this book, but I want to mention two tools that can be used to accomplish it. Both NVIDIA and ATI are developing tools that allow you to do just this.

NVIDIA created a tool called Melody, intended to simplify the whole process. This tool not only generates the mesh LODs for you, but also generates the appropriate texture mapping and bumpmaps to re-create the lost detail.

With the Melody tool, the simplification process takes advantage of an approach similar to the progressive mesh. By using a combination of edge collapse and error metrics, the tool is geared at giving you the best looking LODs available. In addition to the simplification and bumpmapping process, the Melody tool also takes care of optimizing the normal maps it generates for the best possible results.

Unfortunately, at the time of this writing, the Melody tool is still under development but is soon to be released. So keep your eyes open.

On the flip side, ATI Technologies has developed a similar tool called NormalMapper. This tool does not handle the creation of LODs but, given an original mesh and a simplified version, generates the proper texture mapping coordinates and a bumpmap to re-create the lost detail. Their tool is already available from the developer section of their Web site at www.ati.com.

Whether you use one of the existing tools or develop your own utilities, the use of bumpmapping to re-create lost details for your meshes is an awesome way to improve the visual quality of your LOD geometry. In addition, it enables artists to develop their initial mesh at a high resolution so you can use a lesser mesh at run-time but benefit from all the details of the initial mesh for lighting purposes.

Displacement Mapping

In Chapter 13, "Building Materials from Scratch," I discussed how, when dealing with procedural materials, I made a small incursion into modifying the geometry procedurally to create a new effect. In this section, I will introduce a variant on this, where you define a simple piece of geometry and let the hardware determine the final vertex positions.

One thing to keep in mind before I start: This technology is currently available only on 3.0 vertex shader hardware. Because no hardware currently exists that supports this technology, the information presented here is only an introduction to keep you up to date on what could be accomplished in future hardware generations.

Imagine you want to render a landscape. Currently, you would need to generate a grid mesh and assign attributes, including vertex positions, to the whole grid. If you want to represent a huge landscape, you need to store all the vertices for your world even though only a portion is visible at a time. The major issue is that because the geometry for the landscape is along a regular grid, a lot of the geometry is redundant because the only relevant information is the height of the terrain at a particular point. In addition, creating LODs involves creating new sets of geometry, consuming even more resources.

As with terrain, you are dealing with a uniform grid-like mesh, and replicating the grid for each piece of terrain seems useless. Wouldn't it be nice to have a single piece of geometry and reuse it for every segment of landscape?

This is where displacement mapping comes in. By taking a uniform piece of geometry, you will want to procedurally displace the vertices within your vertex shader to achieve the final geometry wanted. If you have a procedurally defined landscape, it would simply be a matter of applying a process similar to what we did in Chapter 13.

If you want the terrain to be artistically defined, you need another way to control the shape of the terrain within the vertex shader. Because the terrain is on a grid, all that is needed to define the final geometry is the height to apply at each vertex. This can easily be stored as part of a texture. But wait! You can't sample textures at the vertex shader level, can you?

You are correct and incorrect at the same time. Although you currently cannot sample textures at the vertex shader level, the 3.0 shader model does allow you to do so, bringing displacement mapping alive and a whole new slew of possibilities for you to use in the vertex shader.

One of the biggest advantages of using such displacement mapping is its independence from the resolution of the initial mesh used. Because the height of the terrain is defined through a texture, you benefit from mipmapping and bilinear filtering. This means that in no way does your terrain mesh have to match your heightmap texture. You can use any resolution of mesh, thus allowing you to fully support LOD on your landscape.

I know, you wish you could use this right now. This section is more of a teaser than anything else, but I think it is a topic of interest and will become more prevalent in the next few years as 3.0 rendering hardware starts appearing on the market.

It's Your Turn!

For this last chapter, I have decided to let you go free without any homework. Enjoy!

Summary

Improving the quality of your graphics isn't always a matter of materials. Manipulating your geometry can enable you to achieve great visual gains and even enhance the performance of your renderings.

With the proper use of level of detail, or LOD, geometry, you can achieve increased performance in your scenes. Static LODs are easy to implement and can let you reduce the overall geometry while giving you control over the quality of your visuals. On the other hand, there are progressive meshes that require more processing but can enable you to have a mesh that seamlessly transitions from one level of detail to another.

Whether you are using static or progressive meshes, it will likely have a negative impact, even though minimal, on the quality of your renderings. Taking advantage of LOD technologies and bumpmapping, you can re-create some of the lost details and even create detail not present before. With this technology, you can take your initial mesh and a lower LOD and use a tool that can re-create this lost detail through the creation of an appropriate bumpmap.

Finally, the future is looking even brighter for procedural geometry. Through the upcoming vertex and pixel shader 3.0 models, you will be able to do proper displacement mapping. By being able to sample textures at the vertex shader level, you will be able to do forms of procedural geometry you never have been able to do before. For example, you could render terrain geometry on-the-fly with a heightmap texture.

What's Next?

You have finally reached the end of your journey into the world of shaders. First of all, I want to thank you personally for reading this book. I hope you enjoyed reading it as much as I did writing it. At this point, you should have a good understanding of shaders in general and have a bag of techniques that you will be able to use in your personal and professional projects.

Shaders are the technology of today and tomorrow. With the advancement of rendering technology, more is possible than ever before. The added flexibility provided by the new shader technologies is bound to make real-time rendering an even more exciting field than ever before. Because technology never sits still, I have dedicated the next few pages to talking about where the technology stands and where it is headed in the future. It seems like the best way to conclude this book—by giving you a glimpse into the future.

It was not that long ago that the only way of doing 3D graphics was through the use of software or through specialized, and expensive, rendering hardware. Back then, you could achieve some real-time graphics, but the quality and realism was so restrictive that its use was mostly restricted to computer-assisted design software and specialized applications such as flight simulators. The introduction of the first consumer level 3D rendering hardware proved to be a true revolution, finally enabling the average joe to enjoy the benefits of real-time 3D graphics.

Even back then, the performance of these devices was limited and the graphical realism was poor, but they did the background work that led us to the current generation of rendering hardware. Over the last decade, rendering hardware made major improvements in terms of performance but was restricted to a fixed rendering pipeline. This pipeline, imposing a set of rendering modes and states allowed relatively good graphics but totally limited you in what you could achieve.

At this point, we were due for a second revolution in terms of graphics hardware. This is where programmable shaders arrived to shake things up. With the introduction of the new shader models came the freedom for developers to separate themselves from the fixed rendering pipeline and explore a new level of creativity. Keeping in mind that the first iteration of programmable shaders offered limited flexibility, they were the first step towards making movie-quality CG possible at run-time on consumer-level hardware.

Recently, with the advent of the 2.0 shader model and supporting hardware, flexibility was even more enhanced, bringing a level of flexibility and power never before imagined. This flexibility has not only increased the creativity of developers but also allowed new algorithms to be implemented that had been possible only in the realm of software rendering.

For example, techniques such as Perlin noise or polynomial texture maps were not possible before the advent of advanced shader support. Even at its current stage, shader technology suffers from some severe limitations. For example, conditional instruction support within pixel shaders is limited and does not give you full control. In addition, texture samplings are currently available only to pixel shaders and cannot be used when processing vertices.

The shader model 3.0 will, in theory, solve some of these problems. Although it's supported by DirectX 9.0, no current hardware supports this model, although you should expect some soon after this book is released. This new version allows for better branching and looping control in addition to some limited texture sampling at the vertex shader level. This new flexibility will allow even more powerful algorithms to be implemented in shader form. To a limited extent, some people have even managed to implement complex algorithms, such as ray tracing or radiosity, using the 3.0 shader models.

What are we to expect from the future? In the short term, you can expect hardware that incorporates the 3.0 shader models. In addition, with improved silicon manufacturing processes, we are bound to see significant improvement in terms of performance. But looking even further into the future, what can you expect?

Of course, this is all speculative at this point, but consider the rate of progression since the release of the first consumer 3D rendering hardware eight years ago. Looking into the future, and the speculation on the next release of DirectX and upcoming hardware such as the Xbox 2, you can see that the future is looking bright.

One of the first improvements you can expect is more widespread support for floating-point textures. By the next version of DirectX, it is expected that all texture operations will be done in floating-point. This also implies that current issues with floating-point textures, such as the lack of alpha blending, will be resolved.

Another significant improvement to expect comes from the increased amount of flexibility being added to the shader model, vertex, and pixel shader functionality. The fact is that with 3.0 specifications, both pixel and vertex shaders are starting to look very much alike. It is safe to assume that very soon, the architecture of rendering hardware will be modified so that it will contain a fixed number of generic shader units that can be used to process both pixels and vertices. This new design will allow a better performance balance by giving the hardware control over the allocation of the processing units, depending on whether the rendering is more vertex- or pixel-intensive.

In addition to the fundamental architectural changes in future hardware, we are bound to see even more of a performance improvement over the next few generations. With faster memory and smaller, yet faster processors, you will not only have more flexibility, but will be able to do even more just because of the extra speed you gain.

How long will it be before you can render movie-quality CG in real-time? This is a question that is hard to answer. We are definitely getting closer, and with the latest technological improvements, it will only be a matter of time. But one thing remains for sure: The future is looking bright when it comes to real-time rendering, and shaders will be at the core!

PART V

APPENDIXES

This section is filled with extra information and reference materials that will be useful to you as a shader developer. The first two appendixes include reference manuals for both Microsoft's High-Level Shader Language and RenderMonkey. The following appendices will give you installation instructions for the content on the CD and solutions to most of the exercises proposed throughout the book.

Appendix A: Serves as a reference manual for the HLSL shader language. This is your best source of information on all the built-in functions and how to make the most of this shading language.

Appendix B: Contains a user manual for RenderMonkey. Use it to familiarize yourself with all the nooks and crannies of RenderMonkey.

Appendix C: Serves as a brief introduction to the content available on the companion CD-ROM.

Appendix D: Contains in-depth solutions to all the exercises developed throughout the book.

Appendix E: A reference shader library. Presents all the important pieces of shader code developed throughout this book in an easy-to-use reference list.

It has been a fun and thrilling journey writing this book. I hope the knowledge I conveyed to you will be helpful and allows you to create the most stunning graphics!

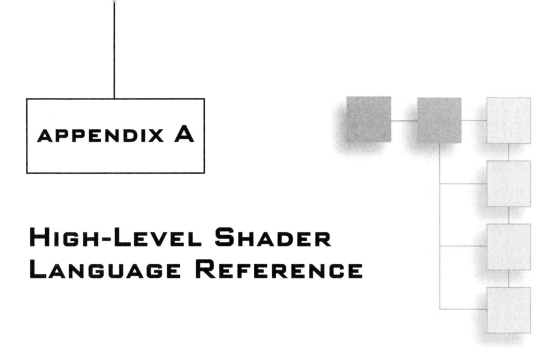

APPENDIX A

HIGH-LEVEL SHADER LANGUAGE REFERENCE

This chapter serves as a reference manual for the *High-Level Shader Language* (HLSL) from Microsoft. Although HLSL was introduced as part of the DirectX 9.0 SDK, I chose this language because of its simplicity and versatility compared to writing shaders in pure assembly. Also, with the introduction of the Cg shading language, which is compatible with HLSL, the knowledge you gain from reading this book is portable to other rendering APIs and platforms without any major modifications.

The big advantage of HLSL over its assembly counterpart is that it brings shaders to you in a more accessible way. It enables you to separate yourself from specific shader support, register allocation, and turn over optimization decisions to the compiler.

The HLSL brings you the development of shaders in a language similar to C. It offers a rich set of features, including functions, statements, user-defined data types, and a wide collection of built-in functions for you to use. All this makes shader development more oriented towards algorithm design and less concerned with figuring out how to code your algorithm.

Keep in mind that this reference manual is loosely inspired by the HLSL reference in DirectX 9's documentation. For a more complete reference, we suggest reading the full reference included as part of the DirectX 9.0 SDK's documentation, which is included on the companion CD-ROM.

Data Types

Microsoft's High-Level Shader Language features a rich set of data types to simplify shader development. It offers types ranging from simple scalar types to vector and matrix types as well. The following section outlines all the different types exposed by HLSL.

Scalar Types

Scalar types are defined by the HLSL standard as singular atomic values. They are the most basic types and are used to compose all the more complex ones. Table A.1 enumerates all the exposed scalar types.

Take note that not all shader targets have native support for integer, half, or double values. If your shader is compiled for a target that does not support a specific format, it will be emulated through use of the `float` type, and results may not be accurate.

Table A.1 Scalar Types Available Through HLSL

Scalar Type	Possible values
bool	True or false
int	32-bit signed integer
half	16-bit floating-point number
float	32-bit floating-point number
double	64-bit floating-point number

Unless you are certain that your target platform supports a specific type, it is better to stick with standard floating-point numbers for the sake of consistency and portability.

Vector Types

The vector type is defined by the HLSL standard as a one-dimensional array composed of one particular scalar type. By default, a vector is an array composed of four floating-point values. However, as shown in Table A.2, you can also manually define arbitrary vectors.

Table A.2 Vector Types Available Through HLSL

Vector Type	Values
vector	A vector of four float components
vector< type, size>	A vector containing `size` components of the specified `type`

Individual vector components may be accessed in many different ways. The following list shows different possible access modes for array components. Take note that for arrays of a size greater than four, the components beyond the fourth must be accessed by the index.

- **By component:** vector.x, vector.y, vector.z, vector.w
- **By color:** vector.r, vector.g, vector.b, vector.a
- **By index:** vector[0], vector[1], vector[2], vector[3]

Vector components can be swizzled by combining multiple components together (ex: vector.xzzy). When swizzling, you need to use the same name set for a particular combination. As seen in the example, you can also repeat components when swizzling; this, however, can only be used for an input value and not for an output. Also take note that you may use the swizzle operator to access individual components of a vector when you need a single scalar from the vector(ex: vector.x).

Matrix Types

Matrix types are defined by the HLSL standard as two-dimensional arrays comprised of one particular scalar type. By default, a matrix is a four-by-four array composed of floating-point values. However, as shown in Table A.3, arbitrary matrices can also be manually defined.

Table A.3 Matrix Types Available Through HLSL

Matrix Type	Values
matrix	A four-by-four matrix of floats
matrix<type,rows,cols>	A matrix of rows rows and cols columns with the specified type

You can address individual row-vectors of matrices by using an array style addressing. For example, you can address a single row of a matrix by using an index such as Matrix[3]. You may also address individual components of a matrix through an indexed row access followed by a standard vector access, such as Matrix[2].x or Matrix[3][2].

Individual components of a matrix can also be accessed on a per-component basis using one of the following two notations:

1-based:

```
_11    _12    _13    _14
_21    _22    _23    _24
_31    _32    _33    _34
_41    _42    _43    _44
```

0-based:

```
_m00    _m01    _m02    _m03
_m10    _m11    _m12    _m13
_m20    _m21    _m22    _m23
_m30    _m31    _m32    _m33
```

Matrices accessed using component addressing can also be swizzled in the same way as you can with vectors (ex: `Matrix._m01_m02_m03_m04`). However, as with vectors, you must ensure that you use the same addressing type. In other words, addressing types such as _m11 and _11 cannot be mixed together. Keep in mind that component matrix access only works for matrices with a dimension of four or less. Larger matrices will need to be accessed by index.

Structure Types

The keyword `struct` is used to declare structure types. Structures are declared as composite types used to group common variables in a single entity. Structures are declared through the following syntax:

```
struct [ID] {members}
```

After a structure is defined, it may be accessed using its identifier (ID). The following is an example of a structure declaration and use:

```
struct Circle
{
   float4   Position;
   float   Radius;
}; // Define a new structure
Circle MyCircle; // Declare a variable of type Circle
```

Predefined Types

The HLSL language specification also defines a set of predefined types, which are there for your convenience and ease of use. Table A.4 lists the types that are already predefined and that you can use in your shaders.

Table A.4 Predefined Types Available Through HLSL

Predefined Type	Values
floatN	A floating-point vector of size N. The value of N can be between 2 and 4.
floatNxM	A floating-point matrix of size N-by-M. The values for N and M can be between 2 and 4.
halfN	A 16-bit floating-point vector of size N. The value of N can be between 2 and 4
halfNxM	A 16-bit floating-point matrix of size N-by-M. The values for N and M can be between 2 and 4.
intN	An integer vector of size N. The value of N can be between 2 and 4.
intNxM	An integer matrix of size N-by-M. The values for N and M can be between 2 and 4.

Typecasts

Typecasts are known in programming jargon as the ability to convert one type to another. HLSL supports many built-in type conversions. Table A.5 summarizes the possible conversions between the built-in types.

Table A.5 Type Conversions in HLSL

Type Conversion	Validity
Scalar-to-scalar	Such conversions are always valid. When casting from bool type to an integer or floating-point type, false is considered to be zero and true is considered to be one. When casting from an integer or floating-point type to bool, a zero value is considered to be false, and a nonzero value is considered to be true. When casting from a floating-point type to an integer type, the value is rounded down to the nearest integer.
Scalar-to-vector	Such conversions are always valid. This cast works by copying the scalar to fill the vector.
Scalar-to-matrix	Such conversions are always valid. This cast works by copying the scalar to fill the matrix.
Scalar-to-object	Such conversions are never valid.
Scalar-to-structure	Valid if all elements of the structure are numeric (objects are considered non-numeric). This cast works by copying the scalar to fill the structure.
Vector-to-scalar	Such conversions are always valid. The conversion selects the first component of the vector to fill the scalar.
Vector-to-vector	The destination vector must not be larger than the source vector. The cast works by keeping the leftmost values and truncating the rest. For this cast, column matrices, row matrices, and numeric structures are treated as vectors.
Vector-to-matrix	For this conversion to be valid, the size of the vector must be equal to the size of the matrix.
Vector-to-object	Such conversions are never valid.
Vector-to-structure	Such conversion is valid only if the structure is not larger than the vector and all components of the structure are numeric.
Matrix-to-scalar	This conversion is always valid. The scalar is filled with the upper-left component of the matrix.
Matrix-to-vector	This conversion is valid only if the size of the matrix equals the size of the vector.
Matrix-to-matrix	For this type conversion to be valid, the destination matrix must not be larger than the source matrix, in both dimensions. The cast works by keeping the upper-left values and truncating the rest.
Matrix-to-object	This type conversion is never valid.
Matrix-to-structure	For this conversion to be valid, the size of the structure must be equal to the size of the matrix, and the components of the structure must all be of a numeric type.
Object-to-scalar	This type conversion is never valid.

Table A.5 Type Conversions in HLSL *(continued)*

Type Conversion	Validity
Object-to-vector	This type conversion is never valid.
Object-to-matrix	This type conversion is never valid.
Object-to-object	This type of conversion is only valid if both object types are of the same type
Object-to-structure	For this type conversion to be valid, the structure must not contain more than one member. The type of that member must be identical with the type of the object.
Structure-to-scalar	For this conversion to be valid, the structure must contain at least one member. This member must be numeric.
Structure-to-vector	For this conversion to be valid, the structure must be at least the size of the vector. The first components must be numeric, up to the size of the vector.
Structure-to-matrix	For this conversion to be valid, the structure must be at least the size of the matrix. The first components must be numeric, up to the size of the matrix.
Structure-to-structure	For this conversion to be valid, the source structure must not be larger than the destination structure. A valid cast must exist between all respective source and destination components.

Variables

The HLSL language allows you to define variables to contain constants, inputs, outputs, and temporary values. By the standard, variables are defined through the following syntax:

```
[static uniform volatile] [const] type id [array_suffix] [:semantics] [= initializers];
```

As you can see from the syntax definition, variables can be prefixed with various keywords, which modify the way the compiler treats the variable. Table A.6 reviews the different prefixes and their effects.

Table A.6 Variable Prefixes and Their Meanings

Prefix	Meaning
static	For global variables, this signals that the value is internal and cannot be exposed to other shaders externally. For local variables, this indicates that its value will persist from call to call. Initialization of static variables is done only once, and if no initialization value is given, zero will be assumed.
uniform	Global variable declarations with the uniform prefix indicate that they do not change, except between draw calls. All non-static global variables are considered to be uniform.
volatile	The volatile keyword is a compiler hint to indicate that the value of this variable is to change often. The usage of this variable prefix allows the compiler to make better optimization decisions.
const	Variables declared as const cannot be modified from their initialization values.

One thing to notice from the syntax of variable declaration is the semantics part. This is used to define a mapping within your shader between a specific variable and either actual vertex shader or pixel shader inputs. The semantics for variables are generally defined for vertex and pixel shader function inputs.

Statements

Statements are used to control the flow of execution of your programs. The HLSL defines multiple types of statements for your use. The syntax for all HLSL-allowed statements is described in the following:

```
{ [statements] }
[expression];
return [expression];
if ( expression ) statement [else statement]
for ( [expression | variable_decleration ] ; [expression] ; [expression]) statement
```

For example, the following piece of code illustrates the statement used to perform a loop within your HLSL code.

```
for (int i=0;i<10;i++)
{
  // Do something…
}
```

Expressions

Expressions are literals, variables, or some combination of literals and variables composed using operators. Available operators and their meanings are described in Table A.7.

Unlike the C language, the evaluation of &&, ||, and ?: expressions never short-circuits because of the way they are evaluated by the hardware.

Many of the operators are labeled as being *per component* (including comparison operators). This indicates that, for each component of the input value, the operation is performed independently from the operations happening on the other components, and the result is placed in the matching component of the output vector.

Functions

The High-Level Shader Language standard, like the C language, allows for the use of both built-in functions and user-defined functions. Functions are a handy way of making your code into reusable components and simplifying your work. In this section, I will overview both how to build your own user-defined functions and how to take advantage of the built-in functions HLSL has to offer.

Table A.7 Operators for Use Within Expressions

Operator	Usage	Meaning	Associativity
()	(value)	Sub expression	Left to right
()	id(arg)	Function call	Left to right
()	type(arg)	Type constructor	Left to right
[]	array[int]	Array subscript	Left to right
.	structure.id	Member selection	Left to right
.	value.swizzle	Component swizzle	Left to right
++	variable++	Postfix increment (per component)	Left to right
--	variable--	Postfix decrement (per component)	Left to right
++	++variable	Prefix increment (per component)	Right to left
--	--variable	Prefix decrement (per component)	Right to left
!	!value	Logical not (per component)	Right to left
-	-value	Unary minus (per component)	Right to left
+	+value	Unary plus (per component)	Right to left
()	(type) value	Typecast	Right to left
*	value*value	Multiplication (per component)	Left to right
/	value/value	Division (per component)	Left to right
%	value%value	Modulus (per component)	Left to right
+	value+value	Addition (per component)	Left to right
-	value-value	Subtraction (per component)	Left to right
<	value < value	Less than (per component)	Left to right
>	value > value	Greater than (per component)	Left to right
<=	value <= value	Less than or equal to (per component)	Left to right
>=	value >= value	Greater than or equal to (per component)	Left to right
==	value == value	Equality (per component)	Left to right
!=	value != value	Inequality (per component)	Left to right
&&	value && value	Logical AND (per component)	Left to right
||	value||value	Logical OR (per component)	Left to right
?:	float?value:value	Conditional	Right to left
=	variable=value	Assignment (per component)	Right to left
*=	variable*=value	Multiplication assignment (per component)	Right to left
/=	variable/=value	Division assignment (per component)	Right to left
%=	variable%=value	Modulus assignment (per component)	Right to left
+=	variable+=value	Addition assignment (per component)	Right to left
-=	variable-=value	Subtraction assignment (per component)	Right to left
,	value,value	Comma	Left to right

User-Defined Functions

Through the HLSL standard, you can define custom functions in a similar way to the C language. Following is the syntax used to define your own functions:

```
[static inline target] return_type id ( [parameter_list] ) { [statement] };
```

As shown in this syntax declaration, functions can be prefixed by several keywords, allowing you to change the compiler's behavior. Table A.8 outlines the possible user-defined function prefixes along with their meaning.

In addition to the function prefixes, all parameters declared with a user-defined function can also be prefixed by special keywords. Table A.9 describes the allowed parameter prefixes with their meaning.

Table A.8 User-Defined Function Prefixes and Their Meanings

Prefix	Meaning
Static	Indicates the function will exist only within the scope of the current shader program and may not be shared.
Inline	Shows the function's instructions are to be copied within the calling code instead of issuing an actual function call. Take note that this is simply a compiler hint and does not guarantee this behavior. Also note that this is the current default behavior for the HLSL compiler.
Target	Indicates which pixel/vertex shader version the code is intended for. This allows the compiler to make the best decisions when building the code. Note that you will not write target in your shader, but will replace it with the name of the target you wish to use, such as ps_2_0.

Table A.9 Function Parameter Prefixes and Their Meanings

Prefix	Meaning
In	Is the default behavior and shows that the parameter is intended to be read only by the function.
Out	Is intended to indicate that the parameter is also a result value and any changes made to its value will be sent back to the caller.
Inout	Essentially combines the behavior of both In and Out.
Uniform	Points out that the value comes from constant data from within the shader.

One last thing to consider is that functions cannot be called recursively themselves. This is because of the way that functions are processed, compiled, and executed by the vertex shader hardware. Following is an example of a user-defined function that performs a simple task:

```
inline float4 lighting(in float3 normal, in float3 light, in float3 halfvector, in
float4 color)
{
   float4 color;
   color = dot(normal,light) * color;
   color += dot(light,halfvector) * color;
   return color;
}
```

Built-In Functions

The High-Level Shader Language contains a wide variety of built-in or intrinsic functions. Those functions will be useful when developing your shaders. The following sections summarize each function, with a review of its functionality and example usage code.

abs

Usage: abs(value *a*)

Return type: same as input

Minimum vertex shader version: 1.1

Minimum pixel shader version: 1.4

Description: This function calculates the absolute value of the input. It will operate on a per-component basis for vector and matrix inputs.

Example:

```
float3 values = float3( -1.0,2.0,0.0 );
float3 res = abs( values );
// res = float3( 1.0,2.0,0.0 );
```

acos

Usage: acos(value *x*)

Return type: same as input

Minimum vertex shader version: 1.1

Minimum pixel shader version: 2.0

Description: This function returns the arccosine of *x*. The result is computed per component for inputs that are vectors or matrices. Input components should be in the range of −1 to 1.

Example:

```
float3 vecA = float3( 1.0, 0.0, 0.0 );
float3 vecB = float3( 0.0, 1.0, 0.0 );
float dotprod = dot( vecA, vecB );
float3 angle = acos( dotprod );
// angle = angle between vecA and vecB, which is pi/2
```

all

Usage: all(value *x*)

Return type: boolean

Minimum vertex shader version: 1.1

Minimum pixel shader version: 1.4

Description: This function tests for non-zero values. The result is calculated per component for inputs that are vectors or matrices. The result of this function is 0 for a zero value input and 1 otherwise.

Example:

```
float3 value = float3( 1,0,2 );
float3 res = all( value );
// res = float3( 0,1,0 );
```

Any

Usage: any(value *x*)

Return type: boolean

Minimum vertex shader version: 1.1

Minimum pixel shader version: 1.4

Description: This function tests for any non-zero values in the input. The result of this function is 0 for a zero value input and 1 otherwise.

Example:

```
float3 value1 = float3( 0,0,0 );
float3 value2 = float3( 1,0,0 );
float2 res;
res.x = any( value1 );
res.y = any( value2 );
// res = float2( 0,1 );
```

Asin

Usage: `asin(value x)`

Return type: same as input

Minimum vertex shader version: 1.1

Minimum pixel shader version: 2.0

Description: This function returns the arcsine of the input. In case the input is either a vector or a matrix, the result is computed per component. Each input component should be in the range of –pi/2 to pi/2.

Example:

```
float value = 0.0;
float res = asin( value );
// res = 1.0;
```

atan

Usage: `atan(value x)`

Return type: same as input

Minimum vertex shader version: 1.1

Minimum pixel shader version: 2.0

Description: This function returns the arctangent of the input. In case the input is either a vector or a matrix, the result is computed per component. Each input component should be in the range –pi/2 to pi/2.

Example:

```
float value = 0.0;
float res = atan( value );
```

atan2

Usage: `atan2(value x)`

Return type: same as input

Minimum vertex shader version: 1.1

Minimum pixel shader version: 2.0

Description: The function returns the arctangent of y/x. The signs of y and x are used to discover the quadrant of the return values in the range –pi to pi. The `atan2` function is well-defined for every point other than the origin, even if x equals 0 and y does not equal 0. If the input is either a vector or a matrix, the output is computed per component.

Example:

```
float valueX = 1.0;
float valueY = 1.0;
float3 res = atan2( valueY, valueX );
```

ceil

Usage: `ceil(value x)`

Return type: same as input

Minimum vertex shader version: 1.1

Minimum pixel shader version: 2.0

Description: This function returns the smallest integer that is greater than or equal to the input value. If the input is either a vector or a matrix, the output is calculated per component.

Example:
```
float4 values = float4( 1.0, 1.2, 2.1, 3.5 );
float4 res = ceil( values );
// res = float4( 1.0, 2.0, 3.0, 4.0 );
```

clamp

Usage: `clamp(value x, value min, value max)`

Return type: same as input

Minimum vertex shader version: 1.1

Minimum pixel shader version: 1.4

Description: This function returns the input clamped to the range [min, max]. If the input is either a vector or a matrix, the output is computed per component.

Example:
```
float4 color = float4( 0.3, 0.5, 0.6, -1.0 );
float4 res = clamp( color * 2.0 , 0.0, 1.0 );
// res = float4( 0.6, 1.0, 1.0, 0.0 );
```

clip

Usage: `clip(value x)`

Return type: none

Minimum vertex shader version: N/A

Minimum pixel shader version: 1.1

Description: This function discards the current pixel, if any component of x is less than zero. This can be used to simulate clip planes, if each component of x represents the distance from a plane. This function can only be used within a pixel shader.

Example:
```
float4 value1 = float4( 1.0, 0.5, 0.0, -1.0 );
float4 value2 = float4( 1.0, 0.5, 0.0, 0.0 );
clip( value1 );
clip( value2 );
// Using value1 discards the pixel, value2 does not
```

cos

Usage: `cos(value x)`

Return type: same as input

Minimum vertex shader version: 1.1

Minimum pixel shader version: 2.0

Description: This function returns the cosine of the input. If the input is either a vector or a matrix, the result is computed per component.

Example:

```
const float pi = 3.14159;
float3 values = float3( 0.0, pi/2, pi );
float3 res = cos( values );
// res = float3( 1.0, 0.0, -1.0 );
```

cosh

Usage: `cosh(value x)`

Return type: same as input

Minimum vertex shader version: 1.1

Minimum pixel shader version: 2.0

Description: This function returns the hyperbolic cosine of the input. If the input is either a vector or a matrix, the result is calculated per component.

Example:

```
const float pi = 3.14159;
float3 values = float3( 0.0, pi/2, pi );
float3 res = cosh( values );
```

cross

Usage: `cross(vector a, vector b)`

Return type: vector

Minimum vertex shader version: 1.1

Minimum pixel shader version: 1.4

Description: This function returns the cross product of two 3D vectors *a* and *b*. The cross product is defined as:

```
float3 a,b;
float3 c = float3(a.y × b.z - a.z × b.y, a.x × b.x - a.z × b.x, a.x × b.y - a.y × b.x);
```

Example:

```
// Compute the normal of a polygon
float3 pos1 = float3( 1.2, 2.4, -1.0);
float3 pos2 = float3( 1.5, 2.9, 0.0);
float3 pos3 = float3( -2.2, -1.4, 1.0);
float3 vectorA = normalize( pos2 - pos1 );
float3 vectorB = normalize( pos3 - pos1 ) ;
float3 res = cross( vectorA, vectorB );
```

D3DCOLORtoUBYTE4

Usage: D3DCOLORtoUBYTE4 (vector *x*)

Return type: vector

Minimum vertex shader version: 1.1

Minimum pixel shader version: 2.0

Description: This function swizzles and scales components of the 4D vector *x* to compensate for the lack of UBYTE4 support in some hardware.

Example:

```
float4 value = float4( 0.1, 0.2, 0.3, 0.4 );
float4 res = D3DCOLORtoUBYTE4( value );
// res = float4( 0.4*255, 0.1*255, 0.2*255, 0.3*255 )
```

ddx

Usage: ddx (vector *x*)

Return type: same as input

Minimum vertex shader version: N/A

Minimum pixel shader version: 2.x

Description: This function returns the partial derivative of *x* for the screen-space x-coordinate. If available, this instruction uses information from other fragments being processed to determine an estimated derivate. In case of vector or matrix inputs, the result is calculated per component. Also note that this function is only available in pixel shaders.

Example:

```
// Assuming color is the interpolated vertex color input for the
// pixel shader in question.
float4 derivate = ddx( color );
// derivate = approximation of the variation of color based on
// x screen space coordinates
```

ddy

Usage: ddy (vector *x*)

Return type: same as input

Minimum vertex shader version: N/A

Minimum pixel shader version: 2.x

Description: This function returns the partial derivative of *x* for the screen-space y-coordinate. If available, this instruction uses information from other fragments being processed to discover an estimated derivate. In case of vector or matrix inputs, the result is calculated per component.

Example:

```
// Assuming color is the interpolated vertex color input for the
// pixel shader in question.
float4 derivate = ddy( color );
// derivate = approximation of the variation of color based on
// y screen space coordinates
```

degrees

Usage: degrees (value *x*)

Return type: same as input

Minimum vertex shader version: 1.1

Minimum pixel shader version: 2,0

Description: This function returns the conversion of the input values from radians to degrees. In case of vector or matrix inputs, the result is calculated per component.

Example:

```
float4 vectA = float4( 1.0, 0.0, 0.0 );
float4 vectB = float4( 0.0, 1.0, 0.0 );
float angle_radians = acos( dot( vectA, vectB ) );
float angle = degrees( angle_radians );
// angle = 90.0
```

determinant

Usage: determinant (matrix *x*)

Return type: scalar

Minimum vertex shader version: 1.1

Minimum pixel shader version: 1.4

Description: This function returns the determinant of the input matrix *x*. Note that the input matrix size must be square. The output of this function is a single scalar value.

Example:

```
float4x4 aMatrix;
float det = determinant( aMatrix );
```

distance

Usage: `distance (vector a, vector b)`

Return type: scalar

Minimum vertex shader version: 1.1

Minimum pixel shader version: 2,0

Description: This function returns the distance between two points *a* and *b*. This operation is defined as *length(b – a)*. Both input values must be vectors, and the output is a scalar.

Example:
```
float4 vectA = float4( 1.0, 0.0, 0.0, 0.0 );
float4 vectB = float4( 0.0, 1.0, 0.0, 0.0 );
float dist = distance( vectA, vectB );
// dist = sqrt(2)
```

dot

Usage: `dot (vector a, vector b)`

Return type: scalar

Minimum vertex shader version: 1.1

Minimum pixel shader version: 2.0

Description: This function returns the dot product of the two vectors *a* and *b*. The dot product is defined as $a.x \times b.x + a.y \times b.y + a.z \times b.z$. This result of the operation is equivalent to the cosine of the angle between the two vectors, if theses vectors are normalized. Both input values must be vectors, and the output is a scalar value.

Example:
```
float4 vectA = float4( 1.0, 0.0, 0.0 );
float4 vectB = float4( 0.0, 1.0, 0.0 );
float angle_radians = acos( dot( vectA, vectB ) );
float angle = degrees( angle_radians );
// angle = 90.0
```

exp

Usage: `exp (value x)`

Return type: same as input

Minimum vertex shader version: 1.1

Minimum pixel shader version: 2.0

Description: This function returns the base-e exponential of the input value *x*. If the input is a vector or a matrix, the output is computed per component.

Example:
```
float4 values = float4( 0.1, 0.5, 1.0, 2.0 );
float4 res = exp( values );
```

exp2

Usage: `exp2 (value x)`

Return type: same as input

Minimum vertex shader version: 1.1

Minimum pixel shader version: 2.0

Description: This function returns the base 2 exponential of the input value x. If the input is a vector or a matrix, the output is calculated per component.

Example:

```
float4 values = float4( 0.1, 0.5, 1.0, 2.0 );
float4 res = exp2( values );
```

faceforward

Usage: `faceforward (value n, value i, value ng)`

Return type: vector

Minimum vertex shader version: 1.1

Minimum pixel shader version: 1.4

Description: This function determines whether a polygon is front facing. The output of this function is defined as `-n × × sign(dot(i,ng))`.

Example:

```
float forward = faceforward( normal, i, ng );
```

floor

Usage: `floor (value x)`

Return type: same as input

Minimum vertex shader version: 1.1

Minimum pixel shader version: 2.0

Description: This function returns the greatest integer that is less than or equal to x. If the input is either a vector or a matrix, the result is calculated per component.

Example:

```
float4 values = float4( 1.0, 1.2, 2.1, 3.5 );
float4 res = floor( values );
// res = float4( 1.0, 1.0, 2.0, 3.0 );
```

fmod

Usage: `fmod (value a, value b)`

Return type: same as input

Minimum vertex shader version: 1.1

Minimum pixel shader version: 2.0

Description: This function returns the floating-point remainder f of a / b such that $a = i \times b + f$, where i is an integer, f has the same sign as x, and the absolute value of f is less than the absolute value of b. If the input is either a vector or a matrix, the result is computed per component.

Example:

```
float reminder = fmod( 10, 3 );
// reminder = 0.3333;
```

frac

Usage: frac (value x)

Return type: same as input

Minimum vertex shader version: 1.1

Minimum pixel shader version: 2.0

Description: This function returns the fractional part f of the input value x such that f is a value greater or equal to 0 and less than 1. If the input is either a vector or a matrix, the result is calculated per component.

Example:

```
float4 values = float4( 1.0, 1.25, 2.1, 3.5 )
float4 res = frac( values );
// res = float4( 0.0, 0.25, 0.1, 0.5 );
```

frexp

Usage: frexp (value x, out exp)

Return type: same as input

Minimum vertex shader version: 1.1

Minimum pixel shader version: 2,0

Description: This function returns the mantissa and exponent of x. frexp returns the mantissa, and the exponent is stored in the output parameter exp. If x is 0, the function returns 0 for both the mantissa and the exponent. If the input is either a vector or a matrix, the result is computed per component.

Example:

```
float exp;
float value = 1100;
float mant = frexp( value, exp ); // mant = 1.1, exp = 2
```

fwidth

Usage: fwidth (value *x*)

Return type: same as input

Minimum vertex shader version: N/A

Minimum pixel shader version: 2.x

Description: This function returns *abs(ddx(x))+abs(ddy(x))*. If the input is either a vector or a matrix, the result is computed per component.

Example:

```
float4 colWidth = fwidth(color);
```

isfinite

Usage: isfinite (value *x*)

Return type: scalar

Minimum vertex shader version: 1.1

Minimum pixel shader version: 2.0

Description: This function returns true if *x* is finite, false otherwise. If the input is either a vector or a matrix, the result is computed per component.

Example:

```
bool res = isfinite( value );
```

isinf

Usage: isinf (value *x*)

Return type: scalar

Minimum vertex shader version: 1.1

Minimum pixel shader version: 2.0

Description: This function returns true if the input value *x* is equal to +INF or –INF, false otherwise. If the input is either a vector or a matrix, the result is calculated per component.

Example:

```
bool res = isinf( value );
```

isnan

Usage: isnan (value *x*)

Return type: same as input

Minimum vertex shader version: 1.1

Minimum pixel shader version: 2.0

Description: This function returns `true` if the input value x is equal to NAN or QNAN, `false` otherwise. If the input is either a vector or a matrix, the result is computed per component.

Example:

```
bool res = isnan( value );
```

ldexp

Usage: `ldexp (value x, value exp)`

Return type: same as input

Minimum vertex shader version: 1.1

Minimum pixel shader version: 2.0

Description: This function is essentially the reverse operation of `frexp` and returns $x \times 2^{exp}$. If the input is either a vector or a matrix, the result is computed per component.

Example:

```
float res = ldexp( mant, exp );
```

len / length

Usage: `len (vector x) / length (vector x)`

Return type: scalar

Minimum vertex shader version: 1.1

Minimum pixel shader version: 2.0

Description: This function returns the length of the input vector x. The result is defined as $sqrt(x.x \times x.x + x.y \times x.y + x.z \times x.z)$. The input to this function must be a vector, and its output is a scalar value.

Example:

```
// Manually normalizing a vector
float4 vect = float4( 1.1, 2.0, -0.6, 3.4 );
float vectlen = len( vect );
float4 normVect = vect / vectlen;
```

lerp

Usage: `lerp (value s, value a, value b)`

Return type: same as input

Minimum vertex shader version: 1.1

Minimum pixel shader version: 1.4

Description: This function returns $a + s \times (b - a)$. This linearly interpolates between a and b, such that the return value is a when s is 0, and b when s is 1. If the input values are either vectors or matrices, the output is computed per component.

Example:

```
float4 Color1 = float4( 0.1, 0.5, 0.0, 1.0 );
float4 Color2 = float4( 0.7, 0.5, 1.0, 0.8 );
float4 res = lerp( 0.5, Color1, Color2 );
// res = float4( 0.4, 0.5, 0.5, 0.9 );
```

lit

Usage: `lit (value ndotl, value ndoth, value m)`

Return type: vector

Minimum vertex shader version: 1.1

Minimum pixel shader version: 2.0

Description: This function returns a lighting vector (ambient, diffuse, specular, 1). The ambient value is always returned as 1. The diffuse value is defined as *diffuse = (ndotl < 0) ? 0 : ndotl*. The specular value is defined as *specular = (ndotl < 0) || (ndoth < 0) ? 0 : (ndoth × m)*. All input values must be scalars, and the output is always a vector.

Example:

```
// Inputs are n = surface normal, l = incoming light direction
// h = half-vector between eye and light vectors
const float specularExponent = 32;
float ndotl = dot( n, l );
float ndoth = dot( n, h );
float4 lighting = lit( ndotl, ndoth, specularExponent );
```

log

Usage: `log (value x)`

Return type: same as input

Minimum vertex shader version: 1.1

Minimum pixel shader version: 2.0

Description: This function returns the base-e logarithm of x. If x is negative, the function returns indefinite. If x is 0, the function returns +INF. If the input is either a vector or a matrix, the result is calculated per component.

Example:

```
float res = log( value );
```

log2

Usage: log2 (value x)

Return type: same as input

Minimum vertex shader version: 1.1

Minimum pixel shader version: 2.0

Description: This function returns the base-2 logarithm of x. If x is negative, the function returns indefinite, or NAN. If x is 0, the function returns +INF. If the input is either a vector or a matrix, the result is computed per component.

Example:

```
float res = log2( value );
```

log10

Usage: log10 (value x)

Return type: same as input

Minimum vertex shader version: 1.1

Minimum pixel shader version: 2.0

Description: This function returns the base-10 logarithm of x. If x is negative, the function returns indefinite, or NAN. If x is 0, the function returns +INF. If the input is either a vector or a matrix, the result is calculated per component.

Example:

```
float res = log10( value );
```

max

Usage: max (value a, value b)

Return type: same as input

Minimum vertex shader version: 1.1

Minimum pixel shader version: 1.4

Description: This function returns the greater of the input values a or b. If the input is either a vector or a matrix, the result is computed per component.

Example:

```
float4 valueA = float4( 1.0, 2.0, 3.0, 4.0 );
float4 valueB = float4( 4.0, 3.0, 2.0, 1.0 );
float res = max( valueA, valueB );
// res = float4( 4.0, 3.0, 3.0, 4.0 );
```

min

Usage: `min (value a, value b)`

Return type: same as input

Minimum vertex shader version: 1.1

Minimum pixel shader version: 1.4

Description: This function returns the lesser of input values a or b. If the input is either a vector or a matrix, the result is computed per component.

Example:

```
float4 valueA = float4( 1.0, 2.0, 3.0, 4.0 );
float4 valueB = float4( 4.0, 3.0, 2.0, 1.0 );
float res = min( valueA, valueB );
// res = float4( 1.0, 2.0, 2.0, 1.0 );
```

modf

Usage: `modf (value x, out ip)`

Return type: same as input

Minimum vertex shader version: 1.1

Minimum pixel shader version: 2.0

Description: This function splits the value x into fractional and integer parts, each of which has the same sign as x. The signed fractional portion of x is returned. The integer portion is stored in the output parameter ip. If the input is either a vector or a matrix, the result is calculated per component.

Example:

```
float4 values = float4( 1.0, 1.2, 3.25, 0.3 );
float4 ip;
float4 res = modf( values, ip );
// res = float4( 0.0, 0.2, 0.25, 0.3 )
// ip = float4( 1.0, 1.0, 3.0, 0.0 )
```

mul

Usage: `mul (matrix a, matrix b)`

Return type: depends on input

Minimum vertex shader version: 1.1

Minimum pixel shader version: 1.1

Description: This function performs matrix multiplication between *a* and *b*. If *a* is a vector, it is treated as a row vector. If *b* is a vector, it is treated as a column vector. The inner dimension *a*(columns) and *b*(rows) must be equal. The result has the dimension *a*(rows) × *b*(columns).

Example:

```
float4x4 modelMtx, viewMtx;
float4x4 finalMtx = mul( modelMtx, viewMtx );
```

normalize

Usage: `normalize (vector x)`

Return type: same as input

Minimum vertex shader version: 1.1

Minimum pixel shader version: 2.0

Description: This function returns the normalized vector, also defined as $x / length(x)$. If the length of *x* is 0, the result is undefined.

Example:

```
// Compute the normal of a polygon
float3 pos1 = float3( 1.2, 2.4, -1.0);
float3 pos2 = float3( 1.5, 2.9, 0.0);
float3 pos3 = float3( -2.2, -1.4, 1.0);
float3 vectorA = normalize( pos2 - pos1 );
float3 vectorB = normalize( pos3 - pos1 );
float3 res = cross( vectorA, vectorB );
```

pow

Usage: `pow (value x, value y)`

Return type: same as input

Minimum vertex shader version: 1.1

Minimum pixel shader version: 2.0

Description: This function returns the input value *x* raised to the power of *y*. If the input *x* is either a vector or a matrix, the operation is performed per component.

Example:

```
float4 value = float4( 1.0, 2.0, 3.0, 4.0 );
float4 res = pow( value, 2 );
// res = float4( 1.0, 4.0, 9.0, 16.0 );
```

radians

Usage: radians (value *x*)

Return type: same as input

Minimum vertex shader version: 1.1

Minimum pixel shader version: 1.1

Description: This function returns conversion of the input value *x* from degrees to radians. If the input *x* is either a vector or a matrix, the operation is performed per component.

Example:

```
float4 vectA = float4( 1.0, 0.0, 0.0 );
float4 vectB = float4( 0.0, 1.0, 0.0 );
float angle_radians = acos( dot( vectA, vectB ) );
float angle = degrees( angle_radians );
// angle_radians == radians( angle );
```

reflect

Usage: reflect (*vector i*, *vector n*)

Return type: same as input

Minimum vertex shader version: 1.1

Minimum pixel shader version: 1.1

Description: This function returns the reflection vector given the entering ray direction *i* and the surface normal *n*. The result is defined as $v = i - 2 \times dot(i, n) \times n$. The input vectors to this function should be normalized.

Example:

```
// Simple environment mapping assuming Normal = surface normal
// and eyeVect = eye vector
float3 reflected = reflect( eyeVect, Normal );
float4 color = texCUBE( envmap, reflected );
```

refract

Usage: refract (*vector i*, *vector n*, value *eta*)

Return type: same as input

Minimum vertex shader version: 1.1

Minimum pixel shader version: 1.1

Description: This function returns the refraction vector *v*, given the entering ray direction *i*, the surface normal *n*, and the relative index of refraction *eta* (which is defined as the ratio between the refraction indexes for the two medias). If the angle between *i* and *n* is too great for a given *eta*, refract returns (0,0,0).

Example:

```
// Simple refraction environment mapping assuming Normal = surface normal
// and eyeVect = eye vector
float eta = 1.0/1.4; // Air-Water refraction index
float3 refracted = refract( eyeVect, Normal, eta );
float4 color = texCUBE( envmap, refracted );
```

round

Usage: round (*vector i, vector n*, value *eta*)

Return type: same as input

Minimum vertex shader version: 1.1

Minimum pixel shader version: 2.0

Description: This function rounds the input to the nearest integer. If the input is either a vector or a matrix, the result is determined per component.

Example:

```
float res = round (10.6);
// res = 11
```

rsqrt

Usage: rsqrt (value *x*)

Return type: same as input

Minimum vertex shader version: 1.1

Minimum pixel shader version: 2.0

Description: This function returns the reciprocal square root of the input value *x* defined as *1/sqrt(x)*. If the input is either a vector or a matrix, the result is computed per component.

Example:

```
// Manual vector length and normalization
float4 vect;
float sqrLen = dot( vect, vect );
float4 normVect = vect * rsqrt( sqrLen );
```

saturate

Usage: `saturate (value x)`

Return type: same as input

Minimum vertex shader version: 1.1

Minimum pixel shader version: 1.1

Description: This function clamps *x* to the range of 0 to 1. This is equal to calling *clamp(x, 0, 1)*. If the input value is either a vector or a matrix, the result of the operation is determined per component.

Example:
```
float4 values = float4( 0.1, 1.5, -0.5, 0.7 );
float4 res = saturate( values );
// res = float4( 0.1, 1.0, 0.0, 0.7 );
```

sign

Usage: `sign (value x)`

Return type: same as input

Minimum vertex shader version: 1.1

Minimum pixel shader version: 1.4

Description: This function computes the sign of *x*. Returns −1 if *x* is less than 0, 0 if *x* equals 0, and 1 if *x* is greater than zero. If the input value is either a vector or a matrix, the result of the operation is determined per component.

Example:
```
float3 values = float3( -10, 10, 0 );
float3 res = sign( values );
// res = (-1, 1, 0)
```

sin

Usage: `sin (value x)`

Return type: same as input

Minimum vertex shader version: 1.1

Minimum pixel shader version: 2.0

Description: This function computes the sine of *x*. If the input value is either a vector or a matrix, the result of the operation is determined per component.

Example:
```
const float pi = 3.14159;
float3 values = float3( 0.0, pi/2, pi );
float3 res = cos( values );
// res = float3( 0.0, 1.0, 0.0 );
```

sincos

Usage: `sincos (value x, out s, out c)`

Return type: same as input

Minimum vertex shader version: 1.1

Minimum pixel shader version: 2.0

Description: This function returns the sine and cosine of *x*. The value *sin(x)* is stored in the output parameter *s*, and *cos(x)* is stored in the output parameter *c*. If the input value is either a vector or a matrix, the result of the operation is determined per component.

Example:
```
const float pi = 3.14159;
float3 values = float3( 0.0, pi/2, pi );
float3 s,c;
sincos( values, s, c );
// s = float3( 0.0, 1.0, 0.0 );
// c = float3( 1.0, 0.0, -1.0 );
```

sinh

Usage: `sinh (value x)`

Return type: same as input

Minimum vertex shader version: 1.1

Minimum pixel shader version: 2.0

Description: This function computes the hyperbolic sine of *x*. If the input value is either a vector or a matrix, the result of the operation is determined per component.

Example:
```
const float pi = 3.14159;
float3 values = float3( 0.0, pi/2, pi );
float3 res = sinh( values );
```

smoothstep

Usage: `sinh (value min, value max, value x)`

Return type: same as input

Minimum vertex shader version: 1.1

Minimum pixel shader version: 2.0

Description: This function returns 0 if *x* < *min*. Returns 1 if *x* > *max*. The function will return a smooth Hermite interpolation between 0 and 1, if *x* is in the range of *min* to *max*. If the input value is either a vector or a matrix, the result of the operation is determined per component.

Example:
```
float res = smoothstep( minVal, maxVal, value );
```

sqrt

Usage: sqrt (value *x*)

Return type: same as input

Minimum vertex shader version: 1.1

Minimum pixel shader version: 2.0

Description: This function returns the square root of the input value *x*. If the input value is either a vector or a matrix, the result of the operation is determined per component.

Example:

```
// Manual vector length and normalization
float4 vect;
float sqrLen = dot( vect, vect );
float4 normVect = vect / sqrt( sqrLen );
```

step

Usage: step (value *a*, value *x*)

Return type: same as input

Minimum vertex shader version: 1.1

Minimum pixel shader version: 1.4

Description: This function returns *(x >= a) ? 1 : 0*. If the input value is either a vector or a matrix, the result of the operation is determined per component.

Example:

```
float3 values = float3( 1.0, 2.0, 0.5 );
float3 res = step( 1.0, values );
// res = float3( 1.0, 1.0, 0.0 );
```

tan

Usage: tan (value *x*)

Return type: same as input

Minimum vertex shader version: 1.1

Minimum pixel shader version: 2.0

Description: This function computes the tangent of *x*. If the input value is either a vector or a matrix, the result of the operation is determined per component.

Example:

```
const float pi = 3.14159;
float3 values = float3( 0.0, pi/2, pi );
float3 res = tan( values );
```

tanh

Usage: `tanh (value x)`

Return type: same as input

Minimum vertex shader version: 1.1

Minimum pixel shader version: 2.0

Description: This function computes the hyperbolic tangent of *x*. If the input value is either a vector or a matrix, the result of the operation is determined per component.

Example:

```
const float pi = 3.14159;
float3 values = float3( 0.0, pi/2, pi );
float3 res = tanh( values );
```

transpose

Usage: `transpose (matrix x)`

Return type: matrix

Minimum vertex shader version: 1.1

Minimum pixel shader version: 1.1

Description: This function returns the transpose of the matrix *m*. If the source is dimension *m*(rows) × *m*(columns), the result is dimension *m*(columns) × *m*(rows). A transpose is equivalent to flipping rows and columns in the matrix.

Example:

```
float4x4 res = transpose( myMatrix );
```

Texture Lookup

The following section covers all built-in HLSL functions used for texture access within fragment shaders. These functions can also be used within a vertex shader if your hardware supports vertex shader texture access.

tex1D

Usage: `tex1D (sampler s, value t)`

Return type: vector

Minimum vertex shader version: N/A

Minimum pixel shader version: 1.1

Description: This function performs a 1D texture lookup. *s* is the sampler used to access the texture, and *t* is a scalar value used as the texture coordinate.

Example:

```
float4 color = tex1D( myTexture, coords );
```

tex1D with Derivates

Usage: `tex1D (sampler s, value t, value ddx, value ddy)`

Return type: vector

Minimum vertex shader version: N/A

Minimum pixel shader version: 2.0

Description: This function performs a 1D texture lookup. *s* is the sampler used to access the texture, and *t* is a scalar value used as texture coordinates. The inputs *ddx* and *ddy* are screen space derivates used to manually override hardware mipmapping.

Example:

```
float4 color = tex1D( myTexture, cords, ddx, ddy );
```

tex1Dproj

Usage: `tex1D proj(sampler s, value t)`

Return type: vector

Minimum vertex shader version: N/A

Minimum pixel shader version: 2.0

Description: This function performs a 1D projective texture lookup. *s* is the sampler used to access the texture, and *t* is a four-component vector where the *t* is divided by its last component before the texture lookup takes place.

Example:

```
float4 color = tex1Dproj( myTexture, coords );
```

tex1Dbias

Usage: `tex1Dbias(sampler s, value t)`

Return type: vector

Minimum vertex shader version: N/A

Minimum pixel shader version: 2.0

Description: This function performs a 1D biased texture lookup. *s* is the sampler used to access the texture, and *t* is a four-component vector. The mipmapping level is biased by *t.w* before the texture lookup takes place.

Example:

```
float4 color = tex1Dbias( myTexture, coords );
```

tex2D

Usage: `tex2D (sampler s, value t)`

Return type: vector

Minimum vertex shader version: N/A

Minimum pixel shader version: 1.1

Description: This function performs a 1D texture lookup. *s* is the sampler used to access the texture, and *t* is a two-component vector used as texture coordinates.

Example:

```
float4 color = tex2D( myTexture, coords );
```

tex2D with Derivates

Usage: `tex2D (sampler s, value t, value ddx, value ddy)`

Return type: vector

Minimum vertex shader version: N/A

Minimum pixel shader version: 2.0

Description: This function performs a 2D texture lookup. *s* is the sampler used to access the texture, and *t* is a two-component vector used as texture coordinates. The inputs *ddx* and *ddy* are screen space derivates used to manually override hardware mipmapping.

Example:

```
float4 color = tex2D( myTexture, cords, ddx, ddy );
```

tex2Dproj

Usage: `tex2Dproj (sampler s, value t)`

Return type: vector

Minimum vertex shader version: N/A

Minimum pixel shader version: 2.0

Description: This function performs a 2D projective texture lookup. *s* is the sampler used to access the texture, and *t* is a four-component vector, where the *t* is divided by its last component before the texture lookup takes place.

Example:

```
float4 color = tex2Dproj( myTexture, coords );
```

tex2Dbias

Usage: `tex2Dbias (sampler s, value t)`

Return type: vector

Minimum vertex shader version: N/A

Minimum pixel shader version: 2.0

Description: This function performs a 2D biased texture lookup. *s* is the sampler used to access the texture, and *t* is a four-component vector. The mipmapping level is biased by *t.w* before the texture lookup takes place.

Example:

```
float4 color = tex2Dbias( myTexture, coords );
```

tex3D

Usage: tex3D (sampler *s*, value *t*)

Return type: vector

Minimum vertex shader version: N/A

Minimum pixel shader version: 1.1

Description: This function performs a 3D texture lookup. *s* is the sampler used to access the texture, and *t* is a three-component vector used as texture coordinates.

Example:

```
float4 color = tex3D( myTexture, coords );
```

tex3D with Derivates

Usage: tex3D (sampler *s*, value *t*, value *ddx*, value *ddy*)

Return type: vector

Minimum vertex shader version: N/A

Minimum pixel shader version: 2.0

Description: This function performs a 3D texture lookup. *s* is the sampler used to access the texture, and *t* is a three-component vector used as texture coordinates. The inputs *ddx* and *ddy* are screen space derivates used to manually override hardware mipmapping.

Example:

```
float4 color = tex3D( myTexture, cords, ddx, ddy );
```

tex3Dproj

Usage: tex3Dproj (sampler *s*, value *t*)

Return type: vector

Minimum vertex shader version: N/A

Minimum pixel shader version: 2.0

Description: This function performs a 3D projective texture lookup. *s* is the sampler used to access the texture, and *t* is a four-component vector where the *t* is divided by its last component before the texture lookup takes place.

Example:

```
float4 color = tcx3Dproj( myTexture, coords );
```

tex3Dbias

Usage: tex3Dbias (sampler *s*, value *t*)

Return type: vector

Minimum vertex shader version: N/A

Minimum pixel shader version: 2.0

Description: This function performs a 3D biased texture lookup. *s* is the sampler used to access the texture, and *t* is a four-component vector. The mipmapping level is biased by *t.w* before the texture lookup takes place.

Example:

```
float4 color = tex3Dbias( myTexture, coords );
```

texCUBE

Usage: texCUBE (sampler *s*, value *t*)

Return type: vector

Minimum vertex shader version: N/A

Minimum pixel shader version: 1.1

Description: This function performs a cubemap texture lookup. *s* is the sampler used to access the texture, and *t* is a three-component vector used as texture coordinates.

Example:

```
float4 color = texCUBE( myTexture, coords );
```

texCUBE with Derivates

Usage: texCUBE (sampler *s*, value *t*, value *ddx*, value *ddy*)

Return type: vector

Minimum vertex shader version: N/A

Minimum pixel shader version: 2.0

Description: This function performs a cubemap texture lookup. *s* is the sampler used to access the texture, and *t* is a three-component vector used as texture coordinates. The inputs *ddx* and *ddy* are screen space derivates used to manually override hardware mipmapping.

Example:

```
float4 color = texCUBE( myTexture, cords, ddx, ddy );
```

texCUBEproj

Usage: texCUBEproj (sampler *s*, value *t*)

Return type: vector

Minimum vertex shader version: N/A

Minimum pixel shader version: 2.0

Description: This function performs a cubemap projective texture lookup. *s* is the sampler used to access the texture, and *t* is a four-component vector where the *t* is divided by its last component before the texture lookup takes place.

Example:

```
float4 color = texCUBEproj( myTexture, coords );
```

texCUBEbias

Usage: texCUBEbias (sampler *s*, value *t*)

Return type: vector

Minimum vertex shader version: N/A

Minimum pixel shader version: 2.0

Description: This function performs a cubemap biased texture lookup. *s* is the sampler used to access the texture, and *t* is a four-component vector. The mipmapping level is biased by *t.w* before the texture lookup takes place.

Example:

```
float4 color = texCUBEbias( myTexture, coords );
```

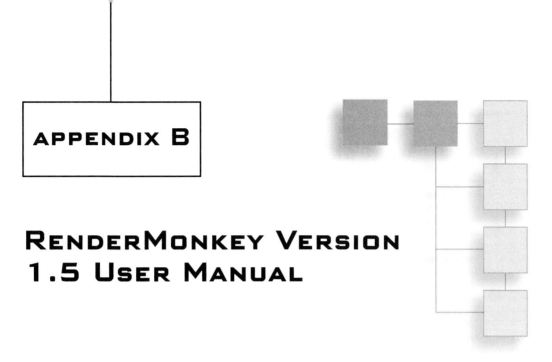

APPENDIX B

RENDERMONKEY VERSION 1.5 USER MANUAL

3 D graphic application developers face many challenges when it comes to rendering. Most of them include taking advantage of the current and continuously changing hardware platforms. With the latest advances and the introduction of the more flexible vertex and pixel shader versions 2.0 and 3.0, developers can now achieve a level of flexibility and graphic realism not previously achievable.

For developers to take advantage of the new advances, a fair amount of development is needed, restricting creativity and making the learning curve steeper. ATI Technologies recently introduced the first fully functional version of its RenderMonkey application. As shown in Figure B.1, this tool serves as an Integrated Development Environment (IDE) focused on simplifying shader development. The main motivations behind RenderMonkey are to provide

- A powerful yet simple development environment for creating shaders
- A standardized means of creating shaders, allowing better collaboration among developers
- A flexible framework not only for today's needs but allowing for future innovation
- An environment that finally bridges the gap between programmers and artists, allowing both of them to work together on the same platform
- A tool that can easily be expanded and customized to meet a particular developer's needs

This appendix serves as an addition to Chapter 3, going into more detail on RenderMonkey's IDE and its use. Keep in mind that this chapter is inspired by ATI's *RenderMonkey User Manual* and that it is included on the CD for a more complete reference.

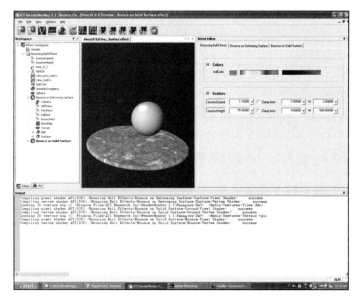

Figure B.1 Taking a look at RenderMonkey in action.

Installation

This section takes you through the simple installation process for RenderMonkey. We have included on the CD the latest version of the software at the time of the printing of this book. If you wish to get the latest version or check for updates, we encourage you to visit the ATI Technologies website at `http://www.ati.com`.

Requirements

RenderMonkey has a few basic computer needs that must be met before you can install and run it. The following list covers the most important ones:

- Although this book assumes Windows XP for consistency, Windows 2000 (Service Pack 2), Windows XP, Windows 98, and Windows ME are supported by Render-Monkey version 1.0.
- DirectX 9.0b (included on the CD).
- At the minimum, you will need a DirectX 9.0-compliant graphics card. However, a card supporting pixel and vertex shaders 2.0 is strongly recommended.
- 128MB of RAM.
- 500MB of free hard drive space.

If your hardware meets those requirements, you can use the following instructions to install the software and get yourself ready to write shaders!

Installing RenderMonkey

Begin the process by selecting Install RenderMonkey from the CD-ROM interface. Once started, you will see a splash screen followed by a warning message. To continue the process, click the Next> button. This brings up a license screen, as shown in Figure B.2.

Although the license agreement is standard, you should still review it. When you are ready to continue, select the option accepting the license agreement and click the Next> button. The following screen asks you for an installation path. Unless you are an advanced user

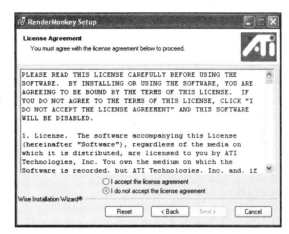

Figure B.2 RenderMonkey's installation license screen.

(in which case you probably are not even reading this), just keep the default value and click Next> to continue. At this point, the software should be installing itself on your machine. The whole process should take less than one minute to complete.

Using RenderMonkey

At this point, the RenderMonkey application should be installed and ready to run. I suggest you fire it up and follow along as I guide you through its different components. I will explain each component's role and use, keeping the explanation as simple and to the point as possible.

Application Toolbar

Figure B.3 illustrates the toolbar as seen in RenderMonkey. The purpose of the tool-bar is to offer you

Figure B.3 Close-up view of RenderMonkey's application toolbar.

shortcuts to common tasks you will need to perform. The following list outlines what each toolbar button accomplishes:

     Open a workspace.

     Save the current workspace.

Toggle on/off the Workspace Window.

 Toggle on/off the Output Window.

 Toggle on/off the Preview Window.

 Toggle on/off the Artist Editor Window.

 Compiles all shaders in the currently active effect. This is equivalent to pressing F7.

 Compiles all the shaders within the current workspace. This can also be done by using the F8 key.

 Changes the Preview Window camera mode to Rotation.

 Changes the Preview Window camera mode to Pan.

 Changes the Preview Window camera mode to Zoom.

 Brings the Preview Window camera back to its original position.

 Changes the Preview Window camera to the overloaded camera mode.

 Enables the camera's mouse input mode.

Application Menu

The menu structure for RenderMonkey is simple. Here I'll break it down by showing you a fully expanded menu structure in Figure B.4. The menu structure should give you a clear idea of which options are available and which ones have shortcut keys associated with them. Tables B.1 through B.5 list each menu item and give a short description of what the option does.

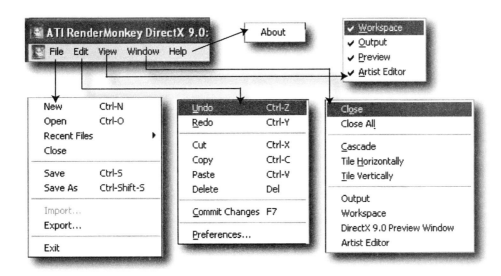

Figure B.4 Expanded view of all menus within RenderMonkey.

Table B.1 File Menu Options

Option	Shortcut	Function
New	Ctrl+N	Creates a new blank workspace. If another unsaved workspace is active, the user will be asked if he wishes to save the current workspace before creating the new one.
Open	Ctrl+O	Opens an existing workspace file.
Recent Files	N/A	Provides a list of the 5 most recently opened workspaces for quick access.
Close	N/A	Closes the currently open workspace. If the current workspace is unsaved, the user will be prompted to save prior to closing it.
Save	Ctrl+S	Saves the current workspace.
Save As	Ctrl+Shift-S	Saves the workspace under a new filename.
Import	N/A	RenderMonkey allows developers to create plug-ins to define their own file formats. You can load 3rd-party file formats through this menu option.
Export	N/A	As with the import option, developers can create export plug-ins. This option allows the user to save her workspace to a third-party format.
Exit	N/A	Quits the application, prompting the user to save any opened workspace.

Table B.2 Edit Menu Options

Option	Shortcut	Function
Undo	Ctrl+Z	Allows the user to undo the last undoable operation.
Redo	Ctrl+Y	Redoes the last undone operation.
Cut	Ctrl+X	Cuts the currently selected item into the clipboard.
Copy	Ctrl+C	Copies the currently selected item into the clipboard.
Paste	Ctrl+V	Pastes the current clipboard item into the workspace.
Delete	Del	Deletes the currently selected workspace node.
Commit Changes	F7	Forces RenderMonkey to compile and commit the currently active shader.
Preferences	N/A	Opens up the Preference dialog box, where some general application options can be set.

Table B.3 View Menu Options

Option	Shortcut	Function
Workspace	N/A	Toggles the visibility of the Workspace Window.
Output	N/A	Toggles the visibility of the Output Window.
Preview	N/A	Toggles the visibility of the Preview Window.
Artist Editor	N/A	Toggles the visibility of the Artist Editor Window.

Table B.4 Window Menu Options

Option	Shortcut	Function
Close	N/A	Closes the currently selected sub-window.
Close All	N/A	Closes all sub-windows.
Cascade	N/A	Cascades all windows.
Tile Horizontal	N/A	Horizontally tiles all windows.
Tile Vertical	N/A	Vertically tiles all windows.

Table B.5 Help Menu Options

Option	Shortcut	Function
About	N/A	Brings up a dialog box with general info about RenderMonkey and how to leave feedback and get support.

Workspace View

Because I have already gone over RenderMonkey's user interface and important windows in Chapter 3, "RenderMonkey Version 1.5," I will go straight to the meat. This section will go over the different operations that can be done within the Workspace view.

The Workspace view, as shown in Figure B.5, is a dockable window usually located to the left of the main window. The two main aspects of this window are its tree view and tab control at the bottom. At the time of this writing, there are two tabs within the Workspace view. The Effect tab is used to view the entire workspace and is intended for the programmer. The Art tab allows editing only of parameters defined as artist-editable within the workspace.

Figure B.5 Close-up view of RenderMonkey's Workspace Window.

The workspace itself is organized as a hierarchical tree-view where each item is represented as a node. As described in Chapter 3, workspace nodes are of various types, but include grouping elements, parameters, states, and resources. Grouping elements include Effect groups, which are intended as a mechanism to organize effects within large workspaces. Effect groups contain one or many individual effects. Each effect, in turn, consists of one or more render passes and global parameters for the effect.

Some types of nodes have built-in editors defined for them. Double-clicking on such a node brings up the associated editor. Some nodes may have multiple editors defined for them; right-clicking and selecting Edit from the menu enables you to pick an editor to use.

tip

By right-clicking on the root node of the workspace, you will notice an option called Add Default Effect. Selecting this option fills your workspace with a simple HLSL shader. A great way to get started on a new shader!

Effect Groups

If you want to create a new Effect Group, you should click on the Effect Workspace node in the Workspace view. You will then see the context menu shown in Figure B.6.

If you pick the Add Effect Group option, you will given the choice of creating a new effect as either being empty or containing a default effect. Picking either option will create a new group for you. If you opt to create an effect group with a default effect, the new group will contain a sample one-pass effect for your convenience. Effect Groups can contain any of the following items:

Figure B.6 Context menu displayed when right-clicking on the workspace root node.

- Variables
- Stream mapping nodes
- Models
- Effects
- Notes
- Renderable textures

note

Any node the RenderMonkey IDE creates for you is automatically named. Because the names created by the application are generic, it is a good idea to rename them to something meaningful by right-clicking on the node and selecting the Rename right-click menu option.

note

As with most other workspace nodes, this node can be deleted, renamed, copied, and pasted. To do any of those operations, select the node within the workspace view, right-click your mouse button, and simply pick the proper operation from the context menu.

caution

Effect Group nodes may only exist as a direct child of the Effect Workspace node. RenderMonkey will not allow you to paste an Effect Group in another location.

Managing Variables

User-defined data is something essential to shader development. RenderMonkey enables you to add variables at any point within the workspace tree, which can be directly referred to by your shader code. If you right-click on any node within the Workspace view, you will see the Add Variable option. From this point, you will be able to select the type of variable or built-in variable you wish to create through a series of menus, such as shown in Figure B.7.

From this menu, you can select which data type and structure you want to use for your new variable. You can currently pick from the following:

- **Boolean:** A single value that is either TRUE or FALSE.
- **Scalar:** A single floating-point, integer, or boolean value.
- **Vector:** A four-component floating-point, integer, or boolean vector.
- **Matrix:** A 4 × 4 floating-point, integer, or boolean matrix.
- **Color:** Defines a color vector (RGBA) editable through a color picker.

tip

Each different type of variable is represented by a different icon within the Workspace view, allowing you to recognize easily how each variable is represented.

Each variable within the Workspace view can be defined as being artist-editable (available within the Art tab of the Workspace view). By default, new scalar, vector, and matrix variables are set as not artist-editable. Color and texture variables are created as artist-editable by default. You can change the artist-editable status and do standard editing operations on a variable by right-clicking on its node in the Workspace view.

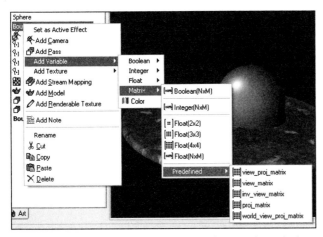

Figure B.7 Adding a variable to a workspace through the use of the right-click menu.

For your convenience, RenderMonkey provides a set of predefined variables that contains general system information sometimes useful for shader development. All of Render-Monkey's built-in variables are outlined in Table B.6.

Table B.6 RenderMonkey's Predefined Variables

Variable Name	Type	Value
time_0_X	Scalar	Provides a time value in seconds which repeats itself based on the Cycle Time value set in the Preferences dialog box.
cos_time_0_X	Scalar	Provides the cosine of time_0_X.
sin_time_0_X	Scalar	Provides the sine of time_0_X.
tan_time_0_X	Scalar	Provides the tangent of time_0_X.
time_cycle_period	Scalar	Provides the Cycle Time value set in the Preferences dialog box.
time_0_1	Scalar	Provides a time value in the range [0..1] which repeats itself based on the Cycle Time value.
time_0_2PI	Scalar	Provides a time value in the range [0..2*PI] which repeats itself based on the Cycle Time value.
cos_time_0_X	Scalar	Provides the cosine of time_0_2PI.
sin_time_0_X	Scalar	Provides the sine of time_0_2PI.
tan_time_0_X	Scalar	Provides the tangent of time_0_2PI.
viewport_width	Scalar	Provides the pixel width of the Preview window.
viewport_height	Scalar	Provides the pixel height of the Preview window.
viewport_inv_width	Scalar	Provides 1 / viewport_width.
viewport_inv_height	Scalar	Provides 1 / viewport_height.
pass_index	Scalar	Provides the index number of the current rendering pass.
mouse_state	Scalar	Provides the current state of the mouse.
mouse_button	Scalar	Provides the button state of the mouse.
mouse_x	Scalar	Provides the X position of the mouse.
mouse_y	Scalar	Provides the Y position of the mouse.
random_fraction_1	Scalar	Provides a random number in the range [0..1].
random_fraction_2	Scalar	Provides a random number in the range [0..1].
random_fraction_3	Scalar	Provides a random number in the range [0..1].
random_fraction_4	Scalar	Provides a random number in the range [0..1].
view_direction	Vector	Provides the view direction vector in world space.
view_position	Vector	Provides the view position in world space.
view_side	Vector	Provides the side view direction in world space.
view_up	Vector	Provides the up view direction in world space.
view_proj_matrix	Matrix	Provides the view-projection matrix.
view_matrix	Matrix	Provides the view matrix.
view_inv_matrix	Matrix	Provides the inverse of the view matrix.
proj_matrix	Matrix	Provides the projection matrix.
world_view_proj_matrix	Matrix	Provides the world-view-projection matrix.

Managing Effects

Effects can be created only as part of an Effect Group. To create an effect, simply right-click on an Effect Group node and pick Add Effect: DirectX from the context menu. This creates a new effect at the bottom of the selected group. RenderMonkey allows effect nodes to contain any of the following:

- Variables (or shader parameters)
- Stream mapping nodes
- Models
- Cameras
- Passes
- Notes
- Renderable textures

note

When a new effect is added to the workspace, it is pre-populated with a sample effect for your convenience.

Because RenderMonkey can only display a single effect at a time, you may need to tell it which effect is current if you have more than one in your workspace. You can activate a specific effect by right-clicking on the effect node and selecting Set As Active Effect from the menu shown in Figure B.8.

As with other nodes, effects can also be renamed, deleted, copied, and pasted with a right-click of your mouse.

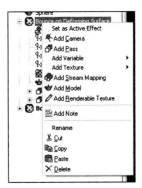

Figure B.8 Context menu displayed when you right-click on an effect node.

Managing Render Passes

Each effect in a workspace may have one of many render passes. A render pass is essentially a way of representing each time a piece of the effect is rendered. A simple example of why multiple passes are needed would be a scene where you want to render a background and then render an object in front of the background. Each of them will need a separate rendering pass.

To create a new rendering pass, you must right-click the mouse to bring up the context menu and select the Add Pass option. Note that passes can only be added as part of an effect node and may only contain the following:

- Variables (or shader parameters)
- **A single** Render State node

- **A single** Vertex Shader node
- **A single** Pixel Shader node
- Textures
- **A single** Camera reference
- **A single** Stream Mapping reference
- **A single** Geometry Model reference
- **A single** Render Target
- Notes

As with other nodes, render passes can be moved, copied, renamed, and deleted. However, because the order of passes is important for rendering and because they are rendered in the order in which they are listed, you can change the position of a render pass in an effect by clicking and dragging it into the proper position. Figure B.9 shows the right-click menu for a Render Pass node.

In addition to standard node operations, you can enable or disable a rendering pass by selecting the Enable/Disable Pass option from the right-click menu. The render pass then appears as crossed-out within the workspace view to show it is disabled.

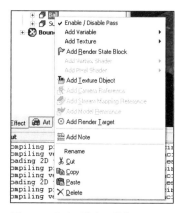

Figure B.9 Right-click context menu for a Render Pass node.

Managing Vertex and Pixel Shaders

The version of RenderMonkey included with this book supports vertex shader version 1.1 through 2.0 and pixel shader version 1.1 through 2.0. Although RenderMonkey supports both HLSL and assembly shaders, this books focuses only on HLSL and will not go into details of assembly level shaders.

To create a new pixel or vertex shader, you must select an effect to which you want to add the shader, and then right-click on that effect. This brings up the context menu, from which you can select either Add Pixel Shader or Add Vertex Shader and then DirectX HLSL to add the wanted shader, as shown in Figure B.10.

Figure B.10 Adding a shader through the context menu.

As with other nodes in RenderMonkey, you may copy, rename, move, and delete shader nodes. Because shaders can only exist within render passes, they may only be copied or moved to other render passes.

This section only discusses creation and management of shaders. The "Shader Editor" section later in this appendix covers editing shaders in more detail.

Managing Render States

Each render pass can have many render states that it may either set explicitly or inherit from a higher level pass or effect. To set hardware render states, you must create render state blocks at any point within your workspace. To create a render state node, simply right-click on any node within your workspace view and select Add Render State Block from the context menu.

If no render state block is created within a rendering pass, the application looks up the workspace hierarchy and inherits the render states of the first block found. If RenderMonkey can't find a render state block to inherit from, it creates one automatically for you.

As with other nodes, render states can be manipulated with standard operations such as Copy, Cut, Paste, Rename, and Delete. However, because render states are inherited and overridden, care must be taken when moving state nodes so that no invalid state occurs.

To edit render states, you can either double-click the node within the workspace or select Edit from the right-click menu. This brings up the render state editor window shown in Figure B.11.

To edit a specific render state, left-click on the Value column for that render state. You can then either pick a value from a drop-down list or input a value directly (depending on the type of render state). If the current render state block inherits values from a higher level node, the inherited values are shown under the Incoming column.

Because RenderMonkey uses the DirectX 9.0 SDK internally, it exposes its render states as Direct3D states. Because you may not be familiar with Direct3D, the following section reviews the available render states.

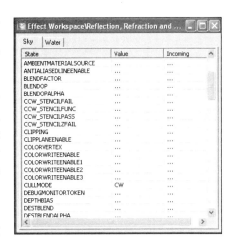

Figure B.11 RenderMonkey's Render State Editor Window.

D3D Render States

In this section we will review the Direct3D render states exposed by RenderMonkey. Keep in mind that this overview is intended as a quick reference and only covers the render states most commonly used. For more details on all render states, you should refer to the DirectX 9.0 SDK Documentation (included on the CD).

ALPHABLENDENABLE, BLENDOP, SRCBLEND, and DESTBLEND

This state controls whether rendering is done with alpha-blended transparency. If blending is disabled (set to FALSE, which is the default behavior), all rendering is opaque and alpha values are ignored. If blending is enabled, the type of alpha blending is determined by the SRCBLEND and DESTBLEND render states. SRCBLEND and DESTBLEND can be set with the values listed in table B.7.

Table B.7 SRCBLEND and DESTBLEND Options

Option	Function
ZERO	Blend factor is (0, 0, 0, 0).
ONE	Blend factor is (1, 1, 1, 1).
SRCCOLOR	Blend factor is (Rs,Gs,Bs,As).
INVSRCCOLOR	Blend factor is (1 - Rs, 1 - Gs, 1 - Bs, 1 - As).
SRCALPHA	Blend factor is (As, As, As, As).
INVSRCALPHA	Blend factor is (1 - As, 1 - As, 1 - As, 1 - As).
DESTALPHA	Blend factor is (Ad, Ad, Ad, Ad).
INVDESTALPHA	Blend factor is (1 - Ad, 1 - Ad, 1 - Ad, 1 - Ad).
DESTCOLOR	Blend factor is (Rd, Gd, Bd, Ad).
INVDESTCOLOR	Blend factor is (1 - Rd, 1 - Gd, 1 - Bd, 1 - Ad).
SRCALPHASAT	Blend factor is (f, f, f, 1); f = min(A, 1 - Ad).
BOTHINVSRCALPHA	Source blend factor is (1 - As, 1 - As, 1 - As, 1 - As), and destination blend factor is (As, As, As, As); the destination blend selection is overridden.
BLENDFACTOR	Constant color-blending factor (BLENDFACTOR).
INVBLENDFACTOR	Inverted constant color-blending factor used.

When the blend factors are defined for both source and destination, the BLENDOP value is used to control how the values are combined. The set of possible blending operations are listed in Table B.8.

Table B.8 BLENDOP Options

Option	Function
ADD	Result = Source + Destination
SUBTRACT	Result = Source - Destination
REVSUBTRACT	Result = Destination - Source
MIN	Result = MIN(Source, Destination)
MAX	Result = MAX(Source, Destination)

ALPHATESTENABLE, ALPHAFUNC, and ALPHAREF

This render state defines whether per-pixel alpha testing is to occur. If the test passes, the pixel is processed by the frame buffer. Otherwise, all frame-buffer processing is skipped for the pixel. The test is accomplished by comparing the incoming alpha value with the value defined by ALPHAREF. The ALPHAFUNC render defines how both alpha values are compared. Possible values are for this render state are

- NEVER
- LESS
- EQUAL
- LESSEQUAL
- GREATER
- NOTEQUAL
- GREATEREQUAL
- ALWAYS

COLORWRITEENABLE*

This render state enables a per-channel write for the render target color buffer. This enables you to selectively turn on or off writing of specific color/alpha channels. Note that COLORWRITEENABLE1, COLORWRITEENABLE2, and COLORWRITEENABLE3 exist to allow support for multiple render targets. Valid values for this render state can be any combination of ALPHA, BLUE, GREEN, or RED.

CULLMODE

Specifies how the hardware will perform its back-facing culling of rendered triangles. This render state can be set to one of the following: CCW, CW, or NONE. For most geometries, front-facing polygons are defined as being counterclockwise, or CCW.

STENCIL*, TWOSIDEDSTENCILMODE, and CCW_STENCIL*

These are miscellaneous render states for controlling the stencil buffer. Stencil buffering enables you to do bit tests and masks out specific regions for rendering. This is especially useful for volume shadows. For more general information on stenciling, refer to the DirectX 9.0 SDK documentation.

ZENABLE and ZFUNC

The depth value of the pixel is compared to the depth-buffer value. If ZENABLE is set to true, the comparison will be used to determine if the fragment should be rendered. The test done is determined by the value of ZFUNC, which compares the current pixel depth with the depth buffer value and can be any of the following:

- NEVER
- LESS
- EQUAL
- LESSEQUAL
- GREATER
- NOTEQUAL
- GREATEREQUAL
- ALWAYS

ZWRITEENABLE

This state determines whether the application writes to the depth buffer when a pixel is drawn. If this render state is set to TRUE, any pixel rendered will overwrite the current depth buffer value with its own value.

Application Preferences

You may change several of RenderMonkey's operating parameters by selecting the Preferences option under the Edit menu. Under the General property page, you can change several options, including

- **Cycle Time:** This setting defines the cycling period, in seconds, for the timer used to fill the time_* predefined shader variables.
- **Auto Refresh:** RenderMonkey can periodically scan the disk for changed textures and models and reload them. This option enables you to set the frequency, in seconds, with which RenderMonkey should scan your computer for updated files.
- **Default Directories:** This option enables you to set the default directories RenderMonkey will use to assess textures and models.
- **Rendering Refresh Rate:** By setting this parameter, the user can control the rate at which the Preview window is updated.

- **Reset Camera on Effect Change**: When a user changes the current active effect, this setting determines whether the camera position and orientation is automatically reset.

Modules

RenderMonkey is built around modules, which construct its functionality. In essence, every subwindow within the tool is considered a module. Although I overviewed many of those modules in Chapter 3, I will now explain more fully how you can use them.

Viewing Your Shaders

As shown in Chapter 3, the preview module enables you to view the results of your effects. To view a particular effect, it must currently be active. To activate an effect, right-click on its node and select the Set as Active Effect from the context menu. In the current version of RenderMonkey, the preview window, as shown in Figure B.12, is displayed using DirectX 9.0. So please make sure you have the latest DirectX drivers installed on your computer.

Figure B.12 RenderMonkey's Preview window showing a sample shader in action.

RenderMonkey provides a simple interface for controlling the camera settings for the effect being rendered. This is accomplished using two features: the camera nodes and camera mode. The use of camera nodes enables you to create multiple cameras with multiple possible camera settings, which can be set by using the Camera Editor. Although you may have multiple cameras associated with a particular effect, only one can be active. To activate a camera, simply right-click the camera reference node in the workspace for the active effect and click the Use Active Camera option.

note

If you do not want to create your own cameras in a RenderMonkey workspace, the software uses a default built-in camera.

When a camera is active, the user can use the mouse to manipulate it within the Preview window through a trackball-like interface. The trackball interface has several modes that can be activated with the right-side toolbar buttons. Table B.9 outlines the different possible camera modes.

Table B.9 Preview Window Camera Modes

Mode	Function
Rotate Camera	Selecting this mode locks the camera into a rotation-only mode. By using the left mouse button, you will be able to change the orientation of the camera. This is the default camera mode.
Pan Camera	Selecting this mode locks the camera into panning mode. By using the left mouse button, you will be able to slide the camera around.
Zoom Camera	Selecting this mode locks the camera into zoom mode. By using the left mouse button, you will be able to control the camera's zoom.
Camera Home	Clicking this button resets the camera to its initial position and orientation.
Overloaded Camera	Selecting this mode uses the overloaded mode for the trackball. The left mouse button rotates the camera, Ctrl+left mouse button pans the camera, and the middle mouse button (or the mouse wheel) controls the zoom.

The right-click context menu for the Preview window, shown in Figure B.13, offers a few extra options to simplify navigation. You can change general rendering properties, switch from hardware to emulated rendering, force the camera to a specific orientation, and even display bounding boxes on the objects in your scene.

Output Window

As discussed in the Chapter 3, this window is located at the bottom of the application interface and offers information regarding shader compilation and other application tasks. Any messages, warnings, or errors originating from your workspace are displayed in this window, as shown in Figure B.14.

Figure B.13 Preview window's right-click context menu.

```
Compiling pixel shader API(D3D) /Reflection, Refraction and Water Effects/Ocean Water (ASM)/Ocean Water Pass/F
Compiling vertex shader API(D3D) /Reflection, Refraction and Water Effects/Ocean Water (ASM)/Ocean Water Pass/
Loading 2D texture map (C:\Program Files\ATI Technologies\RenderMonkey\v1.0\Examples\Dx9\..\Media\Textures\Oce
Loading 2D texture map (C:\Program Files\ATI Technologies\RenderMonkey\v1.0\Examples\Dx9\..\Media\Textures\Oce
Loading 2D texture map (C:\Program Files\ATI Technologies\RenderMonkey\v1.0\Examples\Dx9\..\Media\Textures\Oce
```

Figure B.14 Sample output shown in the Output window.

Stream Mapping

The stream mapping module in RenderMonkey enables you to set up geometry data stream for use by your shaders. The stream contains information such as vertex position and color. However, because of the flexibility of shaders in general, you need to be able to define the format of the data sent to your code.

To create a new stream mapping node, you can right-click your mouse on an effect, pass, workspace, or effect group node, and then select the option named Add Stream Mapping from the context menu. As with other nodes, this node can also be moved, renamed, or deleted with the right-click menu or proper keyboard keys.

After you create a stream mapping node, you can edit it by either double-clicking on the node or by right-clicking and selecting Edit from the context menu. This brings up the stream mapping editor shown in Figure B.15.

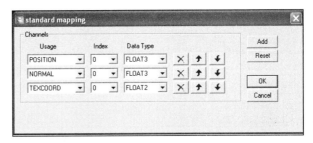

Figure B.15 Close-up view of the stream mapping editor.

At this point, you can add channels with the Add button and adjust each channel's settings by using the drop-down boxes. The Usage and Index columns indicate what kind of data will be stored in the input register. Finally, the Data Type column indicates how the data should be formatted before it is sent to the hardware (mostly useful to test vertex compression). To delete a particular channel, simply click the X button at the end of the row for the channel you wish to delete.

Stream mappings must be created at the Effect workspace level. This enables you to create multiple mappings, which may be used by different effects or passes. To use a stream mapping within a specific pass, you may create a reference to a stream mapping by right-clicking on the pass node and selecting Add Stream Mapping Reference from the context menu.

Shader Editor

To edit a specific shader, you can double-click its workspace node or select Edit… from the context menu that appears when you right-click the node. This opens the shader editor window. Each tab at the top of the window denotes each shader for each pass associated to the current effect.

RenderMonkey and its shader editor currently support two languages for defining shader code (Assembly and HLSL). The shader editor presented in each case is slightly different to account for different features available in each language. However, because I will concentrate only on HLSL in this book, I will not spend time describing the assembly shader editor.

tip

RenderMonkey does not automatically reprocess your shaders when you change their code. To tell RenderMonkey you are done editing, click the Commit Change button on the toolbar. This forces the tool to recompile your shaders and display the appropriate output either in the Preview window or the Output window.

The High Level Shading Language Editor, as shown in Figure B.16, is composed of two separate sections. The top portion is used to manage shader parameters. The bottom section of the editor is the actual code editor where you type in your shader instructions!

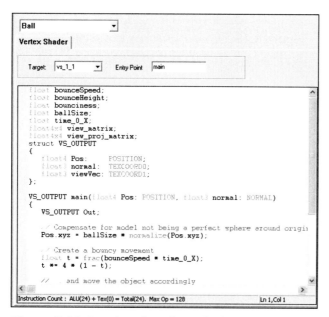

Figure B.16 Snapshot of RenderMonkey's HLSL Shader Editor.

The two last things that are worth mentioning at the moment for the Editor dialog box are the Entry Point and Target fields. The Entry Point field is the name of the HLSL function that will be called within your shader to start execution. Because an HLSL shader can contain sub-routines, you need to let the compiler know which function is the main function. This field is filled with main by default, but you can easily override this value. The second thing of interest is the Target value. This drop-down list defines which different compiler targets to use when processing your shader code. This essentially indicates which version of pixel and vertex shaders you want your compiler to use and turns on proper validation to ensure you do not use features that are not available in a specific shader target.

Editing Variables

To edit any variable in RenderMonkey, simply double-click on its node within the workspace. You may also edit the variables by right-clicking on them and selecting Edit from the context menu.

Boolean Variables

All boolean values can be either TRUE or FALSE only. Boolean values do not have a built-in editor but can be changed by clicking the Boolean Value item when you right-click on their node.

Scalar Variables

All scalar values can be edited by the Scalar Variable Editor shown in Figure B.17. Within the editor, you can edit any number by simply typing in a value in the edit box. Alternatively, you can change the values interactively by clicking the little arrow button next to the edit box, which will bring up a pop-up slider that can be dragged. Also notice the Clamp from field, which allows you to restrict the range of allowable values, which is handy for setting up the artist editor.

Figure B.17 Close-up view of the Scalar Variable Editor.

Vector Variables

The Vector Variable Editor looks and behaves similarly to the Scalar editor, as shown in Figure B.18. All numerical fields behave in the same way as with the Scalar Variable Editor. The only difference to note is the Keep Vector Normalized checkbox, which can be used to force RenderMonkey to always normalize this vector before sending the values off to your shader.

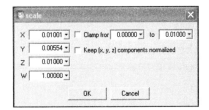

Figure B.18 Close-up view of the Vector Variable Editor.

Matrix Variables

The matrix follows essentially the same scheme as the Vector and Scalar Editor, as shown in Figure B.19. Not much more to say here, with the exception of the Set to Identity Matrix button, which is a quick and easy way to reset the matrix. Also, there is no field to control the range of values.

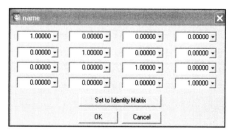

Figure B.19 Close-up view of the Matrix Variable Editor.

Color Variables

Every color variable can be edited with the Color Variable Editor shown in Figure B.20. With the color picker, users can select colors visually or input color values either in RGB or HSV color space (with the use of the drop-down list at the bottom of the dialog box). The final color selected is shown in the little box found at the upper left corner of the editor.

Model, Texture, Cubemap, and Volume Texture Variables

When you edit any of these types of variables, you will be brought to a File Selection dialog box. Models and textures need external data in the form of a file, and you must select a file of the proper format. At the time of this writing, RenderMonkey supports the following file formats:

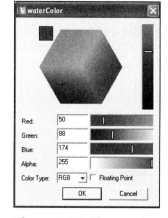

Figure B.20 Close-up view of the Color Variable Editor.

Models: .3DS (3D Studio), .X Microsoft Direct X File
Texture: .DDS (Direct Draw Surface) , .BMP, .JPG, .TGA
Cubemap and Volume Texture: .DDS (Direct Draw Surface)

Artist Editor

One of the problems faced by shader developers is how to allow non-technical artists to experiment with shader parameters to achieve a final wanted effect. RenderMonkey's approach to this problem is known as the artist editor in combination with the Art Tab at the bottom of the workspace window.

During shader development, the programmer can select which variables from his shader are of interest to artists and flag them as artist editable. To do this, simply right-click on any variable node and select the Artist Variable item from the context menu. When a variable is flagged as artist editable, you will notice a little yellow icon overlaid over the regular icon within the workspace view. After variables are flagged, artists can edit them using either the Art tab or through the artist editor, shown in Figure B.21, which can be opened through the painter's palette icon on the toolbar.

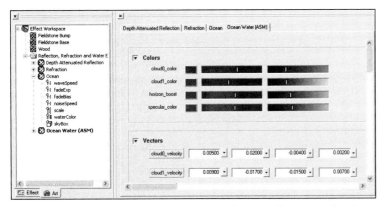

Figure B.21 Screenshot of RenderMonkey's Art Workspace and Artist Editor.

Where Do We Go from Here?

With the content of this appendix and our RenderMonkey introduction in Chapter 3, you should have a good understanding of its use and feel comfortable enough to start writing your own shaders. Don't worry! You shouldn't expect to be a pro right off the bat! As with everything in life, it is always a matter of practice and experience.

If you do need more information about RenderMonkey, technical support, or guidance, please go to ATI Technologies website at http://www.ati.com. There you can find support, articles, demos, and much more.

I would also like to take a few lines to thank ATI Technologies for letting us use Render-Monkey throughout the book. You guys have done a great job with this tool, and I am more than happy to take advantage of it!

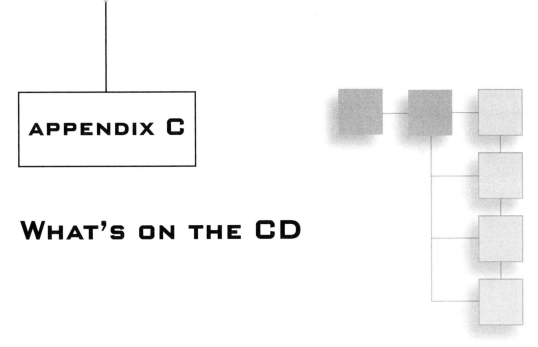

APPENDIX C

WHAT'S ON THE CD

The CD included with this book contains resources intended to be used in conjunction with the text. It includes an auto-installer, so all you have to do is insert the CD into your CD player and the installer will launch itself.

The contents of the CD are detailed in this appendix.

Source Code

Most importantly, the CD includes the full source code for all the shaders developed throughout the book. These are arranged by chapter, with each project having its own directory within the chapter directory. To ensure that every shader in the chapter can be compiled on its own, each directory contains all the necessary assets along with the RenderMonkey workspaces.

Also note that the solutions to each of the exercises are included along with the shaders for each chapter. For example, the solution to the first exercise in Chapter 5 is named shader_ex1.rfx and can be found in the Chapter_5 source code directory.

Installation: The source code to the shaders developed within this book does not require installation. To access the code, simply insert the CD-ROM and pick Source Code from the main menu of the CD-ROM interface. Doing so takes you to a separate menu where you can select the chapter you want to access; this will bring up an explorer window with the shader contents for that chapter.

RenderMonkey

Included on the CD-ROM is the latest version of the RenderMonkey tool developed by ATI Technologies. This is probably the most important part of the CD because all the shaders in this book are developed using RenderMonkey.

At the time of this writing, Version 1.5 of the RenderMonkey tool was the latest version available and is included on the CD-ROM. See Appendix B, "RenderMonkey Version 1.5 User Manual," for more information on how to use this tool.

Installation: To install RenderMonkey, simply insert the CD-ROM into your computer and select the Tool option from the main menu. This will bring you to a separate menu where you can select the Install RenderMonkey 1.5 option. Doing so will start the installation process. For details on this process, please refer to Appendix B.

High Resolution Illustrations

This book is printed in black and white and cannot do complete justice to all the color illustrations and screenshots it contains; therefore, a high resolution color version of each illustration is included on the CD-ROM.

Installation: The illustrations do not require installation and can be browsed directly from the CD-ROM. To facilitate browsing, the illustrations are included in a Web-browsable form. To view them, simply select the Figures option from the CD-ROM's main menu.

DirectX 9.0 SDK

Microsoft developed the DirectX SDK to empower 3D developers and enable them to create 3D applications while taking advantage of hardware acceleration on the Windows platform. Although you will not use the SDK directly, its runtime is required by Render-Monkey. Because of this, we have elected to include the DirectX 9.0 SDK as part of the CD-ROM.

Installation: To install the DirectX SDK, simply insert the CD-ROM into your computer and select the Tool option from the main menu. This will bring you to a separate menu where you can select the Install DirectX option.

NVIDIA Texture Library

NVIDIA has developed a set of free textures that can be used by developers and artists in their own projects. Although this Texture Library can be downloaded online, it is fairly significant in size, which can take a long time to download. Because of this, we have opted to include it on the CD for your use and convenience in your shader development experiences.

Installation: To install the NVIDIA texture library, simply insert the CD-ROM into your computer and select the Tool option from the main menu. This will bring you to a separate menu where you can select the View the NVIDIA Texture Library option. Doing so will bring up an explorer window where the library is located. To install the library, simply open the ZIP package and follow the included instructions.

NVIDIA Photoshop Plug-In

The ability to generate .DDS-compressed textures, cubemaps, and normal maps is crucial as part of shader development. NVIDIA has created a plug-in for use in the Adobe Photoshop image editing tool that enables you to process textures in a format that is more convenient for shader development and for use in DirectX.

Photoshop itself is not included on the CD-ROM because it is a commercial application. However, you can download a trial version for your evaluation at www.adobe.com.

Installation: To install the NVIDIA Photoshop plug-in, simply insert the CD-ROM into your computer and select the Tool option from the main menu. This will bring you to a separate menu where you can select the View the NVIDIA Photoshop Plug-in option. This will bring up an explorer window of where the plug-in is located. To install it, you need to copy it to the proper plug-in folder. For more information on this, please consult your *Adobe Photoshop User Manual.*

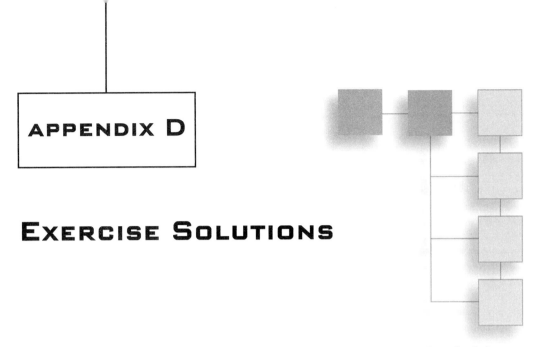

APPENDIX D

EXERCISE SOLUTIONS

This chapter contains complete solutions to all exercises presented in the "It's Your Turn" sections throughout this book. The solutions have been divided by chapter and exercise number for easy reference. I have tried to present solutions in a form as complete as possible and have also included the solutions on the CD-ROM for reference. But keep in mind that with any problem or exercise, there is not always a single valid solution.

Chapter 4

Exercise 1: Animating a Texture

In this exercise, I asked you to do a simple animation on the teapots of the shaders developed during the chapter. For the first part, you need to apply animation to the texture coordinates of the first teapot object. To do this, it was recommended that you use the cos_time_0_X and sin_time_0_X built-in variables.

The first step in creating this shader is to define those variables in your workspace by right-clicking on the Effect node for your shader and selecting Add Variable. Pick the SCALAR type and select the right built-in variable from the Predefined variable menu. Repeat the process for both cos_time_0_X and sin_time_0_X. Those built-in variables will present you a time-varying number based on the sine and cosine of RenderMonkey's internal clock.

With those variables defined in your workspace, bring up the shader editor for your first teapot's vertex shader and add the two variables to your shader. Because the texture coordinates for our object have two components (X and Y), I decided to increment the X component with cos_time_0_X and the Y component with sin_time_0_X. This can be done with the following code:

```
Out.Txr1 = float2(Txr1.x+cos_time_0_X,Txr1.y+sin_time_0_X);
```

Integrating this code into our current vertex shader, we get the following final code:

```
float4x4 view_proj_matrix;
float cos_time_0_X;
float sin_time_0_X;
struct VS_OUTPUT
{
    float4 Pos:     POSITION;
    float2 Txr1:    TEXCOORD0;
};

VS_OUTPUT vs_main(
    float4 inPos: POSITION,
    float2 Txr1: TEXCOORD0)
{
    VS_OUTPUT Out;

    // Output the transformed and projected vertex position
    Out.Pos = mul(view_proj_matrix, inPos);

    // Output the animated texture coordinate
    Out.Txr1 = float2(Txr1.x+cos_time_0_X,Txr1.y+sin_time_0_X);

    return Out;
}
```

For the second part of the shader, you needed to open the pixel shader for the second teapot and animate its color by using the same cos_time_0_X and sin_time_0_X variables. To do this, you needed to add the variable declarations to your pixel shader and then simply change the color output to use those variables instead of our previous color constants. The following code shows an example of how this can be done:

```
sampler Texture0;
float4 ps_main( float4 inDiffuse: COLOR0 ) : COLOR0
{
    //  Output constant color:
    float4 color;
    color[0] = color[3] = cos_time_0_X;
    color[1] = color[2] = sin_time_0_X;
    return color;
}
```

With those changes applied to your shader, you can now compile the workspace and see the final shader through the Preview Window as shown in Figure D.1. The complete RenderMonkey workspace for the solution to this exercise can be found as shader_ex1.rfx under the source code directory for Chapter 4.

Figure D.1 Rendered output for our animating texture and color exercise.

Exercise 2: Blending Two Textures

In this exercise, I asked you to add a texture to the first teapot of the shader from the previous exercise and to blend the two textures together. The first step in performing this is to create a second texture variable within your shader and point it to the supplied texture file distortion.tga. After this is done, you must also create a new Texture Object node within the render pass for the first teapot and point it to the newly created texture variable.

Then you need to modify your vertex shader to pass a second set of texture coordinates to the pixel shader. This is done by changing the VS_OUTPUT structure to add a new texture coordinate with the semantics TEXCOORD1 and to fill this value within your vertex shader. The resulting code for this is as follows:

```
float4x4 view_proj_matrix;
float cos_time_0_X;
float sin_time_0_X;
struct VS_OUTPUT
{
    float4 Pos:     POSITION;
    float2 Txr1:    TEXCOORD0;
    float2 Txr2:    TEXCOORD1;
};

VS_OUTPUT vs_main(
    float4 inPos: POSITION,
    float2 Txr1: TEXCOORD0)
{
    VS_OUTPUT Out;
```

```
// Transform and project the vertex position
Out.Pos = mul(view_proj_matrix, inPos);

// Output the animated texture coordinate
Out.Txr1 = float2(Txr1.x+cos_time_0_X,Txr1.y+sin_time_0_X);

// Output our second texture coordinate
Out.Txr2 = Txr1;
return Out;
}
```

With this vertex shader change, we need to modify our pixel shader to accept the new texture coordinate, add a sampler for the second texture, read pixels from our second texture, and blend the two colors together. The following is the pixel shader code to do this:

```
sampler Texture0;
sampler Texture1;
float4 ps_main(
    float4 inDiffuse: COLOR0,
    float2 inTxr1: TEXCOORD0,
    float2 inTxr2: TEXCOORD1) : COLOR0
{
    // Output blended color
    return tex2D(Texture0,inTxr1)*tex2D(Texture1,inTxr2);
}
```

Compile this new shader, and your Preview Window should show you your new shader in action, as illustrated in Figure D.2. The complete solution to this exercise can be found on the CD-ROM as shader_ex2.rfx in the source code directory for this chapter.

Figure D.2 Rendered output for our texture blending exercise.

Chapter 5

Exercise 1: Old Time Movie

In this simple exercise, I asked you to implement a sepia shader using the general color conversion matrix shader developed in Chapter 5. The only thing you needed to do was to change the grayscale color matrix to account for the tone shift. To add the tone shift, you simply needed to input the tone values in the last column of the matrix and ensure that the alpha component of the incoming colors was set to 1. Figure D.3 shows you the complete color conversion matrix along with the rendered output for the shader. The complete solution for this exercise can be found in the source code directory for this chapter as shader_ex1.rfx on the CD-ROM.

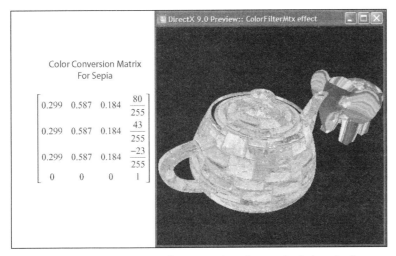

Figure D.3 Rendered output for our sepia color manipulation shader.

Exercise 2: Gauss Filter

In this exercise, you were asked to implement a blurring filter using the seperatable version of a 49 sample Gauss filter. Because of the seperatable nature of the filter, you had to implement two blurring passes. The passes follow the same code architecture used for the other blurring filters and had the following tables:

```
// Horizontal Gauss Filter Pass
const float4 gaussFilterOffset[7] = {
        -3.0f,  0.0f,  0,   1/64,
        -2.0f,  0.0f,  0,   6/64,
        -1.0f,  0.0f,  0,  15/64,
         0.0f,  0.0f,  0,  20/64,
         1.0f,  0.0f,  0,  15/64,
```

```
          2.0f,  0.0f,  0,  6/64,
          3.0f,  0.0f,  0,  1/64
};

// Vertical Gauss Filter Pass
float4 gaussFilterOffset[7] = {
        0.0f,-3.0f,0,1/64,
        0.0f,-2.0f,0,6/64,
        0.0f,-1.0f,0,15/64,
        0.0f,0.0f,0,20/64,
        0.0f,1.0f,0,15/64,
        0.0f,2.0f,0,6/64,
        0.0f,3.0f,0,1/64
};
```

Figure D.4 shows the final rendered output for this exercise. The complete solution for this exercise can be found in the source code directory for this chapter as `shader_ex2.rfx` on the CD-ROM.

Figure D.4 Rendered output for the Gauss filter blurring shader.

Chapter 6

Exercise 1: Multiple Impostors

In this exercise, I asked you to expand on the depth impostor shader developed in Chapter 6. Because the basic shader displayed sharp transitions between the in- and out-of focus areas, I proposed to add extra impostors that introduce less blurring and in turn create a transition region.

To do this effect, you simply needed to create a copy of both your near and far impostors and do a few modifications. The first change needed was to offset the impostor's depth by a small value, thus creating a transition region. Creating a new variable to contain this offset should lead you to the following vertex shader code:

```
float4x4 view_proj_matrix;
float Near_Dist;
float viewport_inv_width;
float viewport_inv_height;
float Near_Dist2;
struct VS_OUTPUT
{
   float4 Pos: POSITION;
   float2 texCoord: TEXCOORD0;
};
```

```
VS_OUTPUT vs_main(float4 Pos: POSITION)
{
    VS_OUTPUT Out;

    // Simply output the position without transforming it
    Out.Pos = float4(Pos.xy, Near_Dist+Near_Dist2, 1);

    // Texture coordinates are setup so that the full texture
    // is mapped completeley onto the screen
    Out.texCoord.x = 0.5 * (1 + Pos.x +viewport_inv_width);
    Out.texCoord.y = 0.5 * (1 - Pos.y +viewport_inv_height);

    return Out;
}
```

In addition, you needed to ensure that the transition impostors did not apply a full blur to the screen. The easiest way to do this is by enabling alpha blending on your impostor. To do this, set the following render states:

```
ALPHABLENDENABLE  = TRUE
BLENDOP           = ADD
SRCBLEND          = SRCALPHA
DESCBLEND         = INVSRCALPHA
```

Finally, you needed to adjust the pixel shader so the alpha output was not equal to 1, or else alpha blending would have been pointless. The resulting pixel shader code is the following:

```
sampler Texture0;
float4 ps_main(float2 texCoord: TEXCOORD0) : COLOR
{
    return float4(tex2D(Texture0,texCoord).rgb,0.6);
}
```

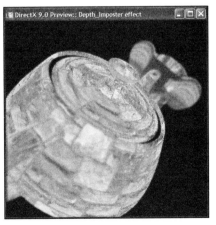

With those modifications, your depth of field effect should now have a smoother transition, as shown in Figure D.5. If you need to make the transition even smoother, you may add extra offset impostors as needed. The complete solution for this exercise can be found on the CD-ROM's source code directory for this chapter as shader_ex1.rfx.

Figure D.5 Rendered output for our multiple impostor exercise.

Exercise 2: Using a Lookup Texture

For this exercise, you were invited to modify the alpha channel DOF effect to make use of a lookup texture. The lookup texture is intended to contain the results of the depth-to-focus equation so you do not have to pay the processing cost for each pixel of each object in your scene.

The first step with this exercise is to create this lookup texture. Generally, you'd generate it offline and use it within your shader. However, for this exercise, you will create it as a separate pass within your effect. The first step is to create a new render target to contain the lookup texture and set up a new render pass. Because the function is static, you will need to make sure your render target is of a constant size, say 512 × 1.

To generate the lookup texture, simply use the same shader you used in the past to copy renderable textures. Because the render target is intended to represent a depth lookup, this means your x texture coordinate will essentially represent the depth to input in your function. The resulting pixel shader for the process is the following:

```
float Near_Dist;
float Far_Dist;
float Near_Range;
float Far_Range;
float4 ps_main(float2 texCoord: TEXCOORD0) : COLOR
{
    float Depth = texCoord.x;
    float Blur = max(clamp(0,1, 1 - (Depth-Near_Dist)/Near_Range),
                clamp(0,1, (Depth-(Far_Dist-Far_Range))/Far_Range));

    return Blur;
}
```

Figure D.6 illustrates a sample output of what the lookup texture may look like once generated.

With your lookup created, all you need to do is add this lookup texture to each pass that renders objects to the scene, and use this texture instead of computing the blurring factor manually. The resulting pixel shader code for the object rendering passes is the following:

Figure D.6 Output for the blur factor lookup texture.

```
float Far_Dist;
float Near_Range;
float Far_Range;
float Near_Dist;
```

```
sampler Texture0;
sampler Texture1;
float4 ps_main(
    float4 inDiffuse: COLOR0,
    float2 inTxr1: TEXCOORD0,
    float1 Depth: TEXCOORD1) : COLOR0
{
  //  Output object color and blurring factor from our previously
  //  generated lookup texture
  return float4(tex2D(Texture0,inTxr1).rgb,tex1D(Texture1,Depth).a);
}
```

The resulting output from this shader is shown in Figure D.7. As usual, you can also find the complete solution to this exercise in the CD-ROM's source code directory for this chapter as shader_ex2.rfx.

Figure D.7 Rendered output for the lookup texture exercise.

Exercise 3: Using Intermediate Blur Textures to Create a Smoother Transition

In this exercise, I invited you to improve upon the two-pass shader developed in Chapter 6 and take advantage of intermediate blurring results to create a smoother transition between the in- and out-of-focus regions. The first task required to accomplish this is to capture the intermediate blurring result and store it in a new render target so you may use it in the shader.

To perform this, create a new renderable texture as with the other blur textures. You must then modify one of the blurring passes, say Blur_2, to render to this new renderable texture, and then make sure to use this render target in the following pass. This ensures that this texture only gets written to once, and you can use the intermediate result in the final blending pass.

The final step required to make this new shader, reality is to change the present pass to combine not only the regular blurred texture, but also the intermediate blur. To do this, you may want to use the `lerp` function to interpolate between all three textures presented to this shader. The following is an example of what your final pixel shader may look like:

```
float4 ps_main(float2 texCoord: TEXCOORD0) : COLOR
{
    // Sample and decode our depth value
    float4 DepthValue = tex2D(Texture2,texCoord);
    float Depth = DepthValue.r + DepthValue.g/127
                  + DepthValue.b/(127*127);

    // Sample our regular and blurred scene
    float4 BlurColor = tex2D(Texture1,texCoord);
    float4 BlurColorInt = tex2D(Texture3,texCoord);
    float4 SceneColor = tex2D(Texture0,texCoord);

    // Use the defined ranges to determine the proper
    // combination of both render targets based on
    // the distance.
    float Blur = max(clamp(0,1, 1 - (Depth-Near_Dist)/Near_Range),
                clamp(0,1, (Depth-(Far_Dist-Far_Range))/Far_Range));

    return lerp(SceneColor,
          lerp(BlurColor,BlurColorInt,clamp(0,1,Blur*2)),Blur);
}
```

Figure D.8 illustrates the final rendering output for this shader. You can also find the complete solution to this exercise on the CD-ROM as `shader_ex3.rfx` in this chapter's source code directory.

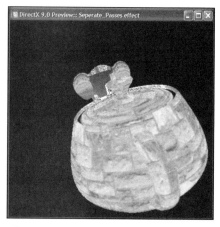

Figure D.8 Rendered output for our intermediate blur exercise.

Chapter 7

Exercise 1: Your Own Refraction Shader

In this exercise, you were invited to implement a full-blown shader performing simple refraction by using the built-in `refract` HLSL function. You were invited to develop this shader on your own using your own creativity and experience.

To start with this exercise, you need a base shader that includes both a background and a teapot object. You can then use the basic shader developed in Chapter 6. To compute refraction, you need to determine the view direction for each vertex in your model. Using the `view_position` variable, you can deduce the view direction by subtracting the vertex position by the `view_position`. After this direction is computed, it can by passed to the pixel shader so that the refraction can be computed in a per-pixel manner. This should yield the following vertex shader code:

```
float4 view_position;
float4x4 view_proj_matrix;
struct VS_OUTPUT
{
    float4 Pos:     POSITION;
    float3 Normal: TEXCOORD0;
    float3 View:    TEXCOORD1;
};

VS_OUTPUT vs_main(float4 inPos: POSITION, float3 inNormal: NORMAL)
{
    VS_OUTPUT Out;

    // Compute the projected position and send out the normal
    Out.Pos = mul(view_proj_matrix, inPos);
    Out.Normal = normalize(inNormal);

    // Determine the view direction (i.e: eye vector) for our
    // refraction calculations
    Out.View = normalize(view_position-inPos);
    return Out;
}
```

On the pixel shader end, you should be receiving both the interpolated surface normal and view vector. Using those two vectors, you can compute the refracted view direction by using the refract function. To render the final teapot color, you need to use the refracted vector to look up into the environment cubemap, as done with the Environment pass. The final pixel shader code is as follows:

```
float indexOfRefractionRatio;
sampler Environment;
float4 ps_main(float3 inNormal: TEXCOORD0, float3 inView: TEXCOORD1) : COLOR
{
    // Make sure all incoming vectors are normalized
    inNormal = normalize(inNormal);
    inView = normalize(inView);

    // Refraction texture lookup
    float3 refrVect = refract(-inView,inNormal,indexOfRefractionRatio).xyz;
    float4 refraction = texCUBE(Environment,refrVect);

    // Output refracted color
    return refraction;
}
```

With these modifications, your refraction should give a result similar to the one shown in Figure D.9. This shader is included on the CD-ROM's source code folder for this chapter as shader_ex1.rfx.

Figure D.9 Rendered output for our refraction shader exercise.

Exercise 2: Making It More Lively

In this exercise, you were invited to improve upon the heat impostor shader developed in Chapter 7. To do this, it was suggest that you sample the distortion texture at two separate offsets and combine the results. To do so, you simply need to sample the distortion texture a second time, using a different set of time variables and offsets.

Once both distortion textures have been sampled, the results can be combined together before they are scaled and offset. With these changes, the pixel shader for the code should look as follows:

```
float OffsetScale;
float time_0_1;
sampler Texture0;
sampler Texture1;
float4 ps_main(float2 texCoord: TEXCOORD0) : COLOR
{
   // Read and scale the distortion offsets
   float2 offset = tex3D(Texture1,
                   float3(8*texCoord.x,8*texCoord.y+2*time_0_1,time_0_1)).xy;
   float2 offset2 = tex3D(Texture1,
                   float3(4*texCoord.y,4*texCoord.x+time_0_1,2*time_0_1)).xy;

   // Combine, offset and scale both distortion values
   offset = ((offset+offset2)-1.0)*OffsetScale;

   return tex2D(Texture0,texCoord+offset);
}
```

With these modifications described above, your preview window should give a result similar to the one shown in Figure D.10. This shader is included on the CD-ROM as shader_ex2.rfx.

Figure D.10 Rendered output for our heat imposter exercise.

Chapter 8

Exercise 1: Using a Big Filter

In this exercise, you were asked to modify the glow shader to use the 49-sample Gauss filter on the glow HDR shader developed in Chapter 8. The idea is to show that you can use a more complex blur filter with fewer passes to accomplish the same task.

The solution to this exercise is simple. You need to go through every glow blur pass with a pixel shader that does the 49-sample Gauss filter. The pixel shader code needed for this is shown in the following:

```
float viewport_inv_width;
float viewport_inv_height;
sampler Texture0;
const float4 samples[7] = {
    -3.0,   0.0,   0,   1.0/64.0,
    -2.0,   0.0,   0,   6.0/64.0,
    -1.0,   0.0,   0,   15.0/64.0,
     0.0,   0.0,   0,   20.0/64.0,
     1.0,   0.0,   0,   15.0/64.0,
     2.0,   0.0,   0,   6.0/64.0,
     3.0,   0.0,   0,   1.0/64.0
};


float4 ps_main(float2 texCoord: TEXCOORD0) : COLOR
{
    float4 col = float4(0,0,0,0);

    // Sample and output the averaged color
    for(int i=0;i<7;i++)
        col += samples[i].w*tex2D(Texture0,texCoord+
          float2(samples[i].x*viewport_inv_width,
                 samples[i].y*viewport_inv_height));
    return col;
}
```

Keep in mind that because of the complexity of the shader, fewer passes are needed to do the same job. You also need to remember that the pixel shader shown is a Gauss shader implemented in a *separated* form. This means for that each blur pass, you need to do an actual horizontal and vertical pass to complete the blur.

With these modifications, you will get a rendering result as shown in Figure D.11. As you can see, the results are very similar to the previous shader developed in Chapter 8. For reference, the complete solution to this exercise has been included on the CD-ROM as `shader_ex1.rfx` in the directory for Chapter 8.

Figure D.11 Rendered output for our enhanced HDR exercise.

Exercise 2: Streaking on Today's Hardware

In Chapter 8, I demonstrated how high dynamic range can be reproduced without the need for floating-point textures by modifying the glow, or bloom, shader. For this exercise, you were asked to apply the same process to the streak shader developed in Chapter 8.

The solution to this exercise is simple. The streaking part of the shader is in essence the same; the only modifications needed are to the object rendering pass, which needs to convert the brightness of pixels into a color+alpha value. The pixel shader code for this is the same as the one developed for the glare shader and is as follows:

```
float Exposure_Level;
sampler Environment;
float4 ps_main(float3 dir: TEXCOORD0) : COLOR
{
    float4 color = texCUBE(Environment, dir);
    return float4(color.rgb, ((1.0+(color.a*64.0))*Exposure_Level)/64.0);
}
```
You also need to make the equivalent changes to the final pass pixel shader, which should give the following pixel shader code:
```
float Glow_Factor;
sampler Texture0;
sampler Texture1;
sampler Texture2;
sampler Texture3;
float4 ps_main(float2 texCoord: TEXCOORD0) : COLOR
{
    // Read in streak colors
```

```
float4 col1 = tex2D(Texture0,texCoord);
float4 col2 = tex2D(Texture1,texCoord);
float4 col3 = tex2D(Texture2,texCoord);
float4 col4 = tex2D(Texture3,texCoord);
// Combine 4 streak directions
return
  min(1.0,
  float4((col1.xyz)*(col1.a*64.0)*Glow_Factor,0.20) +
  float4((col2.xyz)*(col2.a*64.0)*Glow_Factor,0.20) +
  float4((col3.xyz)*(col3.a*64.0)*Glow_Factor,0.20) +
  float4((col4.xyz)*(col4.a*64.0)*Glow_Factor,0.20)
  );
}
```

The rendering result for this exercise is shown in Figure D.12. The solution is included on the CD-ROM as shader_ex2.rfx in this chapter's source code directory.

Figure D.12 Rendered output for our improved streaking shader exercise.

Chapter 9

Exercise 1: Directional Lights

For this exercise, you were asked to take the per-vertex point light shader developed in Chapter 9 and adapt it to make use of a directional light. To accomplish this, you need to make a few minor changes to the RenderMonkey workspace and vertex shader.

To start off, you need to modify the light parameters to change the light position to a direction because directional lights have no position. To complement this, the changes required to the vertex shader are fairly simple. The first modification is to remove the light direction calculation and use the direction supplied in the constant variable. The second change to apply to the vertex shader is to remove the distance-based attenuation because directional light intensities are not distance dependent. What would be the point because there is no position to compute a distance from?

With these modifications, you should have the following vertex shader code:

```
float4x4 view_proj_matrix;
float4 Light_Ambient;
float4 Light1_Direction;
float4 Light1_Attenuation;
float4 Light1_Color;
float4 view_position;
float4x4 inv_view_matrix;
float4x4 view_matrix;
struct VS_OUTPUT
{
   float4 Pos:      POSITION;
   float2 TexCoord: TEXCOORD0;
   float2 Color:    COLOR0;
};

float4 Light_Dir(float3 VertPos, float3 VertNorm, float3 LightDir,
                 float4 LightColor, float3 EyeDir)
{
   // Compute half vector
   float3 HalfVect = normalize(LightDir-EyeDir);

   // Specular
   float SpecularAttn =  max(0,pow(  dot(VertNorm, HalfVect),32));

   // Diffuse
   float AngleAttn = max(0, dot(VertNorm, LightDir) );

   // Compute final lighting
   return LightColor * (SpecularAttn+AngleAttn);
}

VS_OUTPUT vs_main(float4 inPos: POSITION, float3 inNormal: NORMAL,
                  float2 inTxr: TEXCOORD0)
{
   VS_OUTPUT Out;

   // Compute the projected position and send out the texture coordinates
   Out.Pos = mul(view_proj_matrix, inPos);
   Out.TexCoord = inTxr;

   // Output the ambient color
```

```
    float4 Color = Light_Ambient;

    // Determine the eye vector
    float3 EyeVector = -normalize(mul(inv_view_matrix,float4(0,0,10,1))+inPos);

    // Compute light contribution
    Color += Light_Dir(inPos, inNormal, Light1_Direction,
                       Light1_Color, EyeVector);

    // Output Final Color
    Out.Color = Color;

    return Out;
}
```

The rendering result for this exercise is shown in Figure D.13. The solution is included on the CD-ROM as shader_ex1.rfx in this chapter's source code folder.

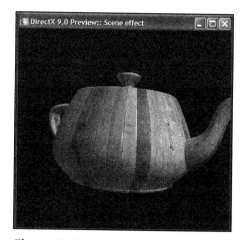

Figure D.13 Rendered output for our directional lights exercise.

Exercise 2: Animating Lights

For this exercise, you were asked to take the point light shader developed in Chapter 9 and to modify it so the light's position would be animated. Creating such an animation can be done through the use of the time_0_2PI built-in variable. The more complex task is to determine how the light is animated. Assuming you want the light to be animated along a circle in the XZ plane with a radius of 60, the following would accomplish this:

```
Light1_Position = float3(60*sin(time_0_2PI),0,60*cos(time_0_2PI));
```

Keep in mind that this is one possible solution to the problem of animating the lights. So by adding the built-in variable to your workspace and changing the vertex shader code to procedurally generate the light's position, you should have the following vertex shader code:

```
float time_0_1;
float4 Light1_Attenuation;
float4 view_position;
float4x4 inv_view_matrix;
float4x4 view_matrix;
float4x4 view_proj_matrix;
float4 Light_Ambient;
float4 Light1_Color;
float time_0_2PI;
struct VS_OUTPUT
{
    float4 Pos:        POSITION;
    float2 TexCoord: TEXCOORD0;
    float2 Color:      COLOR0;
};

float4 Light_Point(float3 VertPos, float3 VertNorm, float3 LightPos,
                   float4 LightColor, float4 LightAttenuation, float3 EyeDir)
{
    // Determine the distance from the light to the vertex and the direction
    float3 LightDir = LightPos - VertPos;
    float  Dist = length(LightDir);
    LightDir = LightDir / Dist;

    // Compute half vector
    float3 HalfVect = normalize(LightDir-EyeDir);

    // Compute distance based attenuation. This is defined as:
    // Attenuation = 1 / ( LA.x + LA.y*Dist + LA.z*Dist*Dist )
    float DistAttn = clamp(0,1, 1 / ( LightAttenuation.x +
                                      LightAttenuation.y * Dist +
                                      LightAttenuation.z * Dist * Dist ));

    // Specular
    float SpecularAttn =  max(0,pow(  dot(VertNorm, HalfVect),32));
```

```
    // Diffuse
    float AngleAttn = max(0, dot(VertNorm, LightDir) );

    // Compute final lighting
    return LightColor * DistAttn * (SpecularAttn+AngleAttn);
}


VS_OUTPUT vs_main(float4 inPos: POSITION, float3 inNormal: NORMAL,
                  float2 inTxr: TEXCOORD0)
{
    VS_OUTPUT Out;

    // Compute the projected position and send out the texture coordinates
    Out.Pos = mul(view_proj_matrix, inPos);
    Out.TexCoord = inTxr;

    // Output the ambient color
    float4 Color = Light_Ambient;

    // Determine the eye vector
    float3 EyeVector = -normalize(mul(inv_view_matrix,float4(0,0,10,1))+inPos);

    // Determine Light_Position
    float3 Light1_Position = float3(0,0,0);
    Light1_Position.x = 60*sin(time_0_2PI);
    Light1_Position.z = 60*cos(time_0_2PI);

    // Animate color
    float4 color = Light1_Color;
    color.x = time_0_1;
    color.y = 1-time_0_1;

    // Compute light contribution
    Color += Light_Point(inPos, inNormal, Light1_Position,
                         color, Light1_Attenuation, EyeVector);

    // Output Final Color
    Out.Color = Color;

    return Out;
}
```

The rendering result for this exercise is shown in Figure D.14. The solution is included on the CD-ROM as `shader_ex2.rfx` in this chapter's source code folder.

Figure D.14 Rendered output for our animating lights exercise.

Chapter 10

Exercise 1: Directional Lights

For this exercise, you were invited to take the per-pixel point light shader and modify it to support a directional light instead of a point light. Although the idea is the same as the first exercise in Chapter 9, the way of achieving the result is slightly different because of the nature of per-pixel lighting.

The effect workspace itself does not need any changes; the only modifications required will be on the vertex and pixel shader. In regards to the vertex shader, because the directional light has a direction and no position, you need to change the code that calculates the tangent space direction vector to use a static direction instead of computing this value from a light position. The second change required is to remove the distance-based attenuation calculation because there is no distance attenuation with a directional light.

With those modifications in place, your resulting vertex shader code should be as follows:

```
float4 Light1_Attenuation;
float4 view_position;
float4x4 view_proj_matrix;
float4x4 inv_view_matrix;
float4x4 view_matrix;
float4 Light1_Color;
float4 Light_Ambient;
struct VS_OUTPUT
{
    float4 Pos:      POSITION;
    float2 TexCoord: TEXCOORD0;
```

```
        float4 LightDir: TEXCOORD1;
        float3 HalfVect: TEXCOORD2;
};


VS_OUTPUT vs_main(float4 inPos: POSITION, float3 inNormal: NORMAL,
                    float3 inTangent:TANGENT, float3 inBinormal:BINORMAL,
                    float2 inTxr: TEXCOORD0)
{
    VS_OUTPUT Out;

    // Compute the projected position and send out the texture coordinates
    Out.Pos = mul(view_proj_matrix, inPos);
    Out.TexCoord = inTxr;

    // Determine the distance from the light to the vertex and the direction
    float4 LightDir = float4(0,0,0,1);
    LightDir.xyz = mul(inv_view_matrix,float3(0.7,00,-0.7));

    // Determine the eye vector
    float3 EyeVector = normalize(view_position-inPos);

    // Transform to tangent space and output
    // half vector and light direction
    float3x3 TangentSpace;
    TangentSpace[0] = inTangent;
    TangentSpace[1] = inBinormal;
    TangentSpace[2] = inNormal;
    Out.HalfVect = mul(TangentSpace,normalize(LightDir.xyz+EyeVector));
    Out.LightDir = float4(mul(TangentSpace,LightDir.xyz),LightDir.w);

    return Out;
}
```

On the pixel shader end, the only change required is to remove the distance attenuation from the final lighting calculations. With this change, the resulting shader should be as follows:

```
float4 Light1_Color;
sampler Texture0;
sampler Bump;
float4 Light_Point(float3 Normal, float3 HalfVect, float4 LightDir,
                    float4 LightColor)
{
```

```
   // Compute both specular and diffuse factors
   float SpecularAttn =  pow( clamp(0, 1,dot(Normal, HalfVect)),16);
   float DiffuseAttn =  clamp(0, 1,dot(Normal, LightDir));

   // Compute final lighting
   return LightColor * (SpecularAttn+DiffuseAttn);
}


float4 ps_main(float2 inTxr:TEXCOORD0,float4 LightDir:TEXCOORD1,
               float3 HalfVect:TEXCOORD2) : COLOR
{
   // Read bump and influence the normal
   float3 normal = tex2D(Bump,inTxr) * 2 - 1;

   // Simply route the vertex color to the output
   return tex2D(Texture0,inTxr)*
          (0.15+Light_Point(normal,HalfVect,LightDir,Light1_Color));
}
```

The rendering result for this exercise is shown in Figure D.15. The solution is included in this chapter's source code directory on the CD-ROM as shader_ex1.rfx.

Figure D.15 Rendered output for our directional lights exercise.

Exercise 2: Multiple Lights

For this exercise, you were asked to add an extra point light to the shader developed in Chapter 10. Because lighting information is passed to the pixel shader for evaluation, the output structure within the vertex shader will need to be modified to pass two sets of lighting vectors. The following shows the structure with the added outputs:

```
struct VS_OUTPUT
{
```

```
    float4 Pos:         POSITION;
    float2 TexCoord:        TEXCOORD0;
    float4 LightDir1:   TEXCOORD1;
    float3 HalfVect1:   TEXCOORD2;
    float4 LightDir2:   TEXCOORD3;
    float3 HalfVect2:   TEXCOORD4;
};
```

On the vertex shader side, you simply need to replicate the code that generates the tangent space light direction and half vector for the second light. The following shows the resulting vertex shader code:

```
float4 Light1_Attenuation;
float4 view_position;
float4x4 view_proj_matrix;
float4x4 inv_view_matrix;
float4x4 view_matrix;
float4 Light1_Color;
float4 Light_Ambient;
struct VS_OUTPUT
{
    float4 Pos:         POSITION;
    float2 TexCoord:    TEXCOORD0;
    float4 LightDir1:   TEXCOORD1;
    float3 HalfVect1:   TEXCOORD2;
    float4 LightDir2:   TEXCOORD3;
    float3 HalfVect2:   TEXCOORD4;
};

VS_OUTPUT vs_main(float4 inPos: POSITION, float3 inNormal: NORMAL,
                float3 inTangent:TANGENT, float3 inBinormal:BINORMAL,
                float2 inTxr: TEXCOORD0)
{
    VS_OUTPUT Out;

    // Compute the projected position and send out the texture coordinates
    Out.Pos = mul(view_proj_matrix, inPos);
    Out.TexCoord = inTxr;

    // Transform to tangent space and output
    // half vector and light direction
    float3x3 TangentSpace;
    TangentSpace[0] = inTangent;
```

```
    TangentSpace[1] = inBinormal;
    TangentSpace[2] = inNormal;

    // Determine the eye vector
    float3 EyeVector = normalize(view_position-inPos);

    // -- Light 1 --
    float4 LightDir;
    LightDir.xyz = mul(inv_view_matrix,float3(80,00,-80)) - inPos;
    float   Dist = length(LightDir.xyz);
    LightDir.xyz = LightDir.xyz / Dist;

    // Compute the per-vertex distance based attenuation
    LightDir.w = clamp(0,1, 1 / ( Light1_Attenuation.x +
                                  Light1_Attenuation.y * Dist +
                                  Light1_Attenuation.z * Dist * Dist ));

    Out.HalfVect1 = mul(TangentSpace,normalize(LightDir.xyz+EyeVector));
    Out.LightDir1 = float4(mul(TangentSpace,LightDir.xyz),LightDir.w);

    // -- Light 2 --
    LightDir.xyz = mul(inv_view_matrix,float3(-80,00,-80)) - inPos;
    Dist = length(LightDir.xyz);
    LightDir.xyz = LightDir.xyz / Dist;

    // Compute the per-vertex distance based attenuation
    LightDir.w = clamp(0,1, 1 / ( Light1_Attenuation.x +
                                  Light1_Attenuation.y * Dist +
                                  Light1_Attenuation.z * Dist * Dist ));

    Out.HalfVect2 = mul(TangentSpace,normalize(LightDir.xyz+EyeVector));
    Out.LightDir2 = float4(mul(TangentSpace,LightDir.xyz),LightDir.w);

    return Out;
}
```

In the pixel shader, you need to add the input parameters for the second set of lighting vectors. Beyond this, the only modification needed to the pixel shader is to call the Light_Point function a second time and add the result to the previously calculated lighting value. The resulting pixel shader code is as follows:

```
float4 Light1_Color;
float4 Light2_Color;
```

```
sampler Texture0;
sampler Bump;
float4 Light_Point(float3 Normal, float3 HalfVect, float4 LightDir,
                   float4 LightColor)
{
   // Compute both specular and diffuse factors
   float SpecularAttn =  pow( clamp(0, 1,dot(Normal, HalfVect)),16);
   float DiffuseAttn =  clamp(0, 1,dot(Normal, LightDir));

   // Compute final lighting
   return LightColor * LightDir.w * (SpecularAttn+DiffuseAttn);
}


float4 ps_main(float2 inTxr:TEXCOORD0,
               float4 LightDir1:TEXCOORD1,float3 HalfVect1:TEXCOORD2,
               float4 LightDir2:TEXCOORD3,float3 HalfVect2:TEXCOORD4) : COLOR
{
   // Read bump and influence the normal
   float3 normal = tex2D(Bump,inTxr) * 2 - 1;

   // Simply route the vertex color to the output
   return tex2D(Texture0,inTxr)*(0.15+
          Light_Point(normal,HalfVect1,LightDir1,Light1_Color)+
          Light_Point(normal,HalfVect2,LightDir2,Light2_Color));
}
```

The rendering result for this exercise is shown in Figure D.16. The solution is included on the CD-ROM as shader_ex2.rfx in this chapter's source code directory.

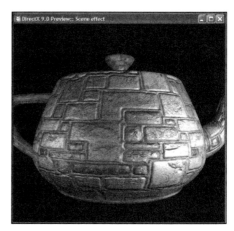

Figure D.16 Rendered output for our multiple lights exercise.

Chapter 11

Exercise 1: Doing It All Per-Pixel

For this exercise, you were asked to take the vertex-based reflection/refraction shader and convert it so that it would operate per-pixel. This task simply involves computing the lighting components within the pixel shader instead of the vertex shader. For this to work, you need to ensure that all the needed components, such as surface normal and eye vector, are passed to the pixel shader, as you have done several times already. The following shader shows how this can be done:

```
float4x4 view_proj_matrix;
float4 view_position;
struct VS_OUTPUT
{
    float4 Pos:      POSITION;
    float2 TexCoord: TEXCOORD0;
    float3 viewVec:  TEXCOORD1;
    float3 Normal:   TEXCOORD2;
};

VS_OUTPUT vs_main(float4 inPos: POSITION, float3 inNormal: NORMAL,
                  float2 inTxr: TEXCOORD0)
{
    VS_OUTPUT Out;

    // Compute the projected position and send out the texture coordinates
    Out.Pos = mul(view_proj_matrix, inPos);
    Out.TexCoord = inTxr;

    Out.viewVec = view_position - inPos;
    Out.Normal = inNormal;

    return Out;
}
```

On the pixel shader side, the code is similar to the vertex shader in the first version, taking in the interpolated vertex lighting components and computing the final reflection/refraction values. The following is the resulting pixel shader:

```
sampler Wood;
sampler EnvMap;
float4 ps_main(float2 inTxr: TEXCOORD0,float3 viewVec: TEXCOORD1,
              float3 inNormal: TEXCOORD2) : COLOR
{
```

```
    viewVec = normalize(viewVec);

    // Compute reflection
    float3 inReflect = reflect(-viewVec,inNormal);

    // Compute the reflection vector using Snell's law
    // the refract HLSL function does not always work properly
    // n_i * sin(theta_i) = n_r  * sin(theta_r)

    // sin(theta_i)
    float cosine = dot(viewVec, inNormal);
    float sine = sqrt(1 - cosine * cosine);

    // sin(theta_r)
    float sine2 = saturate(1.14 * sine);
    float cosine2 = sqrt(1 - sine2 * sine2);

    // Determine the refraction vector be using the normal and tangent
    // vectors as basis to determine the refraction direction
    float3 x = -inNormal;
    float3 y = normalize(cross(cross(viewVec, inNormal), inNormal));
    float3 inRefract = x * cosine2 + y * sine2;

    // Output texture color with reflection map
    return sine * texCUBE(EnvMap,inReflect) +
          ((1 - sine2) * texCUBE(EnvMap,inRefract) + 0.4)
            * tex2D(Wood,inTxr);
}
```

The rendering result for this exercise is shown in Figure D.17. The solution is included in this chapter's source code folder on the CD-ROM as shader_ex1.rfx.

Figure D.17 Rendered output for our per-pixel reflection exercise.

Exercise 2: Color-Based Refraction

For this exercise, you were asked to take a basic refraction shader and expand it to take into account the variation of the index of refraction, or IOR, based on the color of light. Because it is prohibitive to compute the actual wavelength for a particular pixel, the simplest approach is to consider each of the three color components separately and determine its own refraction.

The process to do this is similar to the regular refraction shader, with the exception that you need to sample your refraction texture three times, once for each color component. Each sample is based on a slightly different refraction index.

The following pixel shader code illustrates how this can easily be done:

```
sampler Wood;
sampler EnvMap;
float4 ps_main(float2 inTxr: TEXCOORD0,float3 viewVec: TEXCOORD1,
               float3 inNormal: TEXCOORD2) : COLOR
{
   viewVec = normalize(viewVec);

   // Compute reflection
   float3 inReflect = reflect(-viewVec,inNormal);

   // Compute the reflection vector using Snell's law
   // the refract HLSL function does not always work properly
   // n_i * sin(theta_i) = n_r  * sin(theta_r)

   // sin(theta_i)
   float cosine = dot(viewVec, inNormal);
   float sine = sqrt(1 - cosine * cosine);

   // sin(theta_r)
   float sine2;
   float cosine2;

   // Determine the refraction vector be using the normal and tangent
   // vectors as basis to determine the refraction direction
   float3 x = -inNormal;
   float3 y = normalize(cross(cross(viewVec, inNormal), inNormal));

   // Determine refraction for each color component
   float4 refr = float4(0,0,0,1);
```

```
    // --- RED ---
    sine2 = saturate(1.14 * sine);
    cosine2 = sqrt(1 - sine2 * sine2);
    refr.r = texCUBE(EnvMap,x * cosine2 + y * sine2).r;

    // --- GREEN ---
    sine2 = saturate(1.18 * sine);
    cosine2 = sqrt(1 - sine2 * sine2);
    refr.g = texCUBE(EnvMap,x * cosine2 + y * sine2).g;

    // --- BLUE ---
    sine2 = saturate(1.20 * sine);
    cosine2 = sqrt(1 - sine2 * sine2);
    refr.b = texCUBE(EnvMap,x * cosine2 + y * sine2).b;

    // Output texture color with reflection map
    return sine * texCUBE(EnvMap,inReflect) +
           ((1 - sine2) * refr + 0.2);
}
```

The rendering result for this exercise is shown in Figure D.18. The solution is included on the CD-ROM as shader_ex2.rfx in this chapter's source code folder.

Figure D.18 Rendered output for our color-based refraction exercise.

Chapter 12

Exercise 1: Texture Lookups

For this exercise, you were asked to take the Minneart-based velvet shader developed in Chapter 12 and convert it to take advantage of a texture lookup instead of computing the lighting result for each pixel. Although the texture lookup part is easy, determining the lookup texture may sometimes prove difficult.

One solution is to approximate the results by using a gradient within your image editing program, such as Adobe Photoshop. This works well for simple functions but may not work for more complex ones. The other solution is to set up a simple screen shader that will render your texture in function of screen coordinates.

Doing so in the case of our velvet shader gives the lookup texture shown in Figure D.19.

After you have a lookup texture ready, setting up the shader is simple. Instead of evaluating the full Minneart equation, compute the two angles from your lighting vectors and use them as texture coordinates to perform the lookup. Doing so should yield the following pixel shader code:

Figure D.19 Lookup texture for the velvet BRDF exercise.

```
float Velvet_Exponent;
float4 Light1_Color;
sampler Texture0;
float4 Light_Velvet(float3 Normal, float3 EyeVect, float3 LightDir,
                                float4 LightColor)
{
   // Compute both the light and eye angle about the
   // surface normal
   float l = dot(Normal, LightDir);
   float e = dot(Normal, EyeVect);

   // Compute final lighting. This is simply a matter of looking
   // up our precomputed texture with the light and eye vectors
   return LightColor * 0.2+0.8*tex2D(Texture0,float2(l,e));
}

float4 ps_main(float3 inNormal:TEXCOORD0, float3 LightDir:TEXCOORD1,
            float3 EyeVect:TEXCOORD2) : COLOR
```

```
{
    return Light_Velvet(inNormal,-normalize(EyeVect),
                        normalize(LightDir),Light1_Color);
}
```

The rendering result for this exercise is shown in Figure D.20. The solution is included on the CD-ROM as shader_ex1.rfx in this chapter's source code folder.

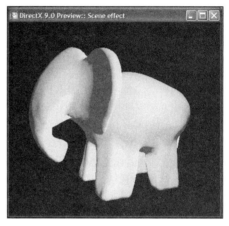

Figure D.20 Rendered output for our BRDF shader exercise.

Exercise 2: Multiple BRDFs

For this exercise, you were asked to take the Oren-Nayer BRDF shader developed within Chapter 12 and use it to render felt, skin, and corduroy. For this exercise, no coding is involved, and all you need to do is look up the proper rho, sigma, and Kd coefficients from Table 12.1 and use the equation in Figure 12.6 to determine the proper A, B, and rho_pi factors.

For felt, once calculated, your coefficients should be as follows: A=0.83, B=0.28, and rho_pi=0.116. With those values input into the Oren-Nayer shader, the rendering should look similar to the one in Figure D.21.

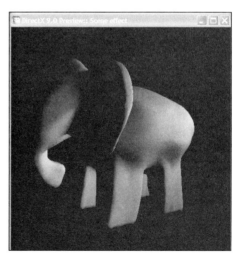

Figure D.21 Rendered output for the felt Oren-Nayer shader.

For human skin, once calculated, your coefficients should be as follows: A=0.748, B=0.345, and rho_pi=0.06. With those values input into the shader, the rendering should look similar to the one in Figure D.22.

And finally, with corduroy, once calculated, your coefficients should be as follows: A=0.7, B=0.38, and rho_pi=0.13. With those values input into the shader, the rendering should look similar to the one in Figure D.23.

Figure D.22 Rendered output for the human skin Oren-Nayer shader.

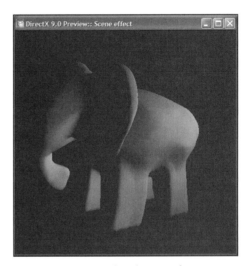

Figure D.23 Rendered output for corduroy Oren-Nayer shader.

Chapter 13

Exercise 1: Animating Clouds

For this exercise, you were asked to take the Perlin noise cloud shader developed during Chapter 13 and expand it to animate the clouds. The first point to consider is taking advantage of the 3D nature of the noise texture to animate the clouds. Animating along this axis causes the clouds to appear as they are evolving. This can simply be done by using the built-in time_0_1 variable for the Z component of the noise texture.

In addition to making the clouds progress over time, you may want to make the clouds move over time. Using the same variable, you can offset the X and Y texture components to create the illusion of movement. One thing to keep in mind is that the speed at which time_0_1 evolves is set within the RenderMonkey properties and may need to be adjusted.

The final pixel shader code for the animating clouds is as follows:

```
float time_0_1;
float persistance;
sampler Texture0;
float4 ps_main(float2 texCoord: TEXCOORD0) : COLOR
{
   // Sample the nouse texture based on time
   float3 txr = float3(texCoord+time_0_1,time_0_1);

   // Combine 2 octaves of noise together.
   // Two octaves are sufficient for cloud rendering
   float final_noise = 0;
   for(int i=0;i<2;i++)
     final_noise +=(1.0/pow(persistance,i))*
                   (tex3D(Texture0, txr*pow(2,i))*2-1);

   // Remove the sign from the noise and prep
   // it for cloud rendering
   return ((final_noise+0.15)*2);
}
```

With this pixel shader, the results look similar to the cloud shader developed in Chapter 13 but will animate over time. Figure D.24 shows several snapshots over time of the animating clouds. This shader can be found in this chapter's source code folder on the CD-ROM as `shader_ex1.rfx`.

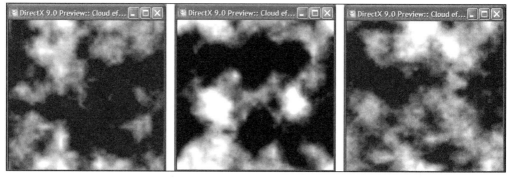

Figure D.24 Rendered output for our animating clouds exercise.

Exercise 2: Rendering Strata

For this exercise, you were asked to use Perlin noise to render a strata-type material. Strata is a rock in which different materials of different color are layered. The set of strata color layers is already provided within the StrataSpline.dds texture.

Because the material is layered in one direction and the color texture is supplied as a 1D texture, you need to pick an axis of the object's vertex coordinates and use them to look up the color texture. Because such material is layered and slightly turbulent, you can then use three octaves of the Perlin noise to offset your lookup into the strata texture. Doing so yields the following pixel shader code:

```
float4 marble_color;
float persistance;
sampler Texture0;
sampler Texture1;
float4 ps_main(float3 txr: TEXCOORD0) : COLOR
{
   // Combine 3 octaves of noise together.
   float final_noise = 0;
   for(int i=0;i<3;i++)
     final_noise += ((1.0/pow(persistance,i))*
                    ((tex3D(Texture0, txr*pow(2,i))*2)-1));

   // Take the Z-coordinate and add some noise before
   // looking into the color map texture
   return tex1D(Texture1,txr.z + final_noise.x/15);
}
```

After it's compiled, the shader should look similar to the rendering shown in Figure D.25. If you need to make the transition even smoother, you may add extra offset imposters as needed. The final shader is included on the CD-ROM as shader_ex2.rfx in this chapter's source code folder.

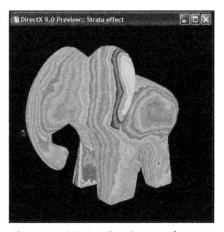

Figure D.25 Rendered output for our strata procedural material exercise.

Chapter 14

Exercise 1: Depth-Based Outline

For this exercise, you were asked to develop a new outline rendering shader using depth, as described in Chapter 14. This shader operates very similarly to the one developed using the edge detection algorithm in this chapter. To accomplish this task, you can start using the shader developed in Chapter 14, but you will need to change the object rendering pass so that the shaders output the object depth instead of a solid color.

To perform this, you need to modify the vertex shader so that it outputs the depth of the object for each vertex. This can easily be done by taking the Z component of the projected position for the vertex. The following is the resulting vertex shader:

```
float4x4 view_proj_matrix;
float depthScale;
struct VS_OUTPUT
{
   float4 Pos: POSITION;
   float texCoord: TEXCOORD;
};

VS_OUTPUT main(float4 Pos: POSITION)
{
   VS_OUTPUT Out;

   // Transform vertex position
   Out.Pos = mul(view_proj_matrix, Pos);

   // Pass the scaled depth value as a texture coordinate
   Out.texCoord = depthScale * mul(view_proj_matrix, Pos).z;

   return Out;
}
```

On the pixel shader side, simply take the depth that was passed as a texture coordinate and output it as a color. The following pixel shader accomplishes this task:

```
float4 main(float depth: TEXCOORD) : COLOR
{
   // Simply output the depth to the texture as a color
   return depth;
}
```

The rest of the shader is essentially the same. The Sobel edge detection filter used in Chapter 14 can also be used to detect discontinuities within the depth values and should give appropriate results. However, I did mention that to create smoother edges, you may want to apply a blurring pass on the result of the edge detection.

To do this, you need to add an extra pass that implements a blur filter. Any good quality blur filter will do. The following is an example of pixel shader using a 12 tap filter:

```
float hardness;
float AA_SampleDist;
sampler EdgeMap;
const float2 samples[12] = {
    -0.326212, -0.405805,
    -0.840144, -0.073580,
    -0.695914,  0.457137,
    -0.203345,  0.620716,
     0.962340, -0.194983,
     0.473434, -0.480026,
     0.519456,  0.767022,
     0.185461, -0.893124,
     0.507431,  0.064425,
     0.896420,  0.412458,
    -0.321940, -0.932615,
    -0.791559, -0.597705,
};

float4 main(float2 texCoord: TEXCOORD) : COLOR
{
    // Apply a simple blur filter to get rid of aliasing and
    // get a wider spread of the edges and a softer image.
    float sum = tex2D(EdgeMap, texCoord);
    for (int i = 0; i < 12; i++){
        sum += tex2D(EdgeMap, texCoord + AA_SampleDist * samples[i]);
    }

    return 1 - hardness * sum;
}
```

After it's compiled and executed, this shader should give results similar to the one shown in Figure D.26. For reference, the shader is included on the CD-ROM as shader_ex1.rfx in the directory for Chapter 14.

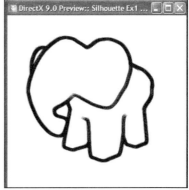

Figure D.26 Rendered output for our depth-based outline exercise.

Exercise 2: Silhouette and Toon Shading

For this exercise, you were asked to combine the depth-based silhouette rendering along with the toon shader developed in Chapter 14. The task itself is trivial because it only involves combining rendering passes previously developed. The one thing you want to keep in mind is that you need to render your object before you render the outline so you can overlay the outline to the geometry. To do this, you need to adjust the render states at the blurring pass so that it only renders where an edge is present, so as not to overwrite the whole object.

With those modifications, your toon shader will look similar to that shown in Figure D.27. The shader is included on the CD-ROM as shader_ex2.rfx in this chapter's source code folder.

Figure D.27 Rendered output for our toon shading exercise.

Chapter 15

Exercise 1: Round Fog

For this exercise, you were asked to take advantage of the hardware-accelerated fog support to implement a twist on the regular fog approach. To prove you can use the hardware to your advantage, you have been asked to implement fog in a circular manner around the center of the screen, thus creating a dream-like illusion.

This shader can easily be developed by starting from the height fog shader developed in Chapter 15. With this shader, you need to change its vertex shader to compute the fog based on a circle around the screen space coordinates of your geometry. This can easily be done by taking the length of the X,Y screen space coordinates. Keep in mind that the fog values are reversed and you will need to negate the result.

Applying this change yields the following final vertex shader code:

```
float4x4 view_proj_matrix;
struct VS_OUTPUT
{
    float4 Pos:     POSITION;
    float2 Txr1:    TEXCOORD0;
    float1 Fog:     FOG;
};

VS_OUTPUT vs_main(
```

```
    float4 inPos: POSITION,
    float2 Txr1: TEXCOORD0)
{
    VS_OUTPUT Out;

    float4 Pos = mul(view_proj_matrix, inPos);
    Out.Pos = Pos;
    Out.Txr1 = Txr1;

    // Set the fog proportional to the Y height.
    // With a vertex shader, the fog can be set to
    // any value you wish.
    Out.Fog = 1-sqrt(dot(Pos.xy/Pos.w,Pos.xy/Pos.w));

    return Out;
}
```

Once completed and compiled, this shader should yield a result similar to the one shown in Figure D.28. The completed shader is included on the CD-ROM as shader_ex1.rfx in the source directory for Chapter 15.

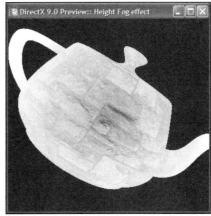

Figure D.28 Rendered output for our round fog exercise.

Chapter 17

Exercise 1: Per-Pixel Spherical Harmonics

For this exercise, you were asked to develop a per-pixel spherical harmonics shader. Because a per-vertex implementation has been created in Chapter 17, the process should be straightforward starting from this shader.

The vertex shader for this task needs some significant changes because most of the computations need to be done within the pixel shader. The vertex shader for this task will need to determine the tangent space for each vertex. However, because the spherical harmonics are represented in view-space, you will need to take your basis and transform it by view_matrix to bring it into view-space.

Beyond this, you simply need to transform the vertex position and send out all the results to the pixel shader. Doing so yields the following vertex shader code:

```
float4x4 view_proj_matrix;
float4x4 view_matrix;
struct VS_OUTPUT
{
   float4 Pos:        POSITION;
   float4 Tex:        TEXCOORD0;
   float3 Normal:     TEXCOORD1;
   float3 Tangent:    TEXCOORD2;
   float3 Binormal:   TEXCOORD3;
};

VS_OUTPUT vs_main(
   float4 inPosition: POSITION,
   float4 inNormal:   NORMAL,
   float4 inTex:      TEXCOORD,
   float4 inTangent:  TANGENT,
   float4 inBinormal: BINORMAL )
{
   VS_OUTPUT Out;

   // Transform and project the position, also output
   // the texture coordinate for this vertex
   Out.Pos = mul(view_proj_matrix, inPosition);
   Out.Tex = inTex;

   // Rotate the basis vectors into view space
   float4 nvector = float4(inNormal.x, inNormal.y, inNormal.z, 0.0);
   float4 tvector = float4(inTangent.x, inTangent.y, inTangent.z, 0.0);
   float4 bvector = float4(inBinormal.x, inBinormal.y, inBinormal.z, 0.0);

   Out.Normal = mul(view_matrix, nvector);
   Out.Tangent = mul(view_matrix, tvector);
   Out.Binormal = mul(view_matrix, bvector);

   return Out;
}
```

The pixel shader will do most of the work for the effect. Initially, it needs to consider the bumpmapping for the surface. To do so, you need to sample the bumpmap and bias the values so they are signed. Because the bumpmap values define the surface normal in tangent space but our lighting is done in view-space, you will then take the normal, tangent, and bi-normal vectors generated within the vertex shader to rotate the normal into the proper space. This can be done by combining the vectors into a matrix and transforming your bumpmap normal by this matrix.

At this point, you have a normal vector pointing into the same space as the spherical harmonic. Because we are dealing simply with diffuse lighting, we can use its value and transform it by the spherical harmonic coefficients. The operation is the same as that done with the vertex-based shader.

Of course, you then need to take the spherical harmonic lighting value and modulate it with the object's color. This yields the following pixel shader code:

```
float4x4 g_matrix;
float4x4 b_matrix;
float4x4 r_matrix;
sampler color_map;
sampler bump_map;
float4 main(
    float4 inTex:       TEXCOORD0,
    float3 inNormal:    TEXCOORD1,
    float3 inTangent:   TEXCOORD2,
    float3 inBinormal:  TEXCOORD3 ) : COLOR
{
    float4 col;
    float3x3 rotation;
    float3 normalbump;
    float4 normal;

    // Define the tangent space matrix for the light
    rotation = float3x3(inTangent, inBinormal, inNormal);

    // Get normal from bumpmap
    normalbump = tex2D(bump_map, inTex) * 2.0 - 1.0;

    // Transform normal into light space
    normal = float4(mul(normalbump, rotation),1.0);
```

```
// Evaluate spherical harmonic
col.r = dot(mul(r_matrix, normal), normal);
col.g = dot(mul(g_matrix, normal), normal);
col.b = dot(mul(b_matrix, normal), normal);
col.a = 1.0;

// Modulate with the texture color
return col * tex2D(color_map, inTex) * 2.0;
}
```

With those modifications, your object should be lit as shown in Figure D.29. The shader is included in this chapter's source code folder on the CD-ROM as shader_ex1.rfx.

Figure D.29 Rendered output for our per-pixel spherical harmonics exercise.

Chapter 18

Exercise 1: Soft Shadow Mapping

For this exercise, you were asked to implement soft shadows by using the shadow mapping shader developed in Chapter 18. Although there are several approaches to this shader, the simplest is to modify the shader to sample multiple shadow values and average the shadow contributions.

To do so, you need to sample the shadow map several times around the current position and repeat the shadow operations. Remember to take advantage of vector operations to optimize the process. After you have multiple shadow values, it is simply a matter of averaging them and using this new value to determine the final shadow. The following pixel shader does exactly this with four shadow samples:

```
float shadowBias;
float backProjectionCut;
float Ka;
float Kd;
float Ks;
float4 modelColor;
sampler ShadowMap;
sampler SpotLight;
float4 ps_main(
    float3 inNormal: TEXCOORD0,
    float3 lightVec: TEXCOORD1,
    float3 viewVec:  TEXCOORD2,
    float4 shadowCrd:TEXCOORD3) : COLOR
{
```

```
// Normalize the normal
inNormal = normalize(inNormal);

// Radial distance and normalize light vector
float depth = length(lightVec);
lightVec /= depth;

// Standard lighting
float diffuse = saturate(dot(lightVec, inNormal));
float specular = pow(saturate(
                dot(reflect(-normalize(viewVec), inNormal), lightVec)),
                16);

// The depth of the fragment closest to the light
float4 shadowMap;
float  offset = (2.0/1024.0)*shadowCrd.w;
shadowMap.x = tex2Dproj(ShadowMap, shadowCrd+float4(offset,0,0,0));
shadowMap.y = tex2Dproj(ShadowMap, shadowCrd+float4(-offset,0,0,0));
shadowMap.z = tex2Dproj(ShadowMap, shadowCrd+float4(0,offset,0,0));
shadowMap.w = tex2Dproj(ShadowMap, shadowCrd+float4(0,-offset,0,0));

// A spot image of the spotlight
float spotLight = tex2Dproj(SpotLight, shadowCrd);

// If the depth is larger than the stored depth, this fragment
// is not the closest to the light, that is we are in shadow.
// Otherwise, we're lit. Add a bias to avoid precision issues.
float shadow;
shadow = (float)(depth < shadowMap.x + shadowBias)/4.0;
shadow += (float)(depth < shadowMap.y + shadowBias)/4.0;
shadow += (float)(depth < shadowMap.z + shadowBias)/4.0;
shadow += (float)(depth < shadowMap.w + shadowBias)/4.0;

// Modulate with spotlight image
float shadowval = spotLight*shadow;

// Shadow any light contribution except ambient
return Ka * platformColor +
       (Kd * diffuse * platformColor + Ks * specular) * shadowval;
}
```

Compiling and running this shader yields results similar to those shown in Figure D.30. You can find the complete version of this exercise in this chapter's source code folder on the CD-ROM as shader_ex1.rfx.

Figure D.30 Rendered output for our soft shadow mapping exercise.

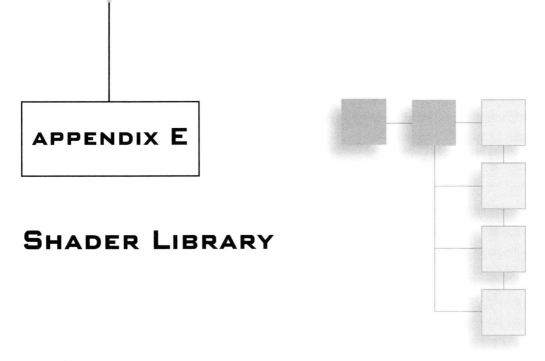

SHADER LIBRARY

Throughout this book we have covered much ground and many different shader techniques. Many of these techniques reuse the same segments of code and could prove useful for other shaders you may develop in the future.

However, because the code is spread throughout this book, it may be difficult for you to find that important piece of code that you need. To help you out, I have created this shader library chapter, which takes all the important code from throughout the book and groups it in one place, divided into categories, making your search even easier. Keep in mind that the code in this chapter is meant as an example that you can reuse in your own shaders; this implies that you might need to change variable names within the code to match your needs.

Basic Components

This section covers the most basic tasks you might need to perform when rendering objects, such as transforming and projecting an object.

Object Transformation and Projection

The most basic task you will need to do is to transform and project an object for rendering. The following code takes the vertex position of an object and transforms it into screen space using the view_proj_matrix variable:

```
VS_OUTPUT vs_main( float4 inPos: POSITION )
{
    VS_OUTPUT Out;
```

```
// Output a transformed and projected vertex position
Out.Pos = mul(view_proj_matrix, inPos);

return Out;
}
```

Basic Texturing

Texturing is an important part of rendering realistic objects. The following code illustrates how you can take the texture coordinates passed from the vertex shader to sample and use the color of a texture within the pixel shader:

```
float4 ps_main(
    float4 inDiffuse: COLOR0,
    float2 inTxr1: TEXCOORD0
) : COLOR0
{
    //  Output the color taken from our texture
    return tex2D(Texture0,inTxr1);
}
```

Color Modulation

In some situations, using a single texture simply isn't enough. Sometimes you need to take two textures or colors and modulate them together. Modulating two colors is simply a matter of multiplying both colors together. The following code shows how this can be done:

```
float4 ps_main(
    float4 inDiffuse: COLOR0,
    float2 inTxr1: TEXCOORD0,
    float2 inTxr2: TEXCOORD1
) : COLOR0
{
    //  Output constant color:
    return tex2D(Texture0,inTxr1)*tex2D(Texture1,inTxr2);
}
```

Depth Encoding and Decoding

Whether you are doing depth of field or per-pixel volumetric fog, you need to take the depth of an object and store it inside a texture for you to reuse. Unfortunately, until support for floating-point texture formats is more widespread, the use of eight bits of precision just isn't enough. By the clever use of several eight-bit color components, you can encode depth with more than enough precision for all your needs.

The following pixel shader code takes care of encoding a floating-point depth value into the color components of a fixed-point texture:

```
float4 ps_main(
    float4 inDepth: TEXCOORD0
) : COLOR0
{
    //  Output the depth as computed by
    //  the vertex shader
    float4 Depth;
    Depth.w = 1.0;
    Depth.x = floor(inDepth.x*127)/127;
    Depth.y = floor((inDepth.x-Depth.x)*127*127)/127;
    Depth.z = 0;

    return Depth;
}
```

After you encode your depth inside a texture, you need to be able to decode this depth for your use. The following pixel shader code fragment illustrates how this can be done:

```
// Sample and decode our depth value
float4 DepthValue = tex2D(Texture2,texCoord);
float Depth = DepthValue.x + DepthValue.y/127
            + DepthValue.z/(127*127);
```

Screen Effects

As you have seen throughout this book, many things can be done using screen effects. Whether you are simply copying from one surface to another or applying a filter to an image, you need to use screen effects. The following section covers some of the most commonly used techniques.

Rendering to a Full Screen Quad

When dealing with screen effects and render targets, you often need to render a texture onto another flat surface. This is most commonly done when applying a filter to a texture or simply copying from one surface to another. The process involves rendering using a full screen quad and adjusting the texture coordinates so that the center of a texel coincides with the center of a screen pixel. The following code does just that:

```
VS_OUTPUT vs_main(float4 Pos: POSITION){
    VS_OUTPUT Out;
```

```
    // Simply output the position without transforming it
    Out.Pos = float4(Pos.xy, 0, 1);

    // Texture coordinates are set up so that the full texture
    // is mapped completly onto the screen
    Out.texCoord.x = 0.5 * (1 + Pos.x - viewport_inv_width);
    Out.texCoord.y = 0.5 * (1 - Pos.y - viewport_inv_height);

    return Out;
}
```

Color Matrix

One of the simplest forms of filtering operations is manipulating the colors in your image. This enables you to render your scene in black and white or even sepia. Generalizing this operation simply involves putting the color modification inside a matrix and multiplying your colors by this matrix, just as the following code does:

```
float4 ps_main(float2 texCoord: TEXCOORD0) : COLOR
{
    // Read the source color
    float4 col = tex2D(Texture0,  texCoord);

    // Apply the matrix to the incoming color
    return mul(color_filter,col);
}
```

Basic Filtering Pixel Shader

Most texture filtering operations involve sampling a texture at several different offsets and combining the results based on specific weights. Because of this, it is simple to take advantage of loops within the HLSL architecture to perform the filtering operation. The following code shows you how you can sample multiple texels from a texture and combine the results:

```
float4 ps_main(float2 texCoord: TEXCOORD0) : COLOR
{
    float4 col = float4(0,0,0,0);

    // Sample and output the box averaged colors
```

```
    for(int i=0;i<4;i++)
        col += samples[i].w*tex2D(Texture0,texCoord+
         float2(samples[i].x*viewport_inv_width,
                samples[i].x*viewport_inv_height));
    return col;
}
```

The next few sections illustrate some of the most commonly used filters overviewed throughout this book.

Box Blur Filter

The following array shows how you can implement a simple box filter.

```
const float4 samples[4] = {
    -1.0,  0.0,  0,  0.25,
     1.0,  0.0,  0,  0.25,
     0.0,  1.0,  0,  0.25,
     0.0, -1.0,  0,  0.25
};
```

Gauss Blur Filter

Although the box blurring filter is simple to implement, its results aren't as impressive. One approach commonly used to improve the quality of the blur is to use a Gauss filter. However, such filters can be prohibitive to implement; a 7×7 filter requires 49 samples to be completed. On the bright side, such filters have a seperatable nature, meaning that you can take a 7×7 filter and separate it into a horizontal and vertical pass, each requiring 7 samples. The following shows you the arrays for a 49-sample Gauss filter.

Horizontal pass:

```
const float4 samples[7] = {
    -3.0,  0.0,  0,  1.0/64.0,
    -2.0,  0.0,  0,  6.0/64.0,
    -1.0,  0.0,  0,  15.0/64.0,
     0.0,  0.0,  0,  20.0/64.0,
     1.0,  0.0,  0,  15.0/64.0,
     2.0,  0.0,  0,  6.0/64.0,
     3.0,  0.0,  0,  1.0/64.0
};
```

Vertical pass:

```
const float4 samples[7] = {
    0.0, -3.0,  0,  1.0/64.0,
    0.0, -2.0,  0,  6.0/64.0,
    0.0, -1.0,  0,  15.0/64.0,
    0.0,  0.0,  0,  20.0/64.0,
    0.0,  1.0,  0,  15.0/64.0,
    0.0,  2.0,  0,  6.0/64.0,
    0.0,  3.0,  0,  1.0/64.0
};
```

Edge Detection Filter

Edge detection is a very powerful technique that can be used in basic image filtering operations. In addition, it can prove handy when doing toon rendering to create an outline around your objects. The following pixel shader implements a basic edge detection algorithm based on the Sobel filter:

```
const float off = 1.0 / 256.0;
float4 ps_main( float2 TexCoord : TEXCOORD0 ) : COLOR
{
   // Sample the neighbor pixels
   float s00 = tex2D(RT, TexCoord + float2(-off, -off));
   float s01 = tex2D(RT, TexCoord + float2( 0,   -off));
   float s02 = tex2D(RT, TexCoord + float2( off, -off));

   float s10 = tex2D(RT, TexCoord + float2(-off,  0));
   float s12 = tex2D(RT, TexCoord + float2( off,  0));

   float s20 = tex2D(RT, TexCoord + float2(-off,  off));
   float s21 = tex2D(RT, TexCoord + float2( 0,    off));
   float s22 = tex2D(RT, TexCoord + float2( off,  off));

   // Sobel filter in X and Y direction
   float sobelX = s00 + 2 * s10 + s20 - s02 - 2 * s12 - s22;
   float sobelY = s00 + 2 * s01 + s02 - s20 - 2 * s21 - s22;

   // Find edge using a threshold of 0.07 which works generally
   // well for general edge detection.
   float edgeSqr = (sobelX * sobelX + sobelY * sobelY);
   return 1.0-(edgeSqr > 0.07 * 0.07);
}
```

Lighting

Lighting is one of the most important components of rendering. The following sections take you through some of the most commonly used pieces of shader code developed throughout this book.

Diffuse Lighting

When rendering rough surfaces, light gets reflected in every direction. This diffusion leads to diffuse lighting. The following function, which can be used either per-vertex or per-pixel, implements diffuse lighting for a simple point light:

```
float4 Light_PointDiffuse(float3 VertPos, float3 VertNorm, float3 LightPos,
                          float4 LightColor, float4 LightAttenuation)
{
   // Determine the distance from the light to the vertex and the direction
   float3 LightDir = LightPos - VertPos;
   float  Dist = length(LightDir);
   LightDir = LightDir / Dist;

   // Compute distance based attenuation. This is defined as:
   // Attenuation = 1 / ( LA.x + LA.y*Dist + LA.z*Dist*Dist )
   float DistAttn = clamp(0,1, 1 / ( LightAttenuation.x +
                                     LightAttenuation.y * Dist +
                                     LightAttenuation.z * Dist * Dist ));

   // Compute suface/light angle based attenuation defined as dot(N,L)
   // Note : This must be clamped as it may become negative.
   float AngleAttn = clamp(0, 1, dot(VertNorm, LightDir) );

   // Compute final lighting
   return LightColor * DistAttn * AngleAttn;
}
```

Specular Lighting

Although diffuse lighting deals mostly with rough surfaces, specular lighting deals with smooth surfaces. Such surfaces reflect light more directly and cause lighting to produce a more distinct highlight. The following function implements a basic specular lighting shader for a basic point light:

```
float4 Light_PointSpecular(float3 VertPos, float3 VertNorm, float3 LightPos,
                           float4 LightColor, float4 LightAttenuation,
                           float3 EyeDir)
```

```
{
    // Determine the distance from the light to the vertex and the direction
    float3 LightDir = LightPos - VertPos;
    float  Dist = length(LightDir);
    LightDir = LightDir / Dist;

    // Compute half vector
    float3 HalfVect = normalize(LightDir-EyeDir);

    // Compute distance based attenuation. This is defined as:
    // Attenuation = 1 / ( LA.x + LA.y*Dist + LA.z*Dist*Dist )
    float DistAttn = clamp(0,1, 1 / ( LightAttenuation.x +
                                      LightAttenuation.y * Dist +
                                      LightAttenuation.z * Dist * Dist ));

    // Compute suface/light angle based attenuation defined as dot(N,L)
    // Note : This must be clamped as it may become negative.
    float SpecularAttn =  pow( clamp(0, 1,dot(VertNorm, HalfVect)),32);

    // Compute final lighting
    return LightColor * DistAttn * SpecularAttn;
}
```

Tangent Space Lighting

Before you can do any complex form of per-pixel lighting, such as bumpmapping, you will need to define your lighting information in tangent space so that the pixel shader can deal with a uniform coordinate system. The following vertex shader code illustrates a basic implementation of how you can determine the tangent space for a simple light:

```
VS_OUTPUT vs_main(float4 inPos: POSITION, float3 inNormal: NORMAL,
                  float3 inTangent:TANGENT, float3 inBinormal:BINORMAL,
                  float2 inTxr: TEXCOORD0)
{
    VS_OUTPUT Out;

    // Compute the projected position and send out the texture coordinates
    Out.Pos = mul(view_proj_matrix, inPos);
    Out.TexCoord = inTxr;

    // Determine the distance from the light to the vertex and the direction
    float4 LightDir;
```

```
LightDir.xyz = mul(inv_view_matrix,LightPosition) - inPos;
float  Dist = length(LightDir.xyz);
LightDir.xyz = LightDir.xyz / Dist;

// Compute the per-vertex distance based attenuation
LightDir.w = clamp(0,1, 1 / ( Light1_Attenuation.x +
                              Light1_Attenuation.y * Dist +
                              Light1_Attenuation.z * Dist * Dist ));


// Determine the eye vector
float3 EyeVector = normalize(view_position-inPos);

// Transform to tangent space and output
// half vector and light direction
float3x3 TangentSpace;
TangentSpace[0] = inTangent;
TangentSpace[1] = inBinormal;
TangentSpace[2] = inNormal;
Out.HalfVect = mul(TangentSpace,normalize(LightDir.xyz+EyeVector));
Out.LightDir = float4(mul(TangentSpace,LightDir.xyz),LightDir.w);

return Out;
}
```

Per-Pixel Bumpmapping

Most objects, even those with high density meshes, can lack detail. The use of bumpmaps can significantly improve rendering quality by adding surface details at the pixel level. The following pixel shader code implements a basic per-pixel bumpmapping shader:

```
float4 Light_Point(float3 Normal, float3 HalfVect, float4 LightDir,
                               float4 LightColor)
{
   // Compute both specular and diffuse factors
   float SpecularAttn =  pow( clamp(0, 1,dot(Normal, HalfVect)),16);
   float DiffuseAttn =  clamp(0, 1,dot(Normal, LightDir));

   // Compute final lighting
   return LightColor * LightDir.w * (SpecularAttn+DiffuseAttn);
}
```

```
float4 ps_main(float2 inTxr:TEXCOORD0,float4 LightDir:TEXCOORD1,
               float3 HalfVect:TEXCOORD2) : COLOR
{
   // Read bump and influence the normal
   float3 normal = tex2D(Bump,inTxr) * 2 - 1;

   // Simply route the vertex color to the output
   return tex2D(Texture0,inTxr)*
          (Light_Ambient+Light_Point(normal,HalfVect,LightDir,Light1_Color));
}
```

Polynomial Texture Mapping

In the search for new lighting techniques, polynomial texture mapping has proven to be
an interesting new candidate as a replacement for regular bumpmapping. By taking an
existing material and sampling it from several different lighting angles, you can construct
a polynomial representation that can be used to represent not only bumpmapping, but
also some of its side effects, such as self-shadowing. The following pixel shader illustrates
how such a shader can be implemented:

```
float4 ps_main(
   float4 inTex: TEXCOORD0,
   float3 inLight:TEXCOORD1 ) : COLOR
{
   float3 lu2_lv2_lulv;
   float4 col;
   float3 a012;
   float3 a345;

   // Normalize light direction
   inLight = normalize(inLight);

   // z-extrapolation
   if (mode > 0.0f && inLight.z < 0.0)
   {
      inLight.xy = normalize(inLight.xy);
      inLight.xy *= (1.0 - inLight.z);
   }
   inLight.z = 1.0;

   // Prepare higher-order terms
   lu2_lv2_lulv = inLight.xyx * inLight.xyy;

   // read terms and bias
```

```
    a012 = tex2D(Poly1,inTex) * 2.0 - 1.0;
    a345 = tex2D(Poly2,inTex) * 2.0 - 1.0;
    a345.z += 1.0;

    // Evaluate polynomial
    col = dot(lu2_lv2_lulv, a012) + dot(inLight, a345);

    // Multiply by rgb factor
    return col * tex2D(color_map, inTex);
}
```

Spherical Harmonics

For a single point in the scene, you can form a representation of all the incoming light at this point. By only considering diffuse lighting, you can simplify the representation with spherical harmonics. This enables you to represent this lighting in a form that is as small as a single matrix per color component. The following shader implements a simple per-vertex spherical harmonics shader:

```
VS_OUTPUT vs_main(
    float4 inPosition: POSITION,
    float4 inNormal:   NORMAL,
    float4 inTex:      TEXCOORD )
{
    VS_OUTPUT Out;

    // Transform the position and output the texture coordinate
    Out.Pos = mul( view_proj_matrix, inPosition);
    Out.Tex = inTex;

    // Rotate normal into view space since the lighting information
    // is in that space
    float4 normal = float4(inNormal.x, inNormal.y, inNormal.z, 0.0);
    normal = mul(view_matrix, normal);
    normal.w = 1.0;

    // Evaluate spherical harmonic
    Out.Diff.r = dot(mul(r_matrix, normal), normal);
    Out.Diff.g = dot(mul(g_matrix, normal), normal);
    Out.Diff.b = dot(mul(b_matrix, normal), normal);
    Out.Diff.a = 1.0;

    return Out;
}
```

Reflection and Refraction

Reflections and refractions are important components in trying to make ● scene livelier. Whether you are rendering glass or water, the following techniques will prove useful in rendering most non-opaque objects.

Reflection

Glossy materials, such as polished metals or glass, will not only produce specular lighting but will also reflect their environment. The following code illustrates how you can implement a shader that determines a reflection vector based on the view vector and surface normal:

```
// Determine the reflection vector by using the normal and view vectors
Out.Reflect = reflect(inNormal,viewVec);
```

Refraction

Any transparent materials will not let light pass straight through. The material has the effect of slightly changing the direction of the light, resulting in an effect called refraction. Because the HLSL function does not always give accurate results, the following code implements a refraction shader based on Snell's Law:

```
// Compute the reflection vector using Snell's law
// the refract HLSL function does not always work properly
// n_i * sin(theta_i) = n_r  * sin(theta_r)

// sin(theta_i)
float cosine = dot(viewVec, inNormal);
float sine = sqrt(1 - cosine * cosine);

// sin(theta_r)
float sine2 = saturate(RefractionIndex * sine);
float cosine2 = sqrt(1 - sine2 * sine2);
// Determine the refraction vector be using the normal and tangent
// vectors as basis to determine the refraction direction
float3 x = -inNormal;
float3 y = normalize(cross(cross(viewVec, inNormal), inNormal));
Out.Refract = x * cosine2 + y * sine2;
```

Materials

Materials help define the surface of an object in more detail than a simple texture can. The following sections cover topics such as procedural materials and BRDF-based lighting.

Velvet

Velvet is one of those materials that seem to defy the laws of physics when it comes to lighting. This is because of its micro-hair structure. The following shader implements a basic velvet-like shader using Minneart's lighting equations:

```
float4 Light_Velvet(float3 Normal, float3 EyeVect, float3 LightDir,
                    float4 LightColor)
{
    // Compute both the light and eye angle about the surface
    // normal for the surface
    float l = pow( clamp(dot(Normal, LightDir),0,1),
              Velvet_Exponent );
    float e = pow( clamp(dot(Normal, EyeVect),0,1),
              Velvet_Exponent );

    // Compute final lighting. Which is defined as the product
    // of the cosine of both the light and eye vectors.
    return LightColor * clamp(l*e,0,1);
}
```

Oren-Nayer Lighting

BRDFs can be expensive to represent accurately. By using data such as the database provided by the Curet group, you can approximate such complex materials through the use of a simplified lighting model. The Oren-Nayer lighting provides an easy and efficient means of representing the BRDFs of multiple classes of materials. The following shader function implements an Oren-Nayer lighting function:

```
float4 Light_OrenNayer(float3 Normal, float3 EyeVect, float3 LightDir,
                       float4 LightColor)
{
    float3 HalfVect = normalize(LightDir+EyeVect);

    // calculate all the dot products
    float EdotH = dot(EyeVect, HalfVect);
    float LdotH = dot(LightDir, HalfVect);
    float NdotH = dot(Normal, HalfVect);
    float NdotL = dot(Normal, LightDir);
    float NdotE = dot(Normal, EyeVect);

    // calculate the zenith angles
    float sinTheta_r = length(cross(EyeVect,Normal));
    float cosTheta_r = max(NdotE,0.001);
```

```
    float sinTheta_i = length(cross(LightDir,Normal));
    float cosTheta_i = max(NdotL,0.001);
    float tanTheta_i = sinTheta_i / cosTheta_i;
    float tanTheta_r = sinTheta_r / cosTheta_r;

    // calculate the azimuth angles
    float3 E_p = normalize(EyeVect-NdotE*Normal);
    float3 L_p = normalize(LightDir-NdotL*Normal);
    float cosAzimuth = dot(E_p, L_p);

    // Compute final lighting
    float inten = rho_pi * cosTheta_i *
        (A + B * max(0, cosAzimuth) *
        max(sinTheta_r, sinTheta_i) * min(tanTheta_i, tanTheta_r));

    return LightColor * clamp(inten,0.0,1);
}
```

Basic Perlin Noise

Not all materials have a nice predictable pattern. Materials such as clouds or wood exhibit
noisy or turbulent patterns that can be re-created procedurally. The advantage of such
materials is that you can use their noisy nature to create a wide variety of instances that
all look different. At the heart of all these materials lies a noise-generating algorithm, of
which the most common is Perlin noise. The following pixel shader shows a basic four-
octave implementation of Perlin noise:

```
float4 ps_main(float2 texCoord: TEXCOORD0) : COLOR
{
    // Sample only the first slice of the noise texture
    float3 txr = float3(texCoord,0);

    // Combine 4 octaves of noise together
    // Note: that the noise is considered signed but read from
    // an unsigned texture so it must be renormalized
    float final_noise = 0;
    for(int i=0;i<4;i++)
        final_noise +=(1.0/pow(persistance,i))*
                    (tex3D(Texture0, txr*pow(2,i))*2-1);

    // Remove the sign from the noise
    return (final_noise+1)/2;
}
```

Marble and Wood Noise Materials

Using Perlin noise, you can implement several classes of noisy or turbulent materials. The following two pixel shaders illustrate how noise can be used to re-create both wood and marble:

```
// Marble
float4 ps_main(float3 txr: TEXCOORD0) : COLOR
{
    // Combine 2 octaves of noise together.
    // Two octaves is sufficient for cloud rendering
    float final_noise = 0;
    for(int i=0;i<2;i++)
        final_noise += ((1.0/pow(persistance,i))*
                    ((tex3D(Texture0, txr*pow(2,i))*2)-1));

    // Remove the sign from the noise and prep
    // it for cloud rendering
    return marble_color * 0.2+(1.2*abs(final_noise));
}


// Wood
float4 ps_main(float3 txr: TEXCOORD0) : COLOR
{
    // Determine two set of coordinates, one for the noise
    // and one for the wood rings
    float3 noisetxr = txr;
    txr = txr/8;

    // Combine 3 octaves of noise together.
    float final_noise = 0;
    for(int i=0;i<2;i++)
        final_noise += ((1.0/pow(persistance,i))*
                    ((tex3D(Texture0, txr*pow(2,i))*2)-1));

    // The wood is defined by a set of concentric rings in the XY
    // plane. Those rings are pertubated by the computed noise.
    final_noise = abs(final_noise);
    float grain = cos(dot(noisetxr.xy,noisetxr.xy) + final_noise*4);
    return wood_color - pow(grain,8)/2;
}
```

INDEX

M

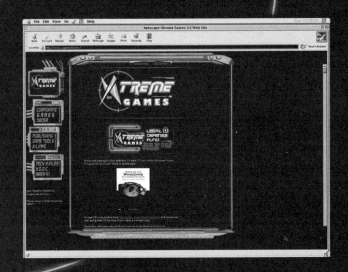

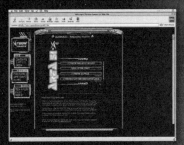

Gamedev.net

The most comprehensive game development resource

- ○ The latest news in game development
- ○ The most active forums and chatrooms anywhere, with insights and tips from experienced game developers
- ○ Links to thousands of additional game development resources
- ○ Thorough book and product reviews
- ○ Over 1000 game development articles!
  Game design
  Graphics
  DirectX
  OpenGL
  AI
  Art
  Music
  Physics
  Source Code
  Sound
  Assembly
  And More!

 Gamedev.net

License Agreement/Notice of Limited Warranty

By opening the sealed disc container in this book, you agree to the following terms and conditions. If, upon reading the following license agreement and notice of limited warranty, you cannot agree to the terms and conditions set forth, return the unused book with unopened disc to the place where you purchased it for a refund.

License:
The enclosed software is copyrighted by the copyright holder(s) indicated on the software disc. You are licensed to copy the software onto a single computer for use by a single user and to a backup disc. You may not reproduce, make copies, or distribute copies or rent or lease the software in whole or in part, except with written permission of the copyright holder(s). You may transfer the enclosed disc only together with this license, and only if you destroy all other copies of the software and the transferee agrees to the terms of the license. You may not decompile, reverse assemble, or reverse engineer the software.

Notice of Limited Warranty:
The enclosed disc is warranted by Course PTR to be free of physical defects in materials and workmanship for a period of sixty (60) days from end user's purchase of the book/disc combination. During the sixty-day term of the limited warranty, Course PTR will provide a replacement disc upon the return of a defective disc.

Limited Liability:
THE SOLE REMEDY FOR BREACH OF THIS LIMITED WARRANTY SHALL CONSIST ENTIRELY OF REPLACEMENT OF THE DEFECTIVE DISC. IN NO EVENT SHALL COURSE PTR OR THE AUTHOR BE LIABLE FOR ANY OTHER DAMAGES, INCLUDING LOSS OR CORRUPTION OF DATA, CHANGES IN THE FUNCTIONAL CHARACTERIS-TICS OF THE HARDWARE OR OPERATING SYSTEM, DELETERIOUS INTERACTION WITH OTHER SOFTWARE, OR ANY OTHER SPECIAL, INCIDENTAL, OR CONSEQUEN-TIAL DAMAGES THAT MAY ARISE, EVEN IF COURSE PTR AND/OR THE AUTHOR HAS PREVIOUSLY BEEN NOTIFIED THAT THE POSSIBILITY OF SUCH DAMAGES EXISTS.

Disclaimer of Warranties:
COURSE PTR AND THE AUTHOR SPECIFICALLY DISCLAIM ANY AND ALL OTHER WARRANTIES, EITHER EXPRESS OR IMPLIED, INCLUDING WARRANTIES OF MER-CHANTABILITY, SUITABILITY TO A PARTICULAR TASK OR PURPOSE, OR FREEDOM FROM ERRORS. SOME STATES DO NOT ALLOW FOR EXCLUSION OF IMPLIED WAR-RANTIES OR LIMITATION OF INCIDENTAL OR CONSEQUENTIAL DAMAGES, SO THESE LIMITATIONS MIGHT NOT APPLY TO YOU.

Other:
This Agreement is governed by the laws of the State of Massachusetts without regard to choice of law principles. The United Convention of Contracts for the International Sale of Goods is specifically disclaimed. This Agreement constitutes the entire agreement between you and Course PTR regarding use of the software.